Readings in Financial Planning

Huebner School Series

Readings in Multiline Insurance Law and Operations
Charles E. Hughes (ed.)

Readings in Financial Planning
Robert M. Crowe (ed.)

Readings in Income Taxation
James F. Ivers III (ed.)

Group Benefits: Basic Concepts and Alternatives
Burton T. Beam, Jr.

Retirement Planning for a Business and Business Owner
Kenn Beam Tacchino

Retirement Planning for Individuals
K. B. Tacchino, W. J. Ruckstuhl, E. E. Graves, and R. J. Doyle, Jr.

Readings in Wealth Accumulation Planning
Robert J. Doyle, Jr., and Eric T. Johnson (eds.)

Readings in Estate Planning I
Ted Kurlowicz (ed.)

Readings in Estate Planning II
Jeffrey B. Kelvin

Planning for Business Owners and Professionals
Ted Kurlowicz, James F. Ivers III, and John J. McFadden

Financial Planning Applications
James F. Ivers III and William J. Ruckstuhl

Tax Planning for Business Operations
Eric T. Johnson

Computerizing a Financial Planning Practice
Edmund W. Fitzpatrick

The primary purpose of this series is to provide timely reading materials tailored to the educational needs of those professionals pursuing the Chartered Life Underwriter and Chartered Financial Consultant designation programs offered by the Solomon S. Huebner School of The American College. These publications should also be of interest to other persons seeking further knowledge in the broad area of financial services.

Huebner School Series

Readings in
Financial Planning
Third Edition

Edited by Robert M. Crowe

The American College/Bryn Mawr, Pennsylvania

This publication is designed to provide accurate and authoritative information about the subject covered. The American College is not engaged in rendering legal, accounting, or other professional service. If legal or other expert advice is required, the services of an appropriate professional should be sought.

*© 1989 The American College
All rights reserved*

*Library of Congress catalog card number 89-080100
ISBN 0-943590-08-6*

Printed in the United States of America

Contents

Preface	*vii*
Financial Planning: The Need, the Process and the Professionals Dale S. Johnson	***1.1***
Standards for a Comprehensive Financial Plan Registry of Financial Planning Practitioners	***2.1***
Effective Communication in Financial Counseling Lewis B. Morgan	***3.1***
The Financial Planning Process: Gathering Client Information Dale S. Johnson	***4.1***
Financial Estate Planning Fact Finder (following 4.44)	
Introduction to Personal Computer Hardware Colin Mick	***5.1***
Introduction to Software Colin Mick	***6.1***
Word Processing Colin Mick	***7.1***
Financial Analysis Colin Mick	***8.1***
Data Base Management Systems Colin Mick	***9.1***
Mailing Support Colin Mick	***10.1***
The Preparation and Use of Personal Financial Statements Burton T. Beam, Jr. William J. Ruckstuhl	***11.1***

Setting Your Objectives
G. Victor Hallman
Jerry S. Rosenbloom **12.1**

The Regulation of Financial Services Professionals
Dale S. Johnson **13.1**

The Impact of the Investment Advisers Act of 1940 on Financial Services Professionals
Dale S. Johnson **14.1**

Relationships between Financial Services Professionals
Gwenda L. Cannon **15.1**

On Professions, Professionals, and Professional Ethics
Ronald C. Horn **16.1**

Code of Ethics
The American College **17.1**

Code of Ethics and Ethical Guideline Procedures
American Society of CLU and ChFC **18.1**

Preface

Few terms have attracted as much national attention in recent years as the term *financial planning*. Surveys have made it clear that the public desperately needs and wants financial planning (though there is still some question as to whether the public is willing to pay for it.) Glossy magazines about financial planning have sprung up and attracted readership in the millions. College professors have begun teaching financial planning at several universities, and a huge trade organization devoted to financial planning has been created. Many financial services practitioners have replaced their old labels—stockbroker, insurance agent, accountant, banker, and so forth—with the new label of financial planner. Undoubtedly financial planning is *in*.

However, there still is very little agreement about what financial planning is. Some argue that it is nothing but a disguise behind which financial product vendors can hide. At the other end of the spectrum are those who regard financial planning as a completely new professional discipline whose practitioners are making major contributions to the financial salvation of mankind.

This book attempts to dispel some of the confusion and contribute to the development of financial planning as a profession. It defines the process of financial planning and describes how it may be used by different types of financial services professionals. It provides an introductory description of some of the tools important to effective financial planning: communication skills, computer knowledge, and the understanding of financial satements. The book includes readings on the regulatory and professional environment within which financial planning occurs. Finally, the subjects of professionalism and professional ethics are explored, topics that are of such critical importance that financial planning is meaningless and probably even harmful without them.

The preparation of this book of readings would not have been possible without the assistance of many people. Among them are

- Burton T. Beam, Jr., CLU, CPCU, associate professor of insurance in the Huebner School at The American College, who made valuable suggestions for improving many of the readings
- Jeanne M. Campo of the Editorial Department, The American College, who provided excellent editorial assistance in all phases of the book's development
- Patricia A. Marruchella, who typed the several drafts and revisions of each reading
- most importantly, Patricia M. Crowe, without whose financial planning skills the Crowe family finances probably would be in a shambles

Robert M. Crowe

Readings in Financial Planning

FINANCIAL PLANNING: THE NEED,
THE PROCESS, AND THE PROFESSIONALS

by Dale S. Johnson*

People rarely attain their financial objectives unless they identify those objectives and then adopt realistic strategies to achieve them. Clearly formulating financial objectives is a particularly complex task, because it involves identifying real needs. Choosing appropriate strategies for satisfying these needs can be even more challenging because it frequently involves changes of behavior. In addition, the financial objectives that people seek are both diverse and often contradictory, reflecting the complexity of human motivations. In short, very few financial objectives are attainable without predetermined objectives and strategies based upon a realistic assessment of needs.

Although a few people are equipped to undertake the responsibility of financial planning, most will require the services of a professional planner. In either case, financial planning involves (1) the thorough collection and impartial analysis of information on a person's or family's personal and financial situation in order to identify needs and problems; (2) the establishment of specific financial objectives; and (3) the formulation, implementation, and continuous monitoring of a financial plan to achieve these objectives. For successful planning, the central focus must be identifying clients' actual financial needs and problems. This is why counseling with clients to gather thorough and accurate information is crucial to successful financial planning.

This reading examines the need for financial planning as a means of achieving personal financial objectives through overcoming the resistances, obstacles, and behavioral habits that typically preclude their attainment. It examines such impediments and suggests the financial planning process as a viable solution. The basic assumption here is that once a person's needs are known and related to available resources, choosing appropriate objective-oriented behaviors leads to successful financial planning, just as it does in any life-planning process.

The reading defines financial planning as a generic client-oriented process, describes its procedural methodology in both single-purpose and comprehensive forms,

---

*Dale S. Johnson, PhD, CFP, is a financial planning consultant and writer headquartered in Villanova, Pa. Robert W. Cooper, PhD, former dean of the Huebner School, also made extensive contributions to this reading.

and delineates the roles that financial services professionals play in the development and implementation phases of planning. Finally, the reading relates these roles to the educational objectives of the Chartered Life Underwriter (CLU) and Chartered Financial Consultant (ChFC) programs.

THE NEED FOR FINANCIAL PLANNING

In the decision-making process, people first establish <u>objectives</u> (goals) that they think will satisfy determined <u>needs</u> and then adopt <u>strategies</u> (behaviors) to achieve their objectives. This process is illustrated in figure 1 below.

FIGURE 1
Relationship of Objectives, Needs, and Strategies

Needs → Strategies → Objectives

A number of things can complicate this decision-making process, especially when it involves financial management. For example, most people are unaware that what they perceive and communicate as needs can be motivated by a variety of underlying desires that are not always related to available resources. The process is also complicated by the fact that people must choose from among a number of strategies that may or may not be appropriate for the achievement of their particular objectives.

For example, if a client's objective is to reduce income tax while funding the children's education, several alternative strategies are available as follows:

- direct gifts to family members
- an irrevocable trust funded with an income-producing asset
- a Uniform Gift to Minors Account, funded annually
- a high write-off exploratory oil drilling program
- a universal life insurance contract on the client

In this example, some of the alternative strategies will be more effective than others in achieving the client's objective. Some will also be more closely integrated with other objectives and strategies determined by the same client.

Once a person has determined an objective and has adopted a good prospective strategy, a decision-making loop is closed. Consequently, the relationship between needs, strategies, and objectives is established by a plan that embodies them as a decision-making process.

As illustrated in figure 2, when a particular objective has been accomplished, the consciously determined need or needs that motivated the successful strategies can be modified or relinquished, thus permitting a reallocation of energy and resources to other objectives. If the initial objective is not achieved, typically a person feels frustration and the need persists.

FIGURE 2
Accomplishment/Nonaccomplishment of Objectives

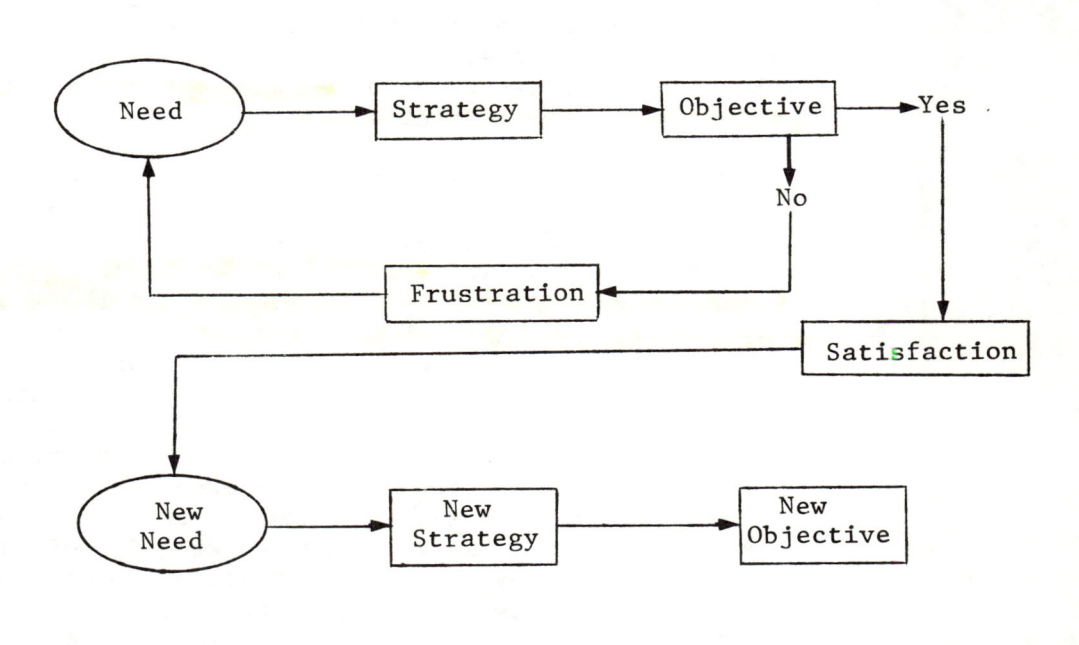

```
   Need ──▶ Strategy ──▶ Objective ──▶ Yes
    ▲                         │
    │                         No
    │                         ▼
    └──────── Frustration ◀───┘
                                        │
                              Satisfaction ◀──┐
    ┌─────────────────────────────────────────┘
    ▼
 New Need ──▶ New Strategy ──▶ New Objective
```

The important point illustrated in figure 2 is that the frustration of not achieving an objective uses up energy and resources in a repetitive cycle. On the other hand, achieving an objective releases these energies and resources and permits new needs to emerge. The whole purpose of counseling in the financial planning process is to help clients refine a decision-making model in which clear, realistic, client-identified relationships are established among needs, objectives, and objective-oriented strategies. They can then identify objectives and select appropriate strategies to achieve them in a life-planning process.

In such a process there are obstacles and resistances to be overcome. Let us examine some of these impediments that may frustrate individuals or prevent them from effectively initiating or carrying out this process.

Obstacles to the Achievement of Financial Objectives

Some of these obstacles are personal: they arise from the psychological makeup of people, the variety and complexity of their needs, and their backgrounds. Others are external, arising from such sources as economic conditions, legislative and social change, the changing financial services marketplace, and the human and technical limitations of financial services professionals. Because the satisfaction of a need usually involves an interaction between people and some aspect of their environment, note that these obstacles are both internal (within people) and external (in the environment).

Distortions of Perception

The most fundamental obstacle people must overcome in order to achieve their financial objectives is grounded in subjective reality--that is, in their perception of the environment in which they function.

Though an impartial observer might describe a situation as "objective reality," it is often perceived differently by different individuals. Because of their personal, subjective involvement, people tend to distort information (usually unconsciously) to make it fit better with their experiences, expectations, or values. These distortions result in part from selective attention, whose counterpart is selective inattention. This means that certain aspects of the environment are screened out and that the perceived environment is evaluated in terms of past experiences, needs, and values. Since the past experiences, needs, and values are never exactly the same for any two people, perceptions of the external environment will differ--will be characterized by an element of distortion that is subjective and does not always match the way "things really are."

Ironically, people's feelings are often the source of both important personal goals and the obstacles and resistances to their effective achievement. Because of this contradiction, the feelings of clients can vitally affect both the formulation and the outcome of financial plans that have been designed to move them from where they are now to where they want to be. The obstacles posed by this conflict can be effectively overcome only through a systematic counseling that enables clients to explore their own particular perception of the world and to come to know their real needs, to formulate realistic objectives, and to choose and adapt to those strategies that are most likely to achieve their objectives. This is the challenge to financial services professionals who attend to clients' needs through the financial planning process and who, as human beings themselves, share virtually the same aspirations, conditions, and obstacles as their clients. Reality, after all, or "things as they really are," is a negotiated and agreeable understanding among those who are involved in it.

Other Personal Obstacles

In addition to distortions of perception, which all individuals are subject to, there are individualistic obstacles to achieving personal financial objectives.

Some obstacles may stem from a person's inability or unwillingness to identify the financial objectives themselves. Since objectives are established in order to satisfy needs, people who are unwilling or unable to give considerable thought to their needs are likely to experience difficulty in setting meaningful objectives. In addition, many people have an obsessive concern with basic needs that prevents the emergence of more complex needs and the establishment of objectives related to those needs. For example, counselors often find clients concerned for their safety needs (security, stability, protection, and freedom from fear) but reluctant to break their old habits and clarify more complex needs and the objectives that might satisfy them. Even when people can articulate their real needs, they may still be unable to establish realistic objectives because of inadequate backgrounds and information. In these instances a financial services professional may help clients overcome obstacles and set priorities among objectives for meeting their needs.

Obstacles and resistances to achieving selected objectives may also arise from people's unwillingness or inability to (1) identify all the alternative strategies for achieving those objectives, (2) obtain the maximum information concerning the potential outcomes of the alternative strategies, and/or (3) select certain potentially successful strategies because they are emotionally threatening. People frequently fail to achieve their financial objectives because they select strategies based on a superficial evaluation of the alternatives available. Again, the services of a professional may be needed to assist clients in dispassionately identifying and evaluating various available strategies.

Procrastination is also a common obstacle to achieving financial objectives. For example, some people put off formulating a plan for achieving their various financial objectives. Reasons for this procrastination may include

- a hesitancy in addressing various painful personal concerns and family problems

1.5

- the lack of time to identify and evaluate wide-ranging planning considerations
- a feeling that one lacks the technical knowledge necessary to assess the alternative strategies for achieving financial objectives
- a sense that there is still plenty of time left for achieving certain objectives

The greatest single cause of procrastination, however, is being confronted by a task looming so large that it is overwhelming. If financial planning itself becomes this kind of obstacle, allowing a financial planner to manage and complete large portions of the task can often solve this problem for clients. At the same time, the planner can encourage them to define their own responsibilities in the planning process and to take on manageable tasks that they can confront and assume.

A properly trained financial services professional may help people deal with these and other sources of procrastination. However, the difficulty of finding a qualified financial services professional may itself be sufficient cause for procrastination. Moreover, if financial plans are formulated--either by individuals or by financial services professionals--procrastination may prevent clients from implementing the plans and/or monitoring and revising them periodically.

Ineffective Communications

Ineffective communications can also be an obstacle to achieving personal financial objectives. For example, the inability to effectively communicate with other family members may distort not only the assessment of a person's needs, but also the selection of appropriate strategies to meet that person's objectives. Similarly, the failure to communicate fully and clearly with financial advisers can result in improperly identified objectives and the formulation of inappropriate planning strategies. The proliferation of advertisements about financial services and products frequently overloads, creates "noise," results in the breakdown of communications, and leaves people confused and uninformed as to their alternatives.

Confusions in the Financial Services Environment

Another obstacle to effective financial planning is posed by the conditions of the financial services marketplace. One source is the communications overload mentioned above. Another source involves people who typically need financial advice but lack the technical information or conceptual knowledge to (1) choose good professional services or product-oriented advice, (2) integrate advice from several sources, or (3) seek advice when it is not readily available. The less than comprehensive advice offered by product and service specialists in all segments of the financial services industry may be uncoordinated even when it is delivered through systematic needs analysis. Too often the products sold by and the advice given by financial services specialists may solve one problem for clients but create others, or fail to address other problems and objectives effectively. However professional this advice may be, the delivery of financial products and services is fragmented because it is not integrated with clients' total financial and personal situations and their interrelated needs. In fact, the specialist adviser or product and service marketer is often unaware of the larger circumstances of the client.

Inflation and Taxes

For typical consumers, inflation has the effect of continuously eroding the purchasing power of their incomes, the accumulation potential of their investment assets, and the prospects of achieving their financial objectives. This leaves them doubtful about what can be done to improve their financial condition in real-dollar terms. Like Alice in Wonderland, in an inflationary environment "it takes all the running you can do to keep in the same place. If you want to get somewhere else, you must run twice as fast."

In addition to inflation, consumers must cope with the obstacles posed by taxation of their incomes and assets and by its negative impact on the achievement of their financial objectives. Frequent legislative, administrative, and judicial changes in the tax code and other regulations force them to modify their strategies every couple of years to avoid being penalized by previously developed financial plans. These factors pose formidable obstacles for people trying to take control of their economic well-being.

Risks to Income and Assets

The risks to people's income and assets in the course of a lifetime are varied and numerous, and any one risk or any combination of them can present serious obstacles to the achievement of personal and financial objectives. For our purposes these risks can be classified as investment risks and pure risks.

Investment risks. In general, risk to investment capital is the possibility that the actual return from an investment will be different from the expected return. In trying to accumulate assets, people are exposed to multiple obstacles that result from the effort to attain a certain level of income and accumulate assets. Obstacles are posed by the bewildering range of alternative investments, each with differing features and benefits. Once investment vehicles have been chosen, there are obstacles posed by the risks associated with achieving expected returns. Both factors--the varying features and benefits of alternative investment vehicles and the uncertainty of their risk/return characteristics--affect the income and appreciation of investment choices.

All of these investment risks can be analyzed in relation to specific investment prospects, and their probable outcomes can be assessed. Most can be evaluated and controlled by informed investment management. Whatever degree of evaluation and management is imposed, however, these risks can prevent achievement of financial objectives, and most people cannot or do not effectively evaluate them.

Pure risks. In addition to the obstacles created by investment risk, there are other areas of clients' personal and financial lives in which they are exposed to risks that may become obstacles also. These are pure risks.

Unlike investment risks, which provide an opportunity for either a gain or a loss, pure risks involve only the chance of loss or no loss. For example, the risks of losing one's home by fire, losing one's income-earning ability due to disability, and losing one's present assets or future income as a result of damages assessed for the negligent injury of another person are pure risks.

Clearly the failure to provide for potentially severe losses arising from pure risks--either by buying insurance or accumulating emergency and retirement funds or both--can produce severe obstacles to achieving personal financial objectives. However, the consequences of pure risks may also affect the achievement of financial objectives in more subtle ways. For example, failure to purchase the correct types of insurance in the correct amounts at the best prices could present a severe obstacle. Failure to evaluate carefully the relative merits of the various protection and accumulation vehicles available for establishing emergency and retirement funds may also create obstacles to achieving financial goals. The assistance of a professional insurance specialist will generally be required in negotiating these obstacles.

What Can Clients Do about the Obstacles Confronting Them?

Confronted by multiple financial needs and objectives, by a bewildering array of alternate strategies, and by personal and external obstacles, typical prospective clients for financial planning are confused. A few people may be able to take charge of their own situations and begin to do their own financial planning; most, however, are not equipped to do so by knowledge or temperament. Without help, most people will fail in their search for economic well-being and the achievement of financial objectives.

Money is a limited resource that can be deployed in a variety of ways with widely varying consequences. Without a systematic plan for acquiring it and allocating it properly, however, most people will not satisfy their overall financial needs. Moreover, they will have no plan for debt financing, balancing income and expenditures, accumulating savings for reserves and investment, protecting against multiple risks and potential liabilities, resolving conflicting financial objectives, providing for retirement, and building an estate. Their economic lives will continue to be buffeted and dislocated by a host of unidentified and uncontrollable variables.

The varying and ever-changing economic environment offers financial services professionals a tremendous challenge and an opportunity to assume responsible roles in helping consumers to enhance and preserve their economic well-being. The following overview of the generic financial planning process and its forms of application will delineate how it responds to consumers' needs and provides appropriate service opportunities for financial services professionals.

WHAT IS FINANCIAL PLANNING?

Financial planning cannot really be defined apart from its process. As opposed to merely selling products or services, financial planning is a generic, client-oriented process that involves

- initial contact with prospective client(s)
- gathering relevant information
- analyzing the prospective client's current position, needs, and problems
- helping the prospective client determine and refine his or her objectives
- developing appropriate plans/recommendations from among alternatives
- presenting plans/recommendations to the prospective client and requesting allocation of resources for implementation and/or payment of a service fee
- reviewing periodically the performance of the implemented plan, and modifying it as necessary and as the client requests

This generic financial planning process can be conducted professionally as either single-purpose financial planning or comprehensive financial planning.

Single-Purpose Financial Planning

Highly professional sales specialists and providers of services are typically problem solvers who meet the needs of their clients not just with products or services, but also with highly proficient technical expertise, a service orientation toward clients, and a needs analysis approach to delivery. It is this group of financial services professionals who first utilized the generic financial planning process. This generic financial planning process is illustrated in figure 3, using tax, insurance, and investment planning as examples of specialized areas. Delivered to clients at the highest level of professionalism and technical expertise, financial plans developed through this process are appropriately characterized as single-purpose or limited-objective plans. They are designed to help clients achieve determined objectives in a single area of their financial situation, or to solve a specific problem. For example, single-purpose financial planning might be directed toward the following specific objectives:

- assembling a portfolio of stocks and bonds for long-range accumulation and income objectives
- planning for the management of risk in a client-owned business
- drafting specific trust instruments to reduce a client's tax liability through income shifting and to provide, simultaneously, funding for the children's education
- providing an accounting opinion of the economic and tax projections for a proposed investment program involving oil and gas developmental drilling and equipment leasing
- determining the needs of a client for life insurance
- drafting buy-sell agreements for the transfer of a client's business interest upon retirement, disability, or death; providing a plan for funding these agreements
- providing legal advice in conjunction with a client's investment program aimed at achieving maximum capital appreciation and tax minimization

Professionally executed, single-purpose financial planning has the following two important characteristics:

- It is client-oriented in that it is a professional service addressed to the needs of clients, who come first in the order of service.
- It produces a plan, a strategy, or a program that is custom-tailored to help individual clients achieve specific objectives and purposes.

FIGURE 3
Types of Single-Purpose Financial Planning

Tax Planning	Insurance Planning	Investment Planning
Initial contact with client	Initial contact with client	Initial contact with client
↓	↓	↓
Gather individual/family data on client	Gather individual/family data on client	Gather individual/family data on client
↓	↓	↓
Analyze client's current position/needs/problems	Analyze client's current position/needs/problems	Analyze client's current position/needs/problems
↓	↓	↓
Help client determine/refine objective(s)	Help client determine/refine objectives(s)	Help client determine/refine objective(s)
↓	↓	↓
Develop plan(s)/recommendation(s) from all realistic alternatives professional adviser can provide	Develop plan(s)/recommendation(s) from all realistic alternatives professional advisers can provide	Develop plan(s)/recomendation(s) from all realistic alternatives professional adviser can provide
↓	↓	↓
Present plan to client, ask for allocation of resources for implementation, payment of service fee	Present plan to client, ask for allocation of resources for implementation, payment of service fee	Present plan to client, ask for allocation of resources for implementation, payment of service fee
↓	↓	↓
Periodic performance review; revise plan as necessary; hold steady if performance is satisfactory	Periodic performance review; revise plan as necessary; hold steady if performance is satisfactory	Periodic performance review; revise plan as necessary; hold steady if performance is satisfactory

1.11

In this sense, single-purpose financial planning helps tremendously to reduce the confusions of the marketplace for consumers by helping clients accomplish limited-objective planning. To the extent that consulting with clients and the delivery of products and services are driven by the process rather than by the motivation to sell, single-purpose financial planning is clearly objective and oriented to the best interests of the client as these interests have been expressed and/or determined in the professional relationship.

Comprehensive Financial Planning

Figure 3 (page 1.11) illustrates how the single-purpose financial planning process is carried out in the tracks of tax planning, insurance planning, and investment planning. These three tracks encompass virtually all of the more specific and narrowly focused financial objectives that individuals typically formulate. As long as financial services professionals conduct their practices solely in one of these three tracks, and adhere to the steps and procedures of the financial planning process, they are providing single-purpose financial planning. As soon as these professionals begin to integrate tax, insurance, and investment planning, however, they begin to move toward providing comprehensive financial planning. When the aspects of tax, insurance, and investment planning are fully integrated, as illustrated in figure 4 (as follows), the process becomes one of comprehensive financial planning.

As figure 4 visually demonstrates, comprehensive (or fully integrated) financial planning considers all aspects of a client's financial position, needs, objectives, and possible planning strategies in an integrated, coordinated approach. The three separate planning tracks of tax, insurance, and investment have now become a comprehensive, fully integrated process. Comprehensive financial planning therefore includes the following two characteristics of single-purpose planning mentioned earlier:

- It is client-oriented in that it is a professional service addressed to the needs of clients, who come first in the order of service.
- It produces a plan, a strategy, or a program that is custom-tailored to help individual clients achieve specific objectives and purposes.

In addition, however, comprehensive financial planning goes beyond single-purpose planning as follows:

- It is comprehensive--that is, it encompasses the total personal and financial situations of clients insofar as these situations can be uncovered, clarified, and addressed through counseling and data gathering.

FIGURE 4
Comprehensive Financial Planning

Tax Planning	Insurance Planning	Investment Planning
Initial contact with client	Initial contact with client	Initial contact with client
Gather individual/family data on client	Gather individual/family data on client	Gather individual/family data on client
Analyze client's current position/needs/problems	Analyze client's current position/needs/problems	Analyze client's current position/needs/problems
Help client determine/refine objective(s)	Help client determine/refine objectives(s)	Help client determine/refine objective(s)
Develop plan(s)/recommendation(s) from all realistic alternatives professional adviser can provide	Develop plan(s)/recommendation(s) from all realistic alternatives professional adviser can provide	Develop plan(s)/recommendation(s) from all realistic alternatives professional adviser can provide
Present plan to client, ask for allocation of resources for implementation, payment of service fee	Present plan to client, ask for allocation of resources for implementation, payment of service fee	Present plan to client, ask for allocation of resources for implementation, payment of service fee
Periodic performance review; revise plan as necessary; hold steady if performance is satisfactory	Periodic performance review; revise plan as necessary; hold steady if performance is satisfactory	Periodic performance review; revise plan as necessary; hold steady if performance is satisfactory

1.13

- It integrates into its own methodology all the facets of the single-purpose planning process, including the expertise of other professional specialists; thus, at more complex and extensive levels of clients' needs, it employs the coordinated team approach to problem solving.

The Comprehensive Financial Planning Process

As we have noted, professionals from all the major segments of the financial services industry--that is, from insurance, securities and investments, banking, law, and accounting--have contributed to the development of the financial planning process in theory and practice. Comprehensive financial planning goes beyond the process of single-purpose financial planning by integrating all financial concerns of clients. Although this integration is effected in the plan development stage of that process, integration characterizes the whole process itself--especially in thorough counseling with clients, gathering complete information about their personal and financial situations, analyzing and diagnosing their current situations, and helping them set realistic and coordinated financial objectives.

Now we will examine more closely the comprehensive financial planning process as schematically illustrated in figure 5 on the following page. In the blocks on the left side are the phases of the process, and in the larger blocks on the right are the primary types of activity these phases trigger. From the starting point (initial client contact) the process moves through several phases and finally to the periodic review of the plan and evaluation of performance (conducted at least annually) after the plan is implemented.

The process begins with the initial contact with the prospective client(s) or with groups for precounseling. This phase of the process, which precedes a formal engagement for comprehensive financial planning, typically involves

- explaining what comprehensive financial planning is, what services are offered, what the planner's compensation arrangements are, what documents and records will be needed, and what relationships with other financial advisers and specialists may be involved
- following up (usually by letter) to suggest an appointment with the individual or members of a group for financial counseling
- sending to each prospective client a list of and receipt for documents and records that will be needed, plus the relevant pages of the planner's information-gathering form for precounseling information

FIGURE 5: The Comprehensive Financial Planning Process

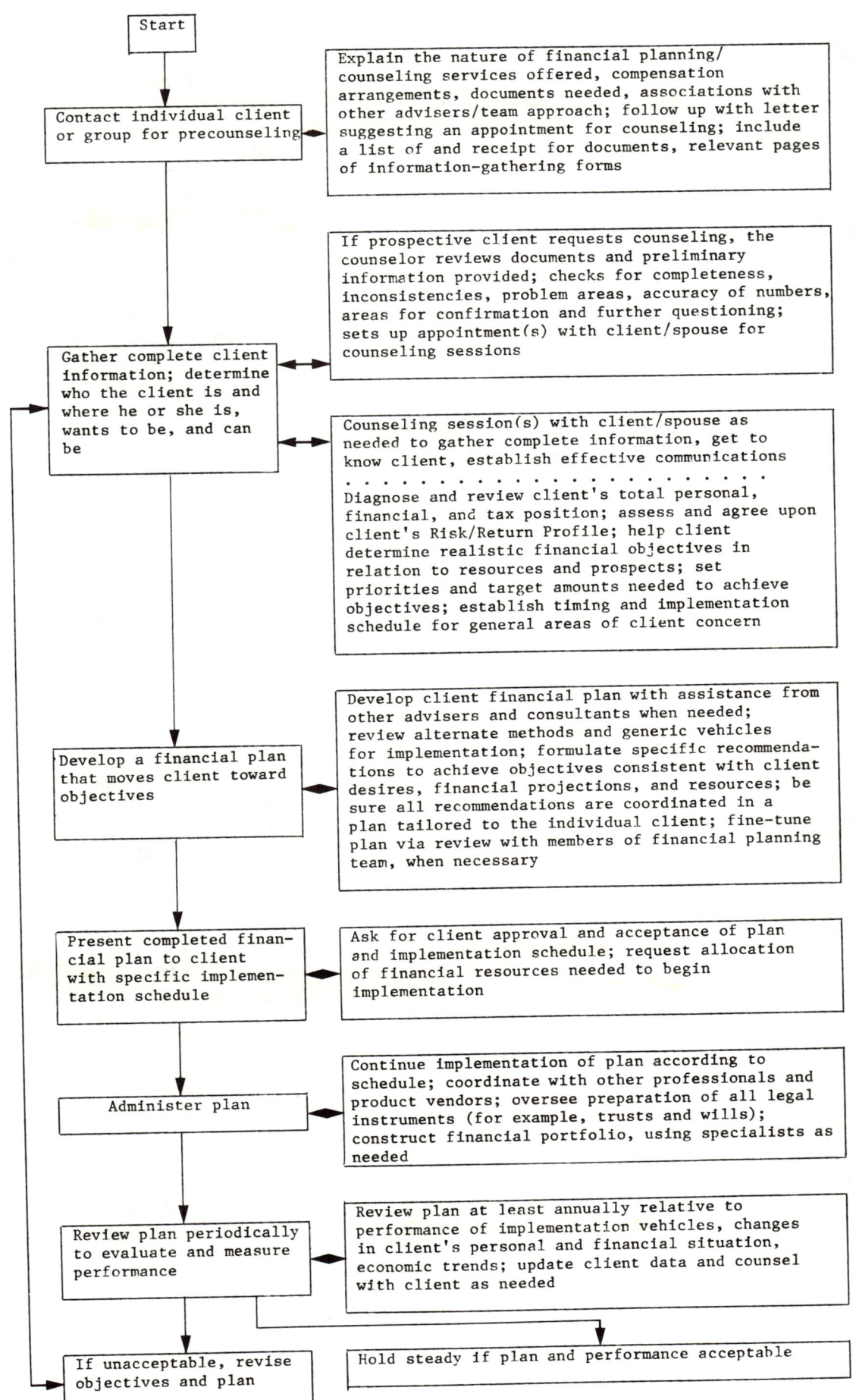

```
┌─────────┐
│  Start  │
└────┬────┘
     ▼
┌──────────────────────┐     ┌─────────────────────────────────────────┐
│ Contact individual   │     │ Explain the nature of financial         │
│ client or group for  │◄───►│ planning/counseling services offered,   │
│ precounseling        │     │ compensation arrangements, documents    │
└──────────┬───────────┘     │ needed, associations with other         │
           │                 │ advisers/team approach; follow up with  │
           │                 │ letter suggesting an appointment for    │
           │                 │ counseling; include a list of and       │
           │                 │ receipt for documents, relevant pages   │
           │                 │ of information-gathering forms          │
           │                 └─────────────────────────────────────────┘
           │
           │                 ┌─────────────────────────────────────────┐
           │                 │ If prospective client requests          │
           │                 │ counseling, the counselor reviews       │
           │                 │ documents and preliminary information   │
           │                 │ provided; checks for completeness,      │
           │                 │ inconsistencies, problem areas,         │
           │                 │ accuracy of numbers, areas for          │
           ▼                 │ confirmation and further questioning;   │
┌──────────────────────┐     │ sets up appointment(s) with             │
│ Gather complete      │     │ client/spouse for counseling sessions   │
│ client information;  │◄───►└─────────────────────────────────────────┘
│ determine who the    │
│ client is and where  │     ┌─────────────────────────────────────────┐
│ he or she is, wants  │     │ Counseling session(s) with              │
│ to be, and can be    │◄───►│ client/spouse as needed to gather       │
└──────────┬───────────┘     │ complete information, get to know       │
           │                 │ client, establish effective             │
           │                 │ communications                          │
           │                 │ . . . . . . . . . . . . . . . . . .     │
           │                 │ Diagnose and review client's total      │
           │                 │ personal, financial, and tax position;  │
           │                 │ assess and agree upon client's          │
           │                 │ Risk/Return Profile; help client        │
           │                 │ determine realistic financial           │
           │                 │ objectives in relation to resources     │
           │                 │ and prospects; set priorities and       │
           │                 │ target amounts needed to achieve        │
           │                 │ objectives; establish timing and        │
           │                 │ implementation schedule for general     │
           │                 │ areas of client concern                 │
           │                 └─────────────────────────────────────────┘
           ▼
┌──────────────────────┐     ┌─────────────────────────────────────────┐
│                      │     │ Develop client financial plan with      │
│                      │     │ assistance from other advisers and      │
│                      │     │ consultants when needed; review         │
│                      │     │ alternate methods and generic vehicles  │
│ Develop a financial  │     │ for implementation; formulate specific  │
│ plan that moves      │◄───►│ recommendations to achieve objectives   │
│ client toward        │     │ consistent with client desires,         │
│ objectives           │     │ financial projections, and resources;   │
│                      │     │ be sure all recommendations are         │
│                      │     │ coordinated in a plan tailored to the   │
│                      │     │ individual client; fine-tune plan via   │
│                      │     │ review with members of financial        │
│                      │     │ planning team, when necessary           │
└──────────┬───────────┘     └─────────────────────────────────────────┘
           ▼
┌──────────────────────┐     ┌─────────────────────────────────────────┐
│ Present completed    │     │ Ask for client approval and acceptance  │
│ financial plan to    │◄───►│ of plan and implementation schedule;    │
│ client with specific │     │ request allocation of financial         │
│ implementation       │     │ resources needed to begin               │
│ schedule             │     │ implementation                          │
└──────────┬───────────┘     └─────────────────────────────────────────┘
           ▼
┌──────────────────────┐     ┌─────────────────────────────────────────┐
│                      │     │ Continue implementation of plan         │
│                      │     │ according to schedule; coordinate with  │
│ Administer plan      │◄───►│ other professionals and product         │
│                      │     │ vendors; oversee preparation of all     │
│                      │     │ legal instruments (for example, trusts  │
│                      │     │ and wills); construct financial         │
│                      │     │ portfolio, using specialists as needed  │
└──────────┬───────────┘     └─────────────────────────────────────────┘
           ▼
┌──────────────────────┐     ┌─────────────────────────────────────────┐
│ Review plan          │     │ Review plan at least annually relative  │
│ periodically to      │◄───►│ to performance of implementation        │
│ evaluate and measure │     │ vehicles, changes in client's personal  │
│ performance          │     │ and financial situation, economic       │
└──────────┬───────────┘     │ trends; update client data and counsel  │
           │                 │ with client as needed                   │
           │                 └─────────────────────────────────────────┘
           ▼
┌──────────────────────┐     ┌─────────────────────────────────────────┐
│ If unacceptable,     │     │ Hold steady if plan and performance     │
│ revise objectives    │     │ acceptable                              │
│ and plan             │     └─────────────────────────────────────────┘
└──────────────────────┘
```

1.15

If prospective clients respond positively to this phase of the comprehensive planning process, the second phase begins with gathering complete information about their personal and financial situation. The purpose of this phase is to determine who the clients are as persons; what the state of their current financial and tax position is; what their needs, problems, and objectives are; and what their financial resources are. This phase involves

- reviewing the documents and preliminary information provided by clients
- determining the completeness (or incompleteness) of information and uncovering any inconsistencies between the information provided by the clients' documents and records and what the clients themselves provide in the information-gathering form or counseling sessions
- setting up appointments with clients and spouses (if any) for thorough counseling about their desires, needs, problems, and objectives
- completing all sections of information requested in the planner's information-gathering form
- establishing effective communications with clients and getting to know personally the details of their lives and relationships that are central to the planner's objective of developing financial plans suited to their circumstances
- diagnosing and reviewing with clients their total personal, financial, and tax position, based upon financial statements
- assessing with clients their risk/return profile
- agreeing with clients about realistic financial objectives based on their resources and prospects
- setting priorities among clients' objectives and determining target amounts needed to achieve them
- establishing a timing and implementation schedule for meeting clients' objectives

The third phase of the comprehensive financial planning process is the development of a comprehensive plan that moves clients toward their financial objectives. In this phase of the process, planners exercise their own specialties and coordinate the participation of other specialists. They rely particularly heavily upon their specialized technical skills, their general overview of available and appropriate planning techniques and strategies, and the specialized services and products that are available through other members of the financial planning team. In this development and planning stage financial planners perform (or coordinate the performance of) the following procedures:

- developing a financial plan, with assistance by other advisers and consultants as needed

- reviewing alternate methods and generic vehicles for plan implementation
- formulating specific recommendations to achieve objectives that are consistent with clients' needs, financial projections, and resources
- coordinating all recommendations to achieve multiple objectives where possible and to provide plans tailored to individual clients
- fine-tuning clients' plans through review with members of the financial planning team, as necessary

The fourth phase of the comprehensive financial planning process is the presentation of completed financial plans to clients in a format that was agreed upon in the initial engagement, along with specific implementation schedules (if this service was included in the original engagement). This stage involves

- asking for and obtaining clients' approval and acceptance of plans and implementation schedules
- requesting the allocation of the financial resources needed to begin the implementation of clients' plans

When clients have accepted their plans and agreed to the implementation schedule, financial planners enter into the fifth phase of the comprehensive financial planning process, the administration of clients' plans, which involves

- implementing plans according to schedule
- coordinating implementation with other financial services professionals and product vendors, as necessary
- overseeing the preparation of all legal instruments associated with plans (such as trusts and wills)
- constructing clients' financial or asset portfolios, using specialists as needed

If carried out effectively and to the clients' satisfaction, the final phase of the comprehensive financial planning process becomes a continuous one. Now, however, the high-level intensity of the initial planning process will be over, and a much-abbreviated version of that process begins.

Specifically this final phase involves

- reviewing clients' plans at least once a year to measure the performance of implementation vehicles, determine changes in clients' personal and financial situations, and evaluate the impact of changes in the economic, legislative, and financial environment
- updating clients' information and further counseling with them as needed to maintain the viability of their plans

If this periodic assessment of financial plans indicates satisfactory performance in relation to the current objectives, then planners should continue in the administration phase. If performance is not acceptable or if there is a significant change in personal or financial circumstances or objectives, planners and clients should revise the initial objectives and modify the plans in light of these changed circumstances. During this revision, of course, planners should repeat only procedures that are necessary. Any changes in the plan must be intricately coordinated with the originally determined plan.

The heart of the comprehensive financial planning process is counseling closely with clients, getting to know them as persons, finding out as much as possible about their current personal and financial situations and how they feel about them, and determining their objectives. Financial services professionals who practice the comprehensive planning process, therefore, will likely begin their role by becoming comprehensive counselors for the client's best interest; as the process proceeds and they learn more and more, they typically become comprehensive planners for the client's best interest.

The next section of the reading examines the results of recently completed research that helps to clarify what the consuming public may really feel that it wants or needs in the way of financial planning.

What Consumers Want in Financial Planning

In recent research studies,[1] Cooper and Ulivi surveyed consumers in two different demographic environments--the state of Arkansas and the California metropolitan statistical areas of Los Angeles/Long Beach and Anaheim/Santa Ana/Garden Grove. The general response rate in both demographic areas was high for this kind of survey. In both surveys, participants were provided with the same somewhat simplified description of the service of comprehensive financial planning, as follows:

> This service involves analyzing an individual's total financial situation, and then designing a comprehensive strategy in the form of a written plan with the purpose of achieving various financial goals. This comprehensive strategy includes specific recommendations in such areas as tax shelters, buying and selling stocks and bonds, the amount of insurance coverage needed (for example, life, disability, fire, etc.), estate planning, and many other areas of finance.

---

1. Robert W. Cooper and Ricardo M. Ulivi, "Comprehensive Personal Financial Planning: A Survey of Consumer Opinions," CLU Journal 37, no. 2 (April 1983): 40-46.

In order to get a general sense of the extent of consumer interest in comprehensive financial planning, the participants in both studies were asked to indicate their degree of interest in obtaining a personal financial plan on a six-point scale ranging from "definitely interested" to "definitely not interested." The responses in both studies indicated relatively high levels of interest in comprehensive financial planning, with 63.7 percent of the California respondents and 45.3 percent of the Arkansas respondents indicating some degree of interest in obtaining a personal financial plan. Although these are rather high percentages, conversely a large percentage of the households in both studies indicated a lack of interest in comprehensive financial planning. These findings suggest that despite the rather extensive interest in comprehensive financial planning, there is still a considerable market for the highly professional single-purpose financial planning traditionally delivered by various financial services specialists.

The research by Cooper and Ulivi also suggests the relative importance that respondents interested in comprehensive financial planning placed on various features that might be included in a personal financial plan. As shown in table 1, the responses of those indicating an interest in comprehensive financial planning in both the California and Arkansas studies assigned a very high degree of importance to the minimization of taxes, minimizing the effects of inflation, and planning for retirement. This suggests that, in general, comprehensive financial plans should place a heavy emphasis on these areas of widespread concern. Respondents also assigned a relatively high degree of importance to features of a plan that would provide analyses of their financial resources and expenses and an understanding of their financial attitudes and goals. These results support the fundamental notion that comprehensive financial planning should help clients understand their present positions and where they would like to be financially, in addition to simply providing them with the most appropriate strategies for getting there. This, in turn, suggests that a comprehensive plan should begin with an analysis of a client's total current financial position and an identification of the client's major financial objectives.

Also, both surveys revealed that features pertaining to the analysis of various types of insurance needs and employer-provided fringe benefits were viewed as relatively more important for inclusion in a financial plan than features related to investment in stocks, bonds, mutual funds, collectibles, and commodities. However, investment in tax shelters was ranked above the insurance-related features in the California study and investment in real estate was viewed as more important in both studies.

TABLE 1

Relative Importance of Various Features That May Be Included in a Personal Financial Plan

Feature	California Study Mean Score Assigned by Group 1	Rank	Arkansas Study Rank
Minimization of taxes	5.53	1	4
Minimizing the effects of inflation	5.34	2	1
Planning for retirement	5.33	3	2
Investment in real estate	5.13	4	7
Understanding of financial attitudes and goals	5.03	5	5
Analysis of your financial resources and expenses	5.01	6	3
Investment in tax shelters	4.87	7	14
A review of the economic outlook	4.64	8	9
Estate planning	4.59	9	13
Preparation of a household budget	4.49	10	6
Analysis of health insurance needs	4.35	11	8
Analysis of property/liability insurance needs	4.21	12	10
Analysis of fringe benefits offered by your employer	3.96	13	11
Analysis of life insurance needs	3.91	14	12
Investment in stocks	3.56	15	16
Investment in mutual funds	3.28	16	17
Investment in bonds	3.25	17	15
Investment in gold or diamonds	2.86	18	18
Investment in commodities	2.55	19	19

The Financial Services Marketplace

In recent years the financial services industry has been undergoing considerable restructuring in response to consumer expectations and needs as described above as well as to increased competition, new technology, and a changing regulatory environment. These structural realignments affect the products available, services provided, and distribution systems. Figure 6 depicts what one observer sees as the new marketplace for financial services that is emerging in the changed industry environment. He sees four fairly distinct tiers, or segments, of financial services

FIGURE 6
Financial Services Market:
The Four Tiers*

		Products & Services	Who Will Service
Net Worth 1+MM Income 250+K	**LEADERSHIP PLANNING MARKET** Tier 4 WEALTHY INDIVIDUALS CHIEF EXECUTIVES	• Specialized products • Integrated tax planning for retirement, corporate benefits, credit lines, cash flow, cash/asset management, wealth maximization/preservation, estate transfer • Comprehensive planning	• Individual financial planners • Interdisciplinary planning firm of specialists
Net Worth 250-500K Income 75-100K	**SOPHISTICATED PLANNING MARKET** Tier 3 PROFESSIONALS SMALL BUSINESS OWNERS UPPER MANAGEMENT "CORPORATE" MARKET	• Private placements, direct investments for specialized needs • Some packaged products • Goal setting, implementation • Counseling, professional relationships	• Individual financial planners • Interdisciplinary specialists • Boutiques (specialty firms) • Large planning firms • Financial supermarkets (minor importance)
Net Worth 50-150K Income 50+K	**DIRECTED PLANNING MARKET** Tier 2 LOWER MANAGEMENT WHITE COLLAR 2-INCOME FAMILIES	• Packaged products (money market funds, mutual funds, REITs, etc.) • Data gathering; computerized packaged plans • Some personal planning services	• Large planning firms • Financial supermarkets • Banks, insurance cos., national securities firms • Financial services specialists
Net Worth 0-25K Income 0-25K	**PRODUCT PLANNING MARKET** Tier 1 1-INCOME FAMILIES BLUE COLLAR MARGINAL SAVERS	• IRAs, life insurance, money market funds (No personal planning services)	• Financial supermarkets • Banks, insurance cos., securities firms • Individual product vendors

*This figure is adapted from a seminar promotion item developed by Richard G. Wollack, president of Consolidated Capital Institutional Advisers Inc., Emeryville, California. It has been modified by the author for use here.

consumers, based on different levels of net worth and income. He suggests that the range of financial products and services that will be of primary appeal differs depending on the market tier or segment. Finally, he has identified which of the many providers of financial services and products now active in the marketplace will, in his judgment, tend to predominate in each market segment.

Although not all experts will necessarily agree with this observer's conclusions, he has nevertheless made it clear that the field of financial services is by no means homogeneous. Let us look more closely at certain types of professionals who are providing financial services in the marketplace today.

THE PROFESSIONALS WHO PROVIDE FINANCIAL SERVICES

In the emerging financial services marketplace, there are many professionals who provide products or services either as specialists or as comprehensive financial planners. In the currently changing marketplace, specialists are becoming even more critical in matching available products and services with consumer needs. Yet, the proliferation and increasing complexity of today's specialized products and services reach well beyond the range of familiarity of most professional specialists.

In this increasingly complex marketplace, consumer demand for financial advice has given rise to distinct markets for comprehensive financial planning. Indeed, this consumer demand plus the deregulation of financial services and the consequential realignment of the producers and distributors of financial products creates an increasing need for generalists in financial services. These generalists do not replace specialists. Rather, they help clients to develop strategies for achieving their economic objectives by coordinating the efforts of various specialists as well as providing their own expertise. These fully professional and competent generalists are comprehensive financial planners.

It is useful at this point to identify the essential functions of the financial services specialists and comprehensive financial planners.

Financial Services Specialists

Professionals who are financial services specialists function primarily in the following ways:

- as single-purpose financial planners, including, for example,
  - tax planners
  - insurance specialists

- investment specialists
- accountants
- bankers and trust officers
- as members of various types of financial planning teams, such as estate planning teams and comprehensive financial planning teams

In short, specialists function either independently, as individuals or firms, or as individual or firm members of financial planning teams. They may be insurance agents, registered securities representatives, bank officers, attorneys, or accountants. Whether they function as independent specialists with their own base of clients or as specialist members of financial planning teams, financial services specialists exercise their primary skills. If they become comprehensive financial planners as well, they add a generalist's function (described below) to their primary specialization. It is through the addition of this generalist's function to an existing specialty that representatives of the professional cadres throughout the financial services industry--in insurance, banking, investments, accounting, and law--have most commonly become comprehensive financial planners.

Comprehensive Financial Planners

Although comprehensive financial planners often serve as a major, if not the principal, source of technical expertise when comprehensive financial planning services are provided to clients, it is their role as generalists that distinguishes them from the other financial services professionals involved in the comprehensive financial planning process. The generalist function performed by the comprehensive financial planner involves the following activities that lie beyond the scope of the functions typically performed by financial services specialists:

- gathering complete information about a client's total personal, financial, and tax situation
- conducting or coordinating a thorough, integrated analysis of the client's current financial and tax position, personal needs, and problems
- helping the client to establish and set priorities among a comprehensive set of financial objectives
- coordinating the development, implementation, and continuous monitoring of an integrated, comprehensive financial plan to achieve the client's objectives

Clearly the comprehensive financial planning process demands both a comprehensive financial planner to direct it and a team of other specialized financial services professionals to provide essential technical expertise (and possibly the financial products and services needed to implement the plan). All teams and organizations are characterized by pecking orders. On the comprehensive financial planning team the comprehensive financial planner who comes to "know" the client through fact finding and earns the client's trust and confidence is the natural leader. In no sense, however, does this relationship diminish the importance of other team specialists. On the contrary, participation in a concerted planning effort for a client <u>enhances</u> the professionalism of the specialists because their efforts are directed not only toward immediate problem solving but also toward preventive strategies that contribute to the client's general well-being into the future. Figure 7 illustrates the relationships between the client, the comprehensive financial planner, and the financial services specialists in the comprehensive financial planning process. Note that the comprehensive financial planner integrates and coordinates the efforts of the various specialists on behalf of the client.

THE RELATIONSHIP BETWEEN THE EDUCATION OF COMPREHENSIVE FINANCIAL PLANNERS AND FINANCIAL SERVICES SPECIALISTS IN INSURANCE

The ChFC and CLU programs of The American College are structured to accommodate and reinforce the relationships between the generalist discipline of comprehensive financial planning and the specialist discipline of counseling clients about their insurance needs and meeting those needs with appropriate plans, strategies, and programs. Accordingly, the CLU and ChFC curricula have been designed to contain certain subject matter that is common to both disciplines and that is fundamental to the education of <u>all</u> professionals providing personal financial services to clients. The common required courses are an introduction to the process of financial planning; an overview of the principal types of insurance products; a survey of investment principles and products; and an examination of the essentials of federal income taxation. Without a firm grasp of these four fundamental areas, neither comprehensive financial planners nor financial services specialists in insurance can provide professional client services.

On the other hand, there is certain additional expertise that all comprehensive financial planners should have that is <u>not</u> the same as the additional expertise that all insurance planning professionals should have. Consequently the ChFC curriculum requires the additional understanding of several advanced, integrated financial and tax planning topics, while the CLU program calls for a more in-depth analysis of insurance products, law, and company operations.

In addition, because of the great diversity that exists among the professional practices of both comprehensive financial planners and financial services specialists in insurance, each of the two educational programs provides an

FIGURE 7
Relationships Between the Client, the Comprehensive
Financial Planner, and Financial Services Specialists

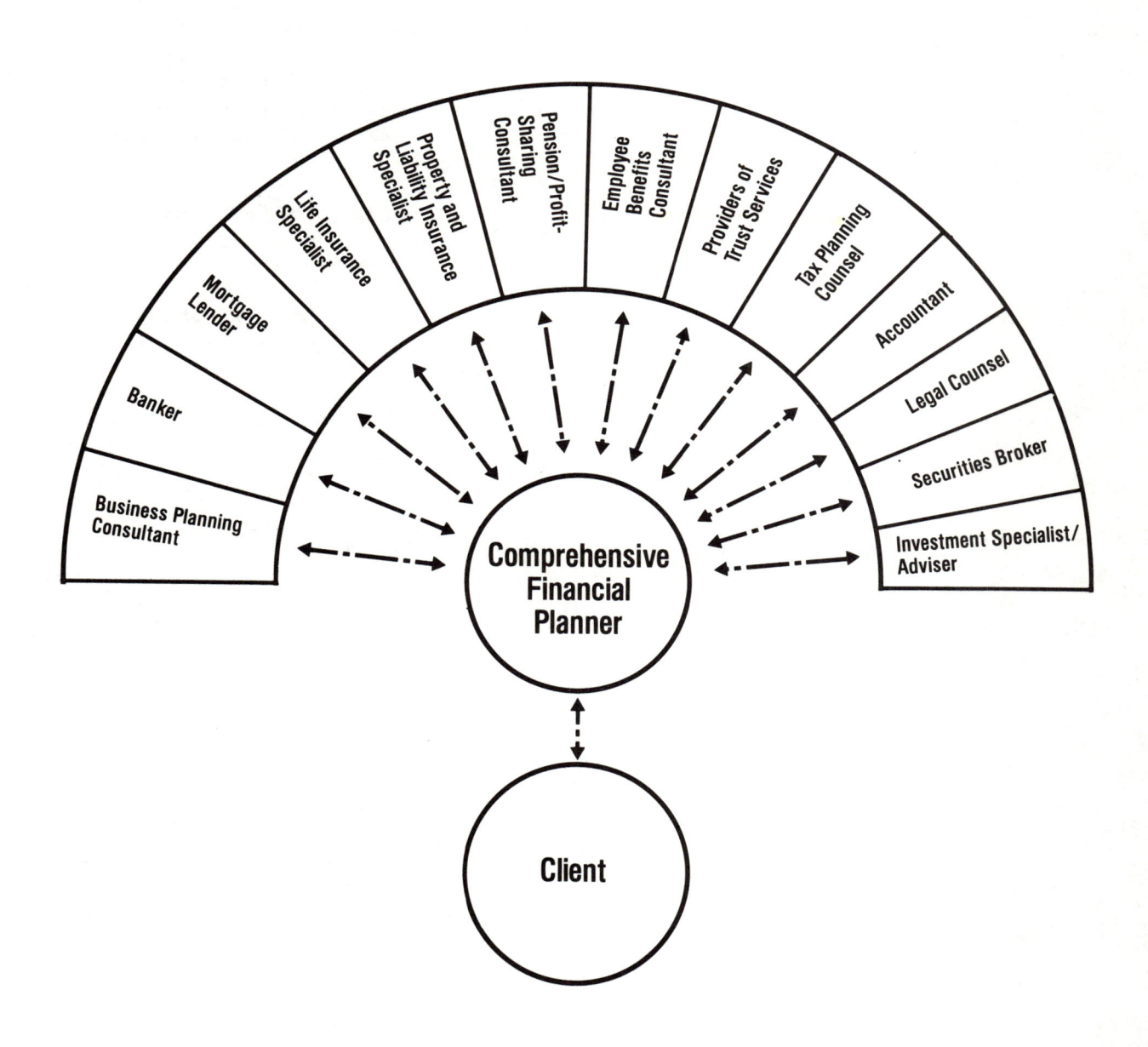

1.25

array of elective courses. Through an appropriate selection of particular electives, each type of professional can develop specialized expertise particularly suited to the needs of his or her own practice and clientele.

Finally, the CLU and ChFC curricula have been designed in view of the fact that many who have developed competency as financial services professionals in the specialized field of insurance will wish to add the generalist's skills needed for comprehensive financial planning, and vice versa. In each case the second educational program may be completed by fulfilling all the course requirements of the second program and completing at least three courses not completed as part of the first program.

To summarize, the educational needs of comprehensive financial planners and financial services specialists in insurance are in several ways similar; in many ways different. Within either category they are varied. Together the two educational programs (ChFC and CLU) can satisfy a broad range of educational needs from all areas of the financial services industry.

STANDARDS FOR A COMPREHENSIVE FINANCIAL PLAN

by the Registry of Financial Planning Practitioners*

INTRODUCTION

The Registry of Financial Planning Practitioners announces its Standards for a Comprehensive Financial Plan, which provides a basis for evaluation of a comprehensive service to clients. It also offers a focal point for dialogue and written commentary to the Registry regarding the evolution of these standards in the months and years ahead. The Registry's goal is to have the public accept financial planning as a profession; these standards are another step toward this objective.

Many clients do not need or want a comprehensive review in all areas covered by these standards. In fact, modular financial plans are more common today and will continue to grow in popularity due to the cost savings of an abbreviated plan or the client's lack of desire for a complete or comprehensive financial plan. It is therefore very likely that areas covered in the plan would be comprehensive in nature but the plan would not be considered a comprehensive financial plan as defined by The Registry. It must be understood that each financial plan and the standards, actions, and elements appropriate to each plan will vary depending upon the individual characteristics or circumstances of the client, the objectives to be reached, and the needs, desires, and requests of the client as presented to the planner.

For example, a financial planner may strictly limit his or her practice to corporate CEO's who do not have a cash-flow problem and who would not want or be willing to pay for a cash-flow analysis. The plan drafted for this type of client would therefore not fall within the Registry definition of a comprehensive financial plan. This does not mean that the plan produced was not excellent and appropriate in the areas covered or that this client was not served professionally, ethically, or competently.

A comprehensive financial plan should contain analysis of all pertinent factors relating to the client. While order and style of presentation may vary, the plan should include, but not be limited to, the following elements:

---

*Copyright © 1987. Registry of Financial Planning Practitioners.

2.1

1. personal data
2. client goals and objectives
3. identification of issues and problems
4. assumptions
5. balance sheet/net worth
6. cash flow management
7. income tax
8. risk management/insurance
9. investments
10. financial independence, retirement planning, education, and other special needs
11. estate planning
12. recommendations
13. implementation

In the development of a comprehensive financial plan, the planner is responsible for the above elements of the plan from data gathering through analysis and presentation to the client. Those elements of the plan that the planner does not personally perform remain the responsibility of the planner to coordinate.

When technical elements such as legal and insurance areas are not personally performed by the planner, the financial plan or supplement should include supporting documentation that these areas have been or will be coordinated by the planner.

Analysis of each element of the plan should consist of a review of pertinent facts, a consideration of the advantage(s) and/or disadvantage(s) of the current situation and a determination of what, if any, further action is required. The plan should include a summary statement providing the planner's comments on the analysis and his or her recommendations where appropriate for each element of the plan.

STANDARDS FOR A COMPREHENSIVE FINANCIAL PLAN

Personal Data

Should include relevant personal and family data for parties covered under the plan

Comments

- This should include, but not be limited to, name, address, social security number, birthdate, and other relevant data.

Client's Goals and Objectives

A reiteration of the client's stated goals and objectives, indicating their priority and including a time frame where applicable

Comments

- The statement of goals and objectives will form the basic framework for the development of the financial plan.
- The client's goals and objectives should be expressed in language as specific and precise as possible. For example, a statement of a goal should read "retire at age 62 in present home and maintain current standard of living" rather than "a comfortable retirement."

Identification of Issues and Problems

A plan must address relevant issues and problems identified by the client, the planner, and/or other advisors.

Comments

- List personal and financial issues and problems that affect the client, such as major illnesses, education costs, and taxes. While the client may be aware of many, if not all, of the issues, the planner may discover other areas that are, or could develop into, a problem.
- These issues and problems, when combined with the client's goals and objectives, will complete the framework and direction for the financial plan. Since style and order are not the primary consideration, the analysis or recommendation section(s) of the plan may be more appropriate for identifying issues and problems.

Assumptions

Identify and state material assumptions used in the plan's preparation.

Comments

- Assumptions should include, but not be limited to, inflation, investment growth rate, and mortality.

Balance Sheet/Net Worth

A presentation and analysis to include, but not be limited to, a schedule listing assets and liabilities with a calculation of net worth and itemized schedules of liabilities and assets to be included as appropriate

Comments

- In addition to the schedules, footnotes should be included as appropriate.

Cash-Flow Management

Statements and analysis to include, but not be limited to, a statement of the client's sources and uses of funds for the current year and for all relevant years, indicating net cash flow, as well as a separate income statement, where appropriate

Comments

- sources--earned income, investment income, sale proceeds, gifts, etc.
- uses--living expenses, debt service, acquisition of assets, taxes paid, etc.
- net cash flow--both positive and negative

Income Tax

An income tax statement and analysis to include, but not be limited to, the income taxes for the current year and for all relevant years covered in the plan

Comments

- Projections should show the nature of the income and deductions in sufficient detail to permit calculation of the tax liability. The analysis should identify marginal tax rate for each year and any special situations such as alternative minimum tax, passive loss limitations, etc., that affect the client's tax liability.
- The financial plan should include footnotes to let the client know which taxes (e.g., state or city) have not been addressed.

Risk Management/Insurance

Analysis of a client's financial exposure relative to mortality, morbidity, liability, and property, including business as appropriate

Comments

- mortality--survivor income and capital needs analysis
- morbidity--impact of loss of health
- liability--legal exposure
- property--loss of value
- business--loss due to business involvement

Listing and analysis of current policies and problems to include, but not be limited to, life, disability, medical, business, property/casualty, and liability

Comments

- Analysis of existing coverage and/or risk exposure in relationship to the client's needs, goals, and objectives.
- If any area of insurance is not within the competency range of the financial planner, the planner has the responsibility to coordinate with other professionals and document such coordination in the financial plan. Documentation of the above areas can include the insurance professional's summary, if completed, or the professional's name and the time frame when such review will be completed.

Investments

A listing of the current investment portfolio and an analysis or discussion of the liquidity, diversification, and investment risk exposure of the portfolio. In addition, the suitability of the investments in relationship to the client's needs, goals, and objectives should be addressed. To include, but not be limited to, risk tolerance, risk management of investments, suitability, liquidity, diversification, and personal management efforts.

Comments

- risk tolerance--addresses the client's willingness to accept investment risk
- risk management--analysis of the client's exposure relative to loss of invested capital
- suitability--appropriateness of the investment for the client
- liquidity--the availability of assets that can be converted into cash at acceptable costs
- diversification--appropriate mix of assets to meet the client's needs, goals, and objectives
- personal management efforts--the degree to which the client wants to manage and is capable of managing his or her assets

Financial Independence, Retirement Planning, Education, and Other Special Needs

An analysis of the capital needed at some future time to provide for financial independence, retirement, education, or other special needs. The analysis should include a projection of resources expected to be available to meet these needs at that time.

Comments

- In achieving the above, inflation, growth of assets, and company benefits should be considered where applicable.
- Special sections of the above topics may require a separate heading in the financial plan. For example, company benefits may require an analysis of types available, pretax and post-tax contributions needed, tax treatment of plans and investment of benefit plan assets.

Estate Planning

Identification of assets includible in the client's estate and an analysis of the control, disposition, and taxation of those assets.

Comments

- control--authority to manage or direct the use of assets by means of title, trusteeship, power of attorney, etc.
- disposition--transfer of ownership by will, trust, beneficiary designation, or operation of the law
- taxation--taxation of the client's estate and the income tax and estate tax consequences to the beneficiaries

Recommendations

Written recommendations that relate to goals and objectives as well as to financial issues and problems

Comments

- Written recommendations should specifically address the client's goals and objectives and all issues and problems identified in the plan as well as determine the actions necessary to compensate for any shortfalls. Recommendations should be clearly identified and stated; they should not be conveyed by implication or inference.

Implementation

A prioritized list of actions required to implement the recommendations, indicating responsible parties, action required, and timing

Comments

- Implementation should include a schedule reflecting actions to be taken as well as priority, dates, and responsible parties.

EFFECTIVE COMMUNICATION
IN FINANCIAL COUNSELING

by Lewis B. Morgan*

INTRODUCTION

Many people take communication for granted. After all, it is an activity that most of us have engaged in since our childhood years, so why not take it for granted? The sad truth, however, is that many of us are ineffective communicators simply because we make that very assumption.

Communication is far too important a skill, especially in the field of counseling, to treat lightly. It is the single most critical skill that a counselor brings to a counseling session.

The purpose of this reading is to examine the communication process as it typically exists in a counselor-client relationship. Our goal is to enable financial planners to become exceptionally effective communicators in their dealings with clients. Perhaps you already consider yourself to be effective in the area of communication; however, there are probably aspects of the communication process in which you can improve. This reading will attempt to bring these aspects into sharper focus and provide you with techniques for becoming the very best communicator/counselor that you have the potential of being.

The reading begins with a delineation of the various types of structured communication: interviewing, counseling, and advising. From there it proceeds to some of the essentials inherent in financial counseling: structuring the counseling relationship; establishing rapport; dealing with resistance. Next it looks at some of the characteristics of effective counseling: unconditional positive regard, empathy, genuineness, and self-awareness.

*Lewis B. Morgan, PhD, is professor of counseling and human relations, Villanova University.

Portions of this reading dealing with elements of nonverbal behaviors and using silence effectively have been excerpted from a two-part article entitled "Practical Communications Skills and Techniques in Financial Counseling," by Dale S. Johnson, PhD, CFP, published in The Financial Planner 11, no. 6 (June 1982): 98-105, and 11, no. 7 (July 1982): 62-71. They are reprinted by arrangement with the editor of that journal.

The second part of the reading focuses on basic communication principles and skills such as nonverbal communication, using the skills of attending to a client, listening and then responding to a client, and asking effective questions.

THREE TYPES OF STRUCTURED COMMUNICATION

Laypeople often use the terms "interviewing," "counseling," and "advising" interchangeably; yet each term has characteristics that are uniquely its own and that differentiate it from the other two. Let us look at each of these three terms and see how they are alike and how they are different.

Interviewing

One of the most common forms of structured communication is interviewing. Interviewing can be defined as a process of communication, most often between two people, with a predetermined and specific purpose, usually involving the asking and answering of questions designed to gather meaningful information. For example, a television sports announcer might interview a coach at halftime to get information about what mistakes his team has made in the first half, what he plans to do differently in the second half, and how he hopes to win. Or an interview might take place in a personnel office where a job applicant is interviewed for a position with the firm. The interviewer will want to know the following: What assets will the applicant bring to the job? What is her employment history? Where does she see herself fitting into the firm? What salary does she expect? In both instances cited, there is a specific purpose to the interview in that relevant information is being sought through a question-and-answer dialogue.

Stewart and Cash, in their book, _Interviewing: Principles and Practices_, refer to two basic types of interviews: the directive and nondirective interview. In the directive interview, the interviewer directs and controls both the pace and the content to be covered. It is a much more formalized and structured style of interaction. Often the interviewer even completes a questionnaire form as the interviewee answers pointed questions--for example, What is your age? Where do you live? Where was your last job? What is the highest level of education completed? The advantages of the directive interview are that it can be brief and that it provides measurable data. Its disadvantages are that it is often inflexible and does not allow the interviewee to choose topics for discussion.

The nondirective interview, on the other hand, allows both the interviewer and the interviewee a wider range of subject areas to be discussed, and the interviewee usually controls the pacing and purpose of the interview. Thus the advantages of the nondirective interview are that there is greater flexibility, more in-depth responses are gathered, and usually a closer relationship between interviewer and interviewee is established. Its disadvantages are that it consumes more time and often generates data that are difficult to measure objectively.

All interviews, whether they are directive or nondirective, share common characteristics. Interviews typically take place in a formal and structured setting. Questions are the primary source of communication used by the interviewer. The subject matter discussed is specific to the overall purpose of the interview, and digressions from the subject are usually not encouraged. Finally, the interview is usually a relatively short-term relationship between interviewer and interviewee.

Counseling

The second term, "counseling," is often confused with interviewing, even though they are not synonymous. Counseling implies help giving, often of a psychotherapeutic nature, and the help-giving aspect is more than implied in counseling; it is built-in and an integral part of the process. Simply stated, a counselor's job is to provide assistance to clients as they explore their present situations, begin to understand where they are in relation to where they would like to be, and then act to get from where they are to where they want to be. Even though this may sound like a simple process, it is not. It usually is a long-term process, typified by struggles, setbacks, and, eventually, insights leading to an ultimate change in behavior as clients strive to live more fulfilling lives.

While financial counseling takes place over a period of time, the interview is usually a one-time interaction. As such, an interpersonal relationship develops between counselor and client, something that usually does not occur in an interview. When we discussed interviewing, we stated that the question was the primary stock-in-trade of the interviewer. While questions are also utilized in counseling, they are not the primary response modality. In certain counseling settings such as mental hospitals and mental health clinics, an intake interview constitutes the first step in the therapeutic process. In this intake interview, many personal questions are asked, either in a written or oral format, but once the intake procedure is concluded, the communication assumes a different form. While questions may still be asked periodically, they are not the predominant form of counselor response. A counselor may paraphrase what the client has said, reflect a feeling, share feedback or perceptions, clarify, summarize, interpret, provide information, and confront. In short, counseling is not as stylized as interviewing because the format is less formal and less structured. Much more of the humanness of both the counselor and the client comes into focus, all with the purpose of providing help to the client.

Advising

Still a third type of structured communication is advising, which is often confused with counseling. In fact, many people who are unfamiliar with counseling think that what they will receive is advice. Perhaps one reason for this misconception stems from the journalistic proliferation of advice such as is offered in newspaper columns by "Dear Abby" and her sister, Ann Landers. This is not to say that advice is never offered by counselors, because it is; but most counselors believe that the very best kind of advice is self-advice, rather than expert advice.

Several situations might require such advice. A college student planning a program of studies is typically assigned an academic adviser in his or her major field of study. The adviser's role is, simply, to advise the student about program sequence, course prerequisites, specific course content, graduation requirements, and possible career opportunities in the major area. In short, the adviser is the expert and, as such, provides excellent advice. A tax adviser might provide advice on tax shelters, investments, tax deferral, and so on. In both instances, advisers know much more about their field of expertise than do their clients, and their clients use this knowledge in order to reach decisions.

In financial counseling, there are bound to be occasions when counselors give advice. After all, financial counselors are the experts and thus their advice has proven value. The danger in offering advice too soon in the counseling relationship is that the client's ability to make decisions is discounted in favor of the expert's opinion. Perhaps the best way to give advice, if advice is given at all, is to hear clients out first in order to understand their situation more completely and to assess their goals, and then to explain what alternatives or options are available.

Advice giving remains a controversial issue in the counseling literature. Its critics maintain that advice fosters dependency and robs clients of the right to make decisions for themselves. It is important for each counselor to question his or her haste in offering ready answers to somewhat complex situations. Is there some inner need like dominance or control being satisfied? Is the advice giver willing to assume the responsibility for another person's life? Is the advice giver projecting his or her own needs, problems, or values into the advice?

So while it is true that many people come to a financial counselor ostensibly looking for advice or the right answer, it is also true that many people choose not to take the advice when it is offered, or if they do take the counselor's advice and later discover that it was unsound, they rightfully blame the counselor.

There is a place for tentative suggestions that leaves the final decision about courses of action entirely up to the client. In this manner, clients are free to make decisions that are right for them and thus assume the responsibility for their own lives. Advisers who do this are functioning in a wholly professional and ethical manner.

ESSENTIALS IN FINANCIAL COUNSELING

In the preceding section we differentiated the three types of planned, purposeful communication: interviewing, counseling, and advising. Each one of these types of communication can be found in the financial counseling relationship. For instance, interviewing in the form of data collection for a fact finder might well constitute the early stages of the communications process.[1] After the data are collected, the second phase would probably consist largely of counseling--listening closely to the client and trying to understand the client's inner world of needs, desires, fears, attitudes, values, and goals. The third and final stage of communication in financial counseling would undoubtedly include giving expert advice, or at least carefully exploring possible alternatives for achieving the client's objectives. Let us look at the dynamics of communication and how it works in actual practice.

Structure

In any kind of planned and purposeful communication setting, the first element that needs to be attended to is structuring. Structuring serves to determine both the format and the subject matter of the interaction that is to follow. The counselor's task is to make the purpose of the session clear to the client at the outset. This would include the inevitable introductions, an explanation of the process involved, a discussion of forms that will be used and the amount of time that will be required, a discussion

---

1. The fact finder, or data-gathering form, that will be used in this course is called the Financial and Estate Planning Fact Finder and will be described in the next reading.

of the confidential nature of the relationship, and some prediction of what kinds of outcomes the client might reasonably expect. This structuring need not be lengthy and cumbersome; in fact, it is far better to structure in a clear, straightforward, and succinct fashion. Consider the following example of structuring:

Counselor: "In order for me to be able to provide the best possible service for you, we'll probably need to see each other on three or four separate occasions, although I want you to know that I'm available to you as often as you need me. Today I thought we'd start by getting some information from you about your own financial situation. To do this, I'll use the fact finder pages, which will remain confidential between the two of us. As we go about our business together, I suspect that we'll be able to come up with a financial plan that will be sensible and help you meet your goals. Do you have any questions?"

The counselor's approach in the foregoing example is friendly and promises cooperation. The client is made to feel important; that he or she is the focal point of the counseling situation. The statement offers hope that the results of client counseling will meet the needs and goals of the client.

In the early stages of counseling, the client may be apprehensive or uncertain about how to begin. A good guide to follow is to begin where the client is. If the client is, in fact, anxious at the outset, some time should be spent discussing the mere difficulty of getting started. Talking about this will invariably alleviate most of the client's anxieties. It is important to keep in mind that whenever feelings emerge, it is best to focus upon those feelings rather than ignore them. If, for example, a client, in the middle of a session, appears distressed over some aspect of his or her situation (for example, an impending divorce), some time must be given to discussing these feelings. Until the feelings are addressed and expressed, a further discussion of content is unproductive and meaningless.

Rapport

Rapport is best established through the personhood of the financial counselor. Attributes that go a long way toward a rapprochement between counselor and client would include a friendly and interested concern; an unhurried, leisurely pace; an accepting, nonjudgmental attitude;

3.6

attentive, active listening; and an egalitarian relationship. In such a climate, clients are free to be themselves, since they don't have to be afraid that what they say will be evaluated in a negative way by the counselor. Furthermore, they begin to realize that the ultimate responsibility for planning, setting goals, and taking action rests with them and not the counselor.

Perhaps the most important attribute of personhood in establishing rapport is the financial counselor's acceptance of the client. This attitude stems from a sincere desire on the part of the counselor to respect the uniqueness of each client and a genuine wish to be of help. And it might be well to add that accepting others is easier said than done, especially with people who are markedly different from us in terms of their values, attitudes, socioeconomic status, and so on. Despite this difficulty, it is absolutely imperative that counselors accept their clients, because unless a client feels accepted by his counselor, the relationship will never really become a partnership of equals.

Resistance

Resistance often occurs in even the best of counseling relationships. It often is expressed in the form of hostility toward the counselor, and the hostility can be either overt or covert. Open hostility is the easiest type to recognize and, in most cases, to handle. We all know what an angry person looks and sounds like: their faces become flushed; their jaws tighten; they clench their fists; their voices rise; their language becomes more expressively angry. The only effective thing to do at this point is to reflect this anger, as in saying "I can sense your anger. You don't like what I've just said, do you?" This allows the clients to vent whatever pent-up feelings of anger they have, and the anger slowly begins to dissipate while the behavior becomes more rational.

Covert hostility is more difficult to recognize and can be more difficult to deal with, since clients themselves may not even be aware of their anger. Some examples of covert hostility are missing appointments; being late for appointments; being sarcastic or cynical; being overly genteel or polite; not getting down to business. Whatever the evidence of covert hostility is, the best approach is not to interpret the behavior for the client as "latent hostility" or "passive-aggressiveness" but simply to focus on the behavior itself and let the client analyze or interpret it. For instance, the counselor might say, "I've noticed that whenever we talk about your spouse's handling of the family budget, you become sarcastic. What do you think might be going on?" Again, this helps the client to focus on the feedback received and allows angry feelings to be vented. Resistance must be addressed as directly as possible if any good is to come of the counseling relationship.

Other types of resistance behaviors that counselors might encounter during counseling relationships would include withdrawal or passivity; dwelling in fantasy or nonreality; ambivalence or vacillation; and the use of inappropriate humor, to name a few. As mentioned, the counselor should not analyze or interpret a client's resistance behavior since analysis tends only to raise the client's defensiveness. Instead the counselor should be aware of what is occurring, note whether it is a recurrent pattern, and at an appropriate point share such observations in a nonjudgmental manner with the client.

Common Areas of Resistance

Client resistance is almost a "given" in a financial counseling relationship, probably because clients, when they enter into a counseling relationship, yield a certain amount of their privacy and personal power over the situation to the counselor. Resistance is a way of defending oneself, or restoring some of the balance of power to oneself. Certain discussion areas, because of their sensitive nature, seem to be particularly vulnerable to client resistance.

One such sensitive subject area is death and dying. Because of its uncertainty, death is extremely anxiety-producing to some people. Dr. Elisabeth Kubler-Ross, an eminent authority on death and dying, postulates that there are five stages that a person facing death passes through: denial, anger, bargaining, depression, and acceptance. The first four of these stages are all different forms of resistance that the person uses for self-protection. Financial counselors, when discussing future plans with older people, need to be particularly sensitive to the feelings of their clients. Counselors must listen and observe very closely what clients communicate when discussing death and dying. Counselors must be empathetic to feelings and communicate accurately what is heard and observed. A genuine concern for the feelings and attitudes of clients must be manifested. Counselors must also be aware of their own feelings about death, so that they do not interfere with what clients are feeling and attempting to communicate.

Counselors can help to restore some control over the future by involving clients fully in decision making and planning for contingencies. This allows clients to feel useful, worthwhile, and somewhat in control of their situation.

Another area where resistance may be encountered involves marital tensions, such as separation/divorce, parent-child disputes, sex, the "empty-nest" syndrome, and mid-life crises. While financial counselors are not expected to be highly qualified marriage or family counselors, they should be astute enough to recognize when a married couple is resisting because of an underlying, unexpressed marital problem. And once it is recognized, counselors should be willing and able to focus with the couple on the problem area. Otherwise, if the problem is ignored, whatever decisions are reached will be less valid than those that would be reached after a full airing of the problem. Besides providing a welcome catharsis for the couple, focusing on the problem also enables them to muster their forces to arrive at a mutually satisfactory solution. In counseling couples who are in disagreement on a crucial subject, the counselor needs to listen closely to what both partners have to say. It is far too common, unfortunately, to let the more dominant partner do most of the speaking and deciding. Since the outcome of the decision affects both partners, both should be involved in the discussion. To do any less than this almost guarantees an unsatisfactory conclusion.

Another sensitive area involves the executive who has failed to attain the degree of success he had dreamed of in his profession. His dreams shattered and unfulfilled, he may resort to cynicism, biting sarcasm, or empty humor in an attempt to endure it. Rather than laugh along with him, the effective counselor <u>reflects</u> the underlying feeling to let the client know that he understands his disappointment. A simple statement like, "I suppose it's a bitter pill to swallow when you've worked so hard to see your personal hopes shattered like that," allows your client to feel understood and appreciated. More often than not, the client will begin to discuss more openly how he feels. And once people are able to express their feelings, they are well on the way to addressing their problems in an effective manner.

Resistance behaviors, in any case, are a certain tip-off that the client is having difficulty subscribing to the counselor's line of reasoning. It does no good for the counselor to proceed with business as usual, ignoring the obvious resistance; nothing can be accomplished as long as the resistance continues. The resistances must be dealt with openly and objectively. Only then is there any chance that they will be diminished and that the participants can get on with the business at hand.

CHARACTERISTICS OF THE EFFECTIVE COUNSELOR

The main thing a counselor brings to the counseling hour is himself or herself. Financial counselors, first and foremost, must be themselves in how they relate to and interact with their clients. Each counselor is a human being, complete with human strengths and frailties. But each counselor is also a professionally trained individual, a person who, ideally, enjoys listening to and trying to understand other human beings and to accept them as they are. The effective counselor is also sincere and genuine in attempting to help others learn how to help themselves. This attitude generates interesting, challenging, and highly gratifying work; and it is--more than anything else--hard work when it is done professionally.

Carl Rogers, in his classic book, Client-Centered Therapy, postulated that there are three conditions necessary to bring about constructive client change: (1) unconditional positive regard, (2) accurate empathy, and (3) genuineness. Most counseling theorists agree that if an effective counselor-client relationship is to exist, the counselor must be open and spontaneous (genuine), must value the client as a unique individual (unconditional positive regard), and must be able to perceive and understand what the client is experiencing (accurate empathy).

A constructive counselor-client relationship serves not only to increase the opportunity for clients to attain the goals that are important to them, but also serves as a model of a good interpersonal relationship. Some questions that all counselors ought to ask themselves from time to time are the following:

- Knowing yourself, do you think it will be possible for you to value your clients, especially those who think, feel, and act differently from you?
- How easy or difficult will it be for you to view the world from another's perspective without imposing your own standards, beliefs, and attitudes on that person? Will your own values, ideas, and feelings hinder your understanding of another person?
- How open do you care, or dare, to be with a client? Will you be able to just "be yourself," or will you role-play how you think a professional counselor should be?

These are important questions to consider before engaging yourself in the dynamics of a counseling relationship. Far too many financial counselors assume that they have the right kind of personality to counsel others without ever scrutinizing themselves in the same way. Let us look a bit more closely at the core conditions to which Rogers refers.

Unconditional Positive Regard

This quality is often misconstrued as agreement or disagreement with the client. Rather, it is an attitude of valuing the client, or being able to express appreciation of the client as a unique and worthwhile person. Liking and respecting another person have a circular effect. When you value clients, your sense of liking will be communicated to them; this by itself will enhance their feelings for themselves and add to their appreciation of themselves as worthwhile human beings.

Accurate Empathy

Accurate empathy means that your sense of the client's world fits the client's self-image. This gives clients the feeling that you are in touch with them. When clients say something like, "Yes, that's it," or "That's exactly right," it indicates that your response was right on target, and that they feel that you are closely following and understanding them.

Learning to understand is not an easy process. It involves the capacity to lay aside your own set of experiences in favor of those of your clients--as seen through their eyes, not yours. It involves skillful listening so that you can hear not only the obvious, but also the subtleties of which, perhaps, even the client is unaware.

Developing accurate empathy also means identifying and resolving your own needs so that they do not interfere with your understanding of the feelings and concerns of your client. The counselor who identifies too strongly with the client's state, however, impedes rather than facilitates the counseling objective.

Genuineness

Genuineness means, simply, that the counselor is a real person. There is no facade, no role-playing of what a professional counselor should be. Professional counselors are wholly aware of themselves and their feelings, thoughts, values, and attitudes. More importantly, genuine counselors are not afraid to express themselves openly and honestly at all times. Financial counselors do not have to become something different for all clients with whom they have relationships. They are "role-free"; they are themselves at all times.

A genuine counselor communicates in a spontaneous and expressive manner and does not conceal anything. A genuine counselor is open and willing to listen to whatever the client is willing to discuss. A genuine counselor is consistent. He or she does not think or feel one thing but say another.

One author suggests that effective counselors can

- express directly to others whatever they are experiencing
- communicate without distorting their messages
- listen to others without distorting their messages
- be spontaneous instead of planned or programmed
- respond openly in a specific and concrete manner
- be willing to manifest their own vulnerabilities and frailties
- learn how to be psychologically close to others
- commit themselves to others

A tall order? Perhaps. And yet, for a financial counseling relationship to be effective, it is mandatory that counselors allow themselves to be genuine with their clients. Otherwise, the relationship deteriorates into a charade of two human beings playing prescribed roles with each other, and this defeats the purpose.

Self-awareness

There is general consensus among counselor educators that counselors need to be highly aware of themselves and particularly aware of their own attitudes and values. Counselors who are aware of their own value systems have a better chance of avoiding the imposition of their values onto their clients. This quality is of vital importance since we want to help our clients make decisions that stem from their own value systems, rather than from ours. The more we know about ourselves, the better we can understand, interpret, evaluate, and control our behavior and the less likely we are to attribute aspects of ourselves to the client, a rather common defense mechanism known as projection. Before we can be aware of others, it is essential that we be solidly grounded in self-awareness.

Barbara Okun, in her book, *Effective Helping*, suggests that counselors should continually try to determine their own needs, feelings, and values by answering the following questions:

- Am I aware when I find myself feeling uncomfortable with a client or with a particular subject area?
- Am I aware of my avoidance strategies?
- Can I really be honest with the client?
- Do I always feel the need to be in control of situations?
- Do I often feel as if I must be omnipotent in that I must do something to make the client "get better" so that I can be successful?

- Am I so problem-oriented that I'm always looking for the negative, for a problem, and never responding to the positive, to the good?
- Am I able to be as open with clients as I want them to be with me?

The adage "Know thyself" should apply to financial counselors and other helping professionals even more than it does to the population at large. A very large part of our responsibility as counselors is to know ourselves as thoroughly as possible, so that we are then able to provide the very best kind of objective, informed counseling to our clients. A counselor who has "blind spots" about himself or herself will surely be less effective in a helping situation than a counselor who is comfortably self-aware. This is not to say that the counselor is a problem-free, completely self-actualized individual; rather, it means that the counselor is a human being, having a multitude of strengths and even some weaknesses, but that the weaknesses are known by the counselor and do not interfere with the dynamics of counseling another person.

Values Orientations

As human beings, financial counselors have value systems that are the result of years of living on this planet. Many of our values are inculcated in us by our parents, by schooling, by religion, by our peers, and by society. However they come to us, they are as much a part of us as our physical and psychological characteristics. This is not to say that they are a permanent, transfixed part of our being, because our values can, and do, change. A vivid example of this type of change came during the decades of the 1960s and early 1970s when a whole society's value system was rocked to the core by momentous events such as the assassinations of the Kennedys and Martin Luther King, the civil rights movement, the war in Vietnam, the women's rights movement, and the Kent State killings. This truly was a time when an entire nation's value system was being challenged, and as a result, certain of our long-cherished values were thrust into a state of flux and some, ultimately, were changed. And what happened to the nation was repeated many times over with many individuals in our midst. People who at first accepted the Vietnam War as a rightful intervention by a powerful nation into the affairs of a far-off country slowly changed their values about not only that war, but about armed conflict in general. And virtually the same thing happened on other controversial issues as well: abortion, human rights, euthanasia, drugs, and the like.

The point here is that values, while deeply internalized, are not immutable. Counselors need to remind themselves of this fact of life as they work with clients who are confused and afraid in approaching important decisions. While it is true that we are in many ways a reflection of our past history, we are--or can be--much more than that. There is no need to be shackled to our past. We can, if we choose, overcome our past and live new lives, based upon who we are now and what we believe in and hold to be valuable to us now and in the future. This is a liberating concept and, as such, frees individuals to think, feel, and behave in ways that are congruent with their present being, rather than dooming them to repeat the past and live in ways that are no longer meaningful.

The financial counselor's role in this situation is to act as a catalyst rather than as a maintainer of the status quo. The implied danger, of course, is that counselors might try to force change in their clients' values and attitudes where none is desired or sought after, or that counselors might subtly or not-so-subtly try to impose their values on clients. Both of these dangers must be consciously guarded against. What counselors must do is listen carefully to clients as they sift through the various value choices faced, so that when clients must finally make the choice, it can be done freely, without encumbrances from the past. Clients must actually be "opened up" to the freedom of making choices that are relevant and meaningful to his or her very existence. Good counselors have a knack of being able to do this.

Values Differences

Each of us has within us a hierarchy of values that makes order of our lives. An older executive facing retirement might, for example, rank security above risk taking in deciding how to invest money. On the other hand, a younger financial counselor might rank risk taking above security in the hierarchy of values. What happens, then, when the risk-taking counselor sits down to counsel the security-minded preretirement executive? If the counselor is sensitive and understanding, he or she will listen to the older person, trying to get a sense of what is important to the client, what the client is willing and unwilling to do. The effective financial counselor does not try to sell the client a product that the counselor believes is right but that the client believes is wrong, unsafe, or risky.

Counseling is caring, and caring means that the counselor cares enough--has enough faith in the client's worth as a unique human being--to permit that client to make value choices that fit his or her value system. The financial counselor can and should provide information that will help the client make the choice, but the choice itself ultimately belongs to the client, not the counselor. Only in this way are we counselors.

3.14

Besides the differences in values, which often are reflective of the differences in age between counselor and client, we also ought to consider several other "isms"--sexism and racism--and how they impinge upon the counselor-client relationship. Let us look first at sex differences. Sexist counseling occurs when the counselor uses his or her own sex ideology as a framework for counseling. In the field of financial counseling this might take place when a male counselor discourages a female client from doing something that has traditionally been thought to be in the "man's world," such as returning to work while there is an infant at home to be cared for. This kind of subtle advice giving, besides reflecting the obvious sex-role bias of the counselor, is not in keeping with what is happening in many households today. Further, it is intrusive in that the responsibility for making that decision is clearly the client's and not the counselor's. It is critical that counselors learn to recognize their own biases and sex-role stereotypes and not inflict them upon people whom they are trying to help.

Since financial counselors typically counsel both husband and wife, it is important to understand what both partners have to say. It is far too common to defer to the male of the household, the "breadwinner," without taking into consideration what the female spouse has to contribute. When both husband and wife are in complete agreement, no problem exists. But when they disagree--and this is often communicated through nonverbal signals like a sigh, a frown, or an angry glance--it is important to make a point of bringing the subject up for a full discussion. It is far better to spend whatever time it takes to get both partners to come up with a mutually acceptable decision than to proceed with one person's plan of action, knowing that it doesn't satisfy the other person.

Racism, despite notable progress in the civil rights movement over the past two decades, is still with us in many forms. Counselors engage in racism when they limit the choices of their clients based solely on their clients' race, or when they make faulty assumptions about their clients because of racist stereotyping.

The issue of whether white counselors can be effective in a relationship with blacks or Hispanics has been the subject of much research, though no conclusive findings exist. An effective counselor should be able to work with people of all races, since all people seem to have the same basic psychological needs and problems. Counselors should be able to relate to their clients as individuals rather than as blacks, Hispanics, or Orientals. Counselors also need to be conscious of their own biases regarding race and to guard against allowing their biases to adversely affect the quality of the counseling relationship. The counseling strategies employed should not differ with regard to what the race of the client is, any more than they should not differ depending on the sex, age, or religion of the client.

BASIC COMMUNICATION PRINCIPLES

In the previous section we discussed attributes of an effective counselor. In this section we will explore communication as a process and attempt to relate fundamental principles of communication to effective financial counseling. An effective counselor is also an effective communicator.

Communication is often thought of as one person sending a message through both verbal and nonverbal channels to another person or persons with the intention of evoking a response. A speaker asks, "How are you?" and the listener (or receiver of the communication) answers, "Just fine--except for my back." Effective communication takes place when the receiver interprets the sender's message in precisely the same fashion in which the sender intended it. Difficulties in communication arise when the receiver misunderstands and/or misinterprets the sender's message. Since any individual's intentions are private and rarely clearly stated, the receiver of the message has the difficult job of decoding the message without knowing for a fact what the sender's intentions are.

In addition, communication failures can also be attributed to the wide variety of stimuli with which individuals are bombarded during the course of a conversation. People try to communicate while watching television or listening to the radio, or they attempt to conduct two conversations simultaneously. But all "noise" is not auditory; some is emotional in nature. How effectively, for example, do you think a Ku Klux Klan member communicates with a Black Muslim? Prejudices and biases, then, are emotionally built-in stimuli that interfere with objective listening and effective communication.

Related to this communication failure is the sad but simple truth that individuals listen in order to evaluate and render judgment about the speaker, which, in turn, makes the speaker guarded and defensive about what he or she is attempting to communicate. Perhaps the best example of this type of ineffective communication is a city council meeting, where one side advocates the raising of taxes, while the other side interrupts, casts aspersions, and generally fights for all it is worth against the tax hike. Whenever there are two people, or two groups, each with a strong vested interest in an emotional issue, the likelihood of there being clear communication is virtually nil.

Communication even in the best of circumstances should not be taken for granted. Let us look now at some basic principles of communication theory.

- Communication is learned by all of us through experience, but experience itself does not necessarily make one an effective communicator. As children, we learn how to communicate by imitating our models--parents, brothers, sisters, neighbors, playmates, babysitters. Unfortunately, not all of our models are effective communicators; thus, we acquire poor habits of communication early, and those habits, like all habits, are difficult to break. A child reared in a home where everyone talks at the same time and no one listens carries this model upon leaving the home.
- The meaning of words is illusory; words do not mean--people do. Words are merely symbols. Consider, for example, a simple word like "rock." The teenager immediately thinks of loud music; the geologist thinks of a hard object created millions of years ago; the burglar thinks of a diamond ring; the old lady thinks of her favorite chair, and so on. The point is that a word can have almost as many meanings as there are people who use it.
- Language is learned; thus, in a sense, we are programmed, and the meaning of words stays within us for future reference. This programming is extremely helpful since, once we learn a word, it usually remains "ours" for a lifetime. However, this programming can also serve as an impediment to open communication with others, in that we often refer back to our original conceptions of words without thinking how others might interpret them. For example, the word "girl," once used to refer to any female, is now clearly inappropriate in referring to an adult woman in this age of ERA and women's rights.
- No two people are programmed alike; therefore no symbol can always be interpreted the same way. Individuals differ in the nature and degree of their understanding. We perceive things differently, from our own frame of reference, so meanings differ.
- It is impossible for any individual to encode or process all parts of a message. Besides the fact that words are often inadequate in describing accurately what we are feeling or thinking, there is also the problem of distortion, that is, an individual's altering the event to suit his or her own purposes. But even if we have the precise word and communicate it without distortion, we still are

3.17

faced with the problem of the receiver's receiving it in the same way in which it was intended.

- Some experts claim that the single greatest problem with communication is the assumption of it. Too many people assume that their messages are automatically understood. We also sometimes assume that our perceptions are more "right" than the perceptions of someone else. Where human communication is concerned, no assumptions can or should be made.

- We can never not communicate. Anything we say or do can be interpreted in a meaningful way as a message. Even during periods of silence, communication takes place. Nonverbal behavior (which will be discussed in some detail shortly) such as eye contact, facial expressions, gestures, body posture, voice inflections, hesitations, and the like, all speak volumes. In fact, most sociological research claims that approximately two-thirds of the total message is communicated via nonverbal channels, especially where human emotions are concerned.

- Listening is communication, too. Unfortunately, not everyone is a good listener; yet, that should not be too surprising, since listening as a communication skill is rarely, if ever, taught formally. To speak precisely and to listen carefully presents a real challenge to all of us. The way in which we listen and respond to another person is crucial for building a fulfilling relationship. When we listen carefully, with understanding and without evaluation, and when we respond relevantly, we implicitly communicate to the speaker, "I care about what you are saying, and I'd like to understand it."

The most effective communication occurs when the receiver of a message gives understanding responses, sometimes called paraphrases. A client might say, "I don't know.....I doubt that we can afford to send both of our kids to college." A financial counselor using an understanding response would respond to the above statement with, "So you're just not sure you have the resources for a college education right now." While it might be tempting to try to convince the clients at this juncture that there is a way to finance their children's college education, the understanding response communicates a desire to understand the clients without evaluating these statements as right or wrong. It also helps the counselor to see the expressed ideas and feelings of clients from their point of view.

Another means available to the counselor to enhance the communication process and the counseling relationship is to personalize messages. The hallmark of personal statements is the use of the personal pronouns, I, me, and my. Using generalized pronouns such as everyone, anyone, or somebody to refer to your own ideas only tends to confuse clients

3.18

and, hence, results in ambiguity and faulty understanding. Personal statements like, "I can appreciate your concern over not having adequate resources," reveals your own feelings to clients and increases the personal quality of the relationship.

ELEMENTS OF NONVERBAL BEHAVIORS

As mentioned above, clients communicate many feelings and attitudes to counselors through nonverbal behaviors, including (but not limited to) fear, anxiety, sincerity, confusion, anger, aggression, happiness, hostility, interest, boredom, and concern. The two main sources of nonverbal behaviors are the body and the voice. From these two sources come four types of nonverbal signs of meaning: body position, body movement, voice tone, and voice pitch. Each of these types of nonlinguistic signs conveys a wealth of information to the observant financial counselor. It should be noted that the counselor's first impressions of the meaning or significance of any body language must be checked out against other clues given by the client.

The Body

When learning to improve one's ability to observe the nonverbal behaviors of clients, it is important to notice the various ways by which the body actually communicates, either in agreement or in variance with what is actually said. In particular, the counselor should notice and learn to interpret the communications that are transmitted by the client's body positions and movements.

Positions

Overall body posture is the first thing the observant counselor notices. Clients who sit erect and comfortably are usually relaxed. If they lean slightly forward, it is usually a sign of interest and involvement in the counseling session. If they slouch, or seem to draw away from the counselor, they may have no interest or trust in the counselor--or they may be bored. Good client posture may indicate self-assurance and positive self-esteem. Poor posture may signal a lack of self-assurance or low self-esteem.

The counselor should also notice the position of the client's arms and legs. When the legs are uncrossed and the arms are positioned comfortably at the sides, the client is usually relaxed and "open." Tightly crossed arms and legs, on the other hand, may indicate distrust or unreceptiveness. The facial position of the client should also be noticed. Most people's faces are expressive of a wide range of ever-changing feelings. The client whose face appears frozen in one position may be signaling fear, anxiety, or anger, or some other prepossessing feeling that could become a block or obstacle to open communication with the counselor.

Movements

The client who frequently changes body positions may be indicating physical or emotional discomfort, or a lack of interest. The counselor should take note of such movements and try to relate them to information gleaned later.

There is reason to believe that body language may be more "honest" or "pure" than verbal communication. In certain positive, straightforward human experiences we know that it is. The impulsive hug or kiss of greeting for people we care for is the most obvious example. But people also communicate through the body when they don't want to communicate, or when they are hiding or contradicting themselves. For example, a client may say, "No, I'm not nervous about investing in a tax shelter," while biting his nails, pulling at his hair, or fidgeting distractedly. People often say what they think they may be expected to say in a given situation or context, not noticing themselves what they are actually communicating through body language.

Gestures

Hand and arm gestures are usually used to illustrate or accent verbal statements. Hands clasped so tightly that the knuckles are whitened and taut certainly signify something, perhaps fear or anxiety. While jerky hand and arm gestures may indicate anxiety, smooth, flowing gestures usually mean that the client is relaxed and interested in the counseling session. Frequent crossing and uncrossing of the legs, or bouncing a leg that is crossed, may indicate nervousness, boredom, or lack of interest.

Facial Expressions

The financial counselor can learn much from a client's facial expressions. Look for frowns, smiles, or nervous habits, such as biting the lips. Look especially to see if the client's facial expressions change as topics change, and note whether the expression is appropriate or incongruent. For example, if the client talks about anger, does she appear angry? If she facially expresses disgust about her husband's spendthrift ways, do her intentions in her last will and testament reflect that feeling by providing for her children through a trust, rather than leaving everything outright to her husband?

Eye Contact

Eye contact, or the lack of it, in the counseling session can indicate the client's feeling. If the client's eyes are downcast and rarely meet the gaze of the counselor, the client could be shy, anxious, or fearful (though not necessarily toward the counselor). On the other hand, if the client stares or glares constantly at the counselor, anger or hostility could be indicated. If the client's eyes rove all around the room, looking at the walls and ceiling while the counselor is filling out the data-gathering form, there could be a serious lack of interest in the relevance of data gathering. A client who is open and interested in the counseling session will usually meet the gaze of the counselor. This eye contact of the client usually indicates interest in the session and a positive and concerned attitude toward counseling. Needless to say, reciprocity from the counselor is likely to be perceived by the client in the same way.

The Voice

Nonverbal voice clues can be observed in the tone and pitch of the client's voice. Tone and pitch are qualities of the voice that may indicate the speaker's feelings, quite apart from what is actually said. They should be observed closely.

The Tone

Tone is loudness or softness. The client who talks very loudly or shouts may be indicating anger or hostility. The client who talks very softly may be exhibiting fear or shyness.

The Pitch

Pitch is the quality of a voice that indicates how high or low the voice is on a musical scale. A high-pitched voice may indicate anxiety, fear, or anger. A low-pitched voice can indicate either comfort or control of strong emotions.

Obviously, some people's voices are naturally louder than others. The natural pitch of different voices also varies greatly. The point is not to type these differences but to observe and determine which vocal qualities are natural to a particular client so as to recognize variations. If these vocal qualities do vary during counseling sessions in relation to personal and financial details, they can be important clues to the strong emotions that often affect a client's motivations, needs, and objectives. The counseling sessions themselves are often an inducement to clients to open up and give vent to feelings about their financial condition. Thus voice tone and pitch are important factors for counselors to observe and consider in relation to all other clues that characterize the client and reveal the individual's self-image.

Interpreting the Meaning of Nonverbal Behaviors

It is important for financial counselors to note that in all the descriptions above of nonverbal behaviors, of "body language," we have stated that a behavior may or usually does indicate one or more feelings. Nonverbal behaviors are clues that must be clearly observed and compared with what the client says in order to determine whether they are appropriate or congruent. For example, if a client blurts out, "I am furious with the broker who sold me that bunch of junk bonds last year!" and strikes the desk, the gesture is congruent with the verbal message--it agrees with what the client says. If the client makes the same statement and sits calmly smiling, however, there is incongruent behavior--the body language does not jibe with the verbal message. When the financial counselor observes incongruent behavior of this sort in a client, it should be mentioned to the client in order to clarify which element of the communication is correct.

Nonverbal behaviors are clues or indicators. While they signify something, their meanings can be clouded by incongruence, distortion, or vagueness. Premature assumptions about what they really mean would be as unprofessional as failing to notice them altogether. For example, a client's palsied hands might be due to one or more of the following causes: nervousness, fear, Parkinson's disease, too much coffee, chemical poisoning, or alcoholism. The client who always talks loudly may be either angry or hard of hearing, or merely an overbearing individual. The client who shows no interest in counseling may be worn out with worrying whether his recent commodities futures trading is going to wipe him out with margin calls, or whether he should buy term or whole life for estate liquidity, or whether he will have an estate. He may be on tranquilizers over worry about a son and heir who himself abuses drugs. For any number of reasons the client may need psychological counseling or therapy before he can undertake financial counseling. In short, not all the problems that clients may bring to financial counseling sessions are financial in origin or nature. When present, these nonfinancial problems will distort client messages and add to the difficulties of clarifying them.

Observant counselors need to be astute enough to discern from among all the verbal and nonverbal clues and be aware that in most client cases there will be a mixture of congruent and noncongruent evidence. Counselors thus understand who clients are, where they are, where they want to go; and can then suggest the optimal ways to help each one get there. DO NOT ASSUME THAT YOU KNOW WHAT A GIVEN BEHAVIOR MEANS. Check it out and clarify your perception with each client.

And do not forget that as a counselor you communicate in both verbal and nonverbal ways, too, just as the client does, and that your communications behaviors very much affect the client. This is particularly true of nonverbal messages. Therefore any of the communications and psychological considerations in this reading that you may agree are important with respect to the client are also important for you. As a financial counseling professional you will want to remove from your own behaviors those elements that present obstacles and barriers to successful communication with the client and with other professionals with whom you deal. The client is then more likely to accept your role in the counseling situation and, ultimately, the plan you develop for meeting his or her financial needs and objectives. Similarly, other professionals whose expertise you will often need to call upon in developing and implementing a plan will respect your role as a financial counselor and planner.

THE SKILLS OF ATTENDING AND LISTENING

Paying attention to clients is a first necessary component in good communication. No matter how expert your other communication skills are, if you are inattentive to your clients' verbal and nonverbal behaviors, you are apt to lose them at the very outset. How often have you been in the company of another person who shies away from looking at you, who glances nervously at his wristwatch, who interrupts you, and who, literally and figuratively, turns his back to you? Surely, if you have had this kind of experience, you recall how uncomfortable and ill at ease you were with this inattentive behavior.

If a counselor's goal is to understand clients, the counselor must first pay close attention to or focus on their verbal and nonverbal messages. Poor attending and poor listening lead to poor understanding.

Physical Attending

Gerard Egan, a renowned counselor educator, categorizes attending behavior into (1) physical attending, or using your body to communicate; and (2) psychological attending, or listening actively. He uses the acronym, SOLER, as a reminder of the five basic attributes associated with physical attending. Let us look at these five attributes.

- S: Face the other person SQUARELY.
  When there is face-to-face, direct contact, the communication process is enhanced. You communicate nonverbally to the other person, "I'm here with you; I'm tuned-in and ready to face the issues with you head-on." Turning your body away lessens your involvement with the other person.

- **O: Adopt an OPEN posture.**
  There is something to be said about receiving a person with "open arms." Crossed arms and crossed legs can inadvertently communicate a "holding-off" of the other person. An open posture--open arms and legs and an open smile--communicates receptiveness to the other person and, hence, increases good communication and decreases defensiveness.
- **L: LEAN toward the other.**
  This is another physical signal of interest, involvement, caring. Two people who care about each other, when involved in conversation, almost always can be seen leaning toward each other. On the other hand, two people who are observed leaning away from one another, or sitting rigidly straight in their chairs, seem to be either bored or disinterested, or extremely cautious and defensive about getting involved with each other.
- **E: Maintain good EYE contact.**
  Good eye contact consists of looking at another individual when you are in conversation. Poor eye contact consists of rarely looking at the other person, or looking away when he or she looks at you or staring constantly with a blank expression on your face. The eye contact should be natural and spontaneous. Since you are interested in your client, you will want to use your eyes as a vehicle of communication.
- **R: Be RELAXED while attending.**
  It is possible to be both intense while focusing on the client and relaxed at the same time. A nervous, fidgety, or rigid counselor communicates these feelings to the client. A counselor who sits in a casual fashion, who speaks naturally and spontaneously, and who uses natural gestures has the advantage of being free to focus intently upon the client and his or her communication, as well as helping to facilitate naturalness and spontaneity in the client.

As has been mentioned previously, it is impossible not to communicate, so as a counselor you might as well use your body--gestures, posture, eyes--to communicate whatever message you wish to communicate. Otherwise, the body may communicate something you do not wish to communicate. In other words, try to make your body work for you on behalf of your counseling relationship.

Active Listening

So far attending has been described as a physical activity; active listening brings in the psychological activity involved in attending. Many of us take listening for granted, but there is a distinct difference between

3.24

simply hearing and actively listening. Hearing means the receiving of auditory signals. A person says, "I have a bad headache," and we hear that message and respond, "That's too bad," or "Here, have a couple of aspirin." An active listener, on the other hand, might respond, "You look as though it's really getting you down." In short, the active listener responds not only to the verbal message received through the auditory channel, but also to the unspoken, or nonverbal message, communicated by the sender's body, facial expression, or tone of voice.

Active listening, then, means putting the nonverbal behavior, the voice, and words together--all the cues sent out by the other person--to get the essence of the communication being sent. An active listener is an understanding listener, one who attempts to see the world from the other's frame of reference. If you can state in your own words what the other person has said, and that person accepts your statement as an accurate reflection of what he or she has said, then it is safe to say that you have listened actively and understood with accuracy.

But it must be stated that active listening is not merely parroting another's words--a computer can be (and has been) programmed to do that. Active listening means involving yourself in the inner world of another person while, at the same time, maintaining your own identity and being able to respond with meaningfulness to the messages of that other person.

Responding during Active Listening

As indicated above, active listening is hard work and requires intense focusing and concentration. Years of not listening have made most of us poor listeners. We are distracted easily; we tend to evaluate and judge what is being said while it is being said, so that we are framing our own responses to the speaker's statement before the speaker is finished talking and, thus, we miss the message.

There are several simple ways of responding to people so that they feel accepted and understood. Let us look at some of these response modalities.

Perhaps the simplest response modality is what Allen Ivey refers to as "minimal encouragers to talk," or "continuing responses." Nonverbally, if you want someone to continue talking, you might smile or nod your head to communicate agreement and/or understanding. Equally as effective in communicating your understanding is a minimal encourager like "uh-huh," "mmmm," "then?" "and...?" These relatively unobtrusive responses encourage the speaker to continue talking. They communicate to the speaker, "Go on, I'm with you."

Another type of response that enhances communication is the restatement-of-content response. The rationale for restatement is to let speakers hear what they have said on the assumption that this may encourage them to go on speaking, examining, and looking deeper. Restatement communicates to the client, "I am listening to you very carefully, so much so that I can repeat what you have said." The most effective restatements are those that are phrased in your own words, a paraphrase of what the speaker has stated. To do this effectively, we must temporarily suspend our own frame of reference and attempt to view the world from the other person's perspective. Suppose the client says to you, "I'm really in a financial bind, what with taxes, inflation, fuel bills; I don't know how we make it from one month to the next." An accurate restatement might be expressed, "So things are tough for you financially. It seems like you can't make ends meet." The client, hearing this understanding response, is encouraged to delve more deeply into the situation, feeling that the counselor has, indeed, "heard" the message on the same wavelength upon which it was transmitted. The bond between client and counselor is, thus, strengthened and greater opportunities for creative problem solving are opened up.

Just as we manifest understanding for our clients by responding to the content of the message, so may we also show our understanding of the client's experience by responding to the feelings expressed. Sometimes feelings are expressed directly, and at other times they are only implied or stated indirectly. In order to respond to a person's feelings, we must observe the behavioral cues like tone of voice, body posture, gestures, and facial expression, as well as listen to the speaker's words. Consider this client statement, "Within the next few months, we need to buy a new refrigerator and another car. (Sighs) I just don't know where the money is going to come from." A reflection-of-feeling response might go, "You sound pretty hopeless about your financial state. It sure is hard to break even, let alone get ahead, these days." Again, by responding in an empathic way to the client's statement, you communicate a deep understanding of the person's experience; in addition, you progress one step further by addressing the unverbalized feelings. We illustrate to the client that we understand so well what he or she is stating that we can paraphrase both words and feelings. It is helpful to both the client and the counselor to struggle to capture in words the uniqueness of the client's experience. The most effective types of understanding responses capsulize both the feeling and the content of the client's message. The basic format for this type of response is "You feel _____ because _____."
                                                       (feeling)   (content)

This response enables clients to get in closer touch with the feelings that are an outgrowth of their situations. And that, in turn, facilitates the working through of the problem, because the counselor involves clients in exploring themselves in the problem. Because you have accurately understood and responded to them, clients will go on to share other personal experiences that bear upon the presented problem.

A word might be added here about the difficulties that some people have in dealing with feelings, either their own or the feelings of others. Problems often arise in interpersonal relationships because one or more of the involved persons choose to repress, distort, or disguise their feelings rather than admit that feelings are present and then discuss them openly. This is particularly true of so-called negative feelings like anger, sadness, anxiety, frustration, discomfort, and confusion. In actuality, no feelings are negative since they all are part of being human. In any case, counselors who wish to communicate effectively need to address their own feelings as well as those of their clients. The mutual expression of feelings is an integral part of building a close, trusting, caring relationship.

Two other types of understanding responses need to be mentioned here. Each is related to the restatement-of-content and the reflection-of-feeling responses; yet, there is a subtle shade of difference. First is the clarifying response that tends to amplify the speaker's statement. The clarifying response does not add anything new to what the speaker has said; it simply expands what has already been stated. The counselor attempts to restate or clarify for the client what the client has had some difficulty in expressing clearly. It is akin to a translation of the client's words into language that is more familiar and understandable to both client and counselor. Suppose a client says, "I'm not sure. Nothing makes sense anymore. Things get more confusing the more I think about them. It's a real puzzle to me." A counselor, by way of clarification, might say, "I can sense your bewilderment. Let me see if I can help out. From what you've said previously, I get the impression that you want to get your mortgage straightened out before you increase your monthly savings. Is that it?" If the financial counselor has, indeed, been following the flow of the client's experience, this statement will help to clarify the client's confusion over the situation. To the extent that the counselor's response is on target, the puzzle becomes suddenly clear and more readily solved.

Another side to the clarifying response concerns the counselor's need to have things clarified. When the counselor is puzzled, then it is certainly legitimate to ask for clarification as, "I'm sorry. I don't follow what you're saying. Can you make that more clear for me?"

Helpful clarifying responses

- facilitate client self-understanding
- attend especially to the client's feelings
- communicate the counselor's understanding
- move the client toward a clearer definition of the problem

The other type of understanding response is the summary. Summaries are especially helpful toward the end of an interview, since they focus and capsulize a series of scattered ideas to present a clear perspective. The summary has the effect of reassuring clients that you have been tuned in to their many messages. For the counselor, it serves as a check on the accuracy with which the various messages have been received.

It is often better to have the client do the summarizing. In this way, the client maintains the responsibility for bringing the messages together into a meaningful conclusion. As in clarifying, themes and emotional overtones should be summarized, and the key ideas should be synthesized into broad statements reflecting basic meanings. An example of an effective summary might go like this: "So today you described your overall financial situation as bleak, although you think that you might be able to increase your savings if you could refinance your mortgage. I know that you're rightly concerned about that." If the financial counselor has accurately summarized the essence of the interview, the client then has a better handle on the intricacies of the situation, and a resolution is closer at hand.

What we have covered thus far are the basics of nonverbal behaviors, the skills of attending and active listening, and the following four basic types of responses associated with active listening:

- restatement of content
- reflection of feeling
- clarification
- summarization

The element common to all four of these response modalities is that the counselor follows, or tracks, the client's lead. A response of this kind communicates a high level of understanding and enables the client not only to experience what it feels like to be understood, but also to progress further toward an ultimate resolution of the situation. Now we will explore other types of counselor responses, responses in which the counselor, to a certain extent, takes the lead and deviates somewhat from the client's preceding responses.

COUNSELOR LEADING RESPONSES

When the financial counselor decides to make a leading response, it is the counselor's frame of reference that comes into focus. Up to this point, the counselor's responses have followed from the client's statements, but here the emphasis shifts. An obvious danger of this shift is that the counselor may move in a direction in which the client is not yet ready or willing to move. Despite this danger, if the counselor has followed the client closely so far, and if a good relationship has been established, then this different kind of response should not threaten the client, as long as it is interposed carefully and tentatively.

The first of the leading responses is known simply as explanation. Explanation is a relatively neutral description of the way things are. It deals in logical, practical, factual information. It is often offered at the client's request, although there are instances when the counselor will offer an explanation without its being requested. A client may be confused by some terminology that the counselor has used and ask, for example, "Exactly what is an annuity?" The counselor's explanation should be simple, concise, and comprehensible. Long-winded explanations tend to become vague and hard to follow. The counselor should also guard against explaining things in a condescending, patronizing, or pedantic tone. The best kinds of explanations are those that are exchanged between equal partners (not superior-subordinates) in a relationship.

Another type of leading response is the interpretive response. Interpretations can be particularly risky when the counselor goes too deep too soon, or when the interpretation is off base. Interpretations often come across as sounding overly clinical, diagnostic, and authoritarian. Despite these drawbacks, interpretations can be extremely effective responses because they often cut to the heart of the matter. When the interpretation makes sense to the client, it definitely accelerates the interview. We should keep in mind that the goal of all interpretive efforts is self-interpretation by the client in order to increase the client's ability to act effectively. An example of a facilitative interpretation would go something like this:

Client: "I'm not sure whether I want to retire early. I like to keep busy, and I don't know what I'd do with all that free time."

Counselor: "So the prospect of an early retirement is a bit frightening. Maybe you're afraid that you'd just waste your time away?"

Notice that the financial counselor's interpretation did not stray too far from what the client had said. The counselor used the words "frightening" and "afraid," but probably did so on the basis of some fear or trepidation detected in the client's voice. Further, the counselor responded tentatively, using qualifiers like "a bit" and "Maybe," and converted the second statement into a question by a raised voice at the end of the sentence. This enables the client to assimilate the counselor's response without feeling as though it has been offered as a fiat from above. The client, thus, is free to accept, modify, or deny the counselor's interpretation, and this is very important. If the counselor's interpretation is inaccurate, it is far better to discover that early than to proceed indefinitely along the wrong path.

A third type of leading response frequently employed by counselors is reassurance, or encouragement. A reassuring response is designed with the intention of making the client feel better, to bolster his or her spirits, and to offer support in a time of need. It communicates clearly to the client that "I am here by your side, ready to aid you in any way that I can." As a means of helping, however, the reassuring response tends to be merely a temporary measure. It is akin to offering a tissue to someone who is crying; the crying may stop temporarily, but the underlying causes have been left untouched. For this reason the counselor must be careful not to use reassurance indiscriminately. The understanding (reflection-of-feeling) response discussed in the previous section on active listening is far more effective when emotions surface. The understanding response communicates accurate empathy; the reassuring response offers only sympathy, and very few people like to feel pitied. Contrast the effect of these two different kinds of responses on our hypothetical client:

Client: "I get *so* furious whenever my broker ignores me! It's almost as though I don't exist!"

Counselor: (using reassuring response): "Well, don't feel so bad. It doesn't do much good to get so worked up. Try not to worry about it, and you'll feel better."

Counselor: (using reflection of feeling): "I can feel the rage as you speak. You feel like a nonperson around your broker, that you are not getting adequate service for the money you are paying, and that infuriates you."

The first counselor response patches a Band-Aid on a deep wound and is therefore ineffectual. The second response reflects the deeply felt anger and, in so doing, helps the client work through the anger. Reassurance, while not a harmful response, promises "pie in the sky" and delivers nothing.

The final type of leading response is called advice, or suggestion. Many people actively seek the advice of others, possibly hoping that the advice giver will make the difficult decision for them, or solve their problems for them. And, as chance or human nature would have it, there is certainly no dearth of people in this world willing to dole out free advice. In a financial counseling relationship, however, the best kind of advice is self-advice. Counselors who have been responding in an understanding fashion are already well on their way toward helping clients discover, in their own way and in their own time, what advice is best for them. There are times within a counseling relationship when proffering advice is acceptable, but these times are few. When advice is given, it should be offered tentatively, in the form of a suggestion, or several suggestions, about which the client has the final decision. Otherwise, the counselor not only leads, but takes over the ultimate responsibility for the client's financial plan, and each person has the right to formulate his or her own plan. Advice giving robs the client of this right.

In the next section, we will look at still another type of counselor response--perhaps the most commonly used response--the question. Questions come in all kinds of hues and colors, some much more effective in communication than others.

THE QUESTION

The question is surely one of the most timeworn response modes used by financial counselors. Many counselors see their main role as an interviewer or an interrogator. The question seems appropriate only when it is an honest attempt to gather information that the counselor requires and to which the client has access. Unfortunately, the question is not always used in this fashion. Moreover, the question-answer dialogue sets up a pattern of communication that is difficult for the participants to break: the client waits for the inevitable question; the question comes, followed by the answer (and not much more), and then the wait for the next question. Questioning almost always casts the counselor in the role of authority figure and the client in the role of somewhat passive subordinate, certainly not the type of interpersonal relationship conducive to effective counseling.

Despite the disadvantages of the question mentioned above, there are times when only a well-phrased question will suffice, particularly when we are seeking data from the client. Even here, though, there is a qualitative difference among the various types of questions that might be asked. Several categories of questions will be discussed in the following section.

Open-ended versus Close-ended Questions

Ideally, questions posed by the counselor should be open-ended and should call for more than just a yes or no response on the part of the client; otherwise, they tend to stifle interaction. The open-ended question allows the client to select a response from his or her full repertory. The close-ended question limits the client to a specific, narrow response, often either a yes or a no. The open-ended question solicits the client's opinions, thoughts, ideas, values, and feelings. The close-ended question typically solicits singular facts or one-word replies.

Contrast the differences in the following sets of questions. The first question in each set is close-ended; the second question in each set is open-ended.

1. a. Are you ready to start an investment program?
   b. How do you feel about starting an investment program?

2. a. Have you given any thought to retirement?
   b. What thoughts do you have about retirement?

3. a. Are you afraid to start saving something now?
   b. Why have you decided to wait to start saving?

As can be readily seen from the above examples, the open-ended questions ask for more complete, comprehensive information. In a way, they force the client to formulate thoughts, ideas, and feelings into fully rounded responses. On the other hand, the close-ended questions solicit only a one-word or short-answer response, requiring little thought.

Leading Questions

Other types of close-ended questions that are not only ineffective but also manipulative are those termed "leading questions." These questions usually begin with, "Don't you think...," or "Do you really feel..."? More often than not they lead the client toward a conclusion that the counselor (not the client) has already formulated, so that there is the element of dishonesty in even asking the question. It is far more effective, and honest, for the counselor to rephrase the leading question into a declarative statement in the form of sharing a perception or opinion with the client. Consider the following leading questions:

"Don't you think you should start an investment program now?"

"Do you really feel that $100 a month is enough?"

"Are you sure you've considered all possibilities?"

With just a bit of reflection, we can see that the counselor is actually saying:

"I think you ought to start an investment program now."

"I don't feel that $100 a month will be enough."

"I'm sure there are other possibilities you haven't considered."

The latter statements are much more honest and to the point than the questions from which they stem. Generally speaking, declarative statements communicate far more clearly than the manipulative leading questions. A good rule of thumb to follow in everyday intercourse is to make as many statements as possible and save the questions for honest information seeking.

The "Either/Or" or "True/False" Question

Another kind of relatively ineffective question is of the "either/or" or "true/false" variety. While this question is not quite as close-ended as the leading question, it is only slightly less closed, since it limits the client to only two options. For example:

"Do you plan to stay in this house or move to an apartment?"

"Are you more apt to take a risk or play it safe?"

Clients might prefer both options, or neither, or a third or fourth option; but here they are forced to choose from what we have offered them. The world is not simply black or white; there are various shades of gray; yet, when we phrase questions so that clients are forced to choose from one of two options, we are ignoring a basic fact of life. In the preceding examples, we can improve on the question format by asking,

"What are your plans after retirement regarding housing?"

"How do you usually make your decisions?"

Again, we see that by opening up the question we allow clients to respond freely from their own frame of reference, and not from ours. And this is what good interviewing is all about.

"Why" Questions

Even though "why" questions can be classified as open-ended questions and, thus, theoretically sound, such is not the case. On the surface, questions beginning with "why" appear to be legitimate enough, signifying the inquiry into causal relationships as in, "Why are you planning to retire at age 62?" Unfortunately, "why" questions carry with them a connotation of implied disapproval by the questioner, thus forcing the person being asked the question to justify or defend his or her thoughts, ideas, or actions. Even when that is not the meaning the questioner intends, that is generally how the "why" question is received. The "why" question tends to question the client's motivation (or lack of motivation) and, thus, creates a certain defensiveness.

Perhaps the chief reason that "why" questions are received so poorly dates back to the manner in which parents put children on the spot: "Why didn't you pick up your room?" "Why don't you have your shoes on?" "Why can't you be more careful?" And, of course, this line of inquiry is later picked up by teachers with students: "Why don't you have your homework?" "Why didn't you study for this test?" In short, as children we learned that when an adult asked us a question beginning with "why," it meant, "Change your behavior; think as I think; behave the way adults do." And we carry that lesson with us throughout life, usually responding to why questions in a defensive, negative manner.

So unless there is a valid reason for asking a why question and when no other type of question will suffice, it is generally better to avoid why questions.

Question Bombardment

Still another kind of faulty questioning technique occurs when we ask double, triple, or even quadruple questions without waiting for a response. This is frequently referred to as "question bombardment." As absurd as this may sound, it occurs far too frequently in interviews to escape comment. For example: "What type of investment program appeals to you most--stock, municipal bonds? Or would you rather look into annuities? When do you think you'd be ready to begin?" The first question in the series is open-ended in nature and can stand by itself quite well; yet the interviewer isn't content to let well enough alone, but instead tacks on other, more restricting close-ended questions. The result then is that the client is caught in a hailstorm of questions all at one time and, more often than not, gets the opportunity to respond to only one of the several questions asked. If more than one question needs to be asked, it is better to ask them as separate questions, waiting for a full response to each question before going on to the next one. The other issue to be addressed, though, is whether so many questions need to be asked in the first place.

Concluding Remarks

Questioning is a major component of the repertory of most interviewers. Yet that need not be so. If we wish to become better communicators, one thing that we can do is to convert some of our questions (especially close-ended, leading, either/or, and why questions) into statements. With a statement, we assume responsibility for what we say. With a question, we shift the responsibility to the other person, which may sometimes be necessary. Far too often, however, we simply shirk our own responsibility for, and involvement in, the interaction when we revert to questioning. As stated previously, counseling is not the same as interviewing. If we hope to do counseling, we need to do far more than simply ask one question after another.

THE FINANCIAL PLANNING PROCESS:
GATHERING CLIENT INFORMATION

by Dale S. Johnson*

A comprehensive financial plan tailored to the needs and objectives of an individual client covers a wide range of areas, including

- an analysis of the client's total financial and tax position
- the identification of personal and family financial objectives
- planning for the management of cash flow, net worth, and taxable income
- planning for tax deferral, conversion, and reduction
- planning for wealth accumulation to meet specific objectives
- planning for business ownership interests to meet personal financial objectives
- planning for retirement
- planning for the estate
- planning for income/asset protection in the event of death, disability, or property-liability losses
- planning for asset and portfolio management

A financial plan that thoroughly integrates and coordinates each of these aspects of a client's concerns and objectives is not arrived at quickly or easily. It is developed through a series of counseling sessions between the client and a financial planner to whom the client has entrusted this responsibility. Normally formulating and implementing the plan will be a team effort involving one or more additional professional specialists. The financial planner chosen by the client to do comprehensive financial planning bears the overall responsibility for ensuring that the client's interests are served and therefore coordinates all team efforts.

THE INITIAL SESSION

To ensure that information-gathering and counseling sessions with the client will be both productive and efficient, financial planning begins with an initial session to determine whether the client is interested in the financial planner's services. While this session will generally involve a single prospective client, the planner

---

*Dale S. Johnson, PhD, CFP, is a financial planning consultant and writer headquartered in Villanova, Pa.

may wish to conduct a seminar for a group of prospective clients, such as the executives of a business firm or members of the local community. In either case the planner will describe the nature and scope of the services to be provided (including referral to other specialists), the modes of operation, the structure of compensation for services, and the form of the financial plan to be produced for the client.

If the planner and the prospective client hope to establish a professional relationship, ground rules must be clarified. Foremost among them should be the understanding that comprehensive financial planning for the client can be done only if complete information about the client's personal and financial situation is revealed. The client should understand the need to furnish extensive records and documents and to engage in counseling sessions with the planner, during which not only the client's financial position but also problems, needs, and personal and financial objectives will be explored.

If a working relationship begins to evolve at this initial meeting, the planner may want to follow up with a letter and a checklist of client documents, records, and information needed for review before the first formal counseling session. In addition, the planner may want to have the client fill out part or all of the information-gathering form used in his or her practice to collect and organize the facts of the client's personal and financial position. Assembling complete information on the client is the single most important task in financial planning. It is therefore imperative that the form on which this information is collected be sufficiently comprehensive to enable the planner to (1) evaluate the client's total financial condition, (2) sense who the client really is as a person, (3) determine where the client wants to be, and (4) formulate the most appropriate strategies for getting there.

Because every financial services professional operates in a complex marketplace of varying services, products, and clients, no single information-gathering form will serve the needs of everyone. The experienced professional will eventually develop a form that meets the needs of his or her practice. As a model of a systematically organized, comprehensive information-gathering form, the Chartered Financial Consultant and CLU programs of The American College use the Financial and Estate Planning Fact Finder (hereafter referred to as the fact finder).[1] Using this form will introduce the areas of financial counseling and planning that require detailed client information and will

---

1. A complete copy of the fact finder is included at the end of this reading.

provide practice in collecting and evaluating complete facts about a client. The fact finder is organized so that information can be interpreted, analyzed, diagnosed, and finally incorporated into a financial plan for the client. When completed it should thoroughly delineate the client's financial condition and enable the client to determine needs and establish objectives in relation to available and anticipated resources.

As a first step the planner may request the client to fill out as many pages of the fact finder as is consistent with the planner's own information-gathering style. In all cases the client should also be provided with a checklist of the various documents and copies of documents that must be made available to the planner. Page 25 of the fact finder is a receipt for documents (shown on the next page) that can be used for this purpose. The new client should provide this preliminary information well in advance of the first formal counseling session to give the planner ample time to (1) review the information, (2) form preliminary impressions of the client's financial condition, and (3) determine those areas in which more detailed information and insight into the client's condition are needed. During this preliminary review of documents and records the planner should record important information from them in the appropriate sections of the fact finder.

It is a rare client who will voluntarily come forth with full information in all of the areas of information provided for in the fact finder. If the client fills out all or part of the fact finder, the planner should consider what the client provides as only provisional. Often the client simply does not know the full details of his or her financial condition or has not kept adequate records. Some of the information must be obtained from other sources, such as the client's employer, attorney, or CPA. The planner may also need to do some research for the client.

If the client is married, the spouse should be fully involved in providing this information and both should be present during the counseling and information-gathering sessions with the planner, unless there are compelling personal reasons to the contrary (such as an impending divorce). Indeed, in households in which both spouses have income and assets, the financial planner often counsels both spouses equally and develops a plan that reflects their respective as well as their mutual concerns and objectives. In such cases, appropriate sections of the fact finder should be duplicated and completed for both the client and spouse.

By now the planner is developing a tentative profile of the client and pinpointing areas where more detailed information is needed. Getting this basic information

RECEIPT FOR DOCUMENTS

Insurance Policies: Life, Health, Property and Liability

Company	Policy Number	✓	Company	Policy Number	✓
_____	_____	☐	_____	_____	☐
_____	_____	☐	_____	_____	☐
_____	_____	☐	_____	_____	☐
_____	_____	☐	_____	_____	☐
_____	_____	☐	_____	_____	☐

Original policies checked ✓ above have been received for review and analysis; they will be returned upon completion of analysis or client request.

_____
(planner)

_____
(address)

_____
(phone)

_____
(date)

All original policies and documents checked in this receipt have been returned to me.

_____
(client)

_____
(date)

Personal/Family Documents (copies)	**Date**	**Business Documents (copies)**	**Date**
☐ Tax returns (3–5 years)	_____	☐ Tax returns (3–5 years)	_____
☐ Wills (client and spouse)	_____	☐ Financial statements (3–5 years)	_____
☐ Trust instruments	_____	☐ Deferred-compensation plan	_____
☐ Financial statements	_____	☐ HR-10 plan (Keogh)	_____
☐ Personal/family budgets	_____	☐ Individual retirement account (IRA)	_____
☐ Sale/purchase contract	_____	☐ Simplified employee pension (SEP)	_____
☐ Current insurance offers	_____	☐ Pension/profit-sharing plan	_____
☐ Current investment offers	_____	☐ Tax-deferred annuity	_____
☐ Deeds, mortgages, land contracts	_____	☐ Stock-option/purchase agreement	_____
☐ Guardian nominations	_____	☐ Buy-sell agreements	_____
☐ Leases (as lessor or lessee)	_____	☐ Employment agreement	_____
☐ Notices of awards, elections	_____	☐ Employee benefits booklet	_____
☐ Power of attorney/appointment	_____	☐ Articles of incorporation	_____
☐ Separation/divorce/nuptial	_____	☐ Merger/acquisition agreement	_____
☐ Patents/copyrights/royalties	_____	☐ Partnership agreement	_____
☐ Employee benefits statement	_____	☐ Company patents	_____
☐ Other (specify)	_____	☐ Equipment leasing agreement(s)	_____
☐ Other (specify)	_____	☐ Other (specify)	_____

© 1984 The American College

beforehand can greatly facilitate the counseling process and enable the planner to use a scheduled counseling session or sessions for reviewing the information, getting to know the client, observing and evaluating the consistency between the client's verbal and nonverbal behaviors, and filling out those sections of the fact finder that the client cannot complete. Valuable time will be saved, there will be more focus in the counseling sessions, and the client will begin to realize that comprehensive information is necessary if the planner is to render a full range of services.

When this preliminary information has been recorded in the fact finder and reviewed, an appointment for the first formal counseling session should be arranged with the client. Since most formal agreements for professional planning services are not effected until during or after this counseling session, the financial planner will devote most of the session to a review of the client's financial position, a clarification of the client's current sense of needs and objectives, and a thorough discussion of the factors that will affect individualized planning. Relevant sections of the fact finder should also be completed if possible. (A fee may be charged for this initial counseling session, or it may be offset against or included in the fee for the comprehensive plan.)

If a professional relationship is established at this point, formal contracts or agreements may be signed as to performance, target dates, and the range of services to be provided by the planner; compensation arrangements will also be agreed upon. This formalization of the professional relationship should also include having the client sign an authorization for information (such as the one contained on page 23 of the fact finder and shown on the next page). This permits the financial planner to inform the client's insurance companies or agents, securities broker, attorney, CPA, and other financial advisers of their current financial planning relationship and thereby obtain additional necessary information. The client should also telephone these advisers to assure them of a willingness to have them discuss his or her personal and business affairs with the financial planner.

The matters discussed above typically precede the complete gathering of client information needed for effective and comprehensive financial planning, which will be the subject of this reading. Before we review the fact finder section by section and page by page to suggest how it should be used and how client information is gathered, verified, analyzed, and incorporated into a plan, a few general comments about the fact finder itself are in order.

AUTHORIZATION FOR INFORMATION

TO: _____

_____

_____

Please provide any information that is in your possession and that is asked for in connection with a survey of my/our financial affairs to

_____

_____
(client's signature)

_____
(spouse's signature)

_____
(date)

TO: _____
    (company)

Please provide any information that is in your possession and that is requested by _____

_____ concerning the following policies of which I am the owner:

_____   _____

_____   _____

_____   _____

Policyowner's
Authorization _____
               (signature of policyowner)

_____
(date)

Notes

© 1984 The American College

4.6

THE FINANCIAL AND ESTATE PLANNING FACT FINDER

The fact finder is designed to elicit the information necessary to formulate and implement a comprehensive financial plan tailored to an individual client's needs. Not all clients will evidence a financial condition, a set of objectives, or the resources or income to make all sections of the fact finder equally relevant. Moreover, not all financial services professionals are engaged in offering comprehensive financial planning. Securities brokers, accountants, attorneys, life insurance agents, bank trust officers, and others who offer specialized financial products or services or single-purpose financial planning may not find all sections of the fact finder relevant to their data-gathering activities. However, the fact finder can be used with a wide array of differing client circumstances, financial needs, and objectives.

Every financial services professional will need a systematic method and format for assembling relevant client information. In some cases where the complete fact finder elicits more information than is needed, the financial services professional can select relevant sections to gather and maintain pertinent client information systematically. In other cases the planner will need more extensive and detailed information than the fact finder gathers. For example, complex estate or tax planning, large-scale or diversified investment portfolio analysis and management, and planning for the owners of closely held corporations will require information and analysis going far beyond that provided by the fact finder. These situations often involve complex legal theory and application or sophisticated calculations, computer analyses, and projections. Since the fact finder provides for comprehensive client information, however, the planner can supplement it with specially designed information and analysis forms and computer software programs for these complex situations.

In summary, the fact finder can impose a systematic method upon the information-gathering process. It makes available a body of logically classified information that can be used directly for comprehensive financial planning strategies, techniques, and methods; that can be used with computer software programs; and that can be shared with other members of a financial services team who are serving an individual client's needs.

A complete copy of the fact finder is included at the end of this reading and in the HS 320 study guide. This reading will proceed through a page-by-page and section-by-section discussion of the kinds of information the fact finder gathers, demonstrating how this information relates to comprehensive financial planning and how it provides the basis for beginning to think and communicate in the professional language of financial planning.

Personal Data

The fact finder begins the accumulation of client information with the personal data section on pages 1-3. After this section has been filled out—either by the client prior to the first formal counseling session or by the planner during that session—the information should be thoroughly reviewed for completeness and accuracy. Moreover, the planner should be alert to the implications and importance of the information gathered.

The first items of personal data, page 1, ask for the home and business addresses and phone numbers of the client and spouse. The two important considerations here are that in a two-wage-earner household, which is quite common, the wife's business address and phone number are as important as the husband's; and the legal domicile of both spouses is extremely important in tax and estate planning. In these first items of page 1 there are also spaces to record the dates of counseling sessions and the dates when the checklist for financial planning review (page 39 of the fact finder, which is illustrated later in this reading) was sent.

It is very important for the planner to know the names, addresses, and telephone numbers of the client's financial, legal, and business advisers. These consultants not only will be important resources for clarifying the client's financial history, but they may also become members of the professional team whose services and products will implement the financial plan ultimately developed for the client. The planner should therefore tactfully inquire whether the client is satisfied with these existing relationships. If so and if the client wants to continue to use the services of these professionals, the planner should ask the client to notify them about his or her professional relationship with the planner. The client should also give permission for the planner to send each of them a brief letter of introduction to ask for their professional collaboration and cooperation in meeting the client's needs.

In discussing these professional relationships with the client, the planner should determine the client's level of awareness and sophistication in dealing with financial services professionals and discover whether the team approach to financial planning is agreeable. The planner may discover, either at this stage or later, that there will be problems in coordinating efforts with those of other team members who also enjoy the client's trust and confidence. These problems will have to be confronted with goodwill, professional tact and courtesy, and a spirit of cooperation. However, as the professional engaged to do comprehensive financial planning for the client, the planner is the captain and coordinator of the professional team and should assume that role with confidence in this unique relationship with the client.

Page 2 of the fact finder asks for detailed information about members of the client's immediate family: ages, social security numbers, occupations, and the amounts of financial support provided for them by the client or spouse. The survey also asks for information about grandchildren and other family members.

Space is also provided on page 2 of the fact finder to list health problems or special needs of the client, spouse, or family members that may affect the client's current financial position or planning for the future. For example, if one of the client's children has a health problem, special consideration might be given to unusual medical expenses or to the need for full or partial support arrangements for that child. Adopted children or stepchildren may require different considerations from natural children. The planner should tactfully explore all client concerns here in order to anticipate later planning considerations. If there are problems, both the client and spouse may want to make some financial arrangement to equalize a particular family member's situation. Quite often the client will want to provide partial or full support for parents or for the spouse's parents, for example.

It is obviously important for the planner to pay particular attention to the number and ages of the client's children, as this information will give some indication of the client's total support obligations to all members of the family, both now and in the future. This is an extremely important consideration in determining the income needs of the client during that person's lifetime, in case of disability, during retirement, and after death. It will also affect decisions about the disposition of income-producing and appreciating assets to fund those needs and decisions about the purchase of appropriate life and disability income insurance coverage in case of premature death and long-term disability.

The personal information asked for on page 3 of the fact finder will reveal a number of potential complications in the client's (or spouse's) circumstances: previous marriages and alimony or child-support obligations; the existence (or lack) of current wills and prenuptial or postnuptial agreements; the existence of trusts or custodial accounts for children or others; guardian nominations for the children; trusts of which the client or spouse is beneficiary; gifts or inheritances pending or anticipated; the educational background; and any benefits resulting from the military service of the client or spouse. Not only are these items important for subsequent financial planning, but they also provide insight into what kind of person the client is and the level of sophistication and complexity of the client's current financial program. No effort is made to gather detailed information concerning existing wills, trusts, nuptial agreements, or guardianships at this point. But the financial planner should know they exist and be able to examine them to determine whether they are in line with the client's expressed wishes and overall financial plan. The client's perceptions of problems in these personal affairs should also be explored so that the planner can have the benefit of the client's current thoughts and feelings about these sensitive matters.

Financial Objectives

The financial objectives section on page 4 of the fact finder permits the client to make preliminary indications of these financial priorities and objectives. They should not be considered to be fixed, since subsequent analysis of the client's actual financial position and prospects may compel radical revisions of the initial objectives or deferment of the target dates for achieving some of the more immediate desires. Often the client will set different priorities as the result of going through the planning process. Nevertheless, these preliminary rankings of objectives give the planner a perception of the client's concerns, which can be explored in counseling sessions and evaluated in the light of the client's total current financial position, the risk/return profile, and reasonable projections for the future. Knowing what the client's real objectives are will permit the planner to provide an appropriate track for the client to run on.

The financial objectives section of the fact finder also contains questions about the client's current monthly budgeting, annual savings, and annual investments. If the client has no financial management program, yet has strongly felt objectives, there is clearly a discrepancy between what the client wants and what he or she is self-disciplined enough to achieve. If the client does have a program but wants to save or invest more, the planner should probe the client's perception of the cause of the disparity. It is often in this area that the planner can help the client realize what obstacles are preventing effective money management. Sometimes the problem is in the client's life-style or in the client's lack of self-discipline; often it is the claims of others (spouse, children, dependents) upon his or her resources or rising tax burdens combined with inflation. The inability to overcome these and other obstacles often gives rise to frustrations that themselves become further obstacles to the achievement of objectives.

If the client is already doing all he or she wants to do in managing personal and family finances, then planning based on the need for tighter financial controls and more savings or investment will probably be unacceptable. On the other hand, if the client wants to save or invest more, then a leaner budget, cutbacks in discretionary spending, and other controls the planner may suggest to accomplish these objectives will be well received. The data in this section of the fact finder will therefore be crucial to the projections into future years that will be made in the cash-management statement and the financial position statement (pages 7 and 35-36 in the fact finder); they may become, in fact, the limits of what the client is willing to undertake in order to start moving toward desired financial objectives. All things considered, willingness is the client's largest resource.

Factors Affecting Your Financial Plan

In the section listing factors affecting the client's financial plan (page 4), there are several items of particular importance to the financial planner's perception of the client's personality and willingness to implement subsequent recommendations. The first two items determine whether the client has made gifts or is willing to consider making gifts to family members, educational institutions, or other tax-exempt organizations, for either philanthropic or tax-planning reasons, and whether charitable giving is consistent with the client's philosophical views. Although positive responses will exhibit an openness to gift giving as a strategy, negative responses do not necessarily indicate the opposite; the client may simply never have considered bequests or may not know how they work or what their advantages are.

If the next two items on page 4 indicate that the client is dissatisfied with the results of previous investments or feels committed to them in any way, these thoughts and feelings should be explored. The risk/return profile on page 21 of the fact finder may reveal the source of such dissatisfaction. The client may have made some investments that were not consistent with his or her personal risk/return profile or chosen investment vehicles that were not appropriate. Perhaps the client has changed objectives, now being less keen on self-directed investing and preferring to place these assets in managed accounts so as to avoid personal involvement. Or the client may be receiving too much taxable income and be seeking means to reduce his or her tax burden.

Since many financial plans ultimately depend upon investments for the accumulation of capital, the client's feelings about previous investment experiences may show how to deploy current assets more compatibly with the client's real investment circumstances. Above all, the client must take management control of current investment assets, no matter how acquired, and use them to best advantage. There are feasible solutions to almost all current investment problems if they are approached realistically.

The next six questions in the section concerning the factors affecting the client's financial plan on page 4 of the fact finder probe the nature of the client's family relationships. These questions, concerning the client's spouse and children, desired age of retirement, and how the estate distribution is to be made, are helpful in discovering both the client's and the spouse's underlying attitudes and motives for a whole range of financial objectives. Answers to these questions, which are extremely personal, may be difficult for the client to articulate. In counseling the client the financial planner must be tactful yet firm in securing clear statements on these matters. If the client and spouse are not of one accord, they must resolve their differences. It is not easy for a client to divulge truthful feelings about a spouse and other family members when these circumstances may be less than ideal or even painful. Yet the client's feelings and perceptions about these matters color the whole financial planning process--indeed, they must, for otherwise the financial plan will not address the human elements that it must accommodate in order to be successful.

The final question in this section--"What do you think financial planning should do for you?"--may bring to a head a whole range of client concerns. Certainly the client's response to this question will show what direction the financial planning process should take by revealing that person's sense of unsatisfied needs.

One final comment about the relevance of the personal client data and information items contained in pages 1 through 4 of the fact finder is necessary. It is in these areas that the client's most sensitive feelings and thoughts are likely to emerge during counseling sessions, that profound human and relational concerns are likely to be discovered. Therefore these areas demand the most sensitive employment of the planner's communications skills and techniques. Even though the client may provide extensive and accurate data and facts before and during the counseling sessions, responses should be thoroughly evaluated for clues to personal, family, and economic problem areas. The planner should ask appropriate clarifying questions in a nonjudgmental way. The client's responses should be compared with other information provided and with facts determined in other sections of the fact finder to ascertain consistency. For example, the forms of ownership of the client's assets shown in the inventory of assets (pages 8-11 of the fact finder) should be analyzed in light of the client's wishes regarding the distribution of the estate.

Objectives Requiring Additional Income/Capital

The section that deals with objectives requiring additional income/capital on page 5 of the fact finder gathers details about specific client financial objectives that may require income or capital beyond what is determined for retirement and estate planning needs. The most common objective will be the client's desire to send the children to college. If the client has considerable holdings in appreciating and/or income-producing assets, achieving this objective may involve little more than allocating these resources (for example, by means of a trust) so as to set them aside for that purpose and perhaps at the same time effect a tax advantage for the client. In other cases the need for additional income or capital to fund college expenses may require the repositioning of assets from nonappreciating or low-income-producing investments or savings media into higher-yielding or growth opportunities, such as Treasury bills or money market funds when yields are high, or deeply discounted good-quality municipal or corporate bonds whose maturities coincide with the need for funds to pay college expenses.

If the client has a high and rising income, he or she may prefer to fund the children's postsecondary education from then-current income. If the client's premature death would jeopardize the funding of this objective (or of any other similar objective), the planner should consider these educational needs when analyzing the client's life insurance program.

In addition, the financial planner should determine whether any help may be available from outside the client's financial resources, such as scholarships, part-time work, and loan funds from federal, state, or family sources. Frequently the children of clients have been designated as beneficiaries of wills or trusts or as donees of gift programs by their grandparents or other relatives to fund all or part of their college education. In the case of remarriage, help toward college expenses may be anticipated from a previous spouse. If such resources are available, the need for funding the client's share of such anticipated future costs could be significantly reduced or even eliminated, thus freeing capital and income for other financial objectives in the client's total plan.

Regardless of how college will be funded, the importance of planning in this area is dramatically illustrated in table 1 on page 3.14. Planning to meet college expenses for the client's children--like all future funding requirements--must realistically consider an inflation factor in relation to the projected rate of return on the investments that are expected to provide the funding. If the client's current assets are producing compound aftertax yields considerably lower than the inflation rate, the net

TABLE 1
Paying for a College Education

Assumptions:
1. Tuition is currently $6,000 per year at a state university and $7,000 per year at a private university.
2. Tuition rates will rise by 6 percent per year.
3. Aftertax rate of return on the savings fund will be 7 percent per year.
4. All the necessary saving will be completed by the time the child enters the freshman year, with the last savings deposit made at that time.
5. Tuition payments will be made at the beginning of each of the 4 years the child attends the university.

	State University		Private University	
# Years Until Child Begins University	4-Yr. Cost When Child Reaches College Age*	Annual Savings Required*	4-Yr. Cost When Child Reaches College Age*	Annual Savings Required*
18	$74,920	$ 2,004	$112,378	$ 3,006
17	70,679	2,079	106,017	3,118
16	66,678	2,162	100,016	3,243
15	62,904	2,256	94,355	3,383
14	59,343	2,362	89,014	3,542
13	55,984	2,460	83,976	3,724
12	52,815	2,622	79,222	3,933
11	49,826	2,785	74,738	4,178
10	47,005	2,978	70,507	4,467
9	44,345	3,210	66,516	4,814
8	41,835	3,493	62,751	5,239
7	39,467	3,847	59,199	5,770
6	37,233	4,302	55,849	6,454
5	35,125	4,910	52,687	7,365
4	33,137	5,762	49,705	8,643
3	31,262	7,041	46,891	10,561
2	29,492	9,174	44,237	13,760
1	27,823	13,441	41,733	20,161
0	26,248	26,248	39,371	39,371

*Estimated

assets working for education objectives will not meet the mark. The client should either consider reallocating these assets to higher-yielding investment media or modify expectations and consider alternatives, such as a state college or university rather than a private one.

4.14

Besides the education objective, the client may have others that require either long- or short-term planning and allocation. These could include a desire to take care of a handicapped child, to provide support for a parent or other relative, or to accumulate funds for a future charitable bequest. The planner should thoroughly explore the client's situation and uncover all objectives beyond the need to provide for personal economic well-being. Then the planner should lead the client to a full determination of all other resources (including the resources of the proposed beneficiary) that may be available to help fund these needs, such as social security benefits, private pensions, part-time work, life insurance proceeds, and income from the proposed beneficiary's own earlier investments.

As with education needs, the client's other specific objectives should be factored into this comprehensive plan and should be funded with the most appropriate and most tax-advantaged investment media available. If possible, part of the client's income should be shifted to a lower-tax-bracket family member so that multiple objectives can be realized in one maneuver. Outright gifts should be considered, including gifts of both cash and appreciating assets that currently produce positive cash flows otherwise taxable to the client. However, the client should be aware that the gift of an income-producing asset to a son or daughter under the age of 14 causes the income to be taxed at the highest marginal rate of the parent.

The primary consideration in financial planning is the comprehensive and efficient use of both financial resources and tax advantages to achieve the client's objectives. Therefore all specific objectives requiring additional income or capital should be considered in relation to the client's total financial condition and to comprehensive lifetime financial objectives and estate planning desires.

Sources of Income

Page 6 of the fact finder is a survey of the client's income from all sources, including the income of spouse and children, if any; income tax obligations; estimated income one, three, and five years in the future; and anticipated salary increases and bonuses.

The financial planner and the client will find it illuminating to analyze the sources of the client's tax liabilities in relation to the sources of income. Clients who suffer from excessive tax burdens usually have not shrewdly managed their sources of income for the tax consequences, much less created them initially with that consideration in mind. The planner should be able to point out why the client is paying so much in taxes.

After the client has provided all the income information, the financial planner should check tax returns to verify the amounts reported. It is crucial that all of this information be correct and complete, as many recommendations the planner may make for family budgeting, savings, investment, funding for specific objectives, additional insurance coverage, tax planning, retirement planning, and estate planning will be related to the current and continuing income sources inventoried on page 6. Using this information, the planner may project the probable growth rate of the client's financial position for years into the future. But planning is only as good as the information on which it is based.

The sources and amounts of the client's income will be transferred to the cash-management statement on page 7 of the fact finder where, along with other types of cash inflows, it will be evaluated in relation to the client's annual cash expenditures.

The Cash-Management Statement

The most important point to be made about the cash-management statement (page 7) is that the figures for all items should be complete and correct. Most individuals and families do not follow a realistic and exacting budget; indeed, many are averse to doing so. For these families the completion of the cash-management statement detailing all items of cash inflows and outflows will be an uncomfortable task for which most will not have kept adequate records--particularly if the client, spouse, and children still living at home are all generating cash inflows and making cash expenditures.

If the client has not used effective budgeting methods before, the exercise of completing this statement and analyzing and evaluating its content relative to both short- and long-term financial objectives can disclose that person's current position and what must be done to achieve the desired objectives. It is usually important for the client to be in a position of positive cash flow so as to permit the client to fund additional financial objectives. No financial plan can work for long if there are consistent net deficits of cash (or, for that matter, net surpluses of cash solely due to liquidating assets or taking on additional debt).

Inventory of Assets and Liabilities

Three fact finder sections, those containing the inventory of assets and of liabilities and that describing the business interest, are pivotal in financial planning. When information about the client's assets and liabilities is transferred to the first column of the financial position statement (pages 35-36 of the fact finder), that person's total financial position and net worth will be reflected. Moreover, this inventory of assets and liabilities will enable the financial planner to understand how the client uses financial resources and debt, what the client's preferences and aversions are, what the liquidity position is, what problems exist, whether all assets (including any business interest) are being used efficiently to meet financial objectives, how diversified these assets are, whether the client is aware of this total financial condition (or even wants to be), and how the client thinks and feels about these present assets and financial resources.

Many clients have an inexact and often only sketchy idea of what their total assets are. Even more have a poor grasp of whether their assets are efficiently working toward their objectives or whether their investment risk exposures are really consistent with their temperament. No other area of the client's financial posture is more crucial for achieving realistic financial objectives than that person's total asset and liability positions and their tax implications, particularly if the client's business interest represents a substantial portion of total assets. Because this area of financial planning is so important and involves so many vital considerations, a major section of this reading is devoted to the nature and significance of the information generated in these three sections of the fact finder.

Inventory of Assets

In the inventory of assets on pages 8-11 of the fact finder, it is of utmost importance not only to list and substantiate all of the client's currently held cash and near-cash equivalents, other financial assets, and property, but also to characterize each asset according to the information called for in the column headings. This information will be crucial in assessing how well the client's assets are performing in relation to personal objectives and in evaluating the relative proportions of each type of asset in the client's total portfolio--that is, the client's asset mix. These column headings will also aid in later decisions as to how some or all of these assets could be liquidated, if desirable, so that the capital thus freed could be redeployed in other investment media whose performances may be more consistent with client-established needs and objectives.

A detailed evaluation of the client's assets might also disclose which assets are most suitable for giving to family members, for meeting short-term liquidity needs, for donating to charity or other tax-exempt organizations, for funding trusts established to meet specific objectives, or for retaining in the estate the client is building. Only a thorough assessment of each asset's features will permit a wise choice of which ones to use for these purposes.

After a course of action has been determined, other factors will come into play. If the asset is owned outright, the client can make the decision alone. If it is held in joint ownership with the spouse, if it is community property, or if it is an asset held in trust or already donated to, let us say, one of their children under a state Uniform Gifts to Minors Act, then the decision may require the cooperation of the spouse or may be precluded entirely by the current form of ownership. In all cases of possible asset liquidation or transfer it is important for the planner to know the form of ownership and the location of the asset--that is, where the certificates, deeds, mortgages, and so on are located.

The headings used in the market-value-and-titled-owners portion of the inventory of assets represent the most common forms of ownership; the value of each asset should be included in the appropriate column. Briefly the common forms of ownership are these:

- Client--Title and ownership are held separately in the name of the client.

- Spouse--Title and ownership are held separately in the name of the spouse.

- Joint (survivor rights)--Title and ownership are held jointly by two or more parties; on the death of one of the joint tenants the deceased's entire interest passes to the survivor(s) by operation of law rather than under the provisions of a will.

- Joint (no survivor rights)--Title and ownership are held jointly by two or more parties; but each tenant may sell, donate, or dispose of his or her proportionate interest by will. Upon the death of a tenant there is no provision of law that passes the tenant's property to other cotenants.

- Community property--Ownership of all property acquired by husband and wife during their marriage, while domiciled in one of the eight community-property states, may be deemed to be owned equally by each.

- Other--Assets and property held in trusts and custodial accounts (such as Uniform Gifts to Minors Act accounts) are in the form of ownership constituted by these instruments and are governed by applicable federal and state law with respect to taxation and transfer. Some of these assets may not be the property of the client, strictly speaking, but the client may still be subject to income or estate taxation under certain circumstances.

In completing and thoroughly discussing the inventory of assets with the client, the planner can discover existing problems in the client's total asset picture, get a sense of what the client's feelings are concerning currently held assets, and begin to look at alternatives for restructuring assets in relation to a comprehensive plan.

Cash and near-cash equivalents. The financial planner begins the client's asset inventory on pages 8 and 9 of the fact finder with the subsection on cash and near-cash equivalents. As this information is gathered and evaluated the planner should consider several critical issues. For instance, how much ready cash is available in checking and savings accounts to meet emergency needs? If more than the equivalent of 3 to 6 months' income is held in low-yielding savings instruments, the client's need for the highest yield on cash equivalents consistent with safety may not be met. Excess cash beyond emergency needs may better be placed in money market funds. In fact, even cash for emergency reserves may be held in money market funds, particularly when yields are high. If the client has large accumulated cash values and dividends in life insurance policies, he or she could free some cash currently held in savings deposits for emergency needs, and reposition it in higher-yielding instruments. If the client seems strongly disposed toward savings and/or to near-cash equivalents, the financial planner should probe to ascertain whether the client is satisfying psychological needs that may obscure unexamined risk attitudes.

Other questions also need to be raised by way of evaluating the client's cash-management program. Optimally the client should have a systematic savings program that both maintains a minimum cash reserve and creates a savings pool from which investments can be made. Does the client's current cash management accomplish this objective? Is a disproportionate amount of the client's savings locked into savings certificates at fixed below-market interest rates? Is the client's cash position large enough to suggest direct investment in high-yielding, short-maturity Treasury bills or commercial paper?

In general, does the client have an efficient cash-management system that places discretionary cash and short-term funds to work at optimum yields consistent with his or her risk profile? In times of high interest rates for short-term cash investments a large proportion of many clients' financial assets (especially common stock) might be abandoned in favor of higher-yielding near-cash vehicles such as money market funds. However, this strategy should be distinguished from savings to maintain a reserve fund, since most of the near-cash vehicles acquired for this purpose should be repositioned into other financial assets or other investments when yields, appreciation potentials, risk elements, and mortgage rates become more favorable.

It is important to observe how much of a client's current income is held in cash and near-cash vehicles in anticipation of future investment opportunities, because this aspect of the client's cash management measures the disposition to save for investment. It is therefore the most important consideration in an assessment of the client's cash and near-cash assets, for it indicates whether the client is willing to forgo a percentage of possible current consumption in favor of saving and investment for the long term to achieve other financial objectives. Evaluating the client in this area, in short, is a way of diagnosing that person's propensity for investing and, ultimately, for getting involved in comprehensive financial planning.

The client's cash and near-cash equivalents will be a revealing figure when compared with other categories of assets and to the total financial condition. There is no real guideline here, especially in times of investment uncertainties, high interest rates, and the varying opportunity cost of money.[2] In general, however, cash in checking and savings deposits should be held for current expenses and emergency and reserve needs (unless the client's life insurance cash values and/or unused debt capacity are adequate for emergency and reserve needs); cash equivalents (such as money market funds and Treasury bills) might be held to take advantage of attractive yields if it seems wise to await more opportune times for making longer-term investments with appreciation potential. A comprehensive financial plan cannot be developed working only with cash and near-cash equivalents, and yet managing one's cash efficiently is a necessary first step toward achieving long-term financial objectives, especially those that are geared to capital appreciation.

Bonds and preferred stock. Maturity and call dates are asked for in the listing of bonds and preferred stock on pages 8 and 9 of the fact finder. Bonds (except U.S. government bonds) and preferred stock are frequently issued with call dates prior to maturity at which the issuer may redeem the bond or preferred stock issue at specified prices relative to their face or par value. (In this respect call dates are merely alternative--and shorter--potential maturity dates for the issues in question.) This flexibility enables the issuer to take advantage of the right to redeem and refund an issue when current interest rates are favorable. To compensate the holder of the bond or preferred stock for the inconvenience, the issuer will usually pay a small premium

---

2. The opportunity cost of money is the difference between the actual yield of an investment and what the yield on the same amount of money might have been in another investment for the same period of time.

over par or face value for the right to call the issue. A client who holds a bond or preferred stock issue that is callable before maturity may have sizable amounts of capital available at the call date for reinvestment in other opportunities or to fund a financial objective. A financial planner who knows these details can plan for uses of future capital in the client's total portfolio.

Bond funds are often unit trust funds of a one-time selection of either corporate or municipal bonds of several issuers with similar maturities. The yield of unit trust funds is a composite yield of all the issues, minus the management fees. As the separate issues mature and are redeemed or are called before maturity, proportionate shares of principal plus accrued interest are returned to holders of unit interests. Bond unit trust funds should be listed in the asset inventory by their fund names. If bond funds are technically mutual funds rather than unit trusts, they should be listed under mutual funds.

Common stock. The inventory of assets proceeds to common stock on pages 8 and 9 of the fact finder. Common stock is either listed (traded on national or regional securities exchanges, or on both), unlisted (traded on the over-the-counter market), or nonmarketable (restricted stock held by the officers of listed or unlisted companies, or shares of closely held corporations for which there is no active market). To enable the planner to evaluate the marketability of the client's holdings of common stock, the code for the stock's category should be noted after the name of the stock issuer.

There are several important points in this inventory of the client's common stock. If most of the client's holdings are in listed issues, there will generally be an active market in those stocks, but prices can fluctuate with market and industry variables at a given time. The same is true for most over-the-counter (OTC) issues. However, some OTC issues are of small companies whose outstanding shares represent relatively small capitalizations and are infrequently traded. Moreover, OTC stock issues are also usually of younger, untried or unseasoned companies. Consequently, OTC issues tend to be more speculative and risky than are listed issues. The financial planner should determine, from the composition of the client's stock portfolio and its total value in relation to other financial assets, whether the portfolio is consistent with his or her risk profile and with the short- and long-term objectives of the comprehensive financial plan. If inconsistencies are uncovered, restructuring the portfolio or repositioning capital out of stocks and into other forms of investment may be called for.

If the client holds restricted stock of publicly traded companies or stock of closely held corporations, there may be problems either in liquidating it or in providing for the redemption of stock upon disability, retirement, or death. The financial planner must consider what the client holds--and why--when recommending appropriate strategies for either retaining, liquidating, or redeeming the stock as part of the client's comprehensive financial plan. For example, it might be appropriate to contemplate buy-sell and/or stock-redemption agreements to dispose of these assets. It should also be noted that in the financial position statement (page 35 of the fact finder), under the column heading Other Financial Assets, client holdings of nonmarketable securities are listed separately from other common stock holdings. This distinction indicates their relative lack of liquidity, for even if there are buyers for those assets, the client usually holds them for long-term financial objectives.

Warrants and options. The warrants and options subsection of client assets on pages 8 and 9 should include warrants held to buy common stock, options to buy the stock of a company for which the client works or has worked, and options bought or sold on the national and regional stock options exchanges. Not many clients trade in warrants anymore, but many are involved in options contracts. Since these contracts can involve sizable blocks of stock that move in and out of the client's portfolio, the financial planner or the client's investment adviser (if they are not the same) needs to know the full details of the client's positions at all times. In addition, the client's preferences about trading in stock options provide additional information regarding this client's risk profile.

If the client holds options to buy, at specified prices, stock in the company where he or she works or has worked, any intentions to exercise those options should be determined. Exercising these options will frequently involve sizable cash outlays that must be funded either from current income, from repositioning capital tied up in other assets, or from bank loans or loans from the client's company. Since the client may know this company better than outsiders do, his or her assessment of the feasibility and desirability of exercising such stock options is a crucial factor for the planner to know. Motivations that are not purely financial are frequently involved; tax-planning implications always are. In any case, the financial planner should discuss stock options held with the client and determine how they relate to that person's total financial position and future plans.

Mutual funds. Mutual funds are typically very liquid (redeemable at net asset value per share) but are usually acquired for long-term purposes. Another common reason for clients to hold mutual funds is that they are managed (for a fee) by the investment companies that issue them, thus relieving the client (or financial adviser) of that responsibility. Mutual funds are classified as to type, the most common classifications being growth, income, balanced (growth and income), indexed (made up of the issues of a common stock market index), and speculative. (Although money market funds are a type of mutual fund, they are included in the cash, near-cash equivalents subsection of the inventory of assets because they are composed of highly liquid, frequently traded, short-term investments.) Income, balanced, and speculative mutual funds may have varying proportions of both stocks and bonds; growth and indexed funds are composed of common stocks.

In the inventory of the client's mutual-fund holdings, the type of fund or funds held is another important indicator of both the client's risk profile and degree of direct involvement in the investment program. These may be important considerations in the evaluation of the client's current position and future planning alternatives and should be carefully looked into by the financial planner. If the client has substantial holdings in growth mutual funds whose performance is both pleasing and consistent with longer-term objectives, those funds are a good index of what suits the client, and alternative investment possibilities should be evaluated accordingly.

Real estate. The inventory of the client's assets proceeds to real estate holdings (pages 10 and 11), which includes real property held as personal residence and seasonal or vacation home(s); residential property held for investment; and commercial property held for income or appreciation purposes. The inventory of the client's real property should be complete and should include (in the inventory of liabilities on page 15 of the fact finder) the interest rate cost of mortgages outstanding on each item. Supplementary sheets will be needed for clients with extensive real estate holdings, and these sheets should record the same type of information on these holdings that the fact finder inventory requests.

Long-term, nonmarketable assets. The next category of client assets, listed on pages 10 and 11 of the fact finder, consists of long-term items. These items are generally illiquid and nonmarketable with benefits that cannot be directly realized until some future date (for example, vested retirement benefits). Listed here among the other items are unit interests in limited partnership investments, for which there is generally no market; these ordinarily cannot be liquidated until the general partners decide to sell or a foreclosure of mortgages or loans occurs. Although these long-term, nonmarketable client assets may be sizable, they do not lend themselves flexibly to financial planning involving a restructuring of client assets. They are simply factored into the client's current financial program and into the financial plan that is developed for the client. But since they are assets and sometimes constitute a significant part of the client's total net worth, it is important for the planner to have complete and accurate information concerning them.

Personal assets. The next subsection of client assets on pages 10 and 11 is personal assets. This category can vary enormously among individual clients in its extensiveness and worth. Some clients own relatively few personal assets apart from household furnishings and automobiles--and even these holdings can be minimal in number and value or extremely costly and extensive. Other clients acquire a whole range of personal items, often with investment as well as personal-use motives. Such clients may have large holdings of jewelry, gems and precious metals, antiques, art, and other collectibles that represent a substantial percentage of their total assets. The typical relatively affluent client may simply have no idea how large this category of assets is until a complete inventory is taken. In this inventory all personal property items of any significant value should be listed.

In reviewing the personal property inventory the financial planner should be looking for several important clues about how the client spends money. Are personal property items acquired for unthinking consumerist reasons, for real personal or family use and enjoyment, for investment purposes, or for some combination of these motives? If such items are acquired for investment purposes, they should be evaluated with respect to their inherent investment characteristics. (They are potentially appreciable but generally produce no income, are often illiquid and unmarketable, and are usually high risk.) Such items should also be viewed in relation to the client's risk profile, comprehensive financial objectives, and need for tax relief.

A client who has acquired large holdings of personal assets to satisfy desires for an affluent life-style and is allocating large amounts of income for this objective may find it difficult or impossible to change these personal tastes and indulgences. However, if the client's overindulgence in the acquisition of personal property is seriously reducing the options available for achieving overall financial objectives, the financial planner should tactfully point this out and allow the client to decide whether to allocate less money to consumption-oriented objectives. Whatever the client's motives for acquiring and holding personal property assets, the inventory of these assets should be complete so that it can be transferred to a property-liability insurance coverage work sheet to determine whether the client has appropriate types and adequate amounts of insurance protection.

Miscellaneous assets. Pages 10 and 11 of the fact finder provide a place to record information about miscellaneous assets such as interests in trusts, accounts or notes receivable, or patents.

When the inventory of assets has been filled out, the appropriate figures for these assets should be transferred to the financial position statement on pages 35-36 of the fact finder as well as to any other appropriate forms the financial planner uses for the client. But before the client's full range of assets can be seen and before that client's net worth can be determined, the value of any business interest owned must be documented.

Business Interest

Pages 12 and 13 of the fact finder ask for detailed information about a client's interest in an ongoing business or in a professional association that operates as a business (such as a professional partnership, sole proprietorship, or corporation of physicians, dentists, or attorneys). Of course not all clients will have such an interest, but those who do may have unusual opportunities for using that business interest to achieve many personal financial objectives.

The questions asked about the business interest on pages 12 and 13 of the fact finder focus on several important aspects of a client's ownership of a substantial business interest:

- the form of the business entity
- the position and degree of ownership by the client and associates
- the client's desires for the disposition of such interest in the event of disability, retirement, or death
- the mechanisms, if any, for transferring the client's interest to a designated survivor or successor or to one or more business associates
- the fair market value of the business and of the client's interest
- the future prospects of the business

Vital information on these issues is requested in this section of the fact finder.

After the name, address, and telephone number of the business have been ascertained, it is important to determine whether the business organization is a sole proprietorship, a partnership, a corporation, or an S corporation. Each form of business organization has its own financial and tax advantages and disadvantages--not only for the business itself, but also for the owners. The nature of the principal business activity, how long the business has been in operation, what state it is incorporated in, how long it has been incorporated, the classes and number of authorized and outstanding shares of stock, and the client's employment position are important for evaluating the economic viability of the business and of the client's relationship to it--in short, for determining its stability as a basis for financial planning for the client.

Under the present owners subsection on page 12, the present owners or major stockholders should be listed by name with an indication of whether there are any insurability problems that might affect the funding of buy-sell agreements or the purchase of additional fringe benefits for the owners. As noted by the asterisk, the relationship of present owners to the client by blood or marriage should be indicated. This information will permit the planner to explore the possibility of retaining ownership in the family in case of the client's disability, retirement, or death and avoid family attribution problems if a redemption is planned. If the business is incorporated, each shareholder's percentage ownership of outstanding common and/or preferred stock is asked for. (In order to provide this information the client may have to permit the planner to examine the list of shareholders or the stock transfer ledger.) If the business is not incorporated, each partner's percentage of ownership is asked for.

Determining the form and distribution of ownership of the business is important because the planner will want to explore, in accordance with the client's wishes, various possibilities for funding the transfer of the business interest in the event of the client's retirement, disability, or death. If the business is incorporated, this may be accomplished either through cross-purchase agreements negotiated between the major stockholders and funded through life insurance or through redemptions by the corporation itself. Redemptions can be funded with life insurance, corporate sinking funds, corporate general revenues, or through a combination of these instruments. Although the possible arrangements for this purpose are numerous, none can be explored or initiated until all the information is known.

The key employees subsection asks for the names of key employees who are not current shareholders of the business, because these key employees might be considered to be potential purchasers of the client's interest in the business. In addition, it may be advantageous to purchase insurance coverage to reimburse the company for the loss of key employees' services owing to their premature death or disability.

The first question on page 13 directly asks for the client's desires for the disposition of his or her interest in the business upon retirement, disability, or death. If the client's interest is to be retained for the benefit of survivors or other family members, it must be determined to whom it will be transferred and through what mechanism and funding. If the business is a partnership and is to be willed to someone other than the client's partner, the partnership agreement must include a provision permitting the partner to dispose of the interest in this manner. If the interest is to be purchased by the heirs of the deceased partner, a significant sum of money may be needed to effect the purchase. If the business is a corporation, the client's stock could be willed, or gifted, or exchanged for consideration, unless it is restricted by prior agreements.

In all cases a formalized agreement that is legally binding and protective of the client's interest needs to be in force and, if appropriate, sufficiently funded to assure that the agreement can be effected without destroying the business. Even though there may be a number of alternatives for disposing of a business interest as such, a person's position and skills in the company are an important asset that cannot be transferred. It is therefore incumbent upon the client to use this current position of influence to make the most advantageous arrangements for the transfer of the interest.

If the client's interest is to be sold outright upon retirement, disability, or death, it is important to arrange for a buyer, determine the means of establishing a fair price, assure that the buyer can pay for the interest, and ascertain the legality of a purchase agreement. If these matters have not been taken care of, the financial planner should advise the client and call in specialists (an attorney, a business valuation specialist, a life insurance agent) to execute the plan for transferring the business interest according to the client's desires. If these arrangements have already been made, but review and analysis show them to be inadequate or not in the client's interest, renegotiation of cross-purchase or stock-redemption agreements and reformulation of business valuation formulas may be possible.

The first six items in the subsection covering valuation of business interest are designed to help both the client and the financial planner determine an acceptable valuation of the business along with the client's percentage of ownership. Attempts to place a value on a client's business interest apart from a professional appraisal can be a nightmare and will always be subjective and inexact. In any of the business valuation methods commonly used, assumptions are central in determining a value for the client's business interest. These assumptions will need to be analyzed in light of the business's financial statements and tax returns for the past several years.

Answers to questions about the potential value of the business will not always be consistent. From the client's responses, however, and especially from the value established by any recent impartial appraisal, a reasonably accurate valuation of the client's business interest can be made. Once this is done, the most appropriate arrangements for estate planning and for disposing of an interest upon retirement, disability, or death can be formulated. No matter what value is established for the client's business interest, real value could be lost or severely eroded if the appropriate instruments for transferring it according to the client's desire are not in place.

In implementing recommendations relating to the client's business interest the client's business attorney and/or accountant should be consulted and integrated into the financial planning team. If the client has a professional consulting relationship with an attorney and accountant but no formal arrangements for disposing of the business interest, this should not reflect negatively upon these professionals. Clients frequently do not move to put these arrangements in place until they have decided to engage in comprehensive financial planning, and implementing these business continuation/transition plans often elicits the eager participation of a client's attorney and accountant in the planning effort.

The answers to the questions on page 13--concerning patents, special processes, and leased equipment and real property used but not owned by the business--could open up several planning possibilities for the client's interest. For example, any patents, manufacturing processes, trademarks or copyrights, equipment, or real property owned by the client who is a sole proprietor pose no particular problem since they are in effect owned by the client. But if the client is a member of a business partnership or a major shareholder of a corporation, ownership of these items will need to be protected for that client's interest. Appropriate legal counsel should be retained if the client's interest is not protected currently or upon disability, retirement, or death--that is, when the partner's or shareholder's association with the business ceases. If the client is a partner or major shareholder and has no formal arrangement for the company's use of any patents, processes, or other owned property, the client may want to consider leasing them to the company rather than assigning them for stock or partnership interest. Such a leasing arrangement can result in substantial tax benefits.

The subsection on survivor control (page 13) asks how the present owners of the business would want ownership and control redistributed in the event of the death of one or more of them. (Disability or retirement could be substituted for death in this section.) Current arrangements for survivor control of the business could be crucial in the financial planner's efforts to ensure that the client's business interest is arranged for optimum advantage in relation to other shares of ownership in the business.

Possibilities to consider for disposing of the client's business interest include the following:

For Sole Proprietorships

- orderly liquidation or sale of the business upon retirement, disability, or death, either by the proprietor or by the estate executor
- family retention of the business through sale to a family member or members (usually funded through life insurance)
- sale of the business to a key employee through a properly funded buy-sell agreement
- incorporation of the business by the estate executor with continued management by a corporate trustee for the benefit of the client's survivors
- family retention of the business by gift or bequest

For Partnerships

- a buy-sell agreement, properly funded, to allow the remaining partner(s) or the partnership itself to buy the client's interest upon retirement, disability, or death
- agreement to sell the business as a going concern upon the retirement, disability, or death of a partner if the law permits (Some partnerships, such as law partnerships, are not allowed to do this.)
- sale of the client's interest to a new partner
- continuation of the partnership with the estate or successor in interest of the deceased partner exercising a management role for the benefit of the client's survivors

For Closely Held Corporations and S Corporations

- a cross-purchase agreement between individual stockholders (usually funded by life insurance)
- a stock-redemption agreement between the corporation and individual stockholders under which the corporation buys the deceased's interest (usually funded by life insurance)
- sale of client's interest to key employee(s)
- an Employee Stock Ownership Plan (ESOP) for purchasing a decedent shareholder's interest (not available to an S corporation)

- succession of a family member or members through gift or bequest, installment sales, or private annuities (but watch for problems if the number of S corporation shareholders exceeds the allowable limits)
- taxable or tax-free sale of stock to an outsider

For Professional Corporations

- a stock-redemption agreement (usually funded by life insurance)
- a cross-purchase agreement with the remaining shareholders (usually funded by life insurance)

Planning for the disposal of a client's business interest is complex; the tax consequences of each alternative for each form of a business entity must be thoroughly analyzed. This planning and analysis should not be undertaken except through the coordinated efforts of a financial planning team that includes competent legal and tax counsel and possibly accountants and business valuation experts. Since effective planning for the client's business interest may also involve other shareholders or partners, the planner may have to deal with a large number of business and legal consultants and coordinate a multiple approach to the development of a comprehensive plan for the client. It is not an area for novices. Most planners who are interested in business planning will develop a clientele among substantial business owners as a specialty, just as others specialize in financial planning for executives or other groups or types of clients.

The employee census on page 14 of the fact finder (shown on the next page) may facilitate a thorough evaluation of a client's business interest. Its relevance will depend upon several considerations: (1) how many employees the client's business has and what the distribution is between key employees (owner-stockholders or partners and indispensable technical or management employees) and other employees; (2) whether the client's position and degree of control permit an influence on company policy with respect to employee benefits; (3) whether improvement in employee benefits for the client would entail prohibitive additional expenditures (because the benefits of the other categories of employees would also have to be upgraded); (4) whether improvement of benefits for the other employees would be advantageous to the company itself--for example, for retention of employees or for improved company morale.

If counseling sessions with the client disclose that improvements in employee benefits are possible and desirable, the client should ask the company's bookkeeper, personnel officer, or other appropriate person to fill out an employee census data form. This information can help the planner evaluate current employee benefits (as

EMPLOYEE CENSUS DATA*

	Sex	Marital Status	Name Last	Name First	M.I.	Date of Birth Month	Day	Year	Date Employed† Month	Day	Year	Full-time‡	Hourly	Salaried	Earnings Annual Salary or Wage	Earnings Additional Compensation	Member of Collective Bargain Unit?	Occupation or Job Title
1																		
2																		
3																		
4																		
5																		
6																		
7																		
8																		
9																		
10																		
11																		
12																		
13																		
14																		
15																		
16																		
17																		
18																		
19																		
20																		
21																		
22																		
23																		
24																		
25																		

*It is suggested that the client request this data directly from bookkeeper or other appropriate person.
†The date of its incorporation is also the date of employment of former proprietors or partners of a business.
‡A full-time employee is one who works 1,000 or more hours per year.

© 1984 The American College

contained in the employee benefits booklet and the client's personal statement of benefits) with a view to substantially improving the client's financial position through the company itself. Depending on the client's associates and/or partners in the business and on the tax laws, these improvements may also be made available to some or all of the other employees of the company.

The value of a client's business interest is an asset--in fact, it may be the client's largest asset. In any case, the value of the business interest, as determined in this section of the fact finder, should be transferred to the financial position statement on page 35. List it under nonmarketable securities if that is the form of the client's interest in a closely held or S corporation, or if this interest is in restricted stock held in a public corporation; list it under value of business interest if the business interest is a sole proprietorship, partnership, or professional service corporation with low stock valuation.

The financial position statement now reflects information from the inventory of assets and the business interest section of the fact finder, thus giving the planner a picture of the client's total assets.

Inventory of Liabilities

The inventory of liabilities on page 15 of the fact finder is not necessarily exhaustive but is intended to cover the typical items found in client liability positions.

The purpose of the information requested in this form for each liability item is to determine not only the amount, length, and term of the client's liabilities, but also the dates when current financial commitments will be fulfilled so that the resources now committed there can be reallocated. This section can also disclose how much credit the client can command. The maximum credit available, present balance, and monthly/annual repayment columns can provide very useful information about the client's current and potential use of debt and leverage to achieve financial objectives. How much the client is paying in interest on current debt indicates the cost efficiency of his or her debt service.

The list of liability items begins with the most current: revolving credit such as retail charge accounts and credit cards. Large outstanding balances in such items may mean that the client is using credit unwisely and is paying exorbitant carrying charges. The aggregate amounts of such overextended credit are frequently rolled over into consolidating loans, with the result that consumables and personal assets are purchased through debt rather than through a controlled budget of balanced income and expenditures. As the debt burden mounts, fewer dollars are available for savings and investments.

The other types of outstanding loans may also reveal how the client uses debt and for what purposes. The financial planner will want to know whether the client uses too much or too little debt in relation to the total financial position and objectives; shops prudently for low-cost debt; overutilizes credit cards and installment buying; has an affluent life-style funded through credit, with concomitantly high interest and repayment drains on cash flow; possesses credit and installment balances that are insured or secured by collateralizing capital assets or other property; and/or has plans that will require the assumption of additional debt.

The remaining items in the inventory of liabilities may or may not be as indicative of the client's attitudes and practices regarding debt financing. Income tax liabilities are fixed by the client's level and kind of income, although these liabilities can almost always be reduced through planning. (It is important to learn, however, whether the client is meeting them currently through withholding rates and cash flow or through borrowing.) Property taxes are also fixed, if they are due and payable, but if they are not included in mortgage payments the planner should determine whether the client is setting aside funds for this obligation in interest-bearing short-term investments.

Although the remaining items in the liability inventory allow little margin of choice if they are applicable to a particular client's situation, it is nevertheless important to gather complete information about them. Answers to the two questions at the end of the inventory about other liabilities against the client's estate and about liabilities planned for the future are also necessary for a complete picture of the client's liability position.

The information gathered in the inventory of liabilities will be transferred to the liabilities category of the financial position statement on page 36 of the fact finder. The completed financial position statement will provide the planner with a summary of the client's current total asset/liability/net worth position.

The Financial Position Statement

Pages 35 and 36 of the fact finder should be used to bring together information on the client's assets and liabilities in the financial position statement, both current and as projected for one or more years into the future. This statement is, in effect, a balance sheet for the client, with the difference that it uses fair market value rather than historical cost for asset items.

All items in this statement have been transferred from the inventory of assets, the business interest, and the inventory of liabilities sections of the fact finder but have been somewhat rearranged here. Client assets are classified in three broad groups: (1) cash and near-cash equivalents, (2) other financial assets, and (3) personal assets. These groups contain the more numerous subsections of the inventory of assets on pages 8-11 of the fact finder, with the addition of the value of business interest item on page 35, which is derived from the estimated value of the client's business interest (page 13).

The client's total liabilities are subtracted from the total assets to determine net worth. To increase this bottom-line figure is, of course, one of the primary objectives of financial planning.

The financial position statement, in conjunction with the cash-management statement on page 7, provides a profile of the client's total financial position as of a particular date. It also provides projections of the client's asset, liability, and net worth positions one or more years into the future--which makes it possible to establish some working objectives. It goes without saying that these objectives should be consistent with the client's wishes, what the resources can realistically support, and the various methods and vehicles of implementation of the client's comprehensive financial plan.

These projections must be based on certain assumptions about the future (such as the inflation rate and the rates of anticipated return on investment). The fact that they <u>are</u> only assumptions should be clarified for the client; otherwise they might be misleading, especially since projections based on them will likely be generated by computer software programs that can give the illusory impression of certainty. Only periodic review, monitoring, and adjustment of client plans can offer any assurance at all that they will achieve client objectives.

<u>Individually Owned Insurance</u>

Pages 16-18 of the fact finder ask for information on risk protection provided by the life, disability income, medical expense, and property-liability insurance policies currently held by the client. Complete information about all the client's insurance policies is important to many aspects of comprehensive financial planning. For example, the amounts provided by the client's personal life and disability income policies will be transferred to page 37 of the fact finder, where they will constitute one element of the client's current resources available for death, disability, and retirement needs. Information regarding personal life insurance will also be a factor in the value of the client's estate and its liquidity position. Personal property and liability insurance coverages will be analyzed to see if they give adequate protection against potential property losses and legal liability. The client's insurance policies that have business uses will be evaluated as to the adequacy of funding for buy-sell or other business-continuation agreements and the adequacy of protection against legal liability arising from the client's business or professional activities.

People typically do not know how to read and interpret the provisions of insurance policies, so information for this survey probably cannot be provided by the client. It must be recorded by the financial planner directly from the client's insurance policies.

Once the planner has reviewed the policies and filled out the appropriate spaces of the fact finder, the amounts, types of coverage, and other relevant provisions of the policies should be reviewed with the client and analyzed in light of the areas of risk in his or her personal and financial situation. By the end of the data-gathering phase of the financial planning process the planner will have enough information about the client and the client's family, occupation, financial objectives, asset and liability position, business interest, income, employee and business benefits, tax-planning position, and general life-style to determine whether the insurance coverages provide adequate protection relative to the overall financial position and degree of exposure to risk. The planner's preliminary assessment of these factors can be passed along to the client at that point.

Pages 12-13 of the fact finder, pertaining to the client's business interest, should also be reviewed with the client during the discussions about insurance protection. This information relates directly to the possible need or desire to fund buy-sell or other business-continuation agreements through disability income and life insurance and to cover various liability risks in the client's particular business or professional practice.

The financial planner who is not an insurance specialist should include appropriate specialists on the financial planning team who will thoroughly analyze all the client's business and personal risk exposures and recommend appropriate coverages to provide protection against the loss of all or part of the income and/or assets that cannot be otherwise replaced without damage to the client's position and objectives. If the planner and client later decide that further insurance protection is needed, professional insurance counsel will also be called for.

Employment-Related Benefits

The employment-related benefits survey on pages 19-20 of the fact finder has several important uses in financial planning. If a client or spouse owns a controlling interest in a business, this section provides a convenient place for not only recording existing employee benefits but also identifying additional benefits that might be implemented in order to put the business ownership to more effective use (and to greater tax advantage) in planning for personal financial objectives. The financial planner will analyze the advantages of possible additional benefits in relation to the client's or spouse's particular form and degree of business ownership. This type of planning will almost always involve bringing other specialists (an attorney for drafting legal instruments, a CPA, an employee benefits specialist, and so on) into the financial planning team at both the planning and the implementation stages of the process.

If a client and spouse have no business ownership interest, or have no control over the kinds of benefits their business interest can provide, pages 19-20 should be used as a survey of the benefits they actually derive from their employment. The client and spouse should each furnish the name and title of the person in their company who can provide detailed information and documents they may not have in their own possession. The documents relating to these benefits are listed on fact finder page 25, receipt for documents, which is also a checklist of information and documents that the client and spouse, or their companies, will need to make available for the financial planner's use. (The receipt for documents is illustrated on the fourth page of this reading.)

The column containing information/comments on the employment-related benefits checklist (page 19) may be used either to describe pertinent details of benefits or to indicate the planner's or the client's feelings about them. The amounts of the existing benefits identified in this survey should be listed on page 37 of the fact finder, which lists the income and lump-sum resources for disability, retirement, and death.

Measuring the Client's Risk/Return Profile

Page 21 of the fact finder is designed to develop a client profile of risk and return that is more precise than are other indicators disclosed by the information-gathering process. By focusing on the risk the client is willing to take and the expected return, the risk/return profile can be of significant value to the financial planner, especially when it is correlated with other indicators and compared with the client's current asset mix, previously stated financial objectives, and ability to achieve these objectives given the constraints imposed by that person's risk temperament.

Risk tolerances are difficult to measure in clients. No matter what method of measurement is employed, the result will be misleading unless it is related to the rate of return the client expects on invested money. It is equally difficult to assess the risk characteristics of investment media themselves, especially in an environment of fluctuating interest rates, an uncertain economy, an unpredictable stock market, and a financial marketplace of evolving concepts and many new and unseasoned investment media. Because nothing in the financial markets stays the same for very long, even the most sophisticated portfolio-management strategies are little more than rules of thumb that require periodic adjustment for changing circumstances. The investment strategy developed for an individual client, therefore, should reflect the client's current risk-taking propensities, the rate of return required to achieve agreed-upon financial objectives, and that person's understanding that both personal circumstances and the financial environment will change over time, thus altering the risk/return profile and requiring modification in the financial plan.

What the risk/return profile intends to measure is dramatically illustrated by figure 1 on the next page. Typical investment media are arranged in a pyramid, with the most conservative, least risky, and (generally) lowest-yielding media at the broad base of the pyramid. The investment media become progressively riskier as they approach the apex, commodities. Toward this apex, however, there is typically a corresponding and commensurate potential for higher return.

The arrows along the sides of the pyramid demonstrate the relationship between risk and return as one ascends or descends through this pyramid of investment possibilities. The figure illustrates that all investments bear an element of risk and that the rate of return is inextricably related to a corresponding degree of risk of loss. There is no way out of this risk/return bind; even investment in the most conservative media risks erosion of capital if the rate of return is less than the rate of inflation. All efforts to manage money, therefore, will involve trade-offs of risks against return. Clients must choose those investment media most closely suited to both their financial objectives and their range of psychological comfort, as represented by their personal risk profiles.

A note about how the risk/return profile is structured is in order here. The upper portion of page 21 of the fact finder asks the client to evaluate, on a scale of 0 to 5, his or her preference for a range of savings and investment media, from savings accounts to commodities. In the lower

FIGURE 1
The Risk/Return Pyramid

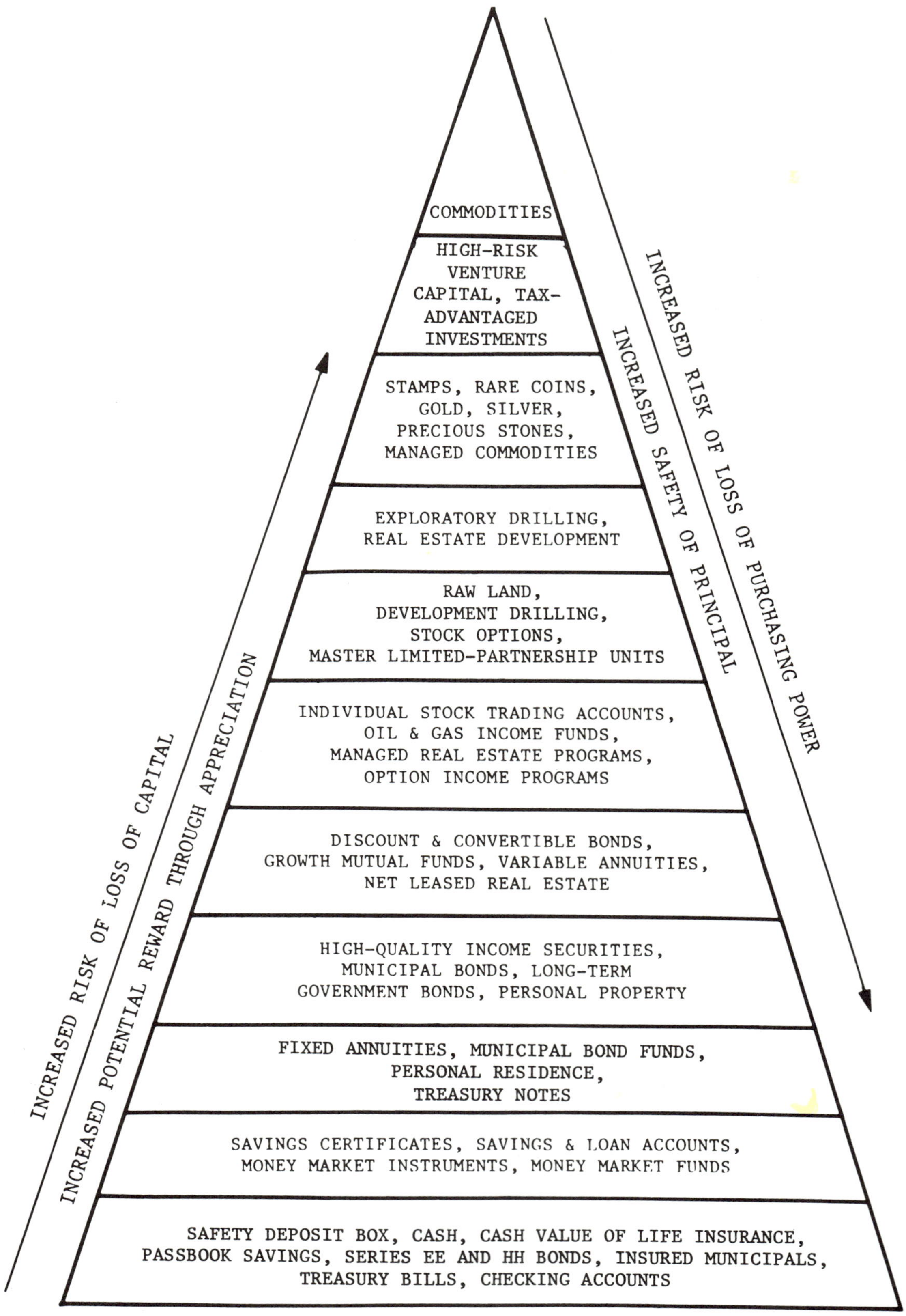
COMMODITIES
HIGH-RISK VENTURE CAPITAL, TAX-ADVANTAGED INVESTMENTS
STAMPS, RARE COINS, GOLD, SILVER, PRECIOUS STONES, MANAGED COMMODITIES
EXPLORATORY DRILLING, REAL ESTATE DEVELOPMENT
RAW LAND, DEVELOPMENT DRILLING, STOCK OPTIONS, MASTER LIMITED-PARTNERSHIP UNITS
INDIVIDUAL STOCK TRADING ACCOUNTS, OIL & GAS INCOME FUNDS, MANAGED REAL ESTATE PROGRAMS, OPTION INCOME PROGRAMS
DISCOUNT & CONVERTIBLE BONDS, GROWTH MUTUAL FUNDS, VARIABLE ANNUITIES, NET LEASED REAL ESTATE
HIGH-QUALITY INCOME SECURITIES, MUNICIPAL BONDS, LONG-TERM GOVERNMENT BONDS, PERSONAL PROPERTY
FIXED ANNUITIES, MUNICIPAL BOND FUNDS, PERSONAL RESIDENCE, TREASURY NOTES
SAVINGS CERTIFICATES, SAVINGS & LOAN ACCOUNTS, MONEY MARKET INSTRUMENTS, MONEY MARKET FUNDS
SAFETY DEPOSIT BOX, CASH, CASH VALUE OF LIFE INSURANCE, PASSBOOK SAVINGS, SERIES EE AND HH BONDS, INSURED MUNICIPALS, TREASURY BILLS, CHECKING ACCOUNTS
INCREASED RISK OF LOSS OF CAPITAL
INCREASED POTENTIAL REWARD THROUGH APPRECIATION
INCREASED RISK OF LOSS OF PURCHASING POWER
INCREASED SAFETY OF PRINCIPAL

portion the client is asked to rate personal financial priorities, also on a scale of 0 to 5. The results of these two portions should correlate with each other. For example, let us say that the client has indicated a preference by circling 4 for commodities, gold, and collectibles and 4 for safety of principal. There is an inconsistency because commodities, gold, and collectibles are speculative and risky. A strong preference for U.S. government bonds, high-quality corporate bonds, and municipal bonds would be much more consistent with the client's financial objective.

The risk/return profile can be useful in another way too. If the client's ultimate objectives can be matched with appropriate planning techniques and implementation vehicles, the risk/return profile can help the planner fine-tune this match. If there are glaring inconsistencies between the client's risk/return profile and the vehicles and instruments supporting the client's current financial position, the financial planner will have to determine whether the client lacks sufficient information for informed decision making. The financial planner should also clarify technical details about various investment media so that the client can make a fully informed choice among alternatives and arrive at a plan that has good prospects of achieving personal objectives without violating risk tolerances.

The results of assessing the client's risk/return profile should be noted at the bottom of the page. Since the profile draws together all indications of the client's profile of risk and return that have been gathered through counseling, there is fertile ground here for probing and clarification involving client and planner. When both are satisfied, the planner's comments and observations at the bottom of page 21 should note the understandings arrived at and the types of investment media most likely to achieve the client's expectations and objectives.

Income and Lump-Sum Needs for Disability, Retirement, and Death

On page 22 of the fact finder the client should record the monthly amounts of income needed if the client or spouse becomes disabled, retires, or dies. These estimates of monthly income needs are expressed in current dollars--that is, in amounts that would be needed now. In formulating a retirement plan for the client, however, the planner will have to adjust the client's estimate of these monthly needs by an agreed-upon inflation factor.

Survivors' monthly income needs in the event of the client's or spouse's death are assessed for three periods: (1) an adjustment period immediately following death when a continuing and unreduced income flow is required until the survivors can adjust to the permanent loss of income from the decedent's earnings; (2) a period of reduced income for the survivors until the youngest child is self-supporting; and (3) the period after the youngest child is self-supporting.

In addition, the survivors may need certain lump sums--to establish an emergency fund, to pay postmortem expenses, to pay off any outstanding mortgage balance on a personal residence, to pay off the decedent's notes and loans, to pay accrued taxes, and to fund college educations for surviving children. These lump-sum needs can be substantial and very real, but often there is not enough ready cash or other assets to meet them.

Close consultation with the client in establishing both income and lump-sum needs upon disability, retirement, and death is always called for. But there is little purpose in establishing precisely what amounts are needed for such events unless there is also a concerted planning effort to assure that adequate resources are available when needed.

Tax Planning

Pages 29-33 of the fact finder inquire in some detail into the client's current and possibly advisable tax-planning strategies. Since the impact of taxation on nearly all types of income and assets is one of the primary concerns of comprehensive financial planning, this section of the fact finder should prove to be especially helpful in evaluating the client's current financial position and for exploring a range of possible methods for reducing the client's tax burden.

Tax planning is a highly complex area of financial planning. Its more technical features are best handled by legal or professional accounting counsel thoroughly conversant with current tax law. Nevertheless, financial planning professionals should know enough about tax planning to be able to explain and evaluate the tax consequences of every move they recommend for clients. If the planner does not have a sufficient knowledge of taxation to assume this responsibility, however, the planner should have an ongoing relationship with a responsible attorney and CPA whose professional expertise can help to formulate tax recommendations for clients. The financial planner should coordinate the team effort to assure that all viable alternatives for achieving the client's financial objectives have been evaluated for the most advantageous tax consequences.

A detailed description of tax-planning principles and strategies is beyond the scope of this reading. However, a brief description of the concept of tax planning and its relationship to comprehensive financial planning is in order.

Tax planning involves the analysis, evaluation, and client acceptance of the tax consequences of every capital and financial transaction--<u>before</u> the transaction is made. It is one thing to look up the tax law and determine the consequences of one's economic activity during the past year--or to pay a tax return preparer a fee for doing that onerous task; it is quite another thing to determine in advance what short- and long-term tax liability will result from every transaction and <u>then</u> to conduct one's transactions so as to achieve financial objectives by the most tax-advantaged means.

For example, a taxpayer who has sold a capital asset during the past year can probably determine the taxable gain or deductible loss on a tax return by looking at the rules concerning basis, holding periods, capital gains and losses, and so on. But through proper tax planning a person can check the potential tax impact before making the sale--or preferably even before making the purchase. It might have been better to postpone the sale until the following year and to use an anticipated gain to offset losses expected for that year.

In the complicated financial conditions of most clients there is almost always at least one alternative (and in most cases several) to the one that may seem most obvious. Financial strategies and products each have their own inherent advantages and disadvantages and therefore are rarely appropriate for every client situation. When tax consequences are considered as well, there is even more divergence--some result in greater, some in lesser, tax liability. But it should be kept in mind that the most apparent route for an immediate (or even long-term) tax saving may not, in the final analysis, be the most advantageous. Tax and economic advantages and disadvantages must be balanced against the risk profiles and the objectives of each client. What works well for one client may not work at all for another in virtually the same position. What works well this year may be a disaster next year or several years down the road.

It should be noted that the tax-planning checklist on pages 29-33 of the fact finder is not intended to be complete or to raise all of the questions that would be relevant to every individual client. At best the checklist introduces some of the more common considerations.

It should also be remembered that every comprehensive financial planner is not a tax expert. Few financial planners will feel comfortable about undertaking the responsibilities of thorough tax planning on their own. They are not authorized to practice law. But the financial planner can gather complete information, counsel closely with the client, determine the person's total position and needs, and discover problem areas. This information can then be shared with members of the financial planning team who can evaluate the tax advantages of the alternatives that the planner is considering to achieve the client's financial objectives. To prepare for this role the planner needs to determine as much about the client's tax position as possible, and the tax-planning checklist and other information gathered in the fact finder will be valuable tools.

Strategies that can be employed in tax planning can be grouped into the three broad categories contained in the tax-planning checklist on pages 29-33 of the fact finder:

- individual planning
- business planning
- estate planning

Prior to the counseling sessions with the client, the planner should review documents and records previously provided to find out whether the client's current financial and tax position involves the use of tax strategies. The client's personal and/or business tax returns for the past several years will be key documents in this analysis.

During the counseling sessions the planner should discuss any potential problems associated with the client's current tax strategies as well as the possible advantages of certain strategies not currently being used. Whether tax strategies not currently being used are advisable for an individual client, now or in the future, will depend on a thorough analysis of each client's position with respect to the types of income and financial resources, and financial objectives--on the client's total position and prospects and disposition toward incorporating these strategies in the financial plan.

The checklist of the client's current position and future possibilities on pages 29-33 will enable the planner to take the client's tax temperature and to factor the information into the comprehensive financial planning process.

Personal Assessment of the Client

Before the client's financial plan is formulated, the financial planner should sum up impressions and observations of the client on page 27 of the fact finder. These impressions are vital to the planning process and to the acceptability and ultimate success of the client's plan, which will incorporate some of the most profound and far-reaching decisions that person will ever have made about life and relationships. But the plan will not be implemented unless it reflects what kind of person the client is; or, if implemented, it will not be monitored and updated. The counseling and planning process will have been wasted and a client relationship lost.

REVIEWING AND MONITORING THE CLIENT PLAN

When the individually tailored financial plan is developed, fine-tuned, presented to and accepted by the client, and implemented, the first cycle of the comprehensive financial planning process will be completed.[3] The process will be renewed periodically, however (though in much abbreviated form), in the ongoing review, monitoring, and restructuring of the plan when necessary during the client's subsequent economic life. If the planning process has met the client's needs and projected that individual toward desired objectives, and if the plan meets the client's expectations reasonably well, a long-term relationship between the client and the financial planner will likely result.

To facilitate this ongoing relationship and to keep in touch with the client's changing circumstances, interests, and needs, the financial planner must have some method for routinely reviewing the client's situation at specified periodic intervals--usually annually. The checklist for financial planning review shown on the next page (page 39 in the fact finder) is a convenient checklist for keeping up with changes in the client's personal life and economic circumstances. Sending this form to the client (in a stamped, self-addressed envelope) or simply going through it quickly in a telephone call will enable the planner to keep up to date.

When significant events have happened in the client's economic life, or are expected to, an appointment should be set up to evaluate the impact of these events on the client's financial plan, and make appropriate adjustments and changes. It goes without saying that when the planner sees or foresees that changes taking place in the financial markets, in tax laws, or in the economy generally will significantly affect the client's plan, the planner should inform the client.

The ever-changing nature of economic conditions and of clients' lives makes it impossible for a financial plan, no matter how well conceived and executed initially, to continue to perform at maximum efficiency indefinitely. Unless it is monitored and updated regularly, the entire planning process will have to be repeated. Both clients and planners will be well served if they recognize and act on this fundamental fact. Financial planning that is done comprehensively and followed up conscientiously, however, serves the interests of both client and planner in an ongoing professional relationship that is characterized by mutual respect and trust.

---

3. The development of financial plans is beyond the scope of this reading on data gathering. HS 332, Financial Planning Applications, will cover how to design and develop individual client plans.

CHECKLIST FOR FINANCIAL PLANNING REVIEW

Change in — Has Occurred / Is Expected

1. Marital status
   - Marriage ☐ ☐
   - Separation ☐ ☐
   - Divorce ☐ ☐
   - Remarriage ☐ ☐

2. Number of dependents
   - Increase ☐ ☐
   - Decrease ☐ ☐

3. Health status
   - Client ☐ ☐
   - Spouse ☐ ☐
   - Dependent ☐ ☐

4. Residence ☐ ☐

5. Occupation
   - Client ☐ ☐
   - Spouse ☐ ☐
   - Dependent ☐ ☐

6. Family financial status
   - Borrowing ☐ ☐
   - Lending ☐ ☐
   - Gifts over $1,000 received ☐ ☐
   - Gifts over $1,000 made ☐ ☐
   - Purchase of property ☐ ☐
   - Sale of property ☐ ☐
   - Investments ☐ ☐
   - Inheritance ☐ ☐
   - Deferred income ☐ ☐
   - Pension plan ☐ ☐
   - Tax-deferred annuity ☐ ☐
   - Dependent's income ☐ ☐

7. Sources of income
   - As employee ☐ ☐
   - From self-employment ☐ ☐
   - From tax-exempt employer ☐ ☐
   - From investments ☐ ☐
   - Inventions, patents, copyrights ☐ ☐
   - Hobbies, avocations ☐ ☐

8. Income tax status
   - From single to joint return ☐ ☐
   - From joint to single return ☐ ☐
   - Capital gains ☐ ☐
   - Capital losses ☐ ☐
   - Substantial contributions ☐ ☐
   - Unreimbursed casualty loss ☐ ☐
   - Sick pay received ☐ ☐
   - Unreimbursed medical expenses ☐ ☐
   - Tax-impact investment(s) ☐ ☐

9. Property ownership
   - Purchase in joint ownership ☐ ☐
   - Purchase, client owned ☐ ☐
   - Purchase, spouse owned ☐ ☐
   - Purchase, dependent owned ☐ ☐
   - Transfer to joint ownership ☐ ☐
   - Transfer to client ☐ ☐
   - Transfer to spouse ☐ ☐
   - Transfer to dependent ☐ ☐
   - Transfer to trustee ☐ ☐

10. Liabilities
    - Leases executed ☐ ☐
    - Mortgage increase ☐ ☐
    - Lawsuit against ☐ ☐
    - Judgment against ☐ ☐
    - Unsecured borrowing ☐ ☐
    - Cosigning of notes ☐ ☐

11. Business ownership
    - New business formation ☐ ☐
    - Interest purchase ☐ ☐
    - Sale of interest ☐ ☐
    - Transfer of interest ☐ ☐
    - Reorganization among owners ☐ ☐
    - Liquidation ☐ ☐
    - Change of carrier ☐ ☐
    - Termination or lapse ☐ ☐
    - Surrender ☐ ☐

12. Legal document status
    - Change in last will ☐ ☐
    - Change in trust ☐ ☐
    - Buy-sell agreement ☐ ☐
    - Agreement to defer income ☐ ☐

13. Insurance status
    - Life insurance ☐ ☐
    - Health insurance ☐ ☐
    - Group insurance ☐ ☐
    - Other employer plan ☐ ☐
    - Property insurance ☐ ☐
    - Liability insurance ☐ ☐
    - Change of plan ☐ ☐

14. Attitudes toward others
    - In family ☐ ☐
    - In business ☐ ☐
    - In accepting professional advice ☐ ☐

15. Interest in
    - Idea previously discussed ☐ ☐
    - Plans seen or heard about ☐ ☐

© 1984 The American College

FINANCIAL AND ESTATE PLANNING FACT FINDER

The information collected and maintained in this document will be held in the utmost confidentiality. It will not be shared except as may be required by law, or as may be authorized in writing by the client.

(signed) _____

The American College

CONTENTS

Personal Data   1

Financial Objectives   4

Factors Affecting Your Financial Plan   4

Objectives Requiring Additional Income/Capital   5

Sources of Income   6

Cash-Management Statement   7

Inventory of Assets   8

Business Interest   12

Employee Census Data   14

Inventory of Liabilities   15

Life Insurance Benefits   16

Health Insurance Benefits   17

Property and Liability Insurance Coverage   18

Employment-Related Benefits Checklist   19

Employment-Related Retirement Benefits/Deferred Compensation   20

Risk/Return Profile   21

Income and Lump-sum Needs for Disability, Retirement, and Death   22

Authorization for Information   23

Receipt for Documents   25

Supplementary Planning Forms

© 1984 The American College

PERSONAL DATA

Name (file no.)	
Spouse's name	
Legal home address	
Business address	*Client*
	Spouse
Phone	Home Business: *Client* / *Spouse*
Dates of counseling sessions	*Initial Interview*					
Dates Checklist for Financial Planning Review was sent						

Consultants for Financial and Business Planning*

		Name	**Address**	**Phone**
Attorney	personal			
	business			
Accountant	personal			
	business			
Trust officer				
Other bank officer				
Life insurance agent				
Property and liability insurance agent				
Securities broker				
Primary financial consultant				

*Indicate source of client with a check.

Notes

© 1984 The American College

PERSONAL DATA (continued)

Client and Spouse

	Date of Birth	Social Security Number	Occupation	Amount of Support by Client/Spouse	Health Problems/ Special Needs
Client*					
Spouse*					

*If not U.S. citizen, indicate nationality.

Children†/Grandchildren

†Indicate whether by prior marriage, adopted, or stepchild.

Client's Parents, Siblings‡

Spouse's Parents, Siblings‡

‡If possible, obtain addresses, phone numbers, and social security numbers of family members, especially those who are, or may become, beneficiaries, executors, guardians, etc.

Notes

© 1984 The American College

PERSONAL DATA (continued)

Marital status	☐ Married ☐ divorced ☐ widowed (check appropriate status) date:
	Any former marriages? ☐ yes ☐ no If yes, to whom? client: spouse:
	Are you paying alimony? ☐ yes ☐ no If yes, amount: Are you paying child support? ☐ yes ☐ no If yes, amount:
	Are there prenuptial or postnuptial agreements? ☐ yes ☐ no
Estate plan	Do you have a basic estate plan? ☐ yes ☐ no If yes, describe briefly.
Wills	Do you have a will? ☐ yes ☐ no date of will:
	Does your spouse have a will? ☐ yes ☐ no date of will:
Executor nominations	Who has been named as executor in your will? in your spouse's will? Name: Name: Address: Address: Phone: Phone:
Guardian nominations	Have guardians been named for your children? ☐ yes ☐ no If yes, who? Name: Address: Phone:
Trust/trustee nominations	Have you created grantor, Clifford, insurance, or testamentary trusts? ☐ yes ☐ no If yes, who is the trustee?
	Who are the beneficiaries?
	Has your spouse created grantor, Clifford, insurance, or testamentary trusts? ☐ yes ☐ no If yes, who is the trustee?
	Who are the beneficiaries?
Custodianships	Have you or your spouse ever made a gift under the Uniform Gifts to Minors Act? ☐ yes ☐ no If yes, in which state?
	Who is the custodian?
	Who are the donees?
Trust beneficiary	Are you or any members of your immediate family beneficiaries of a trust? ☐ yes ☐ no If yes, who? Amount expected:
Gifts/inheritances	Do you, your spouse, or your children expect to receive gifts/inheritances? ☐ yes ☐ no If yes, who? How much? from whom? when?
Education	What is the level of your education?
	What is the level of your spouse's education?
Military service benefits	Are you or your spouse eligible for any benefits deriving from military service? ☐ yes ☐ no If yes, explain.

© 1984 The American College

FINANCIAL OBJECTIVES

Rank from 1 to 8 the importance of having adequate funds in order to do the following:

_____ maintain/expand standard of living
_____ enjoy a comfortable retirement
_____ take care of self and family during a period of long-term disability
_____ invest and accumulate wealth
_____ reduce tax burden
_____ provide college education for children
_____ take care of family in the event of death
_____ develop an estate distribution plan
_____ any others important to you (specify)

Do you have a formal monthly budget?   ☐ yes   ☐ no   If yes, indicate amount:

How much do you save annually?   in what form?   why?

How much do you think you should be able to save annually?   for what purpose?

How much do you invest annually?   in what form?   why?

How much do you think you should be able to invest annually?   for what purpose?

FACTORS AFFECTING YOUR FINANCIAL PLAN

Have you or your spouse ever made substantial gifts to family members or to tax-exempt beneficiaries?   ☐ yes   ☐ no
If yes, give details.

What special bequests are intended, including charity?

Are you satisfied with your previous investment results?   ☐ yes   ☐ no
Explain.

Are there any investments you feel committed to (for past performance, family, or social reasons)?   ☐ yes   ☐ no
If yes, explain.

Is your spouse good at handling money?   ☐ yes   ☐ no

If you die, would your spouse be able to manage family finances?   ☐ yes   ☐ no

In the event of your death, what is your estimate of the emotional and economic maturity of your children?

In the event of your death or of divorce, what are your feelings about the possible remarriage of your spouse?

At what age would you like to retire?

Tax considerations aside, in what manner would you want your estate distributed?

What do you think financial planning should do for you?

© 1984 The American College

OBJECTIVES REQUIRING ADDITIONAL INCOME/CAPITAL

Do your children attend public or private schools?	
If private, annual cost: (elementary) (secondary)	
Do you plan for your children to attend private schools later? ☐ yes ☐ no	
If yes, when?	

Education Fund

Name of Child	Age	No. Years until College	Estimated 4-Year Cost - If Private	Estimated 4-Year Cost - If Public	Estimated Graduate School Costs	Capital Allocated	Monthly Income Allocated

Support for Family Member(s)

Name	Age	Relation	Estimated Cost	Estimated Period of Funding	Capital Allocated	Monthly Income Allocated

Other Objectives

Objective	Target Date	Estimated Cost	Estimated Period of Funding	Capital Allocated	Monthly Income Allocated

Notes

© 1984 The American College

SOURCES OF INCOME

Annual Income

	Client	Spouse*	Dependent Children*
Salary, bonus, etc.			
Income as business owner (self-employment)			
Real estate rental			
Dividends			
Investments (public stock, mutual funds, etc.)			
Close corporation stock			
Interest			
Investments (bonds, money market funds, T-bills, etc.)			
Savings accounts, certificates of deposit			
Loans, notes			
Trust income			
Life insurance settlement options			
Child support/alimony			
Other sources (specify)			
Other sources			
Other sources			
Other sources			
Total annual income			

*If spouse or children are employed, give details here.

Income Tax Last Year

Federal			
State			
Local			
Total income tax paid last year			
Estimated quarterly tax this year			

Future Annual Income Estimate

Next year			
Three years			
Five years			
How often do you expect a salary increase or bonus?			
On the average, how much of a salary increase or bonus do you expect annually?			
Has your total annual income fluctuated significantly during the past three years?			

© 1984 The American College

CASH-MANAGEMENT STATEMENT

Annual Income

	Current Yr. 19____	Projections for Subsequent Years			
		Assumptions	19____	19____	19____	19____
Salary, bonus, etc.						
Income as business owner (self-employment)						
Real estate rental						
Dividends						
Investments						
Close corporation stock						
Interest income						
Investments						
Savings accts., CDs						
Loans, notes, etc.						
Trust income						
Life insurance settlement options						
Child support/alimony						
Other sources (specify)						
Total annual income						

Annual Expenditures: Fixed

Housing (mortgage/rent)						
Utilities and telephone						
Food						
Clothing and cleaning						
Income and social security taxes						
Property taxes						
Transportation (auto/commuting)						
Medical/dental/drugs/health insurance						
Debt repayment						
House upkeep/repairs/maintenance						
Life, property and liability insurance						
Child support/alimony						
Current education expenses						
Total fixed expenses						

Annual Expenditures: Discretionary

Recreation/entertainment/travel						
Contributions/gifts						
Household furnishings						
Education fund						
Savings						
Investments						
Other (specify)						
Total discretionary expenses						
Total annual expenditures						
Net income (total annual income minus total annual expenditures)						

© 1984 The American College

INVENTORY OF ASSETS

Cash, Near-Cash Equivalents

Items	No. Units or Shares	Date Acquired	Amount, Cost, or Other Basis	Client	Spouse	Joint (survivor rights)	Joint (no survivor rights)	Community Property	Other*
Checking accounts/cash									
Savings accounts									
Money-market funds									
Treasury bills									
Commercial paper									
Short-term CDs									
Cash value, life insurance									
Accum. divs., life insurance									
Savings bonds									
Other (specify)									
Subtotal									

Market Value and Titled Owners (column group above Client/Spouse/Joint/etc.)

*Children, custodial accounts, trusts, etc.

U.S. Govt., Municipal, Corporate Bonds, and Bond Funds: Issuer, Maturity, Call Dates

Subtotal									

Preferred Stock: Issuer, Maturity, Call Dates

Subtotal									

Common Stock: Issuer, Listed (L), Unlisted (U), Nonmarketable (NM)

Subtotal									

Warrants and Options: Issuer, Expiration Date

Subtotal									

Mutual Funds and Type: Growth (G), Income (I), Balanced (B), Indexed (IX), Speculative (S)

Subtotal									

© 1984 The American College

INVENTORY OF ASSETS

Cash, Near-Cash Equivalents

Annual Yield %	Annual Yield $	Amount Available for Liquidity	Amount of Indebtedness	Location, Description, Client's Reasons for Holding Asset, etc.	Items
					Checking accounts/cash
					Savings accounts
					Money-market funds
					Treasury bills
					Commercial paper
					Short-term CDs
					Cash value, life insurance
					Accum. divs., life insurance
					Savings bonds
					Other (specify)
					Subtotal

U.S. Govt., Municipal, Corporate Bonds, and Bond Funds: Issuer, Maturity, Call Dates

					Subtotal

Preferred Stock: Issuer, Maturity, Call Dates

					Subtotal

Common Stock: Issuer, Listed (L), Unlisted (U), Nonmarketable (NM)

					Subtotal

Warrants and Options: Issuer, Expiration Date

					Subtotal

Mutual Funds and Type: Growth (G), Income (I), Balanced (B), Indexed (IX), Speculative (S)

					Subtotal

© 1984 The American College

INVENTORY OF ASSETS (continued)

Real Estate

Items	No. Units or Shares	Date Acquired	Amount, Cost or Other Basis	Market Value and Titled Owners					
				Client	Spouse	Joint (survivor rights)	Joint (no survivor rights)	Community Property	Other
Personal residence									
Seasonal residence									
Investment (residential)									
Investment (commercial)									
Land									
Other (specify)									
Subtotal									

Long-term, Nonmarketable Assets

Long-term CDs									
Vested retirement benefits									
Annuities									
HR-10 plan (Keogh)									
IRAs									
Mortgages owned									
Land contracts									
Limited partnership units									
Other (specify)									
Subtotal									

Personal Assets

Household furnishings									
Automobile(s)									
Recreational vehicles									
Boats									
Jewelry/furs									
Collections (art, coins, etc.)									
Hobby equipment									
Other (specify)									
Subtotal									

Miscellaneous Assets

Interest(s) in trust(s)									
Receivables									
Patents, copyrights, royalties									
Other (specify)									
Subtotal									
Totals of all columns									

© 1984 The American College

INVENTORY OF ASSETS (continued)

Real Estate

Annual Yield %	Annual Yield $	Amount Available for Liquidity	Amount of Indebtedness	Location, Description, Client's Reasons for Holding Asset, etc.	Items
					Personal residence
					Seasonal residence
					Investment (residential)
					Investment (commercial)
					Land
					Other (specify)
					Subtotal

Long-term, Nonmarketable Assets

Annual Yield %	Annual Yield $	Amount Available for Liquidity	Amount of Indebtedness	Location, Description, Client's Reasons for Holding Asset, etc.	Items
					Long-term CDs
					Vested retirement benefits
					Annuities
					HR-10 plan (Keogh)
					IRAs
					Mortgages owned
					Land contracts
					Limited partnership units
					Other (specify)
					Subtotal

Personal Assets

Annual Yield %	Annual Yield $	Amount Available for Liquidity	Amount of Indebtedness	Location, Description, Client's Reasons for Holding Asset, etc.	Items
					Household furnishings
					Automobile(s)
					Recreational vehicles
					Boats
					Jewelry/furs
					Collections (art, coins, etc.)
					Hobby equipment
					Other (specify)
					Subtotal

Miscellaneous Assets

Annual Yield %	Annual Yield $	Amount Available for Liquidity	Amount of Indebtedness	Location, Description, Client's Reasons for Holding Asset, etc.	Items
					Interest(s) in trust(s)
					Receivables
					Patents, copyrights, royalties
					Other (specify)
					Subtotal
					Totals of all columns

© 1984 The American College

BUSINESS INTEREST

General Information

Full legal name   Phone
Address
Business now operates as   ☐ proprietorship   ☐ partnership   ☐ corporation   ☐ S corporation
When does the fiscal year end?
What accounting method is used?
What is the principal business activity?
In what year did this business begin operation?
If it began other than as a corporation, what is the date of incorporation?   state of incorporation?
Classes of stock   No. authorized shares   No. outstanding shares
What is your function in the business?
Do you have an employment contract?

Present Owners*

	Insurability Problem? Yes No	Form of Business	
		Corporation	Partnership
(A) _____ Client _____	☐ ☐	owns ____ % common ____ % preferred	____ % _____
(B) _____	☐ ☐	owns ____ % common ____ % preferred	____ % _____
(C) _____	☐ ☐	owns ____ % common ____ % preferred	____ % _____
(D) _____	☐ ☐	owns ____ % common ____ % preferred	____ % _____
(E) _____	☐ ☐	owns ____ % common ____ % preferred	____ % _____

*Indicate relationship to client by blood or marriage.

Key Employees (other than present owners)

	Insurability Problem Yes No		Insurability Problem Yes No
_____	☐ ☐	_____	☐ ☐
_____	☐ ☐	_____	☐ ☐
_____	☐ ☐	_____	☐ ☐
_____	☐ ☐	_____	☐ ☐

© 1984 The American College

BUSINESS INTEREST (continued)

Disposition of Business Interest

Do you want your business interest retained or sold if you
retire? ☐ yes ☐ no   become disabled? ☐ yes ☐ no   die? ☐ yes ☐ no

IF RETAINED
Who will own your interest and how will the person(s) acquire it?

Who will replace you in your job?

IF SOLD
Who will buy your interest?

How is purchase price to be determined?

What is the funding arrangement?

Do you have a buy-sell agreement? ☐ yes ☐ no

    If yes, is it a cross-purchase, entity-purchase, or "wait-and-see" type of agreement?

    Where is it located?

Valuation of Business Interest

Estimate the lowest price for which the entire business might be sold as a going concern today.

What is the lowest price you would accept for your interest today?

If you were not an owner, what is your estimate of the highest price you would pay today for the entire business as a going concern?

What is the highest price you would pay to buy the interest of your coowners today?

Has an impartial valuation of the business been made? ☐ yes ☐ no   If yes, when?
What valuation method was used?   What value was established?

What is the average business indebtedness?
Estimate the highest it has ever been.   Estimate the lowest it has ever been.

Are there patents, special processes, or leased equipment/real property used by but not owned by the business? ☐ yes ☐ no
If yes, who owns what, and under what terms is each used or leased?

What are prospects for growth, sale, merger, or going public?

Survivor Control (letters in parentheses refer to owners named above on page 12)

IF (A) DIES	IF (B) DIES	IF (C) DIES	IF (D) DIES	IF (E) DIES
B wants ____ % control	A wants ____ %	A wants ____ %	A wants ____ %	A wants ____ %
C wants ____ % control	C wants ____ %	B wants ____ %	B wants ____ %	B wants ____ %
D wants ____ % control	D wants ____ %	D wants ____ %	C wants ____ %	C wants ____ %
E wants ____ % control	E wants ____ %	E wants ____ %	E wants ____ %	D wants ____ %
____ wants ____ % control	____ wants ____ %	____ wants ____ %	____ wants ____ %	____ wants ____ %

© 1984 The American College

EMPLOYEE CENSUS DATA*

	Sex	Marital Status	Name Last	First	M.I.	Date of Birth Month	Day	Year	Date Employed† Month	Day	Year	Full-time‡	Hourly	Salaried	Earnings Annual Salary or Wage	Additional Compensation	Member of Collective Bargain Unit?	Occupation or Job Title
1																		
2																		
3																		
4																		
5																		
6																		
7																		
8																		
9																		
10																		
11																		
12																		
13																		
14																		
15																		
16																		
17																		
18																		
19																		
20																		
21																		
22																		
23																		
24																		
25																		

*It is suggested that the client request this data directly from bookkeeper or other appropriate person.
†The date of its incorporation is also the date of employment of former proprietors or partners of a business.
‡A full-time employee is one who works 1,000 or more hours per year.

© 1984 The American College

INVENTORY OF LIABILITIES

Outstanding Obligations of Client or Spouse	Original Amount	Maximum Credit Available	Present Balance	Monthly/ Annual Repayment	Effective Interest Rate	Payments Remaining/ Maturity Date	Secured?	Insured?
Retail charge accounts								
Credit cards								
Family/personal loans								
Securities margin loans								
Investment liabilities								
Bank loans								
Life insurance policy loans								
Income tax liability								
Federal								
State								
Local								
Property taxes								
Mortgage(s)								
Family member support								
Child support/alimony								
Other (specify)								
Total								

Are there any other liabilities your estate might be called upon to pay? ☐ yes ☐ no
If yes, explain.

Do you foresee any future liabilities (business expansion, new home, etc.)? ☐ yes ☐ no
If yes, explain.

© 1984 The American College

LIFE INSURANCE BENEFITS*

Item	Policy 1	Policy 2	Policy 3
Policy number			
Name of insurance company			
Issue age			
Insured			
Owner of policy			
Type of policy			
Annual premium			
Net annual outlay by client			
Current cash value			
Extra benefits (e.g. waiver of premium, accidental death, etc.)			
Amount of base policy			
Dividends (value & option)			
Term rider(s)			
Loan outstanding			
Net amount payable at death			
Primary beneficiary and settlement option elected			
Secondary beneficiary and settlement option elected			

Item	Policy 4	Policy 5	Policy 6
Policy number			
Name of insurance company			
Issue age			
Insured			
Owner of policy			
Type of policy			
Annual premium			
Net annual outlay by client			
Current cash value			
Extra benefits (e.g., waiver of premium, accidental death, etc.)			
Amount of base policy			
Dividends (value & option)			
Term rider(s)			
Loan outstanding			
Net amount payable at death			
Primary beneficiary and settlement option elected			
Secondary beneficiary and settlement option elected			

*Policies and most recent policy anniversary premium notices should be examined for the information recorded on this page.

© 1984 The American College

HEALTH INSURANCE BENEFITS*

Medical/Dental Benefits

	Policy 1	Policy 2	Policy 3	Policy 4
Type of policy				
Policy number				
Name of insurance company or other provider				
Insured				
Annual cost to client				
Type of continuance or renewal provision				
Deductible				
Percentage participation				
Stop-loss limit				
Inside limits				
Overall maximum				

Disability Income Benefits

Policy number				
Name of insurance company or other provider				
Insured				
Annual cost to client				
Type of continuance or renewal provision				
Definition of disability				
Monthly disability income				
Accident				
Sickness				
Partial disability provision				
Waiting period				
Accident				
Sickness				
Benefit period				
Accident				
Sickness				

*Policies should be examined for the information recorded on this page.

© 1984 The American College

PROPERTY AND LIABILITY INSURANCE COVERAGE*

Homeowners Insurance

	Principal Residence	Seasonal Residence	Other Property
Policy number			
Name of insurance company			
Address of property			
HO form # (or other type of policy)			
Coverage on dwelling			
Replacement cost of dwelling			
Replacement cost of contents			
Liability limits			
Endorsements			
Deductibles			
Annual cost			

Automobile Insurance

	Auto #1	Auto #2	Auto #3 (or other vehicles, trailers)
Policy number			
Name of insurance company			
Automobile make/year			
Liability limits			
No-fault/medical benefits			
Uninsured motorist			
Collision/deductible			
Comprehensive/deductible			
Annual cost			

Other Property/Liability Insurance

	Policy 1	Policy 2	Policy 3
Type of policy			
Policy number			
Name of insurance company			
Property covered			
Limits			
Annual cost			

Umbrella Liability Insurance

Policy number	
Name of insurance company	
Liability limits	
Retention	
Annual cost	

*Policies should be examined for the information recorded on this page.

© 1984 The American College

EMPLOYMENT-RELATED BENEFITS CHECKLIST

Name and address of client's employer _____

Name and address of spouse's employer _____

Who can provide detailed information on employee benefits for you and your spouse?

Client
Name _____

Title _____

Department _____

Phone _____

Spouse
Name _____

Title _____

Department _____

Phone _____

	Benefit now provided for client?		Benefit now provided for spouse?		Information/Comments
	Yes	No	Yes	No	
Life and Health Insurance					
Death benefits	☐	☐	☐	☐	_____
Accidental death/dismemberment	☐	☐	☐	☐	_____
Travel accident	☐	☐	☐	☐	_____
Medical expense benefits	☐	☐	☐	☐	_____
Short-term disability income (sick pay)	☐	☐	☐	☐	_____
Long-term disability income	☐	☐	☐	☐	_____
Retirement Benefits/ Deferred Compensation*					
Qualified pension plan	☐	☐	☐	☐	_____
Qualified profit-sharing plan	☐	☐	☐	☐	_____
Nonqualified deferred-compensation plan	☐	☐	☐	☐	_____
Salary reduction plan (401k)	☐	☐	☐	☐	_____
Simplified employee pension (SEP)	☐	☐	☐	☐	_____
Stock bonus plan	☐	☐	☐	☐	_____
Employee stock-ownership plan (ESOP)	☐	☐	☐	☐	_____
Employee stock-purchase plan	☐	☐	☐	☐	_____
Incentive stock-option plan [§422A]	☐	☐	☐	☐	_____
Restricted stock plan [§83(b)]	☐	☐	☐	☐	_____
Phantom stock plan [§83(a)]	☐	☐	☐	☐	_____
Tax-deferred annuity plan	☐	☐	☐	☐	_____
Salary continuation after death	☐	☐	☐	☐	_____
Other (specify)	☐	☐	☐	☐	_____
Miscellaneous Benefits					
Excess medical reimbursement plan	☐	☐	☐	☐	_____
Split-dollar life insurance	☐	☐	☐	☐	_____
Auto/homeowners	☐	☐	☐	☐	_____
Legal expense	☐	☐	☐	☐	_____
Company car	☐	☐	☐	☐	_____
Educational reimbursement	☐	☐	☐	☐	_____
Club membership	☐	☐	☐	☐	_____
Other (specify)	☐	☐	☐	☐	_____

*Describe appropriate benefits on page 20.

© 1987 The American College

EMPLOYMENT-RELATED RETIREMENT BENEFITS/DEFERRED COMPENSATION

Type	Employee's Annual Contribution	Benefits to Client – Lump-sum Pmts.	Benefits to Client – Monthly Income Amount	Benefits to Client – Monthly Income Beginning/Ending	Benefits to Survivors – Beneficiary	Benefits to Survivors – Lump-sum Pmts.	Benefits to Survivors – Monthly Income Amount	Benefits to Survivors – Monthly Income Beginning/Ending
Qualified pension plan								
Qualified profit-sharing plan								
Nonqualified deferred-compensation plan								
Salary reduction plan (401k)								
Stock bonus plan								
Employee stock-ownership plan (ESOP)								
Employee stock-purchase plan								
Incentive stock-option plan [§422A]								
Restricted stock plan [§83(b)]								
Phantom stock plan [§83(a)]								
Tax-deferred annuity plan								
Salary continuation after death								
Other (specify)								
Other (specify)								

Explain and describe pertinent details for planning purposes here (e.g., anticipated benefits not yet in place; client's views on relevance, need, and feasibility of these benefits; problems associated with implementing benefits; etc.).

Social Security Benefits

What are the estimated retirement benefits (in current dollars)?
client only: client and spouse:

What are the estimated disability benefits the client is eligible for if disabled today?
client only: client and family:

What are the estimated survivors' benefits payable to the client's family if death should occur today?

© 1984 The American College

RISK/RETURN PROFILE

On a scale from 0 to 5, with 5 representing a strong preference and 0 representing an aversion, indicate your preference for the following instruments of savings and investment by circling the appropriate number.

Savings account	0	1	2	3	4	5
Money-market fund	0	1	2	3	4	5
U.S. government bond	0	1	2	3	4	5
Corporate bond	0	1	2	3	4	5
Mutual fund (growth)	0	1	2	3	4	5
Common stock (growth)	0	1	2	3	4	5
Mutual fund (income)	0	1	2	3	4	5
Municipal bond	0	1	2	3	4	5
Real estate (direct ownership)	0	1	2	3	4	5
Variable annuity	0	1	2	3	4	5
Limited partnership unit (real estate, oil and gas, cattle, equipment leasing)	0	1	2	3	4	5
Commodities, gold, collectibles	0	1	2	3	4	5

On a scale from 0 to 5, circle the number to the right of each of the items below that most accurately reflects your own financial concerns; 5 indicates a very strong concern and 0 indicates no concern.

Liquidity	0	1	2	3	4	5
Safety of principal	0	1	2	3	4	5
Capital appreciation	0	1	2	3	4	5
Current income	0	1	2	3	4	5
Inflation protection	0	1	2	3	4	5
Future income	0	1	2	3	4	5
Tax reduction/deferral	0	1	2	3	4	5

Planner's comments and observations

© 1984 The American College

INCOME AND LUMP-SUM NEEDS FOR DISABILITY, RETIREMENT, AND DEATH

	Client	Spouse/Children
Disability Income Needs		
Monthly income needed in current dollars	$_____	$_____
Retirement Income Needs		
Monthly income needed in current dollars	$_____	$_____
Survivors' Income Needs*		
Monthly income needed in current dollars for surviving family members during the following periods after death:		
Adjustment period (adjustment of standard of living in a transitional period, as needed)	$_____	$_____
Until youngest child is self-supporting (number of years_____)	$_____	$_____
After youngest child is self-supporting	$_____	$_____
Survivors' Lump-sum Needs*		
Last expenses (final illness and funeral)	$_____	$_____
Emergency fund	$_____	$_____
Mortgage cancellation fund (if appropriate)	$_____	$_____
Notes and loans payable	$_____	$_____
Accrued taxes (income, real estate, etc., if not withheld)	$_____	$_____
Children's education (if not already funded)	$_____	$_____
Estate settlement costs and taxes (if not provided by liquidity)	$_____	$_____
Other (specify)	$_____	$_____
Total lump-sum needs in current dollars	$_____	$_____

*Some survivors' needs may be met by either periodic income or lump-sum payments or by some combination of the two approaches. Double counting in both categories should be avoided.

Notes

© 1984 The American College

AUTHORIZATION FOR INFORMATION

TO: _____

_____

_____

Please provide any information that is in your possession and that is asked for in connection with a survey of my/our financial affairs to

_____.

_____
(client's signature)

_____
(spouse's signature)

_____
(date)

TO: _____
         (company)

Please provide any information that is in your possession and that is requested by _____

_____ concerning the following policies of which I am the owner:

_____   _____

_____   _____

_____   _____

Policyowner's
Authorization _____
                (signature of policyowner)

_____
(date)

Notes

RECEIPT FOR DOCUMENTS

Insurance Policies: Life, Health, Property and Liability

Company	Policy Number	☑	Company	Policy Number	☑
_____	_____	☐	_____	_____	☐
_____	_____	☐	_____	_____	☐
_____	_____	☐	_____	_____	☐
_____	_____	☐	_____	_____	☐
_____	_____	☐	_____	_____	☐

Original policies checked ☑ above have been received for review and analysis; they will be returned upon completion of analysis or client request.

_____
(planner)

_____
(address)

_____
(phone)

_____
(date)

All original policies and documents checked in this receipt have been returned to me.

_____
(client)

_____
(date)

Personal/Family Documents (copies)	**Date**	**Business Documents (copies)**	**Date**
☐ Tax returns (3–5 years)	_____	☐ Tax returns (3–5 years)	_____
☐ Wills (client and spouse)	_____	☐ Financial statements (3–5 years)	_____
☐ Trust instruments	_____	☐ Deferred-compensation plan	_____
☐ Financial statements	_____	☐ HR-10 plan (Keogh)	_____
☐ Personal/family budgets	_____	☐ Individual retirement account (IRA)	_____
☐ Sale/purchase contract	_____	☐ Simplified employee pension (SEP)	_____
☐ Current insurance offers	_____	☐ Pension/profit-sharing plan	_____
☐ Current investment offers	_____	☐ Tax-deferred annuity	_____
☐ Deeds, mortgages, land contracts	_____	☐ Stock-option/purchase agreement	_____
☐ Guardian nominations	_____	☐ Buy-sell agreements	_____
☐ Leases (as lessor or lessee)	_____	☐ Employment agreement	_____
☐ Notices of awards, elections	_____	☐ Employee benefits booklet	_____
☐ Power of attorney/appointment	_____	☐ Articles of incorporation	_____
☐ Separation/divorce/nuptial	_____	☐ Merger/acquisition agreement	_____
☐ Patents/copyrights/royalties	_____	☐ Partnership agreement	_____
☐ Employee benefits statement	_____	☐ Company patents	_____
☐ Other (specify)	_____	☐ Equipment leasing agreement(s)	_____
☐ Other (specify)	_____	☐ Other (specify)	_____

© 1984 The American College

SUPPLEMENTARY PLANNING FORMS

Observations from Counseling Sessions   27

Tax-Planning Checklist   29

Financial Position Statement   35

Income and Lump-sum Resources for Disability, Retirement, and Death   37

Checklist for Financial Planning Review   39

© 1984 The American College

OBSERVATIONS FROM COUNSELING SESSIONS

As soon after counseling sessions as possible the financial planner should record impressions and observations about the client in terms of the following:

Personal appearance _____

Appearance of office or home _____

Personal interests (sports, hobbies, music, etc.) _____
_____

Civic-mindedness _____

Political awareness _____

Financial sophistication _____

College ties _____

Decision-making ability _____

Level of personal goals _____

Consistency of verbal and nonverbal behaviors _____

Condition of health _____

Mental/emotional maturity _____

Attitude toward spouse _____ parents _____

    children _____ other family members _____

Financial risk-taking propensity _____

Attitude toward financial counseling/planning _____

Investment decisions client has made and why _____

Client's financial status (self-made or inherited) _____

Concern with taking care of self during retirement _____

Concern with family after own death _____

Concern with self and family during disability _____

Concern with self right now _____

Concern with self and family right now _____

Other pertinent observations, particularly concerning spouse:

© 1984 The American College

TAX-PLANNING CHECKLIST*

Individual Planning

	At Present Yes	At Present No	Advisable Yes	Advisable No
1. Does the client itemize rather than utilize the standard deduction?	☐	☐	☐	☐
2. Are all personal and dependency exemptions being taken (children, parents, foster children, etc.)? [§§151, 152]	☐	☐	☐	☐
3. Are maximum deductions for all expenses related to the production of income being taken?	☐	☐	☐	☐
4. a. Is optimum utilization being made of retirement plans for tax advantage?	☐	☐	☐	☐
b. Has the appropriate type(s) of plan been chosen?	☐	☐	☐	☐
5. Are contributions to charitable and other tax-exempt organizations being used as fully as the client is disposed to use them? [§170]	☐	☐	☐	☐
6. Are the client's real property investments being fully used for tax advantages?	☐	☐	☐	☐
7. Is the impact of the alternative minimum tax being considered for transactions involving tax-preference items? [§55]	☐	☐	☐	☐
8. Are income and deductions being directed to specific years to avoid drastic fluctuation by				
a. accelerating income	☐	☐	☐	☐
b. postponing deductions	☐	☐	☐	☐
c. postponing income	☐	☐	☐	☐
d. accelerating deductions	☐	☐	☐	☐
e. avoiding constructive receipt	☐	☐	☐	☐
9. To reduce estate taxes				
a. have incidents of life insurance ownership been assigned?	☐	☐	☐	☐
b. is a life insurance trust being used? [§2042]	☐	☐	☐	☐
10. Have installment sales of investments, residences, or other property been arranged to minimize tax? [§453]	☐	☐	☐	☐
11. Is investment in tax-exempt instruments being used?	☐	☐	☐	☐
12. Is income being shifted to lower-bracket taxpayers through outright gifts or other lifetime transfers such as family partnerships or irrevocable trusts?	☐	☐	☐	☐
13. Is a qualified minors [2503(c)] trust being used effectively for income shifting or other tax advantage?	☐	☐	☐	☐
14. Have gifts been made under the Uniform Gifts to Minors Act (UGMA) or the Uniform Transfers to Minors Act (UTMA)?	☐	☐	☐	☐
15. Are gift/sale leasebacks being used?	☐	☐	☐	☐

*All code section references are to the Internal Revenue Code of 1986 as amended.

© 1987 The American College

TAX-PLANNING CHECKLIST (continued)

Individual Planning (continued)

	At Present Yes	At Present No	Advisable Yes	Advisable No
16. Have alternative distribution methods for qualified plans been analyzed for tax consequences?	☐	☐	☐	☐
17. Are capital-loss offsets being used to reduce total income subject to tax?	☐	☐	☐	☐
18. Are plan distributions, rollovers to another qualified plan, or an IRA advisable to defer taxable income?	☐	☐	☐	☐
19. Have like-kind exchanges of property been compared with sale and repurchase and utilized when more advantageous? [§1031]	☐	☐	☐	☐
20. Have loan agreements been negotiated to secure the most tax-advantaged interest payments? [§163]	☐	☐	☐	☐
21. Have returns of capital on investment been distinguished from taxable income? (For example, has the client's basis in the investment been ascertained and any special tax treatment to which that investment is entitled determined?)	☐	☐	☐	☐
22. Is the client suited for tax-advantaged investments?	☐	☐	☐	☐
23. Indicate any situation unique to this client that does not appear above.				

© 1987 The American College

TAX-PLANNING CHECKLIST (continued)

Business Planning

	At Present		Advisable	
	Yes	No	Yes	No
1. Are maximum allowable deductions for all expenses being taken?	☐	☐	☐	☐
2. Are expiring carryovers of credits, net operating losses, and charitable contributions being effectively used through timing of income and deductions? [§§31, 38, 39, 46, 170, 172]	☐	☐	☐	☐
3. a. Is optimum use being made of retirement plans for tax advantage?	☐	☐	☐	☐
b. Has the appropriate type(s) of plan been chosen?	☐	☐	☐	☐
4. Are contributions to charitable and other tax-exempt organizations being used as fully as the client is disposed to use them? [§170]	☐	☐	☐	☐
5. a. Is the form of client's business or investment being fully utilized to maximize personal deductions and credits (e.g., corporation, partnership, trust, S corp.)?	☐	☐	☐	☐
b. Are the business's investments being fully used to maximize deductions and credits to the shareholder(s)?	☐	☐	☐	☐
6. Are income and deductions being directed to specific years to avoid drastic fluctuation by				
a. accelerating income	☐	☐	☐	☐
b. postponing deductions	☐	☐	☐	☐
c. postponing income	☐	☐	☐	☐
d. accelerating deductions	☐	☐	☐	☐
e. avoiding constructive receipt	☐	☐	☐	☐
7. Is the full range of deductible employment fringe benefits being explored and used within the client's limits?	☐	☐	☐	☐
8. Are gift/sale leasebacks being utilized?	☐	☐	☐	☐
9. Have alternative distribution methods for qualified plans been analyzed for tax consequences?	☐	☐	☐	☐
10. Is sale-or-exchange treatment possible for redemption of equity in a closely held corporation? [§§302, 318]	☐	☐	☐	☐
11. Have nonqualified retirement plans been considered? [§83]	☐	☐	☐	☐
12. Are phantom stock plans being used for deferring compensation? [§83]	☐	☐	☐	☐
13. Are stock options possible and advantageous? [§422A]	☐	☐	☐	☐
14. Have simplified employee pensions (SEPs) been compared with other forms of deferred compensation?	☐	☐	☐	☐
15. Are qualified plans designed for maximum employee advantage during employment as well as at retirement? (For example, do they permit loans and rollovers from other plans, etc.?)	☐	☐	☐	☐

© 1987 The American College

TAX-PLANNING CHECKLIST (continued)

Business Planning (continued)

	At Present		Advisable	
	Yes	No	Yes	No
16. Have business continuation plans been developed and formalized by legal agreements?	☐	☐	☐	☐
17. Are employment contracts being used effectively to support the reasonableness of executive compensation?	☐	☐	☐	☐

18. Indicate any situation unique to this client that does not appear above.

TAX-PLANNING CHECKLIST (continued)

Estate Planning

	At Present Yes	At Present No	Advisable Yes	Advisable No
1. Have the client and spouse considered electing not to fully use the marital deduction if such an election is tax advantageous to their cumulative estates? [§2056]	☐	☐	☐	☐
2. Have life insurance policies been properly positioned to minimize estate taxes?	☐	☐	☐	☐
3. Does the estate appear to have sufficient liquidity to fund postmortem expenses and estate tax liabilities?	☐	☐	☐	☐
4. Has consideration been given to generation-skipping transfers? [§§2601-2663]	☐	☐	☐	☐
5. Have testamentary charitable dispositions and their advantages been explored? [§2055]	☐	☐	☐	☐
6. Are lifetime gifting programs being used to shift ownership of assets from the client's estate?	☐	☐	☐	☐
7. Have the client's estate-planning wishes been embodied in appropriate legal documents that have been reviewed recently?	☐	☐	☐	☐
8. Has the value of each estate asset been explored in order to obtain an estimate of potential estate tax liability?	☐	☐	☐	☐
9. Has it been determined that the client can qualify for estate tax deferral? [§6166]	☐	☐	☐	☐
10. If the client qualifies for the requisite percentage of ownership in a corporation, can §303 be utilized to assure sale-or-exchange treatment for stock redeemed to pay administration expenses and estate taxes?	☐	☐	☐	☐
11. Have the client's most personal planning objectives, feelings, and thoughts been given equal weight with tax planning?	☐	☐	☐	☐
12. Has an existing estate plan been evaluated as to the impact of the current unified credit, marital deduction, and gift tax exclusion? [§§2010, 2056, 2503, 2523]	☐	☐	☐	☐
13. Has consideration been given to the potential consequence of certain transfers made within 3 years of death? [§2035]	☐	☐	☐	☐
14. Have rules on valuation of certain property (e.g., family farms and real property used in a family business) been considered? [§2032A]	☐	☐	☐	☐
15. a. Is there any reversionary interest or power of appointment not on the client's balance sheet? b. If so, has it been examined for its potential tax impact?	☐ ☐	☐ ☐	☐ ☐	☐ ☐
16. Have estate-freezing devices such as recapitalizations, personal holding companies, and family partnerships been used?	☐	☐	☐	☐
17. Indicate any situation unique to this client that does not appear above.				

© 1987 The American College

FINANCIAL POSITION STATEMENT

Assets

Cash, Near-Cash Equivalents	Current Value	Assumptions	19___	19___	19___
Checking accounts/cash					
Savings accounts					
Money-market funds					
Treasury bills					
Commercial paper					
Short-term CDs					
Life insurance, cash value					
Life insurance, accumulated dividends					
Savings bonds					
Other (specify)					
Subtotal					

Projections for Subsequent Years

Other Financial Assets

	Current Value	Assumptions	19___	19___	19___
U.S. government bonds					
Municipal bonds					
Corporate bonds					
Preferred stock					
Common stock					
Nonmarketable securities					
Warrants and options					
Mutual funds					
Investment real estate					
Long-term CDs					
Vested retirement benefits					
Annuities					
HR-10 plan (Keogh)					
Individual retirement acct. (IRA)					
Mortgages owned					
Land contracts					
Limited partnership units					
Interest(s) in trust(s)					
Receivables					
Patents, copyrights, royalties					
Value of business interest					
Other (specify)					
Subtotal					

© 1984 The American College

FINANCIAL POSITION STATEMENT (continued)

Assets (continued)

Personal Assets	Current Value	Projections for Subsequent Years			
		Assumptions	19____	19____	19____
Personal residence					
Seasonal residence					
Automobile(s)					
Recreation vehicles					
Household furnishings					
Boats					
Jewelry/furs					
Collections					
Hobby equipment					
Other (specify)					
Subtotal					
Total assets					

Liabilities

Charge accts./credit cards					
Family/personal loans					
Margin/bank/life ins. loans					
Income taxes (fed., state, local)					
Property taxes					
Investment liabilities					
Mortgage(s)					
Child support					
Alimony					
Other (specify)					
Other (specify)					
Other (specify)					
Other (specify)					
Total liabilities					

Net Worth

Total assets minus total liabilities					

© 1984 The American College

INCOME AND LUMP-SUM RESOURCES FOR DISABILITY, RETIREMENT, AND DEATH

Sources of Funds	For Disability – Lump-sum Pmts.	For Disability – Monthly Income Amount	For Disability – Monthly Income Beginning/Ending	For Retirement – Lump-sum Pmts.	For Retirement – Monthly Income Amount	For Retirement – Monthly Income Beginning/Ending	For Death – Lump-sum Pmts.	For Death – Monthly Income Amount	For Death – Monthly Income Beginning/Ending
Continuing income (p. 6)*									
Income of spouse									
Social security benefits									
Pension plan									
Profit-sharing plan									
HR-10 plan (Keogh)									
Individual retirement account (IRA)									
Nonqualified deferred compensation									
Other retirement benefits/ deferred compensation									
Group life insurance									
Personal life insurance									
Annuities									
Group short-term disability income									
Group long-term disability income									
Personal disability income insurance									
Asset liquidation									
Proceeds of sale of business interest									
Other (specify)									
Other (specify)									
Other (specify)									
Totals									

*Be sure to adjust for income sources from p. 6 of the Fact Finder that will terminate or decrease if client or spouse dies, retires, or is disabled.

© 1984 The American College

CHECKLIST FOR FINANCIAL PLANNING REVIEW

Change in	Has Occurred	Is Expected		Has Occurred	Is Expected
1. Marital status			9. Property ownership		
Marriage	☐	☐	Purchase in joint ownership	☐	☐
Separation	☐	☐	Purchase, client owned	☐	☐
Divorce	☐	☐	Purchase, spouse owned	☐	☐
Remarriage	☐	☐	Purchase, dependent owned	☐	☐
			Transfer to joint ownership	☐	☐
2. Number of dependents			Transfer to client	☐	☐
Increase	☐	☐	Transfer to spouse	☐	☐
Decrease	☐	☐	Transfer to dependent	☐	☐
			Transfer to trustee	☐	☐
3. Health status					
Client	☐	☐	10. Liabilities		
Spouse	☐	☐	Leases executed	☐	☐
Dependent	☐	☐	Mortgage increase	☐	☐
			Lawsuit against	☐	☐
4. Residence	☐	☐	Judgment against	☐	☐
			Unsecured borrowing	☐	☐
5. Occupation			Cosigning of notes	☐	☐
Client	☐	☐			
Spouse	☐	☐	11. Business ownership		
Dependent	☐	☐	New business formation	☐	☐
			Interest purchase	☐	☐
6. Family financial status			Sale of interest	☐	☐
Borrowing	☐	☐	Transfer of interest	☐	☐
Lending	☐	☐	Reorganization among owners	☐	☐
Gifts over $1,000 received	☐	☐	Liquidation	☐	☐
Gifts over $1,000 made	☐	☐	Change of carrier	☐	☐
Purchase of property	☐	☐	Termination or lapse	☐	☐
Sale of property	☐	☐	Surrender	☐	☐
Investments	☐	☐			
Inheritance	☐	☐	12. Legal document status		
Deferred income	☐	☐	Change in last will	☐	☐
Pension plan	☐	☐	Change in trust	☐	☐
Tax-deferred annuity	☐	☐	Buy-sell agreement	☐	☐
Dependent's income	☐	☐	Agreement to defer income	☐	☐
7. Sources of income			13. Insurance status		
As employee	☐	☐	Life insurance	☐	☐
From self-employment	☐	☐	Health insurance	☐	☐
From tax-exempt employer	☐	☐	Group insurance	☐	☐
From investments	☐	☐	Other employer plan	☐	☐
Inventions, patents, copyrights	☐	☐	Property insurance	☐	☐
Hobbies, avocations	☐	☐	Liability insurance	☐	☐
			Change of plan	☐	☐
8. Income tax status					
From single to joint return	☐	☐	14. Attitudes toward others		
From joint to single return	☐	☐	In family	☐	☐
Capital gains	☐	☐	In business	☐	☐
Capital losses	☐	☐	In accepting professional		
Substantial contributions	☐	☐	advice	☐	☐
Unreimbursed casualty loss	☐	☐			
Sick pay received	☐	☐	15. Interest in		
Unreimbursed medical			Idea previously discussed	☐	☐
expenses	☐	☐	Plans seen or heard about	☐	☐
Tax-impact investment(s)	☐	☐			

1984 The American College

INTRODUCTION TO PERSONAL COMPUTER HARDWARE

by Colin Mick*

Hardware is a general-purpose term used to refer to all the physical elements of a computer system--the parts you can see, hear, and feel. Hardware items are electronic and mechanical devices.

If hardware represents the physical component of computing, then software represents the intellectual component. Software is a general-purpose term that refers to programs--sets of instructions that tell the computer what to do. We talk more about software in reading 5.

A typical computer system has four components:

The first component is, obviously, the computer. The computer is essentially a general-purpose electronic device designed to process information.

The second component is the terminal. The terminal is the device you use to communicate with the computer. You give the computer instructions by typing them on the terminal keyboard. The computer sends you messages by displaying them on the terminal screen. Some terminals come as a single unit; others come as a separate display screen and keyboard that are connected to the computer.

The third component is the external memory device. External memory devices provide a means for saving information and programs and for moving them into the computer memory when you want to use them. The most common external memory device for personal computers is the floppy disk drive. The floppy disk drive allows you to take information from the computer and store it on the shelf, then send it back to the computer at a later date. The information is stored on a disk of magnetic material, much as music is recorded on a cassette tape.

The final component is the printer. The printer is used to put information on paper for storage or for transmission to people who lack facilities for dealing with electronically stored information.

---

*Reprinted with permission from The Financial Planner's Guide to Using a Personal Computer, by Colin Mick and Jerry Ball (Homewood, Ill.: Dow Jones-Irwin, 1984). Copyright © 1984 by Dow Jones-Irwin.

THE COMPUTER

The computer has four primary units:

1. the CPU, or central processing unit
2. the main memory
3. the external memory controller
4. the peripheral controller

Some computers combine all four of these units on a single printed circuit board. Others have one printed circuit board for each unit.

The most important unit is the CPU. This is the part that actually does the work. It takes electronically stored units of information--called words--and performs operations on them--one unit at a time--following instructions from a program. The size of the information unit or word is determined by the microprocessor.

The units of information are measured in bits. A bit has two values--either 0 or 1. By combining bits, we can develop fairly complex codes to represent information.

Eights bits are called a byte. A byte can have 2 to the 8th power--a total of 256--different values. That's enough to represent all the characters on a typical keyboard-- upper- and lowercase letters, numbers, and punctuation--and still have some left over.

Bits and bytes refer to physical units of information, but you will often hear people refer to a logical unit of information called a word.

A word is a logical chunk of information that the computer actually manipulates. Eight-bit computers use an eight-bit word--a physical byte. This means that they perform all their operations on groups of eight bits. A 16-bit computer uses a 16-bit word.

The key element in the CPU is the microprocessor--the device that makes the entire machine work. Several different microprocessors are used in personal computers. They are generally distinguished by the size of the word they use. Most personal computers use microprocessors that work with either an 8-bit or a 16-bit word.

The second component in the computer is the main memory. Main memory is memory that is operated under the direct control of the CPU. The memory is used to hold information--both program and data--until it is needed by the CPU. The information is stored in special electronic storage circuits. There are two general kinds of memory circuits--RAMs and ROMs.

RAM stands for random access memory. It is general-purpose memory. You can put information in the computer, erase that information, and put in other information. RAM is also volatile information--that means it retains its contents only as long as the computer is operating. When you turn off the computer, RAM circuits lose the information that is stored in them.

ROM is read-only memory. It is used to permanently store information that is needed by the computer on a regular basis. Generally, the computer manufacturer uses ROM to hold program information that the computer uses on start-up.

Memory is measured in words--the number of storage locations available. To simplify matters, we generally refer to memory locations in thousands, which we represent with the symbol K. Thus, a computer with 64K of memory has approximately 64,000 words of storage available.

The amount of memory a computer can control is another measure of its power. To control memory, the microcomputer must be able to pass the address of storage locations through a communications system known as the address bus. The size of this bus controls the amount of memory that can be controlled. We measure that size in bits.

If the address bus were 8 bits wide, then we would have 2 to the 8th power, or 256, unique address codes. Each additional line on the address bus doubles the number of unique address codes. If the address bus were 16 bits wide, we would have 2 to the 16th power, or 65,536, unique address codes.

Most 8-bit microcomputers have 16-bit address buses. This means that they can control about 64,000 words of main memory. Most 16-bit microcomputers have larger address buses and can control between 500,000 and several million words of storage.

The next unit is the external memory controller. It controls the floppy disk drive. We have already discussed why we need external memory--to store programs and information when they don't need to be stored in the main memory of the computer or when the computer is turned off.

The external memory controller is a little computer itself. It is responsible for moving information between the main memory and the external memory. This is much more important than it sounds. Computer main memories really aren't that big--64K is only about 20 pages of text, for example, and you don't have access to all of it; some of it is needed for housekeeping operations.

For most applications the computer holds in its main memory only a portion of a specific program and the data that it is processing. Most of the program and data are actually stored in external memory and are brought into main memory only as they are needed. The external memory controller is responsible for handling these transactions.

The final unit is the peripheral controller. Peripheral is a term used to describe the elements of a computer system that are outside the computer--such as the terminal and the printer. The peripheral controller controls the flow of information between the computer and the peripherals.

This covers the four major elements of a computer--the CPU, the main memory, the external memory controller, and the peripheral controller. However, there are also some support elements that you should know about.

The first is the bus, a series of communication lines that connect the CPU to other components of the computer. We have already mentioned the address bus, but a computer has several other buses as well. One is the data bus, which is one word wide and is used to move data from one component to another. Then there is the control bus, which is used to send synchronizing time pulses that coordinate the various components. And finally, there is the power bus, which is used to bring power to the components.

All computers use a bus to connect components. Some computers put all of their components on a single board. Here the bus is merely a set of printed circuit lines on the board. This is the approach used by many of the small business computers, such as Altos.

The opposite extreme is to build each component on a separate board. The boards are plugged into a series of connected multipin sockets--the bus. This approach is used by small business and scientific machines, such as Cromemco and CompuPro.

A third approach is to put most of the components on a single board and provide a set of bus sockets to add component boards. This is called the pseudobus or expansion bus approach. It is used by many of the popular personal computers, such as Apple and the IBM PC and XT.

Each design approach has its advantages and disadvantages.

The single-board approach is the least expensive and tends to be the most reliable, since there are fewer mechanical connectors. It also gives the smallest package. On the other hand, it is the least flexible approach and the most difficult to service.

The separate board and bus approach provides the greatest flexibility and ease of service. You can build up a system to meet your specific requirements, and it is very easy to replace individual components. On the other hand, it is the most expensive approach and it requires the greatest amount of skill to put the system together.

The pseudobus approach gives the best of both the single-board and the board and bus approach. With the incredible market acceptance of the IBM PC, it is likely to become the most common design approach for personal computers. One catch is that the cooling frequently becomes a problem when all the expansion slots have been filled with add-on components.

Every computer will also have a power supply. The power supply takes 110-volt current from your electrical supply lines and converts it to voltages used by the computer.

All electrical components give off heat. Heat is perhaps the biggest single enemy of electrical equipment, and it is very important to get rid of heat as quickly as possible. Most personal computers do this by putting a fan into each component.

THE TERMINAL

Like the computer, the terminal can be divided into four major components: the display, the keyboard, the controller, and the communications unit.

The display uses a cathode-ray tube, much like the one found on a television set. Normally, however, the displays used with computers have much finer resolution.

Information is shown on the screen of the display using small dots called pixels. Each pixel can be turned on by striking it with electrons under the supervision of the controller. The display is composed of rows and rows of these pixels; the pixels can be combined to form characters and shapes on the screen.

Displays differ in size and resolution quality--the number of pixels they can turn on (which limits the quality of the characters shown on the screen). They come in both color and monochrome. Monochrome displays come with white characters on a black screen, green characters on a black screen, and amber characters on a black screen.

Some displays use "long-persistence phosphors" to keep the characters from flickering on the screen. This does indeed stabilize the characters, but it also creates ghosting when the information on the display changes quickly. Since we feel that the speed of the response is particularly important with personal computers, we would generally not recommend long-persistence phosphors.

The terminal keyboard is very similar to that found on a typewriter. Instead of putting a character on paper, however, hitting a key puts a character on the display screen.

The main difference between a terminal keyboard and a typewriter keyboard is the number of keys. Terminals may have as many as 20 or 30 extra keys--enough to make things thoroughly confusing. Some of these extra keys are included on the regular keyboard. Specific keys to look for are the delete and repeat keys on the right side of the keyboard and the escape, control, and caps lock keys, which are usually on the left side. The delete and repeat keys do just what their name implies, but the remaining three keys require some explanation.

The CONTROL key is very important. It is used in combination with other keys to send software control messages to the computer. It works like a shift key--you hold it down while you press another key to send a particular code to the computer--for example, CONTROL C.

The ESCAPE key works like the control key and is used to send hardware and software control messages to the computer.

The CAPS LOCK or ALPHA LOCK key is a modified shift key that works only on letters. When it is pressed down, you will get capital letters, but the numbers and keys for numbers and punctuation will be unshifted.

Most keyboards include a numeric keypad on the right for fast entry of numbers. It is a godsend to those who are used to working with a ten-key adding machine or calculator.

You will probably also find a set of function keys-- generally labeled with an F and a number. These may be above the regular keyboard, or they may be positioned to the left of it. They are used to send special commands to programs executing on the computer.

The controller is a printed circuit board that controls the display of information on the screen. It takes the information codes from the computer and translates them into patterns of pixels that appear on the screen. The simplest controllers display only capital letters, punctuation, and numbers. More sophisticated controllers display upper- and lowercase letters and have a set of graphics characters. The most sophisticated controllers can create complex graphics on the screen.

The communications interface controls the flow of information between the terminal and the computer.

As we mentioned earlier, terminal components are packaged in a variety of ways. The oldest configuration puts all four components in a single unit. More modern configurations have a removable keyboard to make the terminal more comfortable to use. Modular computers such as the IBM PC and XT package the display and keyboard separately and keep the controller in the computer.

THE DISK DRIVE

Most personal computers use a floppy disk drive. It is a box with slots into which you insert the floppy disks.

The floppy disk itself is a disk of mylar coated with magnetic oxide. It's called a floppy because it is too weak to support itself and must be kept in a protective envelope. The envelope also protects the fragile magnetic oxide coating from damage.

There are three sizes of floppy disks. The regular or maxifloppy is eight inches in diameter. The minifloppy is 5.25 inches in diameter. Standards are not yet fixed for the microfloppy--it ranges from 3 to 4 inches in size, depending on the manufacturer.

Information is recorded magnetically on the surface of these diskettes much as you record music on an audiotape. When a diskette is inserted into the drive, it is rotated at speeds of 300-360 rpm. The rotating disk moves under a read/write head much like the recording head on a tape recorder. The head is pressed against the surface of the diskette to both read from and write to the diskette. Information is stored on the diskette in a series of tracks that are created by moving the read/write head across the surface of the diskette. This forms areas called tracks that are similar to the grooves on a record.

An oval cutout on the protective envelope provides a place for the read/write head to touch the surface of the diskette. There is also an index hole that is used by the drive to compute locations around the diskette.

THE PRINTER

Two basic kinds of printers are used with personal computers. One kind is known as a dot matrix printer--it creates characters by combining dots, much as the terminal creates characters on the display. Dots can be created by striking an inked ribbon with pins (impact) or by squirting small droplets of ink on the paper (ink jet).

The other kind of printer is called a fully formed character printer. It works like a typewriter--striking forms of the letters against an inked ribbon.

Dot matrix printers are less expensive, more flexible, and faster than fully formed character printers (80-100 characters per second versus 20-50 characters per second). In addition to printing text, most will print charts and graphs. Fully formed character printers provide better print quality. We recommend a fully formed character printer and, if you need graphics, either a dot matrix printer or a plotter.

Printers communicate with computers through serial and parallel interfaces. A serial interface sends information serially--one bit at a time--from the computer to the printer. A parallel interface sends eight bits in parallel--a full byte--at one time. Both interfaces can send out information much faster than most printers can print, and interface selection is usually determined by your computer.

Every computer printer should have a forms tractor--this is a device that controls the positioning of continuous form paper and moves it through the printer. It is the most accurate and convenient form of paper control. You can get almost any kind of paper in continuous form--even printed letterheads.

PACKAGING COMPUTERS

Computers are packaged in a variety of configurations. Most of the configurations do not include printers.

The component system represents one packaging extreme--each component is in its own case--computer, terminal, and floppy disk drive. The components are generally made by different manufacturers and are assembled into a system. This system provides maximum flexibility since you can often upgrade individual components. It is also somewhat easier to service. On the other hand, it is more expensive; it has three cases, each with its own power supply. In addition, a component system is more difficult to assemble because you must select components that complement one another and then you must integrate them into a single system.

The opposite extreme is to put all three key components--computer, terminal, and external memory--in a single case. This system looks better and takes up a lot less space on a desk. Also, you don't have to worry about matching and integrating components. On the down side, such a system has less flexibility--it is more difficult to upgrade the basic components, though some of these systems offer an expansion bus.

The third packaging approach is the modular computer. Here the components are in separate cases, but they are made by a single manufacturer and sold as an integrated system. Most modular computers have a separate display; packaging of the other components depends on the manufacturer. Typically, modular systems use an expansion bus, so you can add components to the computer.

Some computers are packaged as portables. The term portable covers a broad range of sizes and capabilities. At the smaller, lower end portables are sophisticated pocket calculators for running programs in BASIC. At the upper end they are full-fledged computer systems that will run the same programs as their desk-bound cousins. Portables range in weight from less than one pound to more than 30 pounds. Small ones fit in a shirt pocket. Larger ones fit in an attache case. Some of the largest will barely fit under an airliner seat.

In addition to these four basic packaging options, there are in-between options. Some of these options put the computer and disk drives together in one box and work with an external terminal. Others put computer and terminal in one box but add external disk drives. Regardless of how they are packaged, however, they all provide the same four functional components.

SUMMARY

The typical computer system has four functional components: the computer, terminal, disk drive, and printer.

The computer also has four functional components: the CPU, main memory, external memory controller, and peripheral controller.

The terminal is the device you use to communicate with your computer. Its functional components include the display, keyboard, controller, and communications interface.

The floppy disk drive is the most common external memory device for personal computers. A floppy disk is inserted into the drive, where it is rotated past a moving read/write head. The disk stores information and programs when the computer is turned off.

The printer is used by the computer to put information on paper. There are two basic kinds of printers, dot matrix printers and fully formed character printers.

Personal computers come in a variety of packages, each with its own advantages and disadvantages. For flexibility, we recommend that you get one that allows you to add boards by plugging them into the bus.

INTRODUCTION TO SOFTWARE

by Colin Mick[*]

Software is a generic term used to describe the instructions we give to the computer so that it will accomplish a specific task. A computer program is software.

Software is used to tell the hardware--the physical components of the computer system--what to do.

Think of a car--the car is hardware and equivalent to the computer. By itself, it is an interesting mix of metal, plastic, and electronics. But to do useful work it needs a driver--someone to tell it what to do and guide it.

Software is the "driver" for the computer system.

There are four basic types of software: operating systems, utilities, languages, and applications programs.

OPERATING SYSTEMS

The operating system provides communication and control between the various hardware components--the computer, the terminal, the external memory or disk drive, and the printer. It handles the scheduling of tasks, disk operations, the allocation of memory, and all of those tedious tasks that keep computing from being fun. The operating system also provides the interface between your hardware and other software products (that is, utilities, languages, and applications programs). This means that your software programs must be compatible with both your computer hardware and your operating system.

Operating systems can be system specific or generic.

System-specific operating systems are developed by hardware manufacturers and are custom tailored to the computer systems of these manufacturers. Such operating systems offer the greatest sophistication and are generally the most user friendly, but at a cost. The cost is that they do not provide a standard software interface, so it is

---

[*]Reprinted with permission from The Financial Planner's Guide to Using a Personal Computer, by Colin Mick and Jerry Ball (Homewood, Ill.: Dow Jones-Irwin, 1984). Copyright © 1984 by Dow Jones-Irwin.

nearly impossible to move programs and languages designed for a system-specific operating system to another computer. Apple, Atari, Commodore, IBM, and Radio Shack computers generally come with system-specific operating systems.

Generic operating systems are developed by software houses and are designed to operate on a variety of different computers. They generally offer less sophistication than do system-specific operating systems because they are designed to operate on a number of different computer systems. On the other hand, since they offer a standardized software interface, they make it possible to move software between different computers. With eight-bit personal computers CP/M-80 is the dominant generic operating system. The overwhelming dominance of IBM in the business and professional portion of the personal computer market has established PC-DOS (IBM's proprietary operating system) as the de facto standard for the current crop of 16-bit machines. MS-DOS, a generic version of PC-DOS, can also be considered a de facto standard. However, just because a computer runs MS-DOS does not mean that it can run all the software that runs on the IBM PC. IBM uses some copyrighted firmware (software permanently stored in a ROM) to control graphics and input-output routines. As a result, some programs that depend on the IBM-specific firmware will not run on some MS-DOS machines. (Be warned, however, that new, more powerful operating systems are on the way for the IBM PC and its clones.)

The operating system is generally located on your floppy disk and is loaded into the computer memory by means of a technique called bootstrap loading. Essentially this means that on start-up a few simple instructions in the computer tell it to go out and read a small section of the operating system of the disk. This section contains instructions that tell the computer to return to the diskette to read and load the remainder of the operating system.

Portions of the operating system always remain in the main memory of your computer while you are using it. These portions contain the basic disk operations and, if you have a generic operating system, the portions that "mate" it to your specific computer. This really doesn't take up too much space--generally less than one fourth of the main memory on a typical eight-bit computer.

UTILITIES

Utilities are primarily simple programs for doing housekeeping operations--operations required to keep your system operating properly. Some utility programs enhance or improve functions provided by the operating system; others go far beyond the operating system.

Here are some examples of utility programs:

- disk-to-disk copy programs that enable you to copy an entire disk with a single command
- cataloging programs that help you keep track of what files are stored on which diskettes. (Cataloging and disk-to-disk copy programs are essential to a good disk backup program.)
- programs to test various hardware components and detect hardware problems
- programs to format floppy disks for use on your system. (If your system uses soft-sectored diskettes, you will have to format the diskettes before they can be used.)
- programs to communicate with another personal computer (generally over telephone lines using a modem). These programs allow you to send messages and files from one machine to another. Often you can even control the other machine remotely.

There is also an entire class of programming utilities that are used to assist in the development and implementation of applications programs.

Utilities may not seem very important, but as you learn to use your computer, you will find that they become essential to effective system management. I use them to perform basic system operations, to support system maintenance, and to configure my system for special functions.

I find that appreciation and use of utilities seem to be related to the sophistication of the use. Starting to look for specific utilities is a sign of emerging sophistication-- aggressive searching for utilities is one of the first major signs of computerphilia.

LANGUAGES

Languages provide a vocabulary and a syntactic structure for organizing instructions for the computer. They come in a bewildering variety of levels and variations. The levels range from the simple binary code of machine language up to higher-level languages that have an English-like vocabulary and syntax.

Computer languages can be classified on a simple scale that reflects how they work. At one end are languages that focus on telling the computer what to do. Languages at this end of the scale are called high-level languages because they use sophisticated commands, have a structure similar to that of English, and are the easiest to understand. Examples of high-level languages include Pascal and LOGO.

At the other end of the scale are languages that focus on telling the computer how to do something. Languages at this end of the scale are called low-level languages because they are rigidly structured, require a large number of very simple commands, and are difficult for novices to understand. Examples include FORTH and assembly language.

Since all instructions for a computer must, in the end, be reduced to machine code, higher-level languages require mechanisms to convert their easier-to-understand statements into machine code so that the computer can execute them.

Two such mechanisms are used, interpreters and compilers.

Interpreters convert instructions from the higher-level language to machine code on a line-by-line basis, providing flexibility (you get feedback on each instruction as it is decoded and executed) at the cost of speed and efficiency.

Compilers work in bulk, converting the entire program. They generally work in two steps, converting the entire program to some intermediate code and then converting that code into machine code at execution time. This enables compilers to execute programs much faster than interpreters but makes it much more complex to deal with errors in the program.

One of the interesting things about computer languages is the development of dialects--variations on the general language. Software engineering is an extremely dynamic field, and languages are constantly being upgraded and adapted to add features. Differences in these expansions give rise to dialects.

BASIC is a good example. Originally developed at Dartmouth College as a teaching language, it gained popularity as a simple-to-learn, though far from elegant, language. Ease of use made BASIC a natural choice for computer hobbyists but resulted in the development of a number of generally incompatible dialects. On my shelf I have essentially six different versions of BASIC--CBASIC, Microsoft BASIC-80, SBASIC, North Star BASIC, Applesoft BASIC, and the BASIC I originally learned on an IBM 360-67. Although the basic vocabulary and syntax are the same, variations in concept and implementation mean that programs written in one dialect require significant revision to run on another.

The end result is that you have to be very careful when you are dealing with languages. It's not enough to say you want BASIC. You have to specify the dialect (CBASIC-2, BASIC-80, SBASIC, and so forth).

There are also variations within dialects caused by upgrades and revisions.

Software publishers try their best to make their products as foolproof as possible, but no matter how hard they try, errors always appear after the product has been released to the market. When errors have been identified and corrected, the publisher will generally release an upgraded version of the product. Upgrades are identified by the version number. For example, version 3.0 of a program generally includes improvements over version 2.5.

Newer versions of languages are generally designed to be compatible with previous versions, but programs written in languages may not be so forgiving. Recent programs, in particular, may use features provided by the latest revision of their language and not run on earlier versions of the language.

APPLICATIONS PROGRAMS

Applications programs and the packaged software industry that produces them are the primary reasons for the success of the personal computer. Applications programs provide instructions telling the computer how to perform specific functions and tasks such as word processing and financial analysis. Applications programs make it possible for you to use your personal computer to perform a host of useful functions without really knowing very much about how your computer works or how to program. In short, they allow you to focus on doing useful work rather than on dealing with the computer.

SOME BACKGROUND ON SOFTWARE

The package software industry is by and large a creation of the microcomputer. Until the advent of the micro, software was provided primarily on a custom basis. A number of software packages were available, but they were large and expensive and they generally required extensive (and expensive) customized fitting to each hardware system.

Two developments created the package software industry. The first was the development of the microcomputer, which resulted in a large installed base (read "market") of generally similar machines, all in need of software. The second was the development of the generic operating system--an operating system that could be installed on a large variety of machines so that they provided a common interface for dealing with other software.

These elements didn't really come together until 1979-80, when CP/M, an operating system for eight-bit microcomputers, became a de facto standard.

The computer business has historically been unalterably opposed to standards. Standards are defined as bad for manufacturers because they allow users (like you and me) to mix and match hardware and software products from different manufacturers. Without standards, you would be "locked into" the products of a single manufacturer.

In the space of about 3 years the package software industry has become big business. Other kinds of de facto standard programs are beginning to appear. I define a standard program as an applications program that is a major contender in its area and that inspires a number of manufacturers to develop add-on products that extend the scope and power of the original program and to provide sophisticated publications that teach you how to use it. A standard program may not be the best program in its area, but by virtue of market acceptance it has become the standard. Here are three examples:

1. WordStar by MicroPro International has emerged as the de facto standard for word processing. The program has consistently been the top-selling word processing software package in the country. Initially designed for machines running CP/M-80, the program has been extended to other machines such as the Apple and the IBM personal computer. Although WordStar itself is an extremely powerful program, its value is increased significantly by add-on products that extend its capabilities, such as spelling, thesaurus access, and automatic indexing.
2. Ashton-Tate's dBase II is a more specialized example. It is a data base management system, a highly sophisticated program used to generate and manage complex data files. It is probably the top-selling program of its type in the country, and it has generated a host of add-on products--screen managers, application shells (prototype systems developed on dBASE II that make bringing up a custom application even easier).
3. VisiCalc, the spreadsheet program from VisiCorp for the Apple, IBM, and Hewlett-Packard computers, is another example. VisiCalc was the first software management tool that achieved wide acceptance from the business world. It has inspired a host of add-on software programs and support publications.

The purpose of this digression is to alert you to de facto standards in applications programs because I think that these are the standards against which other, similar programs should be measured.

The package software industry is extremely new. It is growing and changing very rapidly, making it extremely difficult to predict what will happen. Predictions about software have, in general, proved far less reliable than predictions about hardware (which themselves have been no paragons of reliability).

When in doubt, play conservative and go with the standards. A "standard program" may not be the best of its type, but it is probably your best bet for purchase. Here are four reasons why:

1. Documentation of most applications software is abominable. The best documentation generally comes from "second source publishers" whose sales depends on the quality of their documentation, not the quality of their software. You get a better choice of such documentation on standard programs.
2. Support is easier to get with standard programs. There is a better chance that local dealers will know such programs well. There is also a better chance that you can find other end users like yourself who already know the programs.
3. Standard programs have more add-on programs to increase their power.
4. Standard programs are more likely to be carried onto new hardware and software systems. This is extremely important. Over the long run, your major investment in your system will be the time you have spent in learning how to use the applications software. Hardware will change, and you should anticipate hardware upgrades by getting software that can migrate with you to a new system.

If you buy a language, or for that matter any program, the publisher should provide an update service. This allows you to purchase revisions and corrections for substantially less than the original purchase price. To take advantage of this, you will have to register your copy (almost all software has a serial number) and send in your serial number when you request the update. Some publishers require you to send in the serial number of the diskette on which you received your original program. This is why I recommend that you always safeguard such diskettes.

One problem with the software business is that it is extremely new and still going through growing pains. For example, software houses are not yet certain exactly what it is they are selling (or ought to be selling). The typical software package consists of the program(s), generally stored on a floppy diskette; documentation; and some kind of support service. Currently all three are bundled in the purchase price, although you may have to pay extra for updates and new versions. However, it is not clear that this is the best way to charge for software.

I identify three phases of software use for work programs--programs designed to help you do useful work. The phases represent increasing acceptance of and reliance on such programs.

The first phase is trial. The mode here is exploration and testing. The emphasis is on getting a copy of the software. It is at this stage that most informal software piracy occurs--people "borrow" copies of the software to play with.

The second phase is learning. Here the emphasis is on learning how to use the program effectively. The major concern is obtaining and using the documentation. Ironically, obtaining the documentation is more expensive than obtaining the software itself. Diskettes can be copied in a matter of minutes, but documentation is in print and must be copied at a cost of $.05 or more per page.

The third phase is dependence. Here the emphasis is on using the program to do useful work. The major concerns are maintaining the program, dealing with errors, and upgrading the program with improvements as these become available. The key to this phase is the support relationship with the software house.

Each phase emphasizes a different part of the software package and has different economic considerations. Ideally, software pricing would be unbundled to accommodate these phases, but as yet this is not the case. As a result, we have great concern about software piracy and protection and a low (but hopefully increasing) level of concern about documentation and long-term support. In the long run, software houses stand to gain much more from long-term support and maintenance agreements than from initial purchase of their products, but industry pricing policies do not yet reflect this.

Over the long run, the greatest investment you will make in a personal computer system is not the hardware or the software but the time you invest in learning how to use your system and software.

From this, it follows that in buying software, your strategy should be to minimize learning cost and to ensure that any software you purchase will be able to move with you from one computer to another. In computing, happiness is directly related to the availability of good, reliable, well-known software. Here's how to get it.

Software, not hardware, will be your major investment. The ratio of software to hardware expenditures is already greater than one-to-one and is changing rapidly in favor of software. Hardware changes rapidly--expect most of your hardware to be obsolete in 2 or 3 years. Good software, on the other hand, can stay with you for many years. It takes far longer to use software effectively than it does to use hardware effectively.

All software can be judged by three factors: how user friendly it is, how powerful it is, and how generic it is.

User friendliness determines how easy it is to use the software system. It is most apparent in the command structure and the feedback messages.

The commands are instructions you give to the computer to tell it to do specific tasks. The easiest, most user-friendly way to call a command is to press a clearly labeled key. The most friendly way to use a command is to have it prompt you with a list of all the options. The more difficult it is to remember a command or give it to the computer correctly, the less user friendly the software is.

Program feedback is the messages that the program gives you to tell you what is happening. Some programs offer very cryptic error messages that are difficult to interpret or provide very little useful information. More friendly programs make this information easy to understand and, if you must make a decision, provide alternatives.

More powerful programs give you greater control over what the computer is doing and a greater number of commands to control it. In word processing, for example, low-power programs may have only a few, simple commands that allow you to type in text, make corrections, and print the text out. More powerful programs may have as many as 100 commands and allow you to search the text for unique words, move whole chunks of text around, insert text from other files, and format documents for printing.

As power increases, programs become more complex to use and less user friendly.

BUYING SOFTWARE

Enough philosophy and background. Let's turn to buying software. Here are eight tips to help guide you in doing so.

Buy Generic Software

Generic programs are designed to work on a variety of different machines. Nongeneric programs are designed to work on a specific computer or family of computers. The nongeneric programs tend to be more user friendly and powerful because they can be closely tailored to the host computer. This allows the program designers to take full advantage of functions keys. For example, a graphics program designed specifically for the IBM PC takes full advantage of the function keys to send commands to the computer. The advantage of generic programs is that they can be easily transferred from one computer to another, giving greater flexibility and less reliance on a particular computer. I recommend that you stick with generic programs because I feel that the flexibility and hardware independence gained more than offset slight disadvantages in user friendliness.

Buy for Long-Term Use

In buying software, I recommend that you look beyond initial encounters toward long-term use. You will be amazed at how rapidly you become "computer literate" and how your use of the computer changes. If you make judgments based on initial impressions (and while you are still a computer novice), you may outgrow your software. Try to look ahead. Extra features and flexibility may seem useless now, but in the future you may wish you'd got them.

Good Documentation Is Essential

Documentation should include the following:

- a discussion of how the program works
- a discussion of how to install the program
- a tutorial to help you learn to use the program
- a reference listing commands by function
- a diagnostics or troubleshooting section
- applications examples

Check Out the Software House

Software houses come and go. If your program is a simple one, this is no problem, but if it is a complex program that you plan to use for years, you had best check out the software house and make certain that it will be there when you need it for support and assistance. Find out how long it has been in business and what other programs it offers. Find out what its policy is on consulting and providing updates. Try and find out how many copies of the program you are considering have already been sold. (When in doubt, I give the company a call. When you are talking about laying out hundreds of dollars, a phone call is not out of order.)

Talk to Other People

Find people who are using the software you are considering. Ask how they like it. Find out what problems they have had--both with the software and with support. Computer stores and dealers are one source of information, but remember that they make their living selling software. A better source would be a local computer club or user's group. You can also check out the reviews in the various publications.

Try Before You Buy!

If at all possible, try out applications programs before you buy them. Most advertisements are exercises in creative packaging--they imply and promise far more than they deliver. The best way to find out whether a program is right for you is to try it. This will take some time. Plan on spending a couple of hours so that you will have time to go over the manual and get some hands-on experience. Sometimes dealers will let you "test-drive." Often you can find another user who has the program and is willing to give you some time.

If you can't try the program in advance, see if there is some kind of trial program. Ashton-Tate has a very clever program for dBASE II, a data base management program. It sends you two sealed diskettes. The first is a sample that you can use for a test drive. It allows you to play with the program, see how it works, and try some applications (it will only allow 15 records). If you don't like it, you return the package with the second diskette (which contains the complete program) with the seal unbroken and you get a refund. Open the program diskette, and you keep it. A couple of even braver software houses will send you packages on approval, trusting your honesty. I don't know how well they are doing, but I hope they are doing well.

Don't Buy Copy-Protected Software!

Some software houses (primarily those supplying Apple software) are so concerned about piracy that they build protection routines into their program diskettes so that these cannot be copied. They then offer backup diskettes for a modest fee ($5-$10).

Although I sympathize with concerns about the piracy problem, I feel that it is essential to have a number of backup diskettes. The diskette is the most fragile part of a microcomputer system, and it is extremely vulnerable to damage. If you are going to depend on your software, you must have multiple backup copies immediately at hand. Accordingly, I cannot recommend buying any copy-protected software.

If You Are Going to Depend on It, Buy It!

The software piracy theme has been drifting all through this discussion, and it deserves some attention. Piracy occurs at a number of levels:

- A single organization (or individual) buys one copy of a software package and makes multiple copies so that it can run the program on several machines.
- An individual gets a copy of a software program to

try and, finding that it is a useful program, then buys it.
- Scenario as above, but the individual continues to use the pirated copy.
- A computer club has a stop-and-copy program in which members bring in copies of their favorite software and allow other members to copy them.
- A "grey" vendor duplicates and sells illegal copies without paying the licensing fee to the software publisher.

It's a fact of life that everybody has access to pirated software. If you are just going to play with it, you probably won't do yourself or the software house any harm. Remember, however, that once you start to use software, the key issue is not initial cost but support and updates that can be well worth the cost of the software.

SUMMARY

There are four basic kinds of software:

1. operating systems
2. utilities
3. languages
4. applications programs

Operating systems coordinate and control operation of the computer and provide an interface between the hardware and other software. Utilities are used to support and maintain the hardware and to simplify the use of other software.

Languages provide semantic and syntactic structure for creating programs.

Applications programs and prewritten sets of instructions tell the computer how to perform specific functions and tasks.

In buying software, be conservative, look for de facto standards, and follow my eight rules:

1. When possible, buy generic, machine-independent software.
2. Buy for long-term use.
3. Demand good documentation for your software.
4. Check out your software publisher.
5. Talk to other users.
6. Try it before you buy it.
7. Check out the backup policy.
8. If you are going to depend on it, buy it.

WORD PROCESSING

by Colin Mick[*]

Given the vast amount of information that we generate--most of it text--word processing is probably the most important application for personal computers in the office/work environment today.

As you begin looking at word processing, you will encounter a bewildering array of programs, features, and claims. The purpose of this reading is to help you through this maze.

The reading is divided into four parts. In the first part, we'll discuss the process of generating text and explain how word processing programs can help in the process. In the second part, we'll discuss some of the features and attributes of word processing programs and look at some examples of word processing programs to see how they differ.

Next we'll briefly cover some of the available word processing support programs. Then we'll conclude with some suggestions on how to compare and evaluate word processing programs.

WHAT IS WORD PROCESSING?

Let's start by defining word processing. Word processing is nothing more than using a computer--a general-purpose information machine--to help create letters and documents. Word processing can be divided into four specific operations.

Input is the operation of moving words from your head to the machine--today this is done by typing the text at a keyboard.

Editing is the process of organizing and revising the words so they express your thoughts as clearly as possible.

---

[*]Reprinted with permission from The Financial Planner's Guide to Using a Personal Computer, by Colin Mick and Jerry Ball (Homewood, Ill.: Dow Jones-Irwin, 1984). Copyright © 1984 by Dow Jones-Irwin.

Formatting is the process of organizing the text visually so as to give it the best possible appearance and impact on a page.

Output is the process of actually printing the text onto paper.

Each of these operations puts different demands on both the author and the word processor, so let's look at them in greater detail.

Input

In input, your major concern is to get the ideas that are in your head into the computer. Speed is the name of the game here--you want to get those ideas down as quickly as possible so that you don't forget them.

You don't want anything to disturb the flow of information into the computer. Excess feedback from the program--reports and requests for commands--just get in the way. In this phase, you shouldn't be terribly concerned about grammar or form; you can clean that up during editing.

Most of the professional writers I know who use computers try to stay in this mode as long as they can. If they complete one topic or get bored with it, they immediately start work on another. They don't even worry about logical organization. All of that comes later.

Editing

Editing is where you clean up the text.

You can correct words and sentences. You can move portions of the text around to improve organization. You can even insert information from other documents.

It is at the editing phase that you really become aware of the power of the computer. The key to good writing is rewriting, and the computer, together with a good word processing program, can make rewriting relatively painless. With the computer, you can do as many revisions as you wish for relatively little cost. How many revisions would you be willing to make if you had to retype after each one?

One of the most tedious parts of editing is checking for spelling errors and typos. This can take hours, and no matter how hard you try, a couple always seem to sneak back in. Spelling programs can make this pesky chore a breeze. A good spelling program should be able to check 20 pages in less than a minute and be ready to show you all the words it can't find in its dictionary. The program will automatically mark errors so that you can find them with your word processing program, or it may show them "in context" on the screen for immediate correction.

Formatting

After you have finished editing your text, it's time to format it for printing.

Here your concern is to make the text look as good as possible on the page. You can center heads, indent paragraphs, and change page boundaries.

You can also enter commands to call for special printing effects such as boldface and underline.

For that little touch of class, you can instruct the word processor to print the title and/or your name on each page. You can also modify the page margins, the amount of space between characters, and the amount of space between lines of text.

Printing

The final step is to actually print the document. Many word processing programs actually control the printer during printing. This allows them to further improve the text through techniques such as microjustification which inserts small spaces--each one 1/120 of an inch--between characters and words to give an even right margin. Some word processing programs even given a true proportionate spacing.

The above was just a quick overview of what goes on in word processing, but it does give you some feel for what you can do with a personal computer. Essentially you get two big advantages: increased productivity and higher document quality.

Since the greatest advantages of word processing are achieved in the input and editing phases--essentially the creative parts--it's important to get the word processing program into the hands of the author if you want maximum productivity and quality gains.

A FEATURE ANALYSIS OF WORD PROCESSING

Here are some features to look for in word processing programs.

With word processing, you need to be concerned about attributes of both the hardware (the computer equipment itself) and the software (the word processing program that runs on the hardware). Let's start with a hardware element: the display.

The Display

The display is the hardware component with the most impact on word processing. Most personal computers give you a display that is 80 characters wide by 24 lines deep. This allows you to see full lines as they will appear on paper. You can't see a full page, of course, but you can scroll the text past the display.

The display itself is part of personal computer hardware--the physical elements of the system. There are two things to be concerned about with displays: size and character quality.

The size of the display limits how much text you can see at a time. We don't recommend anything smaller than 80 characters by 24 lines.

Character quality is important in determining how easy it is to see text on the display. Look for characters that are easy to read and well defined.

I think display color is a matter of personal preference. I have worked with all three colors--white, green, and amber--and I can't say that I have noticed any great difference between them. You should, however, look for a nonglare display, as it is much easier on the eyes.

Program Display Characteristics

Now let's look at how the word processing program uses the display, one of the most important attributes of the software.

Text is displayed on the screen as you type it in. Most systems provide automatic wraparound. This means that when you come to the end of the line, the system automatically takes the last word down to the next line and continues.

The cursor is a bright, blinking bar in the screen that indicates where you are working on the display.

Some programs provide a ruler to show margins and tabs. It can be located at either the top or the bottom of the display.

Some programs allow you to extend the margin beyond the edge of the screen and then move the text over. This allows you to work with and see lines that are longer than 80 characters.

Some displays offer a feature called reverse video. This feature can be used to make some operations and commands easier to see.

Command Structure

Command complexity is probably the second most important feature to consider in a word processing program.

Word processors are complex programs and can have a lot of different commands. WordStar, the most popular program, has more than 120 different commands. Commands are generally shown on the display screen with menus. Some programs also provide reference cards that summarize all the commands.

Commands are often organized by function. The functions include file management, cursor movement, scrolling, editing, formatting, moving text, searching text, printer controls, and formatting controls.

Other, less complex programs have smaller sets of commands. The CONTEXT MBA program for the IBM personal computer, for example, combines spreadsheet, data base, and word processing functions in a single program. Its word processing support focuses on input and editing and requires only 14 commands.

Just how powerful a word processor you need depends on what you are doing. If all you want is something for short letters and memos, then a simple program with a limited set of commands could be just the thing. If you are producing long documents or performing a variety of text operations, you should probably look at more powerful programs. Remember, the more powerful the program, the more complex the command structure.

Menus

With more complex word processing programs, on-screen command menus become very important. Unfortunately, the display area is very limited and the space used for menus can't be used to display text.

Some programs use very abbreviated menus. Others allow you to turn off menus once you have learned commands. Some programs bring up menus if you don't complete a command in a certain amount of time.

Command Codes

There are two approaches to the coding of commands for programs--the home key approach and the function key approach.

The home key approach assumes that you know your way around a keyboard and that you like to keep your hands on home keys--the left and right sides of the a-to-l row of typewriter keys or the "5" key on a numeric keypad. All command codes are therefore designed to minimize travel from the home keys. The commands are generally composed of regular keys--for example, a, s, d, f--used in conjunction with the CONTROL and ESCAPE keys. WordStar is the best example of the home key approach in word processing programs.

The function key approach assumes that you aren't comfortable with a keyboard and that you would prefer to have labeled keys dedicated to specific functions. This approach requires the availability of function keys on the keyboard. Some function keys control such things as cursor movement. Others have generic labels and can be custom configured by the program to perform certain functions.

The function key approach used to be difficult to implement since there was no standard for function keys. However, the rapid acceptance of the IBM PC format is making the IBM function key layout a de facto standard. This layout provides a numeric keypad on the right side of the keyboard and a row of function keys on the left side. Many of the new programs on the market take advantage of these function keys.

Which command code approach is right for you depends on your particular circumstances. You should go over the command sequences very carefully to determine how they will affect you. This is very important if you are used to a numeric keypad, as most keyboards do not properly support numeric keypads.

Now that we've talked about commands, let's talk about some of the different kinds of commands and what they do.

Cursor Control and Scrolling Commands

Let's start with the way you move information around on the screen. This is done with cursor controls and scrolling.

The cursor is a bright spot on the screen that indicates where you are working. You should be able to move the cursor up, down, left, right, to the top of the screen, and to the bottom of the screen.

Scrolling moves the text on the display. Vertical scrolling moves the text up and down on the screen. You should be able to move the text on a line-by-line basis, a screen at a time, and continuously.

Horizontal scrolling moves the text left and right on the display. It is handy when you want to work with line lengths greater than the terminal can display.

Basic Editing Commands

Now let's look at some basic editing commands. The simplest are delete, insert, and replace. You should be able to delete a character, a word, and a line with one command. Some programs also allow you to delete sentences and paragraphs. Insert means to put in new text at the cursor position, moving the existing text to the right. Replace means to type over the top of existing text and replace it.

Block Commands

In editing, you often want to physically manipulate sections of text--cutting them out of one location and pasting them into another. In word processing, we call these sections blocks and we call the commands block commands. To do a block move, we first mark the block and then indicate where we want to move it. We can also copy a block to a number of different locations. Some programs offer a column block command to move a specified set of columns from one place to another. This command is very useful in doing tables.

Search and Replace Commands

Search and replace commands are also important. They allow you to search through your text for a specified combination of characters and, if you wish, to replace them with another set. First, you give the program a character sequence--called a string. The program searches through your document and displays the first occurrence of the string that it finds in the text. You can instruct the program to keep on searching until it reaches the end of the document. You can also tell the program to search for one string and replace it with another.

Formatting Commands

Now let's take a look at some formatting commands. We use these to prepare the document for printing.

You should be able to center a line. You should be able to reformat a paragraph to any size.

Controlling page breaks can be a problem. You don't want to have one line of a paragraph on one page and the rest of the paragraph on another. You should have a command that will create a page break.

File Commands

You also need commands to save your text. These are used to make permanent copies of your document so that you won't lose it when you turn off the computer.

When you are working on a document with a word processing program, the document is stored in what is called a working file. This is a temporary file that exists only as long as the computer is turned on. If you wish to keep a copy of the document so that you can work with it on the word processor at a later date, you must copy it to a permanent file.

A permanent file is a representation of the document that is recorded on an external memory device such as a floppy disk. The external memory device can be taken out of the computer and stored. Later it can be reinserted in the computer so that the computer can access information recorded on it.

To transfer the information in a working file to a permanent file, you must use a save file command.

There are two different types of save commands that you should look for. The first is a full save--you use this when you are done with the document and wish to quit or work on another document. When you do a full save, the program saves a copy of the document and then erases the working file. The program will then either let you start a new working file or exit to the operating system.

An intermediate save is used to save your document periodically, while you are still working on it, without erasing the working file. The intermediate save is a very important command because it protects you against accidental loss of the working file. You should do intermediate saves frequently while you are working on a document--at least every 10 minutes. That way, if you experience a computer failure, the most you will lose is 10 minutes' work.

Print Commands

In general, word processing programs use two kinds of print commands.

First, there are commands that control the way the text is printed. These commands are embedded in the text and are used to call for printing effects such as boldface, underline, subscripts, and superscripts. They can also be used to vary line spacing and character spacing.

Printer commands of the second kind are used to control the operation of the printer. They are used to tell the printer to print a file, to print a particular part of the file, and to stop and start.

WORD PROCESSING SUPPORT PROGRAMS

The information presented so far should give you some feeling for what you can do with a word processing program, but the benefits don't stop there.

You can also get a variety of support programs that will significantly improve your document production. Here are some examples:

- Spelling programs will automatically check your text against a dictionary to help you identify words that might be spelled incorrectly. With most spelling programs, you can check more than 20 pages of text in less than a minute.
- Word count programs help you keep track of how long your document is. Word frequency count programs show you which words you have used in the text and how many times you have used them. They are very handy for eliminating jargon and overworked words.
- A new electronic thesaurus program will give you on-line access to a thesaurus right on the screen while you are typing.
- Grammar checkers check for simple mistakes such as repeated words (for example, the the) and unbalanced parentheses and quotation marks.
- Footnote programs make dealing with these pesky critters easy. You just mark the terms you want footnoted and keep on writing. Later you type the footnotes and the program numbers and insert them automatically.
- Indexing and table of contents programs will automatically create an index or a table of contents for your document, indexing terms or sections to the appropriate pages.

SELECTING A WORD PROCESSING PROGRAM

This introduction to word processing should give you some feel for word processing programs and for the features of such programs that are most important for your needs.

I strongly recommend that you do some research before buying a program. Start by checking software reviews in the computer magazines and by getting suggestions from people you know who already use personal computers for word processing. Then go out to visit the dealers and try to test-drive programs that appear promising.

For your test drive, I recommend that you standardize your procedures. Try to get at least an hour for each session. Remember, you are looking at the program, not the computer, the terminal, or the printer.

I recommend that you go through the routine shown below and that you then make notes of your impressions.

1. Type in three or four paragraphs of text to see how it is displayed on the screen.
2. Go back and change part of one paragraph. Try both the insert and replace text commands. Now delete one paragraph.
3. Insert a new sentence into one paragraph. Delete one sentence or one line of text.
4. Do a block command--copy the top paragraph to the bottom of the text.
5. Change several words in the text to boldface.
6. Reformat one paragraph so that it is indented five spaces.
7. Insert a page break between two paragraphs.
8. Print out the text.

After going through this routine with a couple of programs, you'll begin to develop a feel for the features that are important to you.

In addition to the features of the program itself, you should also consider the availability of add-on programs. Some of the word processing support programs we described earlier are only available for particular programs.

FINANCIAL ANALYSIS

by Colin Mick[*]

WHAT IS A SPREADSHEET?

A spreadsheet is nothing more than a paper tool to help you structure numeric information for analysis. All you need to create a spreadsheet are a columnar pad, a pencil (and a good eraser), and, hopefully, a calculator--it's awfully tedious without one.

To use a spreadsheet, you develop a model to represent a particular process--for example, a budget. Then you label the rows and columns as shown in the accompanying form. Here the rows are used to define expense categories and the columns are used to represent months. The intersection of each row and column is called a cell.

The cells contain numeric information called constants and variables. A constant is a fixed amount--a value that will not change. An independent variable is an amount that you can control--for example, your salary, your expenses, or your markup. A dependent variable is a value that is calculated by applying a formula to other variables and constants--it is the result of a calculation.

Here's a simple spreadsheet--a budget form that can be used to project expenses for the first 6 months of the year.

	January	February	March	April	May	June	Total
Salaries		cell					
Rent							
Utilities							
Telephone							
Postage							
Travel							
Total							

[*]Reprinted with permission from The Financial Planner's Guide to Using a Personal Computer, by Colin Mick and Jerry Ball (Homewood, Ill.: Dow Jones-Irwin, 1984). Copyright © 1984 by Dow Jones-Irwin.

Doing spreadsheets with paper and pencil can get very tedious because all the math has to be done by hand or with a calculator. Both methods offer plenty of opportunity for error.

I used to do spreadsheets by hand. For me, it was mostly a question of getting the column and row to agree--and of course they seldom did.

Then I discovered computer spreadsheet programs and all that changed. Once I created my model and entered it into the computer, the math problems were trivialized. The computer took care of all the calculations--row and column totals were always right. I had time to experiment--to vary assumptions and try different ways of doing things. All at once, the spreadsheet was a creative tool limited only by my imagination.

This is the real power of the computerized spreadsheet-- the ability to test different assumptions once the model has been created.

Today spreadsheet programs are used in an incredible array of situations. They allow you to create a model to represent the variables affecting virtually any kind of decision and to examine what happens as the variables change.

Among the applications are the following:

- financial planning
- budgeting
- sales forecasts
- business plans
- tax calculations
- accounting

HOW A COMPUTER SPREADSHEET WORKS

Let's take a look at how you use a spreadsheet program. For this analysis, I'll break spreadsheet work into six functions to make it easier to understand. The functions are planning, setup, input, calculation, formatting, and output.

Planning

Let's start with planning. This is where you decide how to represent your problem--the types of variables you will use to represent it, the rows and columns for the spreadsheet, and the formulas you will use to calculate dependent variables.

Planning is probably the most neglected function in spreadsheet analysis. Too many people try to save time by ignoring planning only to find that the model they built left out crucial variables or features. Proper planning should produce a good, solid model which can be used with few problems.

Issues that you should consider in planning include the following:

- What is the process you want to model?
- How do you plan to use the model? Will you use it only once, or many times? How generic should the model be?
- What are the key variables for the model? Which variables are fixed, which are dependent, and which do you want to manipulate in the analysis?

You should also consider how to model the process, given the limits of your spreadsheet program. I see many users who try to model a very long process--for example, a 5-year month-by-month financial plan--only to discover that the model is too large to fit in the main memory of their computer. Rather than modeling the entire 5 years, they could develop a one-year model that can be applied to any year and calculates starting values based on which year is being modeled.

Setup

Setup is the process of initially organizing the model on the computer. Here you create the spreadsheet and label the columns and rows. You also enter the formulas used to calculate values in the model.

If you are developing a generic model, it is sometimes a good idea to save it at this point--creating what is called a spreadsheet template. Some spreadsheet manufacturers and second-source publishers sell ready-made templates to model common processes such as real estate analysis, break-even analysis, and income tax calculation.

Input

The third function is input--entering the data to run your model. Input fits the template to your specific problem or situation. This is where you type in your constants and the initial values for your independent variables.

Calculation

Calculation is where you apply the formulas to the constants and the independent variables to calculate the dependent variables.

Calculation is the most rewarding part of spreadsheet analysis. Once you have seen the initial results, you can modify the independent variables and run the analysis again, or, if you wish, you can even modify the calculation formulas. This is an iterative process--you do it again and again until you get either the best possible answer to your problem or a range of answers that describe the results of various approaches.

You may wish to save or print out the results of several of these analyses. This brings us to the last two functions, formatting and output.

Formatting

Formatting is the process of organizing the results of your analysis for output. Some spreadsheet programs allow you to totally reorganize and summarize the results of your analysis in a report. Others print out portions or all of the spreadsheet as it appears on the display screen. Some programs can present the results of your analysis graphically.

Output

Output is the process of putting the formatted results of your analysis on paper or storing them in a computer file. The quality of your output is determined by your output devices. Spreadsheets and reports are best displayed using full-character printers, which give maximum print quality. Graphs and charts are best shown using plotters--these give the best graphics output. Dot matrix printers offer a compromise--they can print both tables and graphics. They are faster than full-character printers and plotters, but the quality of their output is somewhat lower.

TYPES OF SPREADSHEET PROGRAMS

Now let's look at the different kinds of financial analysis programs. A vast number of these programs are on the market, ranging in price from under $30 to more than $600. Their names include more permutations on the words calculate and plan than I ever dreamed possible.

The easiest way to deal with all of these programs is to categorize them. I categorize them in two ways--how generic they are and how they work.

Generic Versus System-Specific Programs

By generic, I mean how many different computers can use the program. My basic philosophy of computing states that unless there are overriding reasons to the contrary, you should always select software programs that are designed to run on as many different computers as possible. This allows you to upgrade different parts of your system without having to buy and learn to use new programs.

Accordingly, the first thing I look at in any program is whether it runs on a common operating system--say, CP/M or MS-DOS--or whether it is designed to run on a single computer and a unique operating system.

How the Programs Work

Next I look at how the programs work. I start by looking at the way a program is designed. There are basically two approaches.

One approach starts with the spreadsheet--a matrix of cells organized in rows and columns. When you start out, that's what you see on the screen. You put labels, numbers, and formulas in the cells. You locate yourself by cell--giving your position in terms of row and column numbers. This is a very visual format, and the easiest to use. To make a change, you just go to the specific cell, type in the change, and recalculate the dependent variables.

The second approach--called either the modeling language or the compiler approach--operates more like a computer program. You use an English-like language to define the matrix in terms of rows and columns. The cells have names rather than addresses. Once you have written your description of a model, the program creates a spreadsheet to show the model visually on the screen. This approach is less visual than the straight spreadsheet approach, but it allows you to use named variables in your calculations. The best of these programs are somewhat more powerful than spreadsheets because they allow more complex formulas. One problem with this approach is that if you want to make a change in a formula or modify the spreadsheet, you must return to the modeling language to make the change. This takes longer and is more complex than making a change with a straight spreadsheet program.

Next, I consider memory representation--how the program stores the spreadsheet data. Again, there are two approaches.

The most common approach is to keep the entire spreadsheet in the main memory of the computer. This provides immediate access to each cell and makes the program very fast--all of the data are immediately available to the computer. On the other hand, it limits the size of the spreadsheet you can use, particularly if you are going to run the program on an 8-bit computer, which typically can hold only about 300 cells. The newer 16-bit computers can control more memory, which gives them more cells, but again, the total number of cells available is determined by the particular computer configuration.

The second approach is to keep the spreadsheet in a working file that is stored partially in main memory and partially in external memory. This allows a much larger spreadsheet, but the response time is slower because cells have to be swapped between main and external memory.

Program Power

Finally, I look at how much power the program has--how many features and functions it has. By features, I mean the number of operations and options that the program offers for doing spreadsheets. By functions, I mean what other work the program will do besides spreadsheet analysis.

There is a lot of variation in features, primarily in the number of operations that the program provides. Some programs provide sophisticated calculations such as linear regressions and percentage increases. Others allow you to read information from one spreadsheet into another. This can be very useful if you are working with related spreadsheets. Some programs offer options in how the information is presented visually on the screen--for example, split screens and windows so that you can see different parts of the sheet at one time. You will find that extra features add to the cost of a program.

Some new programs--for example, CONTEXT MBA, Lotus 1-2-3, and Symphony--offer multiple functions such as spreadsheet analysis, data base management, graphics, text processing, and communications in a single program. The argument for these programs is that they enable you to do with one program what would otherwise take several. You only have to learn a single set of commands to perform work that formerly took several programs. The argument against these programs is that they are more difficult to learn, require considerably more main memory, and often offer less sophisticated functions than those you would find in programs focusing on a single function, such as spreadsheets or word processing.

A FEATURE ANALYSIS OF SPREADSHEETS

Now let's switch gears and look at the features you can expect to find in spreadsheet programs. I'll focus on commands, mathematical functions and operators, screen displays, and how commands are coded and entered into the computer.

Commands

Let's start with cursor control. You should be able to move the cursor from cell to cell--left, right, up, or down--to select a cell for input. You should also be able to move quickly to a specific cell by specifying an address, or home--the upper left corner of the spreadsheet.

When you reach a specific cell, you should be able to choose between entering text, a formula, or data (generally, not all three exist in compiler-type programs).

Editing commands should allow you to change the contents of any cell.

You should be able to delete a row of cells or a column of cells.

You should be able to clear or erase the contents of a specific cell, row, or column or of the entire spreadsheet.

You should be able to move a row or column of cells from one position to another.

You should be able to insert new rows and columns.

You should be able to change the format of the spreadsheet--to change the size or type of a row of cells.

You should be able to copy the contents of one cell in another or in a group of cells. If you are copying a formula, you should be able to change the labels of the cells automatically.

The lock command allows you to protect specific cells, rows, or columns against accidental erasure.

The calculate command tells the program to calculate the new value for a specific cell or for the entire spreadsheet. You use it to see the results of changes in either data or formulas in the spreadsheet. Some programs allow you to specify the order in which values are calculated. This can be very important in complex analyses.

You need several file commands. You need a command to save your spreadsheet--to make a permanent copy of the spreadsheet on your disk drive.

Remember, when you are working on the spreadsheet, it is only in a temporary working file. When you turn off the computer--or when there is a power failure--the computer "forgets" the contents of the spreadsheet. The file save command makes certain that you don't lose your work.

The file save command is very important. As a general rule, you should save a working file every 10 minutes or so. Most spreadsheets will allow you to save the working file and keep right on working.

You will also need a read file command. This allows you to read the contents of a permanent file into the working file. You would use this to modify an existing spreadsheet or to continue working on one that you did not complete in a previous session.

Some programs allow you to sort rows and columns to reorganize the spreadsheet.

Print commands are used to format and output results. The number and complexity of print commands depend on the program. Some programs are very simple and prompt you for all decisions. Others allow more control over output formatting but use more complex commands.

The quit command gets you out of the program, back to the operating system. This command may seem very basic, but it's one you have to know.

Menu displays give you a listing of the available commands. They come in various sizes and degrees of detail, depending on the program.

The help command provides more detailed information about commands than you can get in the menu. Some programs have a general help command that calls up a help file. Others allow you to ask for help on a specific command.

Some programs allow you to be working on one spreadsheet while you access information from other spreadsheets stored in permanent files. This can be very useful where you are working on a number of related spreadsheets.

Mathematical Functions and Operators

All spreadsheet programs offer a basic set of mathematical operations that you can use in your formulas. These include addition, subtraction, multiplication, division, summing, counting, and averaging.

Most spreadsheet programs also offer such operations as integer (taking the whole value), rounding (to closest whole value), absolute value, square root, and percent.

Some offer transcendental operations such as log, sine, cosine, tangent, arc sine, and arc tangent.

Some allow operations based on values in the spreadsheet--such as lookups, which look for a specific value stored in another location, or commands that calculate cell values by "growing" from a starting point at a fixed rate--for example, starting at A1 with a value of 10 and telling the program to successively calculate A2 through A10 by increasing each previous value by 10 percent. You can also select the largest or smallest value in a set of values.

Boolean operators allow you to make conditional statements using larger than, equal to, and smaller than as well as conditional operators such as AND, OR, NOT; and IF, THEN, ELSE.

Some programs provide complex operators for standard deviation, linear regression, depreciation, and the like.

Screen Displays

Spreadsheets are very visual programs, and a great deal of information is displayed on the screen. Most of the screen will probably be taken up with the spreadsheet itself--the number of rows and columns displayed depends on the program and their size. However, the screen should also show some other information, including the current cell address, current file name, remaining memory, command menu, and current mode.

Coding and Entering Commands

There are two approaches to the coding of commands for programs--the home key approach and the function key approach. (See the discussion in reading 6.)

Calcstar is the best example of the home key approach spreadsheet programs. Its commands are closely modeled after those used with WordStar--its word processor relative.

The function key approach assumes that you aren't comfortable with a keyboard and that you would prefer to have labeled keys dedicated to specific functions. This approach requires the availability of function keys on the keyboard. Some function keys control such things as cursor movement. Others have generic labels and can be custom configured by the program to perform certain functions.

Lotus 1-2-3 is an example of the function key approach. With function key codes, check very closely to see how they suit your needs. For example, the IBM personal computer does not have an enter key to the right of the keypad, where it should be. In addition, IBM put the cursor controls on the numeric keypad. You merely hit the shift key to switch from entering numbers to moving the cursor.

Programs that use these cursor controls can be very frustrating for people who like to use numeric keypads because it is very awkward to switch between entering numbers and moving the cursor.

ADD-ONS

As spreadsheet programs have become more popular, many software publishers have developed add-on products to supplement the power of the basic program.

Templates

Templates offer a predefined model and save you the time of creating one yourself. Generally, they provide all the row and column labels and formulas to calculate cell values. All you do is load the template, type in the constant data and the model assumptions, and watch it go.

You can find templates for all sorts of applications--for example, financial planning, real estate, income tax, and property management. Generally, independent software publishers create templates only for the most popular financial analysis packages, so if you are interested in templates, check out availability before you select your financial analysis package.

Learning Guides

Learning guides can help you learn how to use your program. They are available in print, as floppy disk tutorials, as audiotapes, and as videotapes. Print guides cost $10-$20. Floppy disk and audiotape tutorials cost $50-$100. Videotape tutorials cost $100-$200.

Support Programs

You should also consider programs that can support and augment a spreadsheet program.

Filing and data base management programs allow you to organize, save, and reuse the results of a particular financial analysis run. Some spreadsheet programs are designed so that they can interface with popular DBMS programs such as dBASE II.

Graphics programs allow you to display the results of your spreadsheet analysis visually. There are a number of graphics programs that will take the results of your spreadsheet analysis and display it for you in a variety of formats.

I must confess that I am particularly attracted to graphics output. It has been my experience that when you get a new technological toy, you flaunt it to excess.

Spreadsheets are no exception. There is an overwhelming temptation to share the results of every analysis with people and totally overwhelm them.

That's why graphics are important. A good graphics program can simplify the results of your spreadsheet so that they can be grasped very quickly. The more powerful graphics programs allow you to show the results of several spreadsheets simultaneously so that you can see the impact of different assumptions.

By itself, the spreadsheet is a very powerful analytic tool. Graphics programs can significantly enhance the power of that tool by giving you a more effective way to present results.

SELECTING A FINANCIAL ANALYSIS PROGRAM

Now that you know what spreadsheet programs are, how to use them, and some of their key features, how do you go about selecting one?

I recommend that you start with a little needs analysis. Ask yourself the following questions:

- What will you do with it?
- How much power do you really need?
- Which functions do you need?
- Do you need graphics?
- How much can you afford to spend?

You can use the answers to these questions to build a set of specifications to help you select candidate programs.

Start by looking at reviews and at articles and ads in the computer publications. Software directories offer a good way to identify a number of candidate programs.

Select several candidate programs for further analysis. I strongly recommend that you go with generic programs rather than with programs that are designed to work only on a specific machine. I also recommend that you look for de facto standard programs. These are programs that, by virtue of market acceptance, have become almost standards for the business. All other things being equal, I always buy de facto standard programs.

Once you have selected your candidate programs, you should compare them on a feature-by-feature basis.

Here are some things to look for:

1. **What information is displayed on the screen?** How many cells can you show at once? Can you display cells selectively?

    How easy is it to get the command menu on the screen?

    How easy is it to get help information on the screen?

2. **How easy is the program to use?** The answer to this question is pretty subjective and requires that you actually try the program out.

3. **The size problem.** How large a spreadsheet can you build on *your* computer in its present configuration? Is it possible to extend the size of the spreadsheet by adding memory?

4. **How does the program handle rounding?** Rounding is frequently a problem with spreadsheet programs. No matter how the numbers are displayed in the cells, they are stored using scientific notation. This means that the value stored generally has more precision--more decimal places--than is shown on the sheet. Operations using the numbers use the stored value, not the displayed one. What does that mean? Here's an example. Suppose you want to total the contents of three cells.

          1.22
          2.54
          5.60

    The sum should be 9.36, right?

    But a spreadsheet program may show 9.37. Why? Because the stored values may have one more digit and look like this:

          1.223
          2.544
          5.603

    The problem here is how the program does its rounding. I used to have great fun at computer shows making spreadsheet programs generate rounding errors. The moral of the story is to find out about rounding errors before you buy.

5. **Interaction between program and hardware**. This is a very subtle area, and it requires a lot of thought. Some programs are poorly designed and don't allow you to take full advantage of your computer. If you are used to using a 10-key pad, make certain that you find a program that will allow you to use it properly on your computer. If you are looking for a computer, make certain that the numeric keypad has an enter key and a minus key.

   In general, make certain that you try out the program on the same kind of computer that you plan to use. If the program uses function keys for commands, make certain that it can be properly installed on your computer.

6. **Documentation**. Documentation is a key issue. Good documentation should include the following:

   - a discussion of how the programs works
   - instructions on how to install the program on your machine
   - a tutorial to teach you how to use the program
   - several application examples
   - a reference guide to commands

7. **Copy policy**. Some manufacturers insist on protecting their programs so that you can't make copies of them. You absolutely must have several backup copies of any program to protect yourself. **Don't buy copy-protected software**.

8. **Support policy**. Does the publisher have a "help" line? How do you get upgrades? Is there a user's group or newsletter?

9. **Availability of add-ons**. Can you get templates to save you the time of planning and setting up common applications?

   Can the program interface with other support programs such as graphics and word processors so that you can use the results of your analysis with these programs?

   Are second-source tutorials available? Tutorials come in print, on floppy disks, on audiotape, and on videotape.

SUMMARY

Now let's quickly recap what we covered.

A spreadsheet program is a program that you use to model a financial problem or a decision process.

Computer spreadsheet programs take care of all the tedious mathematics of spreadsheet analysis and allow you to focus on planning your spreadsheet on varying assumptions about the process you are studying.

Using a spreadsheet involves six functions: planning, setup, input, calculation, formatting, and output.

There are two basic approaches to spreadsheet programs. One allows you to work directly in the spreadsheet; the other creates a spreadsheet based on a model you build in an English-like language.

Some programs require all cells to be in the main memory. Others give you a virtual memory by moving cells between the main memory and the disk drive.

All spreadsheets offer a variety of commands, operations, and features. Some use a home key approach for entering commands; others use function keys.

Despite their similarities, not all spreadsheets are alike. You must compare spreadsheets very closely on a feature-by-feature basis.

When in doubt, buy generic, de facto standard programs.

DATA BASE MANAGEMENT SYSTEMS

by Colin Mick[*]

A data base management system (DBMS) is a sophisticated program that is used to create, manage, and use a group of related files. In order to really understand what a DBMS is, we have to start with a few basic definitions.

A <u>data base</u> is a collection of stored information that has been organized for easy retrieval. The term <u>data base</u> is commonly used to refer to a collection of information stored in computer-readable form so that it can be used for a number of applications. A data base is composed of one or more files.

A <u>file</u> is a collection of information that is stored on the computer as an identifiable unit--generally under a single name. A file is composed of one or more records.

A <u>record</u> is a collection of information that is used to describe a single unit. A record is composed of one or more fields.

A <u>field</u> is a single unit of information. It contains one of three types of information: character data, numeric data, or logical data.

<u>Character data</u> are composed of keyboard symbols--letters, numbers, and punctuation marks.

<u>Numeric data</u> are numbers that are to be used for numeric calculation. (A number stored as character data cannot be used in calculations unless it is converted to numeric data first.)

<u>Logical data</u> are binary data that can have the value true or false. A DBMS has a set of software routines that allow you to

- define a file
- define the records that the file will store
- enter data into the records
- save the file

---

[*]Reprinted with permission from <u>The Financial Planner's Guide to Using a Personal Computer</u>, by Colin Mick and Jerry Ball (Homewood, Ill.: Dow Jones-Irwin, 1984). Copyright © 1984 by Dow Jones-Irwin.

- develop other files and join them into a data base
- add records
- change the file or record definitions
- search a file or data base for specific information
- define and create reports based on information in the files

DBMS programs are among the most complex software packages available. They might best be thought of as a kind of computer language that is designed specifically to work with interconnected files. They are not particularly easy to use. Originally they were designed to support applications programmers who developed custom applications software (for example, accounting packages, data bases). They can be effective tools for end users who have enough applications to justify their cost (both in cash and in the time required to learn how to use them effectively).

WHAT DO YOU DO WITH A DBMS?

You can use a DBMS to organize, store, and use any kind of information. The most common applications are building custom accounting systems and building data bases for organizing collections of complex information.

A Record Store

Here's an example. Assume that you own a record store and that you have decided to build a computer system to manage it.

To begin, you have an inventory of records, so you might start by building an inventory file.

Each record title in your store will be represented as a unique record in the inventory file. In addition to the title, you will need some other information--the name of the artist, the name of the record company, the record ID number, the price code, and the number of copies you have on hand. You might also want a unique inventory code--something like the ISBN numbers used for books. Each piece of information will be stored in a field. Notice that you will need character fields and numeric fields to store the information properly.

You will also need a file to keep track of your bills--your "accounts payable file" in accounting jargon. This file will contain records representing individual transactions. Each record will include the name or code of the supplier, the invoice number, the date of the invoice, and payment data--the date and number of the payment check.

You will need a third file to take care of your sales--an accounts receivable file. Here each record will represent a sales transaction. You will need fields for the date and the amount of the transaction. As long as we're working by computer, let's throw in several fields to hold the ID numbers of the items purchased so that you have the information you need to update your inventory file.

Next you will need some sort of payroll file. Here each record represents a payroll check and includes fields that contain the number of the employee, the amount paid, the taxes withheld, the date, and the check number.

These four files allow you to keep track of the daily business of running your record store, but for accurate control you need a program that periodically evaluates the contents of the files and figures out your overall status. In accounting, this is called a general ledger program. Such a program produces balance sheets that give your overall status and income statements that tell you whether you are making any money. These reports are produced from the data stored in the files.

A report is a compilation of information from the files in a data base. For example, at the end of each day you might want to total up the sales for the day. If you have the computer do this for you, it is a report. You might also want a daily inventory of the records in stock; this is also a report. You might want some other reports as well. For example, if you sell on credit, you could create a program that would examine your accounts receivable file to see who hasn't paid you and for how long. This is called an aged accounts report.

In addition to reports, you could also search the files for specific information. For example, you might want to know whether a particular record is in stock or what the status of a particular account is. This is called a query. A query goes to a file to find one or more specific pieces of information. Now you could buy a ready-made accounting package--you might even find one designed for record stores. The advantage of creating a custom package using a DBMS program is that it allows you to configure the software to your specific circumstances.

An Information File

Now let's take a look at a very different application. Suppose you have a collection of unorganized information--books, magazine articles, and the like. You could build a data base to organize the collection so that you could search for specific kinds of information.

To do this, you would have to store two kinds of data--a summary of the information itself and a set of key words or descriptors that describe the information. Later you could search the file for specific combinations of descriptors to locate information stored in it.

This is actually pretty simple, and you could do it with a filing program. However, a DBMS would also allow you to create an index to speed searching. An index is a different kind of file. Each record would contain a single descriptor and a list of all the records in the main file that contain this descriptor. This greatly speeds the search time because instead of searching all the records in the main file to look for the descriptor, you merely search the index file (which is considerably smaller). This example brings up an additional set of concepts that we should define.

Your main data file is a sequential file. This means that the records are stored in the order in which you input them. To search a sequential file, you start at the beginning and check each record until you find the appropriate one. How long it takes to find a specific record is determined by the position of that record in the file.

In contrast, a random access file allows you to move through a file on some basis other than position.

To use a random access file, you need an index file. An index file causes the main file to look as though it were organized according to the indexing variable. The index file contains the indexing terms and a set of pointers-- addresses of main file records that contain the indexing term stored in the record.

You can sort a file to rank it according to the contents of a specific field. When you do this to an index file, you create what is known as an inverted file.

Indexing terms or descriptors are generally called keys.

There are two approaches to data base management systems. Hierarchical systems maintain the relationships between data elements with sets, linked lists, and pointers. Each data element is tied to a higher-level data element and to one or more lower-level elements. Hierarchical systems are very efficient for storing data and can be searched very quickly. However, they tend to be cumbersome and difficult to use.

Relational systems are more straightforward. Data elements are stored in fields that are organized into records. This is a much simpler structure, one that is easy to work with and manipulate. More space is required to store data, but with the cost of memory dropping almost daily, this is becoming less of a problem.

HOW DO YOU USE IT?

Next let's look at the process of using a DBMS.

For simplicity, I break using a DBMS into five distinct functions or operations: planning, setup, input, modification, and use.

<u>Planning</u> is the most critical step. Here you analyze your problem and decide how to deal with it. You decide how many files you will need and what they will contain. Then you determine how the records for each file will look. In addition, you sketch out what kinds of reports you will need and figure out how they should look.

<u>Setup</u> is the process of defining the file(s) in your DBMS program. You spell out in great detail what each file will look like. You define the record for each file in terms of fields. The fields themselves are defined by name, type, and size.

<u>Input</u> is the process of keyboarding information into the files. Most DBMS programs let you design screens that guide input. The screens prompt you for specific information on a field-by-field basis and display the information as you enter it. Naturally, the screens are designed to make it easy to proof information as it is entered. Some systems allow you to move records to a permanent file as you enter them. Others have you enter new records in a holding file and then load them all into a permanent file with one command.

<u>Modification and update</u> are used to modify the structure of the file (which you defined in setup) or to modify data that have already been entered (during input).

You can use the system in two ways. First, you can generate reports using report formats defined during setup. You can add new report formats at any time. You can also search individual files to find specific information. You can identify specific information by its location (for example, by specifying a record number) or by its attributes (for example, by specifying all of the records that contain specified fields).

COMMANDS

Most DBMS programs have a very complex set of commands--as many as 100. This is really enough to qualify as a computer language. The commands are generally system specific, but here is an overview of what they will do.

9.5

File commands are used to create and manage individual files. You use them to define or modify file structures, to modify data in the files, to copy files, and to create new files by combining information from one or more existing files. For example, you could index one file by creating an index file from a single field, ordering the values in that field, and generating pointers to records associated with each value.

Data input commands are used to facilitate data entry. You use them to enter data field by field; to move the cursor to different characters, fields, and records; to clear fields; and to insert or delete characters, fields, and records. You also have commands for moving a completed record into permanent storage.

You look at files with display, search, and query commands. Display commands let you look at the file structure and at individual records. Search commands help you find specific files by specifying discrete position (by giving an address) or relative position (skip a specific number of records from current position). Query commands are used to locate specific records based on information contained in them. Most systems provide both relational and Boolean operators for building queries.

Report commands are used to design and format reports that the system will create on demand. A simple report might be the number of records in a file. A complex report might compile information from specified fields in several files, process it, and print it out already labeled and ready for distribution. Report commands are used to format reports, specify calculation formulas, and label results. Formulas are built using program operators (described below). You can also build procedures--multistep calculations that are stored in a library and called with a single name. (Some DBMS programs come with procedure libraries. You can also buy procedure libraries for the more popular DBMS programs such as dBASE II).

Operators and functions are the basic units out of which you build formulas and procedures. Any DBMS program should have all of the common mathematical operators ([+], [-], *, [/], (), sum), relational operators (greater than, less than, equal to), and logical operators (and, or, not, etc.). In addition, there should be a set of basic functions such as INT (integer truncation), RND (integer rounding), LEN (length of a field), ULC (uppercase-lowercase conversion), and functions designed to work on strings of characters.

ADD-ONS

The more popular DBMS programs, such as dBASE II, have a host of add-on products that can make them easier to use and extend their utility.

Templates are predefined applications that are already written and ready to go. All you do is modify them to suit your particular circumstances. You can find them for accounting packages, data bases, filing systems, and mailing programs.

Screen generators are utility programs that help you bring up a DBMS application more quickly.

Procedure libraries are collections of predefined functions and formulas that save you the trouble of developing and keyboarding them yourself.

Training aids help you learn how to use your DBMS more quickly. There are live seminars, printed manuals and guides, audiotapes, floppy disk-based tutorials, and videotape tutorials.

Graphics programs take the information from reports and portray it graphically to make it easier to understand. Some graphics programs interface directly with DBMS programs.

HOW TO SELECT A DBMS PROGRAM

The first thing to consider in selecting a DBMS is what you want to do with it. Do you want it to generate a specific application, or do you plan a variety of uses? Try to develop a set of generic specifications for your application. Here are some questions to consider:

- What is your maximum file size?
- How many files will you need?
- Will they be related?
- How many records will there be per file?
- How many fields will there be per record?
- How long will your records be?
- Will you need indexes? How many?
- How much numeric precision will you need?
- What kinds of reports will you need?
- How much use will you make of query features?

The answers to these questions should give you a reasonable set of specifications for what you need. Next go out and identify candidate programs. You can find them by looking at computer magazines and software directories and by talking to dealers and other users.

In looking at programs, you should examine the documentation and support very carefully. Ask yourself the following questions:

- How good is the documentation?
- What kind of support is provided by the dealer? By the publisher?
- Are second-source user aids available?
- Are add-on products available?
- Is there a user's group to which you can go for help?
- Are there any local consultants?

All other things being equal, I suggest that you go with dBASE II, which is the de facto standard DBMS program. It is definitely the most popular DBMS program on the market today. It has the most users, the greatest number of training aids, and the most add-on products. You are more likely to find help with dBASE II than with any other DBMS program on the market today.

However, dBASE II is not the solution to every problem. Some applications may require greater capacity or different features. If dBASE II won't do the job, then look for the program that best matches your specifications and is offered by a reputable software publisher. You will have to lean hard on other people here--your dealer, other users, and, if you can find one, a good consultant.

SUMMARY

A data base management program is a very sophisticated set of computer instructions that are designed to facilitate the development of file-based computer applications. Designed initially for programmers creating custom accounting programs, such programs are now being used in a variety of applications that require building and using information files.

A data base is an organized collection of files. A file is a collection of related information that is stored under a unique identification code. This information is stored in records consisting of one or more fields that hold specific units of information.

A report is a predefined summary of an analysis of information contained in one or more files. A query is a request for a specific piece of information defined in terms of information stored in record fields.

Sequential files store records serially. To locate a specific record, you must start at one end of the file and search to the other. A random access file allows you to go immediately to a specific record based on information contained in one or more fields. This is done by using inverted files, which index sequential files by ordering the values of a specific field and attaching pointers to them that contain the addresses of the records for each value.

There are five basic steps for using a DBMS: planning the application, setting up the data base structure, inputting the data, modifying the structure or updating data, and using the data base.

Because of its overwhelming popularity and the large number of products that simplify and extend its use, dBASE II is currently the best choice in a DBMS program.

DBMS programs are extremely complex and require considerable effort to master. The decision to use one should not be made lightly.

Here is a checklist of features you can use to compare DBMS programs:

- maximum number of fields per record
- maximum number of records per file
- maximum number of characters per field
- simultaneous editing of files
- selective editing of files
- perform calculations during update
- perform logical comparisons during update
- find the last record in a file
- find the previous record
- find the next record
- find a specific record
- merge data files
- append data files
- test input for whole numbers
- test for numeric input
- test for alpha (character) input
- standard file format that can be used by other programs
- availability of sample programs
- availability of second-source tutorials
- availability of templates

MAILING SUPPORT

by Colin Mick[*]

Mailing is a key part of any financial planner's operation. Two obvious applications are maintaining communication with existing clients and reaching out to prospective clients. Both applications require the development and maintenance of mailing lists (names, addresses, etc.) and the production of both general (no unique salutation) and specific (personal) letters. A good computer mailing program can help in these areas.

First, you can develop and maintain sophisticated mailing lists. You can sort these lists by zip code, city, or state. Some programs allow you to add descriptors to mailing labels so that you can search them on other attributes, such as participation in a particular offering.

Second, you can combine your mailing lists with text to produce "custom" letters. You can print the same letter to every addressee, or you can print the same basic information in all of the letters but vary specific elements within the body of each letter.

In addition to using a mailing program to print custom letters, you can use it to address envelopes or print mailing labels.

SOFTWARE OPTIONS

There are three kinds of software support mailing programs. You can use your word processing program in combination with a merge program; you can use a stand-alone mailing program; or you can build a custom mailing program using a DBMS package. Which approach is best for you depends on your particular circumstances.

A Word Processing Program with a Merge Program

If you already have a word processing program, the simplest way to run a mailing program is to use a mail merge program. Such programs operate with your word processing program to merge two files--your address file and a letter file--during printing.

---

[*]Reprinted with permission from The Financial Planner's Guide to Using a Personal Computer, by Colin Mick and Jerry Ball (Homewood, Ill.: Dow Jones-Irwin, 1984). Copyright © 1984 by Dow Jones-Irwin.

You can prepare the address list using your word processor, or you can develop it independently using a compatible address list program. Many of the more powerful word processing programs either have a mail merge function built in or offer it as an add-on option. Sort programs are available to sort your address files.

This is probably the cheapest approach, but it generally requires the most work to use.

A Mailing Program

A somewhat simpler approach is to use a stand-alone mailing program. Here one program does everything from handling input of addresses and letter text to sorting addresses and printing out letters, envelopes, and labels.

Mailing programs generally have fixed address formats, so it's a good idea to check the programs out carefully before you buy. The one I use, for example, limits the address to 3 lines of 22 characters each, plus city, state, and zip. It doesn't have room for a title (for example, president), and it requires some very creative abbreviations for organizational names. It also has problems with foreign addresses. Moreover, the length of the letter body is limited to about 35 lines.

These are all things you should check out when you look at mailing programs. You should also check out the editing functions (used during input of addresses and letter text) and the updating (the changing and purging of records). Don't forget zip codes--someday we may really have to start using nine-digit zip codes, and your mailing program had better support them.

A zip code index is a nice feature if you can find it. It allows a program to "learn" to associate city and state with a specific zip code. Once the program has learned a specific zip code, you only use the zip code; you don't have to type in the city and state. Some programs have a command that takes the address line from the last address. This can save a lot of typing when entering addresses with common street, city, or state names. Mailing programs should output letters, envelopes, and a variety of label formats.

This is the easiest approach to learn and use. It provides the highest concentration of mailing power, but it may be less flexible than a custom program developed from a DBMS package.

A DBMS Program

The third option is to build your own mailing program using a DBMS program. This approach requires the most effort, but it has some advantages in certain circumstances. For example, if you are already using a DBMS program to track your clients, it makes sense to adapt that program to use as a mailing program. A DBMS program might also be used to add data to the address record to indicate those programs in which your clients are participating. Then you could either search your address file to print out a letter to clients participating in a particular program or you could print out different letters to clients participating in different programs.

This approach can also be very easy to use, but it requires the most effort to put together. I certainly wouldn't buy a DBMS program for a mailing application that could be handled just as well with a stand-alone mailing program, but if you already have a DBMS package, this might be a good way to go. Mailing applications are quite simple to program, and many DBMS packages use them as applications examples in their documentation. You can also buy preprogrammed mailing application "templates" for use with many of the common DBMS packages.

MAILING SUPPORT

Plain white paper with a typed letterhead or stick-on address labels aren't going to cut it when you are trying to make a good impression on a customer. To have an effective mailing, you will need some way of moving letterhead paper and envelopes through your printer. There are two ways to do this.

One way is to purchase a sheet feeder for your printer. Sheet feeders automatically insert, position, and remove single sheets. They are available for most common high-end fully formed character printers, including those made by Diablo, NEC, and Qume. Some sheet feeders will hold two different types of paper so that you can print second sheets. Others can be adapted to feed envelopes. Sheet feeders are relatively expensive--they generally cost more than $1,000--and they require both mechanical and electronic interface with your printer.

The other way is to have custom letterheads and envelopes printed on continuous form so that they can be moved through your printer on a forms tractor. Several computer supply firms will print letterheads on continuous form bond paper with very fine perforations. Most of the Classic Laid finishes as well as 25 percent rag bond are available in continuous form. The perforations on these forms are so fine that when the forms are burst, it is very difficult to tell that a letter was printed on a computer printer. The prices vary from around $60-$100 per 1,000 sheets, depending on the firm, the type of paper, and the size of your order. You can get the same papers unprinted for custom-produced multipage documents. You can also get matching envelopes on continuous form.

Personally, I prefer continuous form paper and a tractor feeder over sheet feeders. Tractor feeders are simple and trouble free, and I can buy a lot of continuous form paper and envelopes for the price of a sheet feeder. Also, with continuous forms I can print on any of my printers.

THE PREPARATION AND USE
OF PERSONAL FINANCIAL STATEMENTS

by Burton T. Beam, Jr., and William J. Ruckstuhl*

Many persons--either from a formal study of accounting or from their personal business experiences--realize the importance of accounting-based financial information for business decision-making purposes. This form of accounting emphasizes financial accounting and involves the preparation of financial statements, such as balance sheets and income statements, for reporting to outsiders--including stockholders, current and potential creditors, and regulatory officials. For many business purposes, these financial statements must be based on generally accepted accounting principles (GAAP). In addition to the reports for outsiders, another segment of accounting, managerial accounting, is devoted to the preparation of financial reports, such as budgets and cash-flow statements, for internal use. These statements and reports are planning and control tools for the business. Although managerial-accounting statements and reports are based on the same set of data used to prepare financial reports, they may take any form that is useful to the user.

The preparation of organized financial information is equally important for individuals. Like businesses, individuals must often prepare financial information for outsiders. Banks and other lending institutions will rarely make a loan without first analyzing an individual's current financial position and future ability to repay the loan. State election officials may require a person to disclose certain financial information before that person can run for office.

However, the primary use of financial information in personal financial planning is for internal purposes in the analysis, planning, and control of ongoing personal financial decisions, whether conducted by the individual alone or with the assistance of a financial planner. The focus of this reading is on financial statements useful for such internal purposes. It is difficult, if not

---

*Burton T. Beam, Jr., CLU, CPCU, is associate professor of insurance at The American College.

William J. Ruckstuhl, CLU, ChFC, is assistant professor of finance at The American College.

impossible, to identify financial objectives and formulate strategies for their achievement without knowing a client's current financial situation and resources. In addition, the ongoing analysis of personal financial information is crucial in monitoring whether financial objectives are being achieved.

THE PREPARATION OF PERSONAL FINANCIAL STATEMENTS

The two primary financial statements used in personal financial planning are the financial position statement[1] (often referred to as a personal balance sheet) and the cash-management statement[2] (often referred to as a personal income statement). Before each is discussed in greater detail, a few general comments concerning financial statements are in order.

While it is common to see financial statements that have been prepared only at the end of a calendar or fiscal year, both the timing and frequency of financial statements often vary. When a lending institution needs personal financial information for loan purposes, it will usually require that the information be prepared as of the date of the loan application. Similarly, a financial planner needs financial information at the time the planning process begins and at the time of each subsequent review of a client's financial plan. If reviews take place every 6 months, it will be necessary to prepare updated personal financial statements at these same intervals. In other words, personal financial statements are not prepared at arbitrary points in time, but rather at those times when the information is needed for the financial planning process.

The financial position statement and the cash-management statement result from what has occurred in the past. For purposes of personal financial planning, it is also necessary to prepare pro forma (or projected) financial statements that illustrate future financial statements if certain activities are implemented under specified assumptions. At some later time actual financial statements can then be compared with past projections to see if the results of a financial plan are achieving a client's objectives.

Financial Position Statement — BALANCE SHEET

The financial position statement shows an individual's (or family's) wealth at a certain point in time. It

---

1. See pages 35 and 36 of the Financial and Estate Planning Fact Finder following the reading that begins on page 4.1.

2. See page 7 of the Financial and Estate Planning Fact Finder.

reflects the results of the individual's past financial activities and contains three basic classifications: assets, liabilities, and net worth. The items that make up assets and liabilities are often grouped into subclassifications that better enable the financial planner to analyze the component parts of the client's total financial situation and to evaluate the mix of assets in relation to the client's objectives.

Assets

Assets are items owned by the clients. It is immaterial whether the item was purchased for cash, whether its purchase is being financed by borrowing, or whether it was received as a gift or inheritance. Items that are not owned by the client, such as rented apartments or leased automobiles, are not shown as assets.

It is common practice for personal financial statements to show assets at their current fair market values. These values may vary considerably from the original purchase prices. (This practice is in contrast to the requirement that businesses prepare basic financial statements on the basis of adjusted historical costs.)

At a minimum, assets should be subdivided into two categories: financial assets and personal (or nonfinancial) assets. However, the financial position statement in the fact finder uses three major categories of assets by separating total assets into (1) cash and near-cash equivalents, (2) other financial assets, and (3) personal assets. Other financial assets are sometimes further subdivided, possibly on the basis of their relative liquidity, income characteristics, or growth characteristics.

Liabilities

Liabilities are the debts of the client. While the financial position statement in the fact finder does not separate liabilities into major subcategories, it is not unusual to see liabilities grouped by the time period in which they must be repaid. For example, the statement might show subtotals for short-term liabilities (due in one year or less), intermediate-term liabilities (due in one to five years), and long-term liabilities (due in more than five years).

The liability section of the financial position statement should show all liabilities as of the date of the statement--even if a formal bill has not been received. This practice may require the client to make estimates for such items as taxes due, utility charges owed, and credit-card obligations.

Net Worth

Net worth measures the client's wealth or equity at the date of the financial position statement. It is equal to the client's total assets less his or her total liabilities. In other words, it is what would be left over if all the client's assets were sold at their fair market values and all debts were paid. If a client has a negative net worth, the client is considered to be technically bankrupt.

It is important to note that net worth is not the same as total cash or total assets. It is the difference between assets and liabilities. Note also that the size of a client's net worth reveals little about the nature of the assets or liabilities. A client with a large net worth may have all his or her assets tied up in nonincome-producing assets such as homes, automobiles, and other personal possessions. On the other hand, a client with a modest net worth may hold most assets in the form of financial assets that may be generating income, capital appreciation, or both.

A client's net worth may increase or decrease during a period of time. Other things being equal, a client's net worth will be increased by any one of the following:

- appreciation in the value of assets
- use of a portion of current income to increase ownership of cash, cash equivalents, other financial assets, real estate, or personal assets
- the addition of assets through gifts or inheritances
- a decrease in liabilities through forgiveness or repayment at a discount

The Format of the Financial Position Statement

Obviously, any financial statement should be in a format that is understandable, and some degree of uniformity is desirable. However, the actual format is really secondary to the information being both accurate and usable. It should be noted that the format of a financial position statement (and also a cash-management statement) is often determined by the software system used by the financial planner for analyzing data and producing reports.

Traditionally financial position statements have been presented in two columns--one containing assets, the other containing liabilities and net worth. The term balance sheet is derived from the fact that these two sides must balance. That is,

Total assets = total liabilities + net worth

A client's financial position statement might look like table 1 as follows:

TABLE 1

Financial Position Statement for Mr. & Mrs. John Client as of December 198X

ASSETS		LIABILITIES AND NET WORTH	
Cash, Near-Cash Equivalents		**Liabilities**	
Cash	$ 2,500	Credit-card balances	$ 500
Money market fund	25,000	Automobile loan	6,500
Life insurance cash value	8,000	Mortgage loan	41,000
Subtotal	$35,500	Total liabilities	$ 48,000
Other Financial Assets			
Mutual funds	$10,000		
Vested pension benefits	15,000	Net Worth	$248,500
Subtotal	$25,000		
Personal Assets			
Residence	$170,000		
Automobiles	16,000		
Household furnishings/ personal possessions	50,000		
Subtotal	$236,000		
TOTAL ASSETS	$296,500	TOTAL LIABILITIES AND NET WORTH	$296,500

In recent years it has become more common in personal financial planning to see a financial position statement presented in a single-column format as used in the fact finder and presented on the following pages. The major advantage of the single-column format is that it facilitates the projection of financial position statements and the comparison of consecutive statements over time.

Cash-Management Statement — Income Statement

A cash-management statement shows the cash inflows (or income) that were received by the client and the cash outflows (or expenditures) that were made during some past time period, usually the previous year. As such, a cash-management statement is actually a modified combination of an income statement and a cash-flow statement that are normally prepared for businesses.

MR. & MRS. JOHN CLIENT, DECEMBER 198X

FINANCIAL POSITION STATEMENT

Assets

Cash, Near-Cash Equivalents	Current Value	Assumptions	19___	19___	19___
Checking accounts/cash	$2,500				
Savings accounts					
Money-market funds	25,000				
Treasury bills					
Commercial paper					
Short-term CDs					
Life insurance, cash value	8,000				
Life insurance, accumulated dividends					
Savings bonds					
Other (specify)					
Subtotal	$35,500				

Other Financial Assets

	Current Value	Assumptions	19___	19___	19___
U.S. government bonds					
Municipal bonds					
Corporate bonds					
Preferred stock					
Common stock					
Nonmarketable securities					
Warrants and options					
Mutual funds	$10,000				
Investment real estate					
Long-term CDs					
Vested retirement benefits	15,000				
Annuities					
HR-10 plan (Keogh)					
Individual retirement acct. (IRA)					
Mortgages owned					
Land contracts					
Limited partnership units					
Interest(s) in trust(s)					
Receivables					
Patents, copyrights, royalties					
Value of business interest					
Other (specify)					
Subtotal	$25,000				

© 1984 The American College

11.6

FINANCIAL POSITION STATEMENT (continued)

Assets (continued)

Personal Assets	Current Value	Assumptions	19___	19___	19___
Personal residence	$170,000				
Seasonal residence					
Automobile(s)	16,000				
Recreation vehicles					
Household furnishings	50,000				
Boats					
Jewelry/furs					
Collections					
Hobby equipment					
Other (specify)					
Subtotal	$236,000				
Total assets	$296,500				

Liabilities

	Current Value	Assumptions	19___	19___	19___
Charge accts./credit cards	$ 500				
Family/personal loans	6,500				
Margin/bank/life ins. loans					
Income taxes (fed., state, local)					
Property taxes					
Investment liabilities					
Mortgage(s)	41,000				
Child support					
Alimony					
Other (specify)					
Other (specify)					
Other (specify)					
Other (specify)					
Total liabilities	$ 48,000				

Net Worth

	Current Value	Assumptions	19___	19___	19___
Total assets minus total liabilities	$248,500				

11.7

Income

For purposes of a cash-management statement (as distinct from tax purposes), income includes such inflows as salary, self-employment income, interest received, investment income, alimony received, borrowed funds, and proceeds from the sale of assets.

Expenditures

Expenditures are the uses of income. They can be either fixed or discretionary. Fixed expenditures are those that are essential, will continue over the long run, or arise from contractual commitments. These include such items as housing, food, clothing, taxes, insurance premiums, and debt repayment. Discretionary expenditures are those that can be postponed at any time. These include such items as contributions, travel, savings, and investments.

It should be noted that while fixed expenditures may represent essential items, a client generally has some control over the amount of some of these expenditures, even in the short run. For example, the purchase of clothing can often be postponed or the client can economize on food bills. For this reason, these items are sometimes shown as discretionary expenditures on cash-management statements.

Net Income

The final item on a cash-management statement is net income. It is the difference between total sources of cash and all cash expenditures for a specific time period. If all income were received in cash and all expenditures were made in cash, then net income would be equal to the change in the client's cash position for the period. If income exceeded expenditures, the client would have increased his or her cash holdings; if expenditures exceeded income, the client would have decreased cash holdings.

The Format of a Cash-Management Statement

There is more variation in the format of a cash-management statement than in the format of a financial position statement. For example, income may be figured net of taxes, rather than showing taxes as a fixed-expenditure item. Savings and investments may not be treated as discretionary expenditures, but rather may be viewed as the residual amount after all other expenditures are subtracted from income. The actual format used will be that which is most useful to both the client and the financial planner. For purposes of this reading, the format used in the fact finder will be followed. A client's cash-management statement using this format is shown on the following page.

MR. & MRS. JOHN CLIENT, DECEMBER 198X

CASH-MANAGEMENT STATEMENT

Annual Income

	Current Yr. 19 8X	Projections for Subsequent Years				
		Assumptions	19__	19__	19__	19__
Salary, bonus, etc.	$50,000					
Income as business owner (self-employment)	10,000					
Real estate rental						
Dividends						
Investments	500					
Close corporation stock						
Interest income	2,000					
Investments						
Savings accts., CDs						
Loans, notes, etc.						
Trust income						
Life insurance settlement options						
Child support/alimony						
Other sources (specify) CAPITAL GAINS	100					
Total annual income	$62,600					

Annual Expenditures: Fixed

Housing (mortgage/rent)	$7,000					
Utilities and telephone	1,200					
Food	7,000					
Clothing and cleaning	5,000					
Income and social security taxes	17,000					
Property taxes	2,500					
Transportation (auto/commuting)	2,000					
Medical/dental/drugs/health insurance	1,000					
Debt repayment	3,000					
House upkeep/repairs/maintenance	1,000					
Life, property and liability insurance	1,000					
Child support/alimony						
Current education expenses						
Total fixed expenses	$47,700					

Annual Expenditures: Discretionary

Recreation/entertainment/travel	$8,000					
Contributions/gifts	2,000					
Household furnishings	1,000					
Education fund						
Savings	1,500					
Investments	2,000					
Other (specify)						
Total discretionary expenses	$14,500					
Total annual expenditures	$62,200					
Net income (total annual income minus total annual expenditures)	$400					

1984 The American College

THE USE OF PERSONAL FINANCIAL STATEMENTS

As mentioned previously, personal financial statements can be used as an aid in (1) identifying financial objectives and formulating the strategies for their achievement and (2) monitoring whether these financial objectives are being achieved.

Identifying Financial Objectives and Formulating Strategies

Perhaps an example would best demonstrate how financial statements can aid in identifying realistic financial objectives and formulating strategies for a client. Assume you are approached by the couple whose financial statements were shown previously in this reading. The husband, aged 51, is the controller of a small manufacturing firm and has an annual salary of $50,000. The wife, aged 50, earns $10,000 as a part-time freelance editor. They live comfortably on their relatively high joint income, but the majority of their savings and investments over the years have been liquidated to send three children to expensive private colleges. They would like to retire when the husband reaches age 62 with an income that will enable them to maintain their current life-style. However, they realize that their social security benefits and the husband's retirement benefits will not be adequate to meet this objective.

In analyzing their latest financial position statement, you notice that, with the exception of their home ownership and life insurance cash values, they are not using tax-advantaged savings or investments. Consequently their income tax burden is relatively high. After considerable discussion, you and the clients determine that an additional objective should be the minimization of income taxes.

You also notice that their savings and investments (other than home equity) consist primarily of $25,000 in a money market fund, with smaller amounts in a mutual fund and in life insurance cash values. In addition, during the last year they added about 6 percent of their gross income to additional savings and investments. You estimate that, with inflation, they will need $260,000 in savings and investments (other than home equity) by the time the husband reaches age 62. After extensive calculations you have determined that if current interest rates remain stable and if their current level of contributions to the money market fund and the mutual fund continues, they will accumulate only $120,000 in savings and investments by the planned retirement date. Thus there is a shortfall of $140,000. What can be done?

11.10

The options are many and varied. The assets of the clients could be repositioned so that they would generate a higher yield. For example, a large part of the money market fund might be liquidated and used to purchase a growth mutual fund. If such a repositioning were appropriate, it would of course need to be consistent with the risk profiles of the clients. The clients might also consider borrowing the life insurance cash values and investing the proceeds to yield a higher return than the interest rate on the policy loan. In addition, the clients could put a portion of their assets into tax-advantaged investments, or they could consider the use of an IRA. The wife could also establish a Keogh plan on the basis of her self-employment income. This would lower their taxes and thereby provide additional funds for savings and investment. Since the husband participates in a pension plan with his employer, the clients cannot place tax-deferred principal into an IRA. However, since interest earnings are tax deferred until withdrawn during retirement, an IRA could be attractive. As a final example, the clients might consider selling their home and buying a smaller (and presumably less expensive) home now that their children are grown. This option would either free some of the home equity for alternative investments or, if the equity were totally invested in the new home, might reduce or eliminate a large portion of their monthly housing costs.

Another option would be for the clients to reduce current consumption and increase their level of saving and investment. The potential sources for this increase can be ascertained by analyzing the clients' cash-management statement. For example, you notice that $8,000 was spent on recreation and travel last year, and upon further questioning determine that the clients, who like to travel, take two expensive vacations each year. Perhaps the clients will be willing to take somewhat less frequent or less expensive vacations. Maybe the clients can also reduce expenditures by eating out less frequently, economizing on clothing, or postponing the planned purchase of additional personal assets, such as a new car.

Depending upon the attitudes of the clients, one of the previous options or some combination of two or more options may enable the clients to meet their stated retirement objective. However, what if the clients are averse to riskier investments and are unwilling to reduce current consumption? Then the clients must modify their objective for retirement. Perhaps this modification will be in the form of accepting the fact that they will have to adjust their life-style downward if they retire when the husband reaches age 62; perhaps it will be in the form of accepting the fact that retirement will have to be postponed.

Monitoring Financial Objectives

Assume that after lengthy counseling sessions with the clients, it has been agreed that their objectives can be met by repositioning assets and making additional annual contributions to savings and investments. Some of the funds will come from tax savings by making the maximum contributions to the Keogh plan. The remainder will come from increases in income and decreases in expenditures, particularly travel. The anticipated results of these actions can be shown through pro forma financial statements. In effect, the pro forma cash-management statement becomes a financial plan for the clients. These projected statements can then be compared with actual results to see if the clients are staying on track.

Assume that you contact the clients after one year for a review of their financial plan. At that time you compare their pro forma financial results with the actual financial results for the year. It is also helpful to compare these results with the previous financial results. These comparisons are shown on the work sheets on pages 10.14 and 10.15.

Clearly, financial performance has not gone entirely as planned, particularly with regard to the other financial assets. Is it because the clients have not followed the plan you worked out together? Not necessarily. For example, the stock market may have declined, causing the mutual funds, IRAs, and Keogh plan to decrease in value. For a one-year period, such a fluctuation in the market may not be of great concern. In other years the market may rebound. To fully determine the causes of the differences between plans and results, it is also necessary to examine the pro forma and actual cash-management statements for the year, which are shown on page 10.16.

From these statements it can be seen that the clients liquidated $10,000 of the money market fund and used it, along with other contributions, for IRAs, a Keogh plan, and a substantial contribution to the mutual fund. However, the mutual fund contributions were $3,400 less than projected. In addition, the clients' cash holdings also decreased by $500. Therefore a substantial portion of the less-than-projected net worth has resulted from the clients' failure to follow through with their financial plan. The cash-management statement shows that the major causes of this difference arose from overestimated income and a large increase in house upkeep (a new furnace was needed). Whatever the reasons, however, it will be necessary for the clients to either alter their financial objectives or bring their future financial performance in line with their objectives.

CONCLUSION

This reading has shown how personal financial statements are prepared and may be used in personal financial planning. The example illustrating the use of these statements is actually quite simplistic in that the clients have a small number of financial objectives that are achievable within their resources. In the next reading you will become aware that comprehensive financial planning usually encompasses a much broader range of financial objectives.

MR. + MRS. JOHN CLIENT, DECEMBER 198Y

FINANCIAL POSITION STATEMENT

Assets	ACTUAL DEC. 198X Current Value	Projections for Subsequent Years			
		Assumptions	PRO FORMA DEC. 19 8Y	ACTUAL DEC. 19 8Y	19___
Cash, Near-Cash Equivalents					
Checking accounts/cash	$ 2,500		$ 2,500	$ 2,000	
Savings accounts					
Money-market funds	25,000	MOVE $10K TO MUT. FD. /IRA/ KEOGH	16,200	16,200	
Treasury bills					
Commercial paper					
Short-term CDs					
Life insurance, cash value	8,000		8,500	8,500	
Life insurance, accumulated dividends					
Savings bonds					
Other (specify)					
Subtotal	$35,500		$27,200	$26,700	
Other Financial Assets					
U.S. government bonds					
Municipal bonds					
Corporate bonds					
Preferred stock					
Common stock					
Nonmarketable securities					
Warrants and options					
Mutual funds	$10,000		$27,000	$21,000	
Investment real estate					
Long-term CDs					
Vested retirement benefits	15,000		17,000	17,000	
Annuities					
HR-10 plan (Keogh)		NEW	2,100	2,000	
Individual retirement acct. (IRA)		NEW	4,000	3,500	
Mortgages owned					
Land contracts					
Limited partnership units					
Interest(s) in trust(s)					
Receivables					
Patents, copyrights, royalties					
Value of business interest					
Other (specify)					
Subtotal	$25,000		$50,100	$43,500	

© 1984 The American College

11.14

FINANCIAL POSITION STATEMENT (continued)

Assets (continued)	ACTUAL DEC. 198X Current Value	Projections for Subsequent Years			
Personal Assets		Assumptions	PRO FORMA DEC 19 8Y	ACTUAL DEC 19 8Y	19___
Personal residence	$170,000		$180,000	$180,000	
Personal residence					
Automobile(s)	16,000		14,500	13,000	
Recreation vehicles					
Household furnishings	50,000		52,000	52,000	
Arts					
Jewelry/furs					
Collections					
Hobby equipment					
Other (specify)					
Subtotal	$236,000		$246,500	$245,000	
Total assets	$296,500		$323,800	$315,200	

Liabilities					
Charge accts./credit cards	$ 500		$ 500	$ 600	
Family/personal loans	6,500		4,500	4,500	
Margin/bank/life ins. loans					
Income taxes (fed., state, local)					
Property taxes					
Investment liabilities					
Mortgage(s)	41,000		38,000	38,000	
Child support					
Alimony					
Other (specify)					
Other (specify)					
Other (specify)					
Other (specify)					
Total liabilities	$ 48,000		$ 43,000	$ 43,100	

Net Worth					
Total assets minus total liabilities	$248,500		$280,800	$272,100	

The American College

11.15

MR. +MRS. JOHN CLIENT, DECEMBER 198X

CASH-MANAGEMENT STATEMENT

Annual Income

	ACTUAL DEC. 198X Current Yr. 19___	Assumptions	PRO FORMA, DEC. 198Y 19___	ACTUAL, DEC. 198Y 19___	19___	19___
Salary, bonus, etc.	$50,000		$54,000	$53,000		
Income as business owner (self-employment)	10,000		11,000	10,500		
Real estate rental						
Dividends						
Investments	500		1,100	1,000		
Close corporation stock						
Interest income	2,000		1,200	1,200		
Investments						
Savings accts., CDs						
Loans, notes, etc.						
Trust income						
Life insurance settlement options						
~~Child support/alimony~~ OTHER - MONEY MKT FUND PARTIAL LIQUIDATION			10,000	10,000		
Other sources (specify) CAPITAL GAINS	100		200	200		
Total annual income	$62,600		$77,500	$75,900		

Annual Expenditures: Fixed

Housing (mortgage/rent)	$7,000		$7,000	$7,000		
Utilities and telephone	1,200		1,300	1,700		
Food	7,000		7,000	7,400		
Clothing and cleaning	5,000		5,000	5,200		
Income and social security taxes	17,000		15,000	14,500		
Property taxes	2,500		2,600	2,800		
Transportation (auto/commuting)	2,000		2,200	2,500		
Medical/dental/drugs/health insurance	1,000		1,200	1,100		
Debt repayment	3,000		3,000	3,000		
House upkeep/repairs/maintenance	1,000		1,200	2,500		
Life, property and liability insurance	1,000		1,000	1,000		
Child support/alimony						
Current education expenses						
Total fixed expenses	$47,700		$46,500	$48,700		

Annual Expenditures: Discretionary

Recreation/entertainment/travel	$8,000		$6,000	$6,200		
Contributions/gifts	2,000		2,200	2,300		
Household furnishings	1,000		1,200	1,000		
~~Education fund~~ CONTRIBS: IRA/KEOGH			5,600	5,600		
Savings	1,500*		1,200*	1,200*		
Investments	2,000†		14,800†	11,400†		
Other (specify)						
Total discretionary expenses	$14,500		$31,000	$27,700		
Total annual expenditures	$62,200		$77,500	$76,400		
Net income (total annual income minus total annual expenditures)	$400		0	($500)		

© 1984 The American College
*INCLUDES REINVESTMENT OF INTEREST INCOME.
†INCLUDES REINVESTMENT OF DIVIDENDS + CAPITAL GAINS.

11.16

SETTING YOUR OBJECTIVES*

by G. Victor Hallman and Jerry S. Rosenbloom

Since personal financial planning is concerned primarily with helping people meet their objectives, the nature of those objectives and the ways they can be met are of critical importance in the planning process. A problem defined and broken down into its component parts frequently is half solved. In this reading, we shall analyze the financial objectives common to most people and outline briefly the sources available to help meet these objectives.

IMPORTANCE OF SETTING OBJECTIVES

As a general principle, it is desirable to formulate and then state your objectives as explicitly as possible. This can have several advantages. First, it forces you to think through exactly what your financial objectives are. Second, by doing this you are less likely to overlook some objectives while concentrating unduly on others. Third, when you carefully define your objectives, you may see solutions that had been overlooked before. You also are less likely to be sidetracked by persuasive sales presentations into actions that run counter to your long-range planning. Finally, the explicit determination of your financial objectives establishes a rational basis for you to take appropriate action to realize those objectives.

Once established, a person's financial objectives do not remain static. What may be entirely appropriate for a young married man with small children may prove quite inappropriate for an executive with college-age children or for a husband and wife approaching retirement.

HOW TO ORGANIZE YOUR OBJECTIVES

While the emphasis on particular objectives will change over a family's life cycle, the following classification system of personal financial objectives provides a systematic way for identifying your specific objectives and needs. It is used as a framework for total [comprehensive] financial planning.

*Reprinted with permission from Personal Financial Planning, 3d ed., revised by G. Victor Hallman and Jerry S. Rosenbloom (New York: McGraw-Hill Book Co., 1985), 17-35. Copyright © 1985 by McGraw-Hill.

Protection against Personal Risks

This category recognizes the desire of most people to protect themselves and their families against the risks they face in everyday life. These risks can arise from the possibility of premature death, disability, large medical expenses, loss of their property from various perils, liability they may have to others, and unemployment.

Premature Death

A major objective of most people is to protect their dependents from the financial consequences of their deaths. Some people also are concerned with the impact of their deaths on their business affairs. At this point, let us briefly note the various financial losses that may result from a person's death.

Loss of the deceased's future earning power that would have been available for the benefit of his or her surviving dependents. Most families live on the earned income of the husband or husband and wife combined. The death of an income earner results in the loss of his or her future earnings from the date of death until he or she would have retired or otherwise left the labor force. For most families, this represents a potentially catastrophic loss and usually is the most important financial loss arising out of a person's premature death.

Costs and other obligations arising at death. Certain obligations are either created or tend to come due at a person's death. Perhaps the most important of these are funeral and burial expenses, cost of settlement and administration of the deceased's estate, and any federal estate and/or state death taxes that may be due. The deceased's estate also owes the federal income tax on his or her income during the year of his or her death.

In addition to the costs created by death itself, there often are obligations that tend to come due at death. Most people have balances on charge accounts, credit cards, and other personal debts that their estate must pay in the event of their death. In addition, many people have larger debts outstanding that they may want to be paid at their death. Perhaps the most typical would be the balance due on any mortgages on their homes. While there may be valid reasons why a family would decide not to pay off such a mortgage note after a breadwinner's death, many persons planning their affairs like to think that their families at least would be able to pay off all their debts and thus would not "inherit a mortgage."

Increased expenses for the family. The death of certain family members, especially the wife and mother, results in increased expenses for the family to replace the economic functions she performed as homemaker. This potential loss frequently is overlooked, and yet it can be considerable. Another increasingly significant factor is that in a great many families today, the wife is an important income earner, and her premature death results in the loss of her present and/or future earning power in the outside job market.

Loss of tax advantages. In some cases, the death of a family member can result in substantially increased taxation for the survivors. This results largely from the loss of income, estate, and gift tax advantages accorded to married persons under our tax laws. Generally, the tax benefit most discussed in this regard is the potential loss of the federal estate tax marital deduction on a spouse's death.

Loss of business values because of an owner's or key person's death. When the owner or one of the owners of a business that can be called "closely held" (that is, a sole proprietor, a partner in most partnerships, or a stockholder in many smaller corporations with only a few stockholders who actively run the business) dies, the business may die with him or suffer considerable loss in value. Those potential losses in business values are directly related to the owners' personal financial planning because such closely held business interests frequently constitute the major part of the owners' estates.

Many businesses also have certain key employees, whether owners or not, whose premature death can cause considerable financial loss to the business until they can be replaced.

Sources of Protection against Premature Death

Various kinds of death benefits may be available to a deceased person's family. They are shown here in outline form to give an overview of the planning devices that may be available to meet this important risk.

1. Life insurance
    a. Individual life insurance purchased by the insured, his or her family, or others
    b. Group life insurance
        (1) Through the insured's employer or business
        (2) Through an association group plan provided through a professional association, fraternal association, or similar group
    c. Credit life insurance payable to a creditor of the insured person to pay off a debt
2. Social security survivors' benefits
3. Other government benefits
4. Death benefits under private pension plans

5. Death benefits under deferred profit-sharing plans
6. Death benefits under tax-sheltered annuity (TSA) plans, plans for the self-employed (HR-10 plans), individual retirement account or annuity (IRA) plans, nonqualified deferred compensation plans, personal annuity contracts, and the like
7. Informal employer death benefits or salary-continuation plans
8. Proceeds from the sale of business interests under insured buy-sell agreements or otherwise
9. All other assets and income available to the family after a person's death

Disability Income Losses

Another major objective of most people should be to protect themselves and their dependents from financial losses arising out of their disability, either total and temporary or total and permanent. Disability, particularly total and permanent disability, is a serious risk faced by almost everyone. Yet, surprisingly, it is often neglected in financial planning.

Actually, the probability that someone will suffer a reasonably long-term disability (90 days or more) prior to age 65 is considerably greater than the probability of death at those ages. For example, the data below show that the probability of such a long-term disability at age 32 is about 6½ times the probability of death at that age. This is something for the young family man and woman to think about.

Attained Age	Probability of Disability of 90 Days or More per 1,000 Lives	Probability of Death per 1,000 Lives	Probability of Disability as a Multiple of Probability of Death
22	6.64	0.89	7.46
32	7.78	1.18	6.59
42	12.57	2.95	4.26
52	22.39	8.21	2.73
62	44.27	21.12	2.10

The financial losses from disability generally parallel those resulting from death. An important difference from the consumer's viewpoint, however, is that there is a wide range of possible durations of total disability--from only a week or so to the ultimate, personal catastrophe of total and permanent disability. Thus, a person must recognize in personal financial planning that he or she could become disabled for a variety of durations--from a few days to the rest of his or her life. Virtually all experts agree, however, that the consumer should give greatest planning attention to protecting himself or herself against long-term and total and permanent disability rather than being unduly concerned with disabilities that last only a few weeks. For example, depending on individual circumstances and resources, it often is much more economical for a family to rely upon their emergency investment fund for shorter-term disabilities than to buy disability income insurance to cover such disabilities.

The total and permanent disability of a family breadwinner actually is a much greater catastrophe than his or her premature death because the disabled person remains a consumer, whose consumption needs may even increase because of the disability, and because other family members must devote at least some of their time to caring for him or her, and, of course, his or her spouse is not free to remarry as long as the disabled spouse is alive. In fact, total and permanent disability has been graphically characterized as the "wheelchair death."

One final point about disability risk is in order. The disability of someone who owns property and/or investments may give rise to particular property and investment management problems because the disabled person might be in such a physical or mental state that he or she is unable to manage his or her affairs effectively. Advance planning is desirable to provide a means for handling this unhappy contingency.

Sources of Protection against Disability Income Losses

As was done in the case of premature death, the various sources of protection against disability income losses are outlined below.

1. Health insurance
    a. Individual disability income insurance purchased by the insured, his or her family, or others
    b. Group disability income insurance
        (1) Through the insured's employer or business
        (2) Through an association group plan
    c. Credit disability income insurance payable to a creditor of the insured person to pay off a debt
2. Disability benefits under life insurance policies
    a. Disability income riders added to some individual life insurance policies
    b. Waiver of premium benefits included with, or added to, most individual life insurance policies
    c. Disability benefits under group life insurance
3. Social security disability benefits
4. Workers' compensation disability benefits
5. Other government benefits

6. Disability benefits under private pension, profit-sharing, and nonqualified deferred compensation plans
7. Noninsured employer salary-continuation (sick-pay) plans
8. All other income, investment or otherwise, available to the family

This outline, and that for premature death, show that there often are more sources of protection available than many people may think. The problem is to recognize these sources and use them efficiently to meet your and your family's needs.

Medical Care Expenses

There is little need to convince most people of the need to protect themselves and their family against medical care costs. Mounting medical care costs have become a national problem, and they are no less so for you and your family.

For your personal financial planning, it may be helpful to divide family medical care costs into three categories, as follows.

"Normal" or budgetable expenses. These are the medical expenses the family more or less expects to pay out of its regular monthly budget, such as routine visits to physicians, routine outpatient laboratory tests and X-rays, expenses of minor illnesses, and small drug purchases. Just what expenses are "normal" or budgetable depends a great deal on the needs, other resources, and desires of the individual or family. The federal income tax law seems to imply that about 7½ percent of your income is considered "normal" medical expense for tax purposes because medical expenses of less than this amount cannot be taken as itemized deductions for income tax purposes. But as a general principle, the larger the amount of annual expenses a family can afford to assume, the lower will be its overall costs. This is true because buying insurance against relatively small potential losses results in what is called "trading dollars with the insurance company," which usually is an uneconomical practice for the insured. Also, to the extent an emergency fund is established to meet unexpected expenses and losses (of all kinds), the investment earnings on this fund would be available to the consumer.

"Larger than normal" expenses. These are medical expenses that exceed those that are expected or budgetable. If they occur, they probably cannot be met out of the family's regular income. To meet such expenses, most people need insurance. The cutoff point between "normal" and "larger than normal" expenses depends upon the family's circumstances.

Catastrophic medical expenses. These are expenses so large as to cause severe financial strain on a family. They are important to plan for because they are potentially so damaging. Again, the dividing line between "larger than normal losses" and "catastrophic losses" depends on individual circumstances. One family, for example, may feel that uninsured medical expenses of over $500 in a year would be a severe financial strain. Another family, however, with a larger income and an emergency fund, may feel that uninsured medical expenses of several thousand dollars could be tolerated, provided the annual cost savings were significant enough for the family to assume this much risk. The significance of the dividing line lies in the fact that insurance generally is necessary to protect the family against truly catastrophic medical expenses, while the family may elect to assume at least some of the larger than normal expenses. In many cases, however, this decision is, in effect, taken away from the individual because his or her employer provides group medical expense insurance which the employee must either accept or, in rare cases, reject.

The traditional approach for protecting your family against catastrophic medical expenses is coverage under so-called "major medical expense" insurance. But even major medical expense insurance may prove inadequate to meet some of the really large medical bills that are possible. As an example, The Wall Street Journal reported the case of a 2½ year-old girl suffering from nephrosis (a kidney disease) whose father (a corporate executive) had incurred medical expenses on her behalf of $57,794 over a 21-month period and still expected at least 4 more years of treatment. The father's group major medical expense insurance reimbursed only $13,082 of these expenses before its benefits were exhausted.[1] While such instances are relatively infrequent, they nevertheless point up the need for planning to meet this risk.

There really is no way for you to know in advance just how large catastrophic medical expenses might be. Because they could be <u>very</u> large, you should plan for that possibility.

Sources of Protection against Medical Care Expenses

The following are the major sources to which consumers may look for coverage of medical care costs.

1. Health insurance
   a. Employer-provided medical expense coverage (including insured plans, Blue Cross-Blue Shield plans, and health maintenance organization (HMO) plans)

---

1. "The Cost of Illness: Medical Bills Burden Even Affluent Families," The Wall Street Journal, May 7, 1970, p. 1.

b. Individual medical expense insurance
 2. Medical payments coverage under liability insurance policies and "no-fault" automobile coverages
 3. Social security medical benefits (Medicare)
 4. Workers' compensation medical benefits
 5. Other government benefits
 6. Other employer medical reimbursement benefits
 7. Other assets available to the family

Property and Liability Losses

All families are exposed to the risk of property and/or liability losses. For planning purposes, it is helpful to consider property exposures and liability exposures separately because somewhat different approaches may be used for each.

Property losses. Ownership of property brings with it the risk of loss to the property itself, or <u>direct losses</u>, and the risk of indirect losses arising out of loss or damage to the property, called <u>consequential</u> losses. Direct and consequential losses to property can result from a wide variety of perils, some of which, such as fire, theft, windstorm, and automobile collision, are common, while others, such as earthquake and flood, are rather rare except in certain geographical areas.

Some of the kinds of property owned by individuals and families that may be exposed to direct loss include:

  residence
  summer home
  investment real estate
  furniture, clothing, and other personal property
  automobiles
  boats (and aircraft)
  furs, jewelry, silverware, and fine art works
  securities, credit cards, cash, and the like
  professional equipment
  assets held as an executor, trustee, or guardian and assets in which the person has a beneficial interest

Some of the consequential losses that may arise out of a direct loss to such property are as follows:

  loss of use of the damaged property (including additional living expenses while a residence is being rebuilt, rental of a substitute automobile while a car is being repaired, etc.)
  loss or rental income from damaged property
  depreciation losses (or the difference between the cost to replace damaged property with new property and the depreciated value, called "actual cash value," of the damaged property)
  cost of debris removal

12.8

Many property losses are comparatively small in size, but some are of major importance. As with disability income losses and medical care expenses, what constitutes a "small" loss depends upon the resources and attitudes of those involved. Also, like disability income and medical expense exposures, a financial planning decision needs to be made as to how much of your property loss exposure should be assumed and how much insured. Another decision is what property to insure against what perils.

Liability losses. By virtue of almost everything you do, you are exposed to possible liability claims made by others. Such liability claims can arise out of your own negligent acts; the negligent acts of others for whom you may be held legally responsible; liability you may have assumed under contract (such as a lease); and the liability imposed on you by statute (such as workers' compensation laws).

Some of the exposures that may result in a liability claim are:

- ownership of property (for example, residence premises, vacation home)
- rental of property (for example, vacation home)
- ownership, rental, or use of automobiles
- ownership, rental, or use of boats, aircraft, snowmobiles, etc.
- hiring of employees (for example, domestic and casual)
- other personal activities
- professional and business activities (including officerships and directorships)
- any contractual or contingent liability

Most people realize the financial consequences that could occur as a result of liability claims against them. However, they may not recognize all the liability exposures they have and may not protect themselves against the possibility of very large claims. Like medical expenses, there really is no way you can know in advance just how large a liability loss you may suffer. Judgments and settlements for $1 million and more are not unheard of by any means. Therefore, prudent financial planning calls for the assumption that the worst can happen and providing for it.

Sources of Protection against Property and Liability Losses

For most persons, the main source of protection against property and liability losses is insurance. This insurance generally is available under individually marketed property and liability policies, but also may be available under so-called "mass (or collective) merchandised" plans, usually through the person's employer. In some cases, it may be possible for some individuals to protect themselves by not assuming liability under contract or by transferring a liability risk to others by contract. But this really is not feasible for most people.

Capital Accumulation

Many people and families do not spend all their disposable income, and thus they have an investible surplus; many also have various semiautomatic plans, such as profit-sharing plans, that help them build up capital; and some receive gifts and/or inheritances that must be invested. Thus, in one way or another, an important and desirable financial objective for many is to accumulate and invest capital.

There are a number of reasons why people want to accumulate capital. Some of the more important are for an emergency fund, for the education of their children, for retirement purpose, and for a general investment fund to provide them with capital and additional income for their own financial security. In other words, people want to accumulate capital to promote their own personal financial freedom. People also save with certain consumption goals in mind, such as the purchase of a new car or taking an extended trip or vacation.

The relative importance of these reasons naturally varies with individual circumstances and attitudes. A woman in her fifties may be primarily interested in preparing for retirement, while a younger family man or woman may be more concerned with educating his or her children or the capital growth of a general investment fund.

Emergency Fund

An emergency fund may be needed to meet unexpected expenses that are not planned for in the family budget; to pay for the "smaller" disability losses, medical expenses, and property losses that purposely are not covered by insurance; and to provide a financial cushion against such personal problems as prolonged unemployment.

This need for an emergency unemployment fund has received greater attention in recent years as many capable persons have lost their jobs because of economic uncertainties. A reasonable emergency fund can help prevent the problem of temporary unemployment from becoming a crisis by giving the affected family time to adjust without having to change their living standards drastically or disturb their other investments.

The size of the needed emergency fund varies greatly and depends upon such factors as family income, number of income earners, stability of employment, assets, debts, insurance deductibles and uncovered health and property insurance exposures, and the family's general attitudes toward risk and security. The size of the emergency fund can be expressed as so many months of family income--such as 3 to 6 months.

By its very nature, the emergency fund should be invested conservatively. There should be almost complete security of principal, marketability, and liquidity. Within these investment constraints, the fund should be invested so as to secure a reasonable yield, given the primary investment objective of safety of principal. Logical investment outlets for the emergency fund include:

    bank savings accounts (regular accounts)
    savings and loan association accounts (regular accounts)
    money market mutual funds
    United States savings bonds
    life insurance cash values
    short-term United States Treasury securities

The careful person also may want to have some ready cash available for emergencies, even if it is noninterest-earning.

Education Needs

The cost of higher education has increased dramatically, particularly at private colleges and universities. For example, it may cost $15,000 or more per year in tuition, fees, and room and board only for a student to attend some private colleges. This can result in a tremendous financial drain for a family with college-age children, and yet it is a predictable drain that can be prepared for by setting up an education fund.

The size of the fund obviously depends upon the number of children, their ages, their educational plans, any scholarships and student loans that may be available to them, and the size of the family income. It also depends upon the attitudes of the family toward education. Some people feel they should provide their children with all the education they can profit from and want. Others, however, feel that children should help earn at least a part of their educational expenses themselves. There is also the idea in some cases that older children should help send their younger brothers and sisters through school after their parents have helped them. What types of schools the children plan to attend also has a considerable bearing on the costs involved.

An investment fund for educational needs often is a relatively long-term objective, and it is set up with the hope that the fund will not be needed in the meantime. Therefore, wider investment latitude seems justified than in the case of the emergency fund to secure a more attractive investment yield. All that is really necessary is for the ... [funds] to be there by the time each child is ready for school.

Retirement Needs

This is a very important objective for many people in accumulating capital. They want to make sure they can live independently and decently during their retired years. Because of the importance and unique characteristics of retirement planning, it is dealt with as a separate objective later in this reading.

General Investment Fund

People often accumulate capital for general investment purposes. They may want a better standard of living in the future, a second income in addition to the earnings from their employment or profession, greater financial security or a sense of personal financial freedom, the ability to retire early or to "take it easier" in their work in the future, or a capital fund to pass on to their children or grandchildren; or they may simply enjoy the investment process. In any event, people normally invest money for the purpose of maximizing their after-tax returns, consistent with their objectives and the investment constraints under which they must operate.

The size of a person's investment fund depends upon how much capital there originally was to invest, how much the person can save each year, any other sources of capital, and how successful the person or his or her advisers are. There are, of course, wide variations in how much different people have to invest. However, one investment advisory organization has estimated that there are 10 million people in the United States who have $5,000 or more available for investment.

There are a number of ways people can accumulate capital and many possible investment policies they might follow. However, in terms of the objective of capital accumulation, an individual basically has the following factors to consider: (1) an estimate of how much capital will be needed at various times in the future (perhaps including an estimate for future inflation or deflation); (2) the amount of funds available to invest; (3) an estimate of how much will be saved each year in the future; (4) the amount of time left to meet your objectives; (5) the general investment constraints under which you must operate in terms of security of principal, stability of income, stability of principal, tax status, and the like; and (6) the adoption of an investment program that will give the best chance of achieving as many of your financial objectives as possible, within the limitation of the investment constraints.

Tables 1 and 2 give some growth rates for capital at assumed rates of return over various time periods. Table 1 shows how much an investment fund of $1,000 would grow to at certain assumed rates of return for the number of years indicated. This is known as the future value of a sum.

The dramatic effect of compound rates of return over a number of years can be seen from table 1. Suppose you are age 35 and have $10,000 to invest. If you receive a net rate of return (after investment expenses and income taxes) of only 4 percent, you can accumulate $14,800 by the time you are age 45, $21,910 by the time you are 55, and $32,430 when you reach 65. But if you can increase this net rate of return to 6 percent, you can accumulate $17,910 by 45,

---

TABLE 1
Values of a $1,000 Investment Fund Invested for Specified Numbers of Years at Various Rates of Return (Future Value of a Sum)

Percent Annual Net Rate of Return (Compounded)	\multicolumn{8}{c}{Number of Years the $1,000 Is Invested}
	5	8	10	12	15	20	25	30
3	$1,159	$1,267	$1,344	$1,426	$1,558	$1,806	$2,094	$2,427
4	1,217	1,369	1,480	1,601	1,801	2,191	2,666	3,243
5	1,276	1,478	1,629	1,796	2,079	2,653	3,386	4,322
6	1,338	1,594	1,791	2,012	2,397	3,207	4,292	5,744
8	1,469	1,851	2,159	2,518	3,172	4,661	6,848	10,064
10	1,611	2,144	2,594	3,138	4,177	6,727	10,835	17,449
15	2,011	3,059	4,046	5,350	8,137	16,367	32,919	66,212

TABLE 2
Values of a Periodic Investment of $100 per Year at the End of Specified Numbers of Years at Various Rates of Return (Future Value of an Annuity)

Percent Annual Net Rate of Return (Compounded)	\multicolumn{8}{c}{Number of Years at $100 per Year}
	5	8	10	12	15	20	25	30
3	$531	$889	$1,146	$1,419	$1,860	$2,687	$3,646	$4,758
4	542	921	1,201	1,503	2,002	2,978	4,165	5,608
5	553	955	1,258	1,592	2,158	3,307	4,773	6,644
6	564	990	1,318	1,687	2,328	3,679	5,486	7,906
8	587	1,064	1,449	1,898	2,715	4,576	7,311	11,328
10	611	1,144	1,594	2,138	3,177	5,728	9,835	16,449
15	674	1,373	2,030	2,900	4,758	10,244	21,279	43,474

$32,070 by 55, and $57,440 by 65. And if you can increase this net return to 10 percent, the comparable figures would be $25,940 by 45, $67,727 by 55, and $174,490 by 65.

Approached in a somewhat different manner, if a man aged 35 with a $10,000 investment fund feels that he needs approximately $20,000 in 12 years for his children's education, he can see from table 1 that he will have to earn a net rate of return of about 6 percent on the money to accomplish his goal ($10,000 at 6 percent per year for 12 years = $20,120).

You also may want to know to how much a certain amount saved each year will accumulate in a specified period, known as the future value of an annuity. This can be determined from table 2, which shows to how much $100 per year would grow at certain assumed rates of return for the number of years indicated. Now assume that you are 35 and can save $1,200 per year (about $100 per month). If you receive a net rate of return of 8 percent on the money, you can accumulate $17,388 by the time you are 45 ($1,449 x 12), $54,912 by the time you are 55, and $135,936 by the time you reach age 65. This kind of analysis is often used to show the growth of a periodic savings program for retirement.

It often is helpful to combine the results of tables 1 and 2. People frequently have an investment fund and also are saving so much each year. Suppose, for example, that you are age 35 and have $10,000 to invest now and expect to save about $1,200 per year that you can invest in the future. If you can invest these amounts at a net annual rate of return of 8 percent, you will accumulate $38,978 by age 45 ($21,590 from table 1 and $17,388 from table 2), $101,522 by age 55, and $236,576 by age 65. You can see from the tables that substantially higher accumulations could be achieved by securing a net rate of return even 1 or 2 percentage points higher than the 8 percent assumed above. It also is clear that consistent saving and investment can produce rather startling results.

Investment Instruments for Capital Accumulation

There is a wide variety of possible investment instruments (or media) that you can use as investment outlets. The instruments are classified as fixed-dollar and variable-dollar (or equity) investments. Fixed-dollar investments mean those whose principal and/or income are contractually set in advance in terms of a specified or determinable number of dollars. Variable-dollar (or equity) investments are those where neither the principal nor the income is contractually set in advance in terms of dollars. In other words, both the value and the income of variable-dollar investments can change in dollar amount, either up or down, with changes in economic conditions.

1. **Fixed-dollar investments**
   a. Bonds
   b. Savings accounts and certificates
   c. Certificates of deposit, Treasury bills and notes, and other short-term debt investments
   d. Money market funds
   e. Preferred stock
   f. Life insurance cash values*
2. **Variable-dollar investments**
   a. Common stock
   b. Mutual funds (stock and balanced funds)
   c. Real estate
   d. Variable annuities
   e. Tax-sheltered investments
   f. Ownership of business interests
   g. Commodities
   h. Fine arts, precious metals, and other miscellaneous assets

Provision for Retirement Income

We noted above that a basic personal objective is to provide a retirement income for an individual and also for his or her spouse. This objective has become increasingly important in modern times because of changes in our socioeconomic institutions and because most people now can anticipate living to enjoy their retirement years. As you can see from the figures below, the life expectancy at all these ages exceeds the typical retirement age in the United States of 65. Also, at all these ages the probability of survival to age 65 considerably exceeds the probability of death before age 65.

Age	Life Expectancy in Years[†]	Probability of Death before Age 65[†]	Probability of Survival to Age 65 (1—Probability of Death)
25	46	0.29	0.71
30	41	0.28	0.72
35	37	0.27	0.73
40	32	0.26	0.74
45	28	0.25	0.75
50	24	0.22	0.78
55	20	0.18	0.82
60	16	0.12	0.88
65	13	--	--

*Editor's note: The cash values of a number of currently available life insurance contracts are actually variable rather than fixed (for example, variable life, whose cash values are a function of investment performance rather than contractual determination).

[†]Computed from the 1958 Commissioners Standard Ordinary Mortality Table.

Today, there are many ways a person can plan for retirement--some involve government programs while others rely primarily on private means, and some involve tax advantages while others do not. The following is a brief outline of these sources.

1. Social security retirement benefits
2. Other government benefits
3. Private pension plans
   a. Employer-provided pension plans
   b. Retirement plans for the self-employed (HR-10 plans)
   c. Individual retirement accounts and annuities (IRA plans)
   d. Voluntary employee contributions to an employer-sponsored plan
   e. Tax-sheltered annuity (TSA) plans
4. Deferred profit-sharing and other employee benefit plans
5. Nonqualified deferred compensation plans
6. Individually purchased annuities
7. Life insurance cash values
8. Investments and other assets owned by the individual

Many of these instruments for providing retirement income offer substantial tax advantages to the individual if the plan meets the requirements of the tax laws.

Because many persons today do have a variety of retirement benefits available to them, coordination of these benefits becomes increasingly important. It does not make sense to either underprovide or overprovide for retirement income.

Reducing the Tax Burden

In many ways, we have a tax-oriented economy in the United States. Most people have the legitimate objective of reducing their tax burden as much as legally possible, consistent with their nontax objectives. Also, the tax implications of most transactions at least must be considered, and some transactions are entered into because of their tax advantages. Thus, tax planning has an important role in personal financial planning.

People are subject to many different taxes. These include sales taxes, real estate taxes, social security taxes, federal income taxes, state and/or local income taxes, federal estate tax, state inheritance and/or estate taxes, federal (and sometimes state) gift taxes, and potentially the federal tax on generation-skipping transfers. The relative importance of these taxes varies considerably among families, depending upon their circumstances and income levels. When engaging in tax planning, however, most people are concerned primarily with income taxes, death taxes, and perhaps gift taxes.

A wide variety of specific tax-saving plans are being used or proposed today. In general, however, they fall under one or more of the following basic tax-saving techniques: (1) tax elimination or reduction, (2) shifting the tax burden to others who are in lower brackets, and (3) postponing taxation.

Planning for Your Heirs

This is commonly referred to as "estate planning." An estate plan has been defined as "an arrangement for the devolution of one's wealth." For a great many people, such an arrangement can be relatively simple and inexpensive to set up. But for larger estates or estates with special problems, estate plans can become quite complex. Estate planning is a technical and specialized field where such diverse areas of knowledge as wills, trusts, tax law, insurance, investments, and accounting are important. Thus, it frequently is desirable to bring together several professionals or specialists into an estate planning team to develop a well-rounded plan.

Unfortunately, the impression has developed over the years that estate planning is only for the wealthy. However, many persons who would not regard themselves as wealthy actually do have potential estates large enough to justify the use of estate planning techniques.

Investment and Property Management

Need for Management

The need and desire to obtain outside investment or property management vary greatly among individuals and families. Some people have a keen interest in investments and property management and hence seek little, if any, help in managing their affairs. Others who may be knowledgeable enough to handle their own investment and property management nevertheless prefer to devote their full time and energies to their business or profession and leave the management of their personal financial affairs to professionals in that field. Then, of course, there are those who by temperament or training are not equipped to manage their own financial affairs.

However, the increasing complexity of dealing with investments, tax problems, insurance, and the like generally has increased the need for investment and property management. Also, these complexities tend to increase as personal incomes and wealth increase in our society.

Sources of Aid in Management

There are many such sources now available. They vary considerably in the nature and scope of the aid they offer.

Use of financial intermediaries. Broadly speaking, a financial intermediary is a financial institution that invests other people's money and pays them a rate of return on that money. Such institutions serve as conduits for savings into appropriate investments. In effect, then, they take over the investment and money management tasks with respect to those savings. They may also offer subsidiary financial advice, but normally only within their particular areas of interest. The important financial intermediaries as far as most individuals are concerned include:

- commercial banks (offering various types of savings accounts)
- savings and loan associations
- mutual savings banks
- life insurance companies
- investment companies (mutual funds and closed-end investment companies)

Trusts. One of the basic reasons for establishing trusts is to provide experienced and knowledgeable investment property management services for the beneficiary(ies) of the trust. There are various uses of personal trusts, including the use of revocable living trusts to provide investment and property management services for the person creating the trust.

Investment advisory services. There are more than 1,500 investment advisory firms that offer their clients professional investment advice on a fee basis. These firms range from small advisory firms of one or a few persons to large firms handling hundreds or even thousands of clients and having sizable staffs of specialists in various phases of investments. Many banks and some investment banking firms also offer investment advisory services on a fee basis.

The investment advisory services that may be rendered include: (1) analysis of the client's investment needs and objectives, (2) recommendation of an investment program and specific investment policies to achieve the client's objectives, (3) recommendation of specific security issues to implement the policies, and (4) continuous supervision and review of the client's investment portfolio. Banks and some investment advisory firms also provide custody services for their clients, which include safekeeping of securities, handling buy and sell orders with brokers, collection of dividends, dealing with rights under securities, and record keeping, as a part of their advisory services. Banks also provide custody services separately if that is all the customer wants.

In terms of investment decision-making authority, investment advisers may operate in one of three ways: (1) on a strictly discretionary basis, under which the adviser actually makes investment decisions and buys and sells securities for the client without prior consultation on the transactions with the client; (2) under an arrangement whereby the adviser basically makes the investment decisions but does consult with the client to inform him or her of the reasons for the decisions before taking action; and (3) an arrangement under which the adviser and clients consult extensively before investment decisions are made, but clients reserve the actual decision making for themselves. There are advantages and disadvantages for the adviser and client in each of these methods of operation. In the final analysis, however, the worth of any investment adviser basically lies in how good his or her advice turns out to be over the long pull in terms of the client's objectives.

Annual fees charged by investment advisers vary, depending upon such factors as the size of the client's portfolio, the extent of the services rendered, whether it is a discretionary or nondiscretionary account, and the kinds of securities (or property) in the portfolio. For example, an annual fee might start at 3/4 of 1 percent of principal with a minimum annual fee of, say, $500, $1,000, or more. Unfortunately, use of investment advisers by smaller investors frequently is made impractical by the relatively large minimum annual fees charged. For an investor with a $20,000 portfolio, for example, even a $500 minimum annual fee would constitute an annual charge of 2½ percent of principal. For this reason, many investment advisers discourage accounts of less than, say, $75,000. Some advisers, however, encourage smaller accounts, but with proportionally higher fees.

Investors, small and large, also can obtain valuable investment advice from account executives and others with stock brokerage firms. Many brokerage houses have active and well-staffed research departments that provide their customers with considerable investment information and often helpful recommendations. It must be pointed out, however, that the relationship between stockbrokers and their customers is not the same as that of investment advisers and their clients. Brokers typically are paid commissions based on the transactions in their customers' accounts, while advisers are paid on an annual-fee basis as described above. However, professional-minded brokers recognize that long-term success ultimately depends upon the investment success of their customers and act accordingly.

Other advisers. There obviously are other important sources from which individuals can secure aid in managing their affairs. Attorneys provide necessary legal and other advice. The old adage, "The person who acts as his or her own lawyer has a fool for a client," still holds true. In the area of estate planning, for example, costly mistakes can be made in the absence of professional advice. Accountants are depended upon by many persons for advice concerning their financial affairs, particularly in the tax area. Mutual fund representatives and persons offering various tax-sheltered investments provide important advice on investments and how they can be used in financial planning. Life insurance agents can offer valuable advice concerning life insurance, health insurance, and pensions, as well as the other financial products and services their companies may offer. Similarly, property and liability insurance agents and brokers are becoming increasingly important for the advice they can provide on personal risk management, property and liability insurance coverages, and the other financial products and services their companies may offer.

The total-financial-services concept also has fostered the development of a new kind of financial services or financial planning organization. These organizations typically attempt to provide coordinated planning for their clients in such areas as investments, insurance, pensions and other employee benefits, and tax and estate planning. Their goal is to deal with the client's total picture. Some banks, insurance companies, stockbrokers, independent financial planners, and others offer this kind of service.

ADJUSTING YOUR OBJECTIVES FOR INFLATION AND DEFLATION

Inflation has been a persistent worldwide economic problem for many years. Also, as the experience of the depression of the 1930s shows, deflation and even depression cannot be ruled out as economic phenomena which one must at least consider in his or her personal financial planning. However, how to plan for inflation and perhaps deflation is difficult indeed. Obviously, since we cannot foretell the future, we cannot be sure which will occur, and when, and in what magnitude.

However, it is possible to adjust one's objectives as to future financial needs for assumed rates of inflation (or deflation) on the basis of the person's perceptions and belief as to what will happen in the future. Let us say, for example, that Mr. Jones, age 50, estimates that he and his wife will need a retirement income (after income taxes) of about $2,000 per month by the time he reaches age 65, or in 15 years. If it is assumed that the price level in the economy (as measured, for example, by the Consumer Price Index or CPI) will remain stable over this 15-year period, then Mr. Jones and his wife need only plan to have a retirement income of $2,000 per month at his age 65. If, however, this assumption is not deemed to be realistic in view of past inflationary trends, and if an inflation rate of, let us say, 6 percent is assumed for the next 15 years (perhaps even a conservative assumption), then their retirement income objective, to be realistic, should be adjusted for the expected inflation. Assuming a 6 percent compounded annual diminution in the value of the dollar, $1 today will be worth only 41.73 cents in 15 years. This is also the present value of $1 due at the end of 15 years at 6 percent compounded interest. (This present value is 0.4173; similar present values for different interest rates and/or time periods can be secured from present value tables published in financial texts or reference books.)

Therefore, to convert a retirement income objective of $2,000 per month in current dollars to a corresponding dollar amount of equal purchasing power starting 15 years hence, assuming a 6 percent per year inflation rate for the 15-year period, we should divide the $2,000 per month by the present value of $1 due at the end of 15 years at 6 percent compound interest (or 0.4173). The result is a retirement income objective expressed in terms of the assumed price levels (purchasing power) that will exist when Mr. Jones reaches age 65 (assuming 6 percent inflation) of $4,793 ($2,000 ÷ 0.4173). When thus adjusted for assumed inflation, the Jones's retirement income objective might require somewhat different planning than otherwise would have been the case.

THE REGULATION OF FINANCIAL
SERVICES PROFESSIONALS

by Dale S. Johnson*

Financial services professionals operate in one of the most fragmented and confusing environments insofar as professional standards and regulations are concerned. There is no one set of professional or regulatory standards that applies to everybody. Even for a given segment of the financial services industry--such as insurance, banking, or securities--regulatory jurisdictions are divided between state and federal levels and regulatory requirements often vary considerably from one jurisdiction to another.

This reading addresses some key aspects of the regulatory environment faced by financial services professionals--especially the legal responsibilities of insurance agents, brokers, and consultants and of registered securities representatives. Although the reading briefly discusses the unauthorized practice of law, it does not address the issues of regulation specific to banking, accounting, and law.[1] The focus of the reading on the regulation of sales professionals in financial services is useful because the insurance and securities industries provide the predominant numbers of practicing professionals. The next reading in this volume addresses the impact of the Investment Advisers Act of 1940 on financial services professionals of all types.

---

*Dale S. Johnson, PhD, CFP, is a financial planning consultant and writer headquartered in Villanova, Pa. The author acknowledges significant critical contributions to this reading by three Huebner School faculty colleagues: Robert W. Cooper, dean of the Huebner School; Edward E. Graves, assistant professor of insurance; and Burton T. Beam, Jr., associate professor of insurance and director of curriculum development.

1. To the extent that professionals from the banking industry are moving into broader-based financial services, they are moving into the marketing of securities and insurance products. Current regulatory trends suggest strongly that they will therefore become subject to the same regulatory environment that this reading addresses. Accounting and law are accepted, essentially self-regulating professions. However, to the extent that practitioners from these fields become involved in the activities covered in this reading, they, too, may become subject to the regulations that apply to insurance and securities professionals.

REGULATION AND LICENSING OF INSURANCE AGENTS, BROKERS, AND CONSULTANTS

The professionals who operate as agents, brokers, and consultants in the insurance industry encounter a somewhat different regulatory environment from that of the securities industry. Regulation for the insurance industry is primarily at the state level, whereas regulation for the securities industry is primarily at the federal level. State laws governing life, health, and property and casualty insurance activities vary, often significantly, from state to state. Nevertheless, there are important similarities, especially within the three major industry groupings of life, health, and property and casualty insurance.

Students should remember the essential differences between an agent, a broker, and a consultant. An insurance agent is a person who sells insurance contracts for an insurer to third parties (clients) and owes primary fiduciary responsibility to the insurer. A broker is a person who represents buyers of insurance contracts and owes primary fiduciary responsibility to those buyers. However, a broker may also owe a fiduciary responsibility to sellers (that is, insurers) in matters involving premiums and other funds payable to insurers. A consultant is a person who provides insurance counseling, advising, analysis or other specialist consulting service to clients irrespective of any insurer relationship and owes unequivocal fiduciary responsibility to clients.

All of the states have licensing laws that govern each type of insurance agent doing business in those states. All of the states require applicants to pass an examination before they can sell insurance within the state. However, in some states, possession of the CLU or CPCU designation exempts licensing applicants from all or part of the examination requirements. Some states require a certain number of classroom hours before initial licensing; among these, some accept course work or program completion in the CLU or CPCU professional designation programs as substitutes for classroom training.

Some states recognize and license brokers; others do not. Among the states that recognize insurance consultants in either life, health, or property and casualty insurance, some require licenses; others do not. In states that do not license consultants and/or brokers, persons acting in these capacities and selling insurance contracts will still be required to be licensed as agents. In some states, licensed agents may be forbidden by law to act as either broker or consultant, or both. In some other states, licensed agents may be permitted to act as either broker or consultant, but not as both.

In addition to state licensure laws pertaining to agents, brokers, and consultants, other state laws regulate a wide range of activities of insurance professionals. Generally speaking, insurance agents who do business in states where they are not residents must obtain a nonresident license. Temporary licenses are issued without examination in some states to allow an applicant for a permanent license to sell insurance while engaged in qualifying for a permanent license or to allow a representative of a disabled or deceased agent or broker to continue the disabled agent or broker's business. Temporary licenses are usually limited to a duration of 90 days. Limited licenses are issued in some states to permit the solicitation of certain types of business, such as the sale of travel accident policies or the employment of a solicitor by a licensed agent or broker. In some states, agents licensed under the auspices of a contract with one insurer may submit insurance applications to an insurer with which they have no contract. In all cases other than those excepted by special circumstances, however, the activities of an insurance agent require that the person be appropriately licensed for the type of insurance involved and have a contract with an insurer licensed to do business in the state of the agent's business activities.

Licensed insurance agents must also conform to several general rules of practice in the states in which they do business. One such rule is the requirement that agents can sell only those policy forms that insurers have filed with and/or had approved by the state insurance department. It is illegal for agents to misrepresent coverage or, except in Florida where the legal status is still uncertain, to rebate to clients any part of commissions paid on the sale of contracts. Laws regarding disclosure, replacement, and timely and competent service must also be observed. In some states there are specific prohibitions against agents, brokers, and consultants engaging in the unauthorized practice of law. (Of course, in no state do insurance regulations and laws promote the unauthorized practice of law.) Separate licenses to sell health insurance may be required unless they are included in the examinations and licenses for life or property and casualty agents.

Accurate business records must be kept in accordance with state laws. These laws often specify how bank accounts are to be set up and what reports are to be filed with state insurance departments (including address changes and notices of appointments and terminations). Agents of record in the sale of insurance contracts are entitled to commissions according to arrangements that are usually spelled out in their agency contracts. Commissions can sometimes be shared between an agent of record and another agent if both agents are licensed and the laws of the state(s) in which they do business do not prohibit the sharing.

The foregoing summary provides a sketch of the general legal and regulatory environment in which insurance professionals operate. Because this environment is defined primarily at the state level, it is imperative that all questions and issues be clarified by practitioners in all of the states in which they conduct business.[2] As noted, the issue of foremost importance is that of being appropriately licensed for the activities and services in which agents, brokers, and consultants engage. Normally, for insurance agents this procedure is supervised by the insurers that recruit and train the agents who handle their business. As principals in the relationship with agents, insurers exercise a controlling responsibility to ensure that company operations are in compliance with the laws of the states in which they do business and issue agency contracts. Insurers exercise considerably less control over insurance brokers than insurers do over agents because of the more independent nature of the broker-insurer relationship. Consultants operating in compliance with state law concerning licensure are independent of insurer control.

The Law of Agency

In addition to the administrative regulation of insurance professionals at the state level, persons who engage in insurance sales, brokerage, and consulting activities are governed at a more fundamental level by the general law of agency. The law of agency is a concept of common law that applies to agents, brokers, and consultants in differing ways and degrees. In addition, there are important distinctions between agency in the life and health insurance field and agency in the property and liability field. Both state laws and state insurance departments generally take these differences and distinctions into account in spelling out and enforcing regulations applying to each type of agent, broker, or consultant operating in their states.

The distinctions between agents, brokers, and consultants are clarified by the agency concept. This

---

2. Federal regulation of insurance professionals does apply in some areas. For example, the federal Employee Retirement Income Security Act of 1974 (ERISA) applies to professionals in the areas of pension planning and administration. Moreover, the sale of variable annuity and variable life insurance contracts is regulated by SEC licensing and regulation through the NASD Series 6 examination.

concept can be applied to these distinctions through this question: "For whom is an agent, broker, or consultant primarily acting in their respective capacities?" If we remember that an insurance agent solicits the purchase of insurance contracts, an insurance broker represents buyers of insurance contracts, and an insurance consultant provides counseling, advice, or analysis irrespective of an insurer relationship, the following definitions and discussion of the activities that are typical for these three types of insurance professionals will be clearer.

Definition of Agent

An agent is a person who acts for an insurer, the principal, in soliciting the purchase of insurance contracts by third parties. The essence of agency is power; it means that an agent has the power to subject a principal to contractual liability and to create contractual rights for the principal. Acts of the agent, within the scope of his or her power, are acts of the principal. The knowledge of the agent is considered to be the principal's knowledge in matters concerning business transactions conducted by the agent for the principal. A life insurance agent generally does not have the power to create binding contractual coverages without approval by the insurer of the individual risk. A property and liability agent, on the other hand, often does have the power to bind coverage.

An agent's relationship with the principal can be created by an explicit or implied grant of authority by the principal. The relationship can also be created by apparent authority if this authority is coupled with the principal's ratification of the agent's acts after they are done, even if these acts were not otherwise authorized by the principal's grant of authority to the agent. Within the scope of the agent's authority, the acts of the agent are binding upon the principal. Crucial to the agency relationship is the agent's fiduciary responsibility of loyalty and obedience to the principal and of reasonable care and skill in exercising the duties of an agent. Thus, an insurance agent acts primarily to secure and maintain contracts in the best interests of the principal.

The principal is the party for whom the agent acts. A principal can limit and control the agent's authority. When such limitations are clearly communicated to third parties, they are binding. The principal can initiate legal action or terminate the agency relationship to enforce agency duties. In turn, in most instances the principal has a duty to provide the agent with an opportunity to work, to compensate the agent, and to keep accounts of what is owed to the agent. The principal is bound by a contract made by the agent with a third person when the agent is functioning within the scope of his or her authority. The principal can also enforce such a contract against the third person, or initiate a cause of action against a third person who colludes with the agent to violate fiduciary duties.

Definition of Broker

In some instances, persons licensed to sell insurance for more than one insurer are misleadingly called brokers. Legally, in most of these cases, such persons are actually agents of each insurer rather than brokers. A broker is a person whose business is to represent buyers in bringing both buyers and sellers together in a contractual relationship. In insurance, a broker is usually a person who procures insurance contracts upon request. In this sense, an insurance broker is usually the client's agent and therefore the client's fiduciary for purposes of procuring the insurance or of making the application. However, the broker may be the insurer's fiduciary for other purposes, such as the collection of the premiums or delivery of the policy.

Life insurance brokers may procure policies from a number of insurers for their clients, and often sell other types of insurance as well. Property and liability brokers typically procure insurance contracts from an even larger number of companies according to their clients' needs. Over half the states recognize and license life and health insurance brokers. Most states recognize and license property and liability insurance brokers. Most companies require proof of a valid broker's license before accepting applications from purported brokers because they cannot legally accept applications that are not lawfully solicited.

Definition of Consultant

An insurance consultant (in some states counselor, specialist, analyst, or adviser) is a person who provides counseling, analysis, or advice regarding insurance policies. If this consultation involves a prospective sale of specific contracts, or the subsequent purchase of these contracts by consulting clients, the consultant will need to be licensed as an agent or broker. State laws regarding insurance consultants vary considerably. The laws of some states do not even address the issue. Some require a consultant's license. Some that require consultant licenses also require examinations for licensing. Some permit the charging of a consultant's fee by a licensed agent, broker, or consultant; others do not. Some permit a consultant's fee but not a fee plus commissions on contracts sold. The variability of state laws in defining consultants and their activities is perhaps more confusing than the variability of laws applying to the activities of agents and brokers. With the emergence of consulting as a more distinct service now being provided to clients by both insurance and other financial services professionals, this variability in state laws has become a critical issue. The key elements of the issue are addressed by the Agents and Brokers Licensing Model Act that the National Association of Insurance Commissioners (NAIC) has proposed for adoption by the states as a uniform law.

The NAIC Model Act contains the following provisions concerning consultants:

- Agents, brokers, attorneys, bank trust officers, actuaries, and public accountants, acting in their professional capacities, do not have to be licensed as consultants.
- A licensed insurance consultant cannot hold an agent's or broker's license or receive remuneration from agents, brokers, or insurers.
- A written examination is required before a person can be licensed as an insurance consultant.
- The commissioner of insurance in each state may investigate the other qualifications of an applicant for an insurance consultant's license.
- There should be a written agreement between the consultant and his or her client before the insurance consultant can render service.
- The written agreement must be signed by both consultant and client and must outline the work to be performed and the fee to be charged.

Section 7h of the NAIC Model Act defines the nature of the service provided that would qualify as licensable consulting as follows:

A consultant is obligated under his license to serve with objectivity and complete loyalty the interest of his client alone; and to render his client such information, counsel, and service as within the knowledge, understanding, and opinion, in good faith of the licensee, best serves the client's needs and interests.

The NAIC Model Act is in no way binding unless and until a state adopts it. However, the model does clarify some central issues, such as the potential conflict of interest inherent in both charging fees for consulting and receiving commissions as agent or broker. It is also unequivocal in defining a consultant as a professional who acts for the client's best interests, therefore as the client's fiduciary.

The Need for Licenses

The importance of the foregoing discussion of the regulatory environment for insurance agents, brokers, and consultants is that each must decide which examinations and licenses are required for various lines of insurance and for each type of practice--that is, as agent, broker, or consultant--in each state in which the person operates. These licenses exist to define legal practice in insurance, to protect the public, and to minimize the possible liabilities for errors and omissions in providing client service and for breach of contract in agency relationships. To the extent that persons sell insurance contracts that qualify as securities (for example, a variable annuity or variable life insurance contract), or other clearly definable investment products (such as tax shelters, mutual funds, or stocks and bonds), they must also be appropriately licensed to sell securities. Conversely, registered representatives from the securities industry who sell insurance must be appropriately licensed to do so by the states in which they solicit business. Insurance agents whose clientele encompasses several states must be licensed in each state in which they conduct business.

Meeting these base-level requirements is obligatory for compliance with the applicable statutes, procedures, and rules of practice set forth in the regulatory environment of the insurance industry.

REGULATION, REGISTRATION, AND LICENSING OF SECURITIES REPRESENTATIVES AND PRINCIPALS

The licensing and registration requirements of sales representatives and principals in the securities field is also a confusing subject for a great many financial services professionals, especially those who have just begun or are preparing to sell securities. As in the insurance industry, regulation exists on two levels, federal and state. However, federal regulation of the securities industry is far more significant and compelling than state regulation.

The federal government has passed numerous laws to ensure that the securities markets are fair and reasonably honest places where both big and small savers and borrowers can place or raise their funds according to their objectives. Laws forbidding fraud and price manipulation have been passed and federal agencies established to enforce them. Moreover, professional associations (such as the Financial Analysts Federation) and trade associations (such as the National Association of Securities Dealers or NASD) have established codes of ethics and standards of practice with which members must comply.

13.8

Congress has enacted a variety of legislation to curb fraudulent practices, excessive debt pyramiding, dissemination of misleading or fraudulent information, market breaks such as the great crash of 1929, trading on insider information, and other potential abuses. In addition, this legislation imposes rules of practice and regulates the business conduct of issuers, underwriters, and sellers of securities--that is, of corporations that issue securities, of investment bankers or syndicators of securities issues, and of sales representatives who market those issues to the public.

For example, in addition to requirements pertaining to full disclosure of information about securities issues, the Securities Act of 1933 sets forth antifraud criteria that provide recourse by investors against securities salespersons who disseminate false or misleading information. Recourse is through court-imposed injunctions and other civil law remedies (such as reimbursement for damages). Recourse is also through criminal law when fraud is involved in the issuance of securities. The act limits the techniques that can be used to sell securities. Furthermore, it provides the basis for a subsequent ruling of the Securities and Exchange Commission that, by offering their services to the public, all securities dealers imply that they will deal fairly. This ruling in turn provides a basis for prosecuting securities salespersons who issue misleading advice or information or commit other frauds.

NASD and SEC Registration and Licensing

Many financial services professionals are confused about the purposes of registration and licensing through the NASD qualifying examinations and registration as an investment adviser with the SEC and/or with the state securities commissions. NASD registration and licensing has nothing to do with registration as an investment adviser under the Investment Advisers Act of 1940; each type of registration is designed for a different purpose and function. NASD registrations apply to persons who sell securities or act as managers of securities salespersons. The Investment Advisers Act applies to persons who give investment advice under conditions defined by the act. (The requirements of the Investment Advisers Act of 1940 are addressed in the reading immediately following.) The fact is that a financial services professional may require one or more of the NASD registrations to sell particular securities product lines and in no way be required to register as an investment adviser under either federal or state law. Or, a financial services professional may be subject to investment adviser registration requirements at either the state or federal level, or both, as well as NASD registration requirements for selling securities. Finally, a financial services professional may be subject to investment adviser registration at either the state or federal level, or both, and not be subject to NASD registration because he or she sells no securities at all. Here we are concerned with NASD registrations and licensing of securities salespersons as required by both federal and state law.

Self-Regulation through NASD Membership and Compliance

The National Association of Securities Dealers is a self-regulating trade association authorized by the Maloney Act of 1938. The NASD includes about 2,800 member broker-dealer firms with approximately 200,000 securities salespersons operating in the over-the-counter securities markets. In addition to this number of NASD registrations, the member firms of national securities exchanges (such as the New York and American Stock Exchanges) include some 70,000 additional registered securities representatives, who are regulated not by the NASD but by the rules of the exchanges and by their member firms.[3] The NASD does, however, administer the qualifying examinations for the securities exchanges.

As part of its regulation of the activities of its members, the NASD has established the following: a set of "Rules of Fair Practice" forbidding fraud, manipulation of securities markets, and excessive profit-taking from clients; a uniform practices code that standardizes and expedites routine transactions such as payments and deliveries; and an enforcement program to discipline its members for illegal or unethical acts. The discipline procedures of both the NASD and its member firms, and of the securities exchanges and their member firms, are strictly enforceable for proven misconduct, with penalties ranging from censor to suspension to fines. The severest penalty is expulsion from the NASD or revocation of exchange licensing for specific periods of time or permanently. Both types of penalties effectively remove individuals involved from further activities in the securities industry while either of the penalties is in force.

---

3. It should be noted that the NASD examinations and securities registrations qualify persons to be licensed in the states in which their member firms do business. There is no <u>federal</u> license in securities. In addition, although the NASD administers the qualifying examinations for the national and regional securities exchanges, the actual licenses to function as registered securities representatives are also issued by the individual states in which the representatives conduct securities transactions.

As a means of promoting technical competency and legal and ethical compliance, the NASD develops and administers a series of qualifying examinations for the registration and licensing of securities salespersons (called registered representatives) in various specialized segments of the securities industry. In each of these segments of the industry the association also administers the qualifying principals' examinations. The individual may not act alone as a securities salesperson or principal or practice unless he or she has an affiliation with a broker-dealer firm.

A principal is any person associated in a management or supervisory capacity with a securities broker-dealer firm. Registered principals are controllers of registered representatives. A registered representative is any person who is engaged in securities sales as the representative of a broker-dealer in securities, or who is engaged in the training of salespersons associated with a member firm. In other words, sales personnel for NASD member firms and national exchanges must be registered and licensed as representatives; management personnel must be registered and licensed as principals.[4]

Special Brokering Activities

In some cases, however, it is possible to engage in activities that are not fully in compliance with the legal requirements for securities transactions as stated above. For example, a financial services professional who is a registered representative for one broker-dealer may engage in compensated securities transactions for clients through a broker-dealer with which he or she is not a registered representative. Another financial services professional may engage in such transactions with no NASD securities registrations or broker-dealer affiliation at all (as an adviser or consultant could do). Because of the nature of these types of transactions, both persons may be required to register as broker-dealers under the Securities Exchange

---

4. The principals' examinations are administered by the NASD on behalf of the North American Securities Administrators Association (except Series 12) and consist of the following series: Series 4, Registered Options Principal; Series 8, General Securities Sales Supervisor; Series 12, Branch Office Managers (for those who manage a branch office for a NYSE member firm); Series 24, General Securities Principal; Series 26, Investment Company/Variable Contract Principal; Series 27, Financial and Operations Principal; Series 39, Direct Participation Programs Limited Principal.

Act of 1934, which is administered and enforced by the Securities and Exchange Commission.

A dealer effects securities transactions for his or her own account; a broker effects securities transactions for the accounts of others. It is in brokering activities that financial services professionals most often confront the possible need to be registered under the 1934 act.

It is crucial in determining the status of securities brokering activities to examine all relevant facts and circumstances of each case in point. It is important also to differentiate each case from the "finders" activity of bringing together buyers and sellers of securities who thereafter deal directly with each other, with no special compensation paid to the "finder," since this activity will not require broker-dealer registration. The relevant circumstances to be examined in determining whether a financial services professional is acting as a broker in securities transactions and may therefore need to be registered as a broker-dealer are as follows:

- whether there is a substantive role in the marketing, negotiating, or settling of clients' purchases and sales of securities
- whether the person acts as an intermediary for his or her customers in placing buy or sell orders for securities and maintains custody or possession of clients' funds or securities
- whether the person, operating without appropriate NASD registration and without the control of an affiliated broker-dealer, channels business to and receives compensation from a registered broker-dealer in connection with effecting securities transactions for clients
- whether the person is acting as a "purchaser representative" for clients or others in connection with private offerings of limited partnership or tax-sheltered investments that are exempt from securities registration under Regulation D of the Securities Act of 1933, and is receiving compensation for that activity on a transactions basis rather than through a general advisory fee
- whether the person's brokering activities for clients go beyond those that are incidental to activities as a registered representative of a broker-dealer and special compensation is paid for the brokering activities
- whether the brokering activities referred to above involve transactions of an interstate nature for several clients or are wholly intrastate and of very limited application

- whether the brokering activities involve securities in general, private offerings of Regulation D securities marketed interstate to several clients, or only transactions in securities that are specifically exempted from registration requirements, such as certain bank trust funds, tax-qualified insurance contracts, commercial paper, bankers' acceptances, and commercial bills

Engaging in these securities brokering activities (as financial services professionals and financial planners may do even inadvertently) without complying with registration requirements and statutory provisions and rules for broker-dealer activities can lead to the voiding of contractual advisory relationships with clients. It can also subject professionals to serious sanctions and liabilities, including injunctive relief, criminal penalties, imprisonment, rescinding of transactions, judgment for damages, and the barring of applicants from subsequent SEC registrations.[5]

NASD Examinations and Registrations

Figure 1 delineates the qualifying examinations and licenses required to sell various types of securities, with an indication of the various types of firms through which typical products are sold. It should be noted that there are three common approaches to registration: (1) the full securities approach wherein the Series 7 examination qualifying for the sale of all securities except commodities and certain options is taken; (2) the limited registration approach wherein, typically, the Series 6 and Series 22 examinations are taken; (3) the state level or blue-sky approach, in which, in addition to the Series 7 or Series 6 and 22 examinations, the Series 63 (Uniform Securities Agent State Law Examination) is taken by individuals in states that require it and offer no exemption by reciprocity for successful completion of other NASD-administered examinations.

In addition to its own qualifying examinations, the NASD also administers programs for other regulatory agencies, including the Municipal Securities Rulemaking Board, the Chicago Board of Trade, the New York Stock Exchange (for principals and representatives of all of the member firms that deal in listed securities trading on the major

---

5. For a more complete analysis of broker-dealer activities covered by the Securities Exchange Act of 1934, see Arthur H. Bill, "A Walk Through the Jungle," *Financial Planning* 13, no. 2 (February 1984), 125-130, and "Regulation Landmarks," *Financial Planning* 13, no. 3 (March 1984), 125-128. The second article is particularly useful for its description of registration procedures and requirements for broker-dealers under the Securities Exchange Act of 1934.

FIGURE 1
Registered Securities Representative Licenses

Types of securities sold	License required	License typical for securities salespersons associated with these firms
Mutual funds, variable contracts, investment company products	NASD Series 6, Investment Company (Mutual Funds)/ Variable Contract Representative, or NASD Series 7, General Securities Representative	-Insurance companies -Investment companies
Limited partnerships, gas programs, tax shelters, real estate syndications, real estate limited partnerships	NASD Series 22, Direct Participation Programs, or NASD Series 7	-Oil and gas specialty firms -Real estate specialty firms -Tax-sheltering firms -Some insurance companies -Registered broker-dealers
Municipal, state and local government securities	MSRB Series 52, Municipal Securities, or NASD Series 7	-Banks
Stocks, bonds, options, mutual funds, tax shelters, municipal securities	NASD Series 7, General Securities Representative (can be held in lieu of Series 6, 22, or 52, or all three)	-NASD broker-dealers -NYSE member firms
Futures trading-- grain, livestock, broilers, plywood, silver, gold, interest rates, stock indexes	NASD Series 3, Commodities	-Commodities trading firms -Specialist departments, NYSE and NASD firms
General securities in certain states	NASD Series 63 Uniform Securities Agent State Law Examination (blue-sky)	-Securities salespersons in states where Series 63 is required, unless exempted by reciprocity with NYSE/ NASD qualifying exams

exchanges), the Securities and Exchange Commission, and the options trading exchanges. The NASD also administers the Uniform Securities Agent State Law Examination, which is currently required in addition to NASD qualification requirements by some 30 states. (The other 20 states either require no further examination or they license by reciprocity those who have successfully qualified through NASD-administered examinations.) Financial services professionals who sell or intend to sell securities must determine the requirements of the state in which they practice if their affiliated broker-dealer does not make this determination reliably.

THE UNAUTHORIZED PRACTICE OF LAW

A final and major consideration of financial services professionals is their need to avoid the unauthorized practice of law. Again, the issues are not clear-cut. All financial transactions have legal and tax consequences. Practice in the environment of financial services poses many possibilities for infringement upon the prerogatives and authorized practices of numerous professionals, especially the practicing attorney.

Although financial services professionals must know a great deal about tax issues and the tax laws in order to effectively gather appropriate information about clients and their family situations and identify potential problem areas, most are not attorneys. For these professionals the specter of a possible charge of the unauthorized practice of law can be troubling.

The American Bar Association's recently adopted Model Rules of Professional Conduct are not particularly helpful in this area; nor was the earlier Code of Professional Responsibility they replaced. It is quite clear that no one other than a lawyer is permitted to engage in the practice of law. What constitutes the practice of law, however, is not definitively delineated. The earlier Code of Professional Responsibility stated that "It is neither necessary nor desirable to attempt the formulation of a single, specific definition of what constitutes the practice of law. Functionally, the practice of law relates to the rendition of services for others that call for the professional judgment of a lawyer. The essence of the professional judgment of the lawyer is his educated ability to relate the general body and philosophy of law to a specific legal problem of a client . . . ." The subsequently adopted Model Rules state only that "The definition of the practice of law is established by law and varies from one jurisdiction to another. Whatever the definition, limiting the practice of law to members of the bar protects the public against rendition of legal services by unqualified persons."

Despite the Bar Association's ambiguous definition of what constitutes the practice of law, there are some activities that are universally regarded as the practice of law and as such are to be engaged in only by lawyers. An example of one such activity is the drafting of legal documents.

The line between the unauthorized practice of law and the permissible giving of advice is much more difficult to ascertain, especially in fields such as accounting and financial planning. At what point does the giving of tax information or information about a particular proposed transaction or tax technique by a CPA or financial planner become "legal advice" and as such become the exclusive right of the lawyer? There is no unambiguous way to answer this question.

There is, however, some guidance available to assist the nonlawyer in avoiding potential problems in the unauthorized practice area. If the advice given is couched in general informational terms--for example, if the general principles of a technique are explained for the client's information--such an approach should not be viewed as the unauthorized practice of law. Moreover, even advice that is specifically related to a client's situation should not constitute an unauthorized-practice violation as long as the subject matter of the advice is settled in the law and is a matter of common knowledge in the adviser's field.

The safest way to deal with the unauthorized-practice issue is to involve an attorney as a member of the professional planning team early in the process of providing financial services to clients. It is prudent also to continue this involvement throughout the planning process in those areas in which it is difficult to separate legal advice from advice or information that can legitimately be offered by nonlegal advisers.

THE IMPACT OF THE INVESTMENT ADVISERS ACT OF
1940 ON FINANCIAL SERVICES PROFESSIONALS

by Dale S. Johnson*

In the current financial services environment many professionals and specialists functioning in a vending, advisory, or administrative capacity in the securities, insurance, investment company, estate planning, investment advisory, and pension, retirement, and employee benefit consulting fields may at one time or another be subject to the Investment Advisers Act of 1940. In recent years the specific provisions and broad scope of this act have taken on new significance with the emergence of the financial planning movement, the passage of the Employee Retirement Income Security Act in 1974, the extended scope of financial products and services offered by all major financial institutions, and the more vigorous compliance and enforcement posture assumed by the Securities and Exchange Commission. The act empowers the SEC to administer and enforce its extensive regulatory requirements, to promulgate additional rules, to propose congressional amendments, and to recommend cases to the attorney general for prosecution.

In recent years the SEC has carried out its mandate with increasing attention to the fast-changing financial services environment and to the activities of professionals who function in investment advisory capacities. These include

- the large national companies operating in the insurance and securities industries
- independent broker-dealerships and agencies
- individuals whose compensation is derived from client fees or commissions or some combination of the two
- individuals who are primarily investment advisers, financial planners, or product-oriented salespeople

Since the Investment Advisers Act covers the activities of so many people, it behooves all financial services professionals to determine whether they are subject to registration as investment advisers and to become aware

---

*Dale S. Johnson, PhD, CFP, is a financial planning consultant and writer headquartered in Villanova, Pa.

of the potential impact of the act upon further aspects of their client relationships.

Motivated by a number of factors, including the desire to serve their clients more effectively, the need to enhance and/or stabilize their earnings, the desire to retain their existing clients, and the availability of a wider range of financial products and advisory services in the contemporary marketplace, financial services professionals have been rapidly expanding their products and services to clients in recent years. To give broader service, many are providing or are exploring the possibility of providing comprehensive financial planning for their clients. As these professionals become involved in financial planning and the recommendation and/or sale of various investments, they may become subject to the provisions of a number of federal and state securities statutes, as well as the supervision of regulatory agencies at both levels.

Although professional securities salespeople are licensed as registered securities representatives of the companies or independent broker-dealerships they represent, many of them are apparently unaware of the possible need to register with the SEC under the provisions of the Investment Advisers Act. Even if they are exempt from registering, all persons characterized by the Investment Advisers Act as investment advisers need to understand how they are subject to its antifraud provisions. The purpose of this reading, therefore, is twofold. First, it summarizes the various factors that should be considered by financial services professionals in determining whether they are required to register with the SEC as investment advisers under the provisions of the Investment Advisers Act, as well as the additional requirements imposed on Registered Investment Advisers. (The discussion draws heavily from the contents of SEC Release No. IA-770 issued on August 13, 1981, which presents the views of the Investment Advisers Study Group of the Division of Investment Management concerning the applicability of the Investment Advisers Act of 1940 to financial planners and other professionals who provide investment advisory services to others for compensation.) Second, the reading explores the antifraud provisions of the Investment Advisers Act, which are applicable to all financial services professionals whose activities characterize them as investment advisers as defined by the act.

STATUS AS AN INVESTMENT ADVISER

The Investment Advisers Act of 1940 was intended by Congress to accomplish the following four objectives:

- correct the abuses of fraud in the securities industry
- promulgate and clarify fiduciary standards in investment advisory relationships by characterizing an investment adviser as a fiduciary, thus subjecting the adviser to fiduciary law
- mandate and promote full disclosure of all pertinent facts in investment contracts
- define what constitutes "investment adviser" and monitor (through the requirement of registration) the activities of those who offer investment advice for compensation

Let us look first at the last of these four objectives—the definition of an investment adviser.

Definition of an Investment Adviser

Section 202(a)(11) of the Investment Advisers Act defines the term <u>investment adviser</u> as

> any person who, for compensation, engages in the business of advising others, either directly or through publications or writings, as to the value of securities or as to the advisability of investing in, purchasing, or selling securities, or who, for compensation and as part of a regular business, issues or promulgates analyses or reports concerning securities.

Since the act's definition of an investment adviser determines whether its provisions apply to a particular financial services professional, the three main elements of that definition, as well as the exceptions to it, must be carefully examined. These elements are as follows:

- A person provides advice, or issues reports or analyses, regarding securities.
- A person is in the business of providing such services.
- A person provides such services for compensation.[1]

---

1. For purposes of the act a "person" is defined as either a natural person or a company. A company is defined in the act as a corporation, a partnership, an association, a joint-stock company, a trust, or any organized group of persons, whether incorporated or not; or any receiver, trustee in bankruptcy, or similar official, or any liquidating agent for any of the foregoing, in that agent's capacity as such.

Although a final determination of whether an individual providing financial services would be an investment adviser within the meaning of the act depends upon all relevant facts and circumstances in a particular case, in general a person meeting all three of these test elements (which are described in greater detail below) is subject to the provisions of the Investment Advisers Act unless otherwise specifically excepted.

Financial services professionals who are uncertain as to whether their activities fall within the scope of the above definition or any exceptions contained in the act can request interpretive advice from the SEC, in accordance with the procedures set forth in Investment Advisers Act Release No. 281 (January 25, 1971). The SEC has indicated that it will respond to routine requests for interpretive advice relating to the status of persons engaged in various types of financial planning activities by referring such persons to SEC Release No. IA-770 unless the requests present novel factual or interpretive issues--such as material departures from the nature and types of services and compensation arrangements discussed in the release.

The final determination as to whether an individual is an investment adviser depends upon whether one qualifies under all three elements in the definition quoted above. Let us examine more closely the meaning of those three elements.

Advice or Analysis Concerning Securities

The first element in the definition of an investment adviser pertains to investment advice, or the issuance of reports or analyses, regarding securities. It is important to understand what is meant by the term security and what is meant by providing investment advice, or issuing reports or analyses, regarding securities.

> The Investment Advisers Act defines a security as any note, stock, treasury stock, bond, debenture, evidence of indebtedness, certificate of interest or participation in any profit-sharing agreement, collateral-trust certificate, preorganization certificate or subscription, transferable share, investment contract, voting-trust certificate, certificate of deposit for a security, fractional undivided interest in oil, gas or other mineral rights, or, in general, any instrument or interest commonly known as a "security," or any certificate of interest or participation in, temporary or interim certificate for, receipt for, or guaranty of, or warrant or right to subscribe to or purchase any of the foregoing.

A critical and often controversial question raised by this definition of a security is the meaning of the term investment contract. The Supreme Court has stated on several occasions that the test for determining what constitutes an investment contract under various federal securities laws is whether the scheme involves an investment of money in a common enterprise, with profits to come solely from the efforts of others. A series of court decisions over the years suggests that the sale of a security by one party to another constitutes an investment contract. The seller of a security, then, becomes a party to an investment contract. In this capacity the seller conforms to state and federal securities law if that individual passes qualifying NASD examinations and becomes a registered securities representative of a broker-dealer. However, if in addition to or apart from this vending role in placing securities with clients the seller also provides advice concerning investments and securities under the conditions spelled out in the Investment Advisers Act, such an individual may be required to become registered as an investment adviser as well.

Any person who gives advice or makes recommendations or issues reports or analyses with respect to specific securities would clearly be considered to be an investment adviser under Section 202(a)(11)--assuming, of course, that the other two elements of the definition of an investment adviser are met and that the person is not specifically excepted from the definition of an investment adviser by Clauses (A) to (E) of Section 202(a)(11) of the act, which are described below. Moreover, the SEC would generally view as an investment adviser a person who provides advice or issues or promulgates reports or analyses that concern securities but do not relate to specific securities--assuming such services are performed as part of a business and for compensation. Thus, for example, the SEC has interpreted the definition of an investment adviser to include persons who advise clients either directly or through publications or writings concerning the relative advantages and disadvantages of investing in securities in general as compared with other investment media. A person who, in the course of developing a financial program for a client, advises a client as to the desirability of investing in securities as opposed to stamps, coins, commodities, or other investment vehicles would also be "advising" others, according to the definition contained in the act. Likewise a person who advises employee benefit plans on funding plan benefits by investing in securities, instead of, say, insurance products, real estate, or other funding media, would be "advising" others within the SEC's interpretation of the definition of an investment adviser.

The "Business" Standard

The second element in the definition of an investment adviser requires that a person must for compensation either (1) engage "in the business of advising others. . .as to the value of securities or as to the advisability of investing in, purchasing, or selling securities," or (2) issue or promulgate "analyses or reports concerning securities" as part of a regular business. It is important to note that these activities need not constitute the principal business activity or any particular portion of the business activities of a person in order for the person to be considered an investment adviser. However, a person who provides investment advice for compensation but is not in the business of advising others as to the value of securities or the advisability of investing in securities, or who does not issue reports or analyses concerning securities as part of a regular business, does not come within the definition of an investment adviser contained in the act.

Whether or not a person's activities meet the "business" standard contained in the definition of an investment adviser will depend on the following criteria, developed as part of the SEC's ongoing review of earlier staff interpretive letters:

- whether the investment advice being provided is incidental to a noninvestment advisory business that is the primary business of the person providing the advice
- how specific the advice being given is
- whether the provider of the advice is receiving, directly or indirectly, any special compensation for the advice

In general, the SEC would take the position that a person who provides financial services including investment advice for compensation is in the business of providing investment advice within the meaning of Section 202(a)(11), unless the advice being provided by that person is (1) incidental to that person's noninvestment advisory business, (2) nonspecific, and (3) not rewarded by special compensation for the advice. If one presents oneself as an investment adviser or as an individual who provides investment advice, he or she would be considered to be in the business of providing investment advice. However, the SEC has indicated that a person whose principal business is providing financial services other than investment advice would not be regarded as being in the business of giving investment advice if, as part of this service, the person merely discusses in general terms the advisability of investing in securities--for example, during a discussion of economic matters or the role of investments in securities in a client's overall financial plan.

The SEC takes the position that a person is *in the business* of providing investment advice if, on anything other than rare and isolated incidences, that person discusses the advisability of investing in or issues reports or analyses as to specific categories of securities (for example, bonds, mutual funds, technology stocks, and so forth). A person who provides market timing services would also be viewed as being in the business of giving investment advice. Finally, the SEC regards a person as being *in the business* of providing investment advice if that person receives any special compensation for the advice or receives any direct or indirect remuneration for a client's purchase or sale of securities. However, a person would generally not be considered to be receiving special compensation for providing advisory services if the individual makes no charge for the advisory portion of these services or charges an overall fee for financial advisory services of which the investment advice is an incidental part.

Compensation

The third element in the definition of an investment adviser requires that a person *receive compensation* for giving investment advice. The compensation element is satisfied by the receipt of any economic benefit, whether in the form of an advisory fee, some other fee relating to the total services rendered, commissions, or some combination of these forms of compensation. SEC Release No. IA-770 points out that it is not necessary for a person who provides investment advisory and other services to a client to charge a separate fee for the investment advisory portion of the services. The compensation element is satisfied if a single fee is charged for a number of different services, including giving investment advice or issuing reports or analyses concerning securities. As mentioned, however, the fact that no separate fee is charged for the investment advisory portion of the service could be relevant in determining whether the person is *in the business* of giving investment advice.

SEC Release No. IA-770 also indicates that it is not necessary that an adviser's compensation be paid directly by the person receiving the investment advisory services, but only that the investment adviser receive compensation from some source. Thus a person providing a variety of services to a client, including investment advisory services, for which that person receives any economic benefit (such as a single fee or commissions upon the sale to the client of insurance products or investments) would be performing such advisory services *for compensation* within the meaning of Section 202(a)(11) of the Investment Advisers Act.

Exceptions to the Definition of an Investment Adviser

Even if the activities of a financial services professional, a financial institution, or a financial services firm meet all three test elements of the definition of an investment adviser, the professional or business would not be considered an investment adviser within the scope of the act--and thus would not be subject to its registration provisions--if it fell into one of the categories of exceptions contained in Clauses (A) to (E) of Section 202(a)(11):

(A) a bank, or any bank holding company as defined in the Bank Holding Company Act of 1956, which is not an investment company

(B) any lawyer, accountant, engineer, or teacher whose performance of such [advisory] services is solely incidental to the practice of his profession

(C) any broker or dealer whose performance of [advisory] services is solely incidental to the conduct of his business as a broker or dealer and who receives no special compensation therefor

(D) the publisher of any bona fide newspaper, news magazine or business or financial publication of general and regular circulation

(E) any person whose advice, analyses, or reports relate to no securities other than securities which are direct obligations of or obligations guaranteed as to principal or interest by the United States, or securities issued or guaranteed by corporations in which the United States has a direct or indirect interest which shall be designated by the Secretary of the Treasury, pursuant to Section 3(a)(12) of the Securities Exchange Act of 1934, as exempted securities for the purpose of the act

Section 202(a)(11)(F) also excepts from the definition of investment adviser certain other persons not within the intent of this paragraph as the SEC may designate by rules and regulations or order.

Whether financial services professionals or financial services firms providing investment advisory services are excepted from the definition of an investment adviser will depend upon the relevant facts and circumstances surrounding the particular case. In addition, SEC Release No. IA-770 points out that persons relying on an exception from the definition of an investment adviser must meet all the requirements of that particular exception. For example, the SEC has indicated that the exception contained in Clause (B) would not be available to attorneys or accountants who offered themselves to the public as persons who provide financial planning, pension consulting, or other financial advisory services. The SEC feels that in such cases the performance of investment advisory services would be incidental to the practice of their financial planning or pension consulting profession and not incidental to their practice as lawyers or accountants. Similarly, the exception for brokers or dealers contained in Clause (C) would not be available to brokers or dealers, or associated persons of brokers or dealers, acting within the scope of their business as brokers or dealers, if such persons receive any special compensation for the provision of investment advisory services. Moreover, the exception from the definition of investment adviser contained in Clause (C) would not be available to associated persons of broker-dealers or registered securities representatives who provide investment advisory services to clients outside of the scope of such persons' employment with the broker-dealers. For example, even if insurance agents are also registered securities representatives or associated persons of a broker-dealer, they would not qualify under the exception to the definition of an investment adviser contained in Clause (C) if they either receive any special compensation from their company for providing investment advisory services or engage in investment advising for compensation independently of their company affiliations, such as to a private clientele. (For a general statement of the views of the SEC regarding special compensation under Section 202(a)(11)(C), see Investment Advisers Act Release No. 640 [October 5, 1978].) In this case insurance agents would be considered to be investment advisers within the scope of the act.

REGISTRATION AS AN INVESTMENT ADVISER

Who Must Register

Any person who is an investment adviser within the meaning of Section 202(a)(11) of the Investment Advisers Act (unless excepted by Sections 202(a)(11)(A) to (F)), and who uses the mails or any instrumentality of interstate commerce in his or her business as an investment adviser, is required by Section 203(a) of the act to register with the SEC as an investment adviser unless specifically excepted from registration by Section 203(b). Section 203(b) excepts the following investment advisers from registration:

- any investment advisers whose clients are all residents of the state where they maintain their principal place of business, and who do not furnish advice or issue analyses or reports about securities that are listed or admitted to unlisted trading privileges on any national securities exchange
- any investment advisers whose only clients are insurance companies

- any investment advisers who during the preceding 12 months have had fewer than 15 clients and who neither present themselves generally to the public as investment advisers nor act as investment advisers to any investment company registered under the Investment Company Act

---

Editor's note: In September of 1988 the S.E.C. issued a new release, IA-1140, proposing important liberalizations of two of the foregoing exemptions, the "intrastate" exemption and the "small adviser" exemption. These liberalizations had not been made official at the time this book was being prepared.

The new intrastate exemption would eliminate the registration requirement for an adviser who operated in only one state, had no more than 50 clients in the preceding 12 months, and managed securities portfolios with a total market value of not more than $10 million at the end of the adviser's last fiscal year.

The new small-adviser exemption would allow the adviser to hold himself or herself out as an investment adviser if the adviser had no more than 25 clients during the preceding 12 months and if the adviser managed securities portfolios with a total fair market value of not more than $1 million at the end of the adviser's last fiscal year.

However, neither of these exemptions will be available unless three conditions are present: (1) the adviser must be registered with the appropriate securities regulatory authority in each state in which the adviser conducts business; (2) the adviser may not advise any investment company registered under the Investment Company Act of 1940 or a business development company regulated as such under that act; and (3) the adviser must not have custody of any client funds or securities.

Procedure for Registering as an Investment Adviser

The materials necessary for registering with the SEC as an investment adviser can be obtained by writing to the Publications Unit, Securities and Exchange Commission, Washington, DC 20549. Application for registration involves filing with the Washington headquarters of the SEC three executed copies of Form ADV (Uniform Application for Investment Advisers Registration), along with a filing fee of $150. Form ADV consists of two parts and a number of supplementary schedules. Part I of Form ADV requires information on the type and location of the registrant's business and associates, as well as on the registrant's background and fiduciary relationships with clients. Part II of Form ADV requires more detailed information concerning the nature of the applicant's business, basic operations, types of services offered, and fees charged. Further questions are asked about the adviser's clients and about investment advisory services and methods of operation, including specific business associations within the securities industry and the degree and kind of direct involvement undertaken in securities transactions for clients. Other questions elicit information about the educational and business standards and background of the adviser and certain associates. The registrant is also asked to provide a balance sheet.

If the SEC finds that the applicant has satisfied the requirements upon which registration is normally accepted, it must grant registration within 45 days of the filing date or institute proceedings to determine whether registration should be denied. Registration will be denied if these requirements have not been met or if the SEC determines that registration, if granted, would be subject to suspension or revocation. For example, registration might be denied, suspended, or revoked if the proposed conduct of the adviser's business does not meet the standards defined by the Investment Advisers Act or if a previously undisclosed securities law conviction in the applicant's past was discovered.

In addition to filing this initial application for registration, each year the Registered Investment Adviser must file with the SEC an updated Form ADV-S.[2] Full and factual disclosure in Form ADV and in the annual updates of Form ADV (as well as in the brochures provided annually to clients, as discussed below) is mandatory.

Additional Requirements for a Registered Investment Adviser

Once accepted by the SEC as a Registered Investment Adviser, the adviser must comply with certain other requirements, including the delivery of written disclosures to clients and the maintenance of certain records required by SEC rules.[3]

A Written Disclosure Statement

A Registered Investment Adviser must deliver a written disclosure, or brochure, to each current and prospective client before or at the time of entering into a written investment advisory contract. This disclosure may be Part II of Form ADV or it may be a separate document containing the information required in Part II. The purpose of this "brochure rule" (Rule 204-3 adopted by the SEC) is to compel full disclosure of an adviser's qualifications, including educational qualifications. Each year the Registered Investment Adviser must deliver (or offer in writing to deliver) an updated brochure to all current and prospective clients. Therefore it is advisable that all Registered Investment Advisers maintain a procedure and schedule to conform to this rule.

---

2. Form ADV-S, containing information about the Registered Investment Adviser's fiscal year, is intended to inform

the SEC whether the adviser is still in business and whether there has been an address change, to remind the adviser to make any necessary amendments to Form ADV, and to provide for the submission of a balance sheet annually.

3. In addition, an investment adviser subject to registration (whether actually registered or not) is prohibited by Section 205 of the act from basing client fees upon a share of the capital appreciation of the funds or any portion of the funds of a client, unless the client is a registered investment company or unless the investment advisory contract relates to the investment of assets in excess of $1 million. Section 205 also prohibits the assignment of an investment advisory contract by the adviser unless the client consents. Finally, Section 208(c) prohibits a Registered Investment Adviser from using the term <u>investment counsel</u> unless that adviser's principal business consists of acting as an investment adviser and a substantial part of this business consists of rendering <u>investment supervisory services</u>, as that term is defined in Section 202(a)(13) of the act.

<u>Record Keeping for Registered Investment Advisers</u>

Rule 204-2 sets forth detailed requirements for the maintenance and retention of certain records, including

- journals and ledgers reflecting asset, liability, reserve, capital, income, and expense accounts
- memoranda of orders given for the purchase or sale of client securities and all client instructions concerning the purchase, sale, receipt, or delivery of a security
- original copies of all written communications recommending or advising clients on courses of action; the receipt, disbursement, or delivery of funds or securities; or the execution of purchase or sales orders
- copies of all written agreements with clients
- copies of all written recommendations for the purchase or sale of a specific security distributed to more than nine people and a memorandum stating the reason for each recommendation (if not stated in the communication itself)
- records of transactions in securities in which the investment adviser or any advisory representative thereof has, or by reason of a transaction acquires, beneficial ownership

Rule 204-2 imposes even more stringent record-keeping requirements on advisers who assume custody of client funds or exercise investment supervisory services. Advisers must keep copies of client acknowledgment of the receipt of two disclosure documents (the brochure plus a statement disclosing how and where client funds are being kept and used) as well as written disclosure statements by anyone who solicited the client's business for the adviser. In addition, copies and continuous records must be kept showing that documents required by the brochure rule, including dates, were furnished to clients and prospective clients. (Records kept and maintained in compliance with Rules 17a-3 and 17a-4 of the Securities Exchange Act of 1934 may be substituted for those required by Rule 204-2, being substantially identical.)

These books and records must be kept in a safe and accessible place for not less than 5 years from the end of the fiscal year of the last recorded entry. Even if the adviser ceases business operations, these records must be kept for this 5-year period. Moreover, these records are subject to SEC examination and audit at any time. To protect the identity and often delicate personal data of clients, client files may be coded--in which case a master code must be kept for client names should any of the adviser's business become a part of an official SEC investigation or compliance proceeding. These records are quasi-public and may be accessed without violation of fourth-amendment protections. Failure to produce records upon request may lead to revocation of registration.

ANTIFRAUD PROVISIONS OF THE ACT

The antifraud provisions of the Investment Advisers Act, as well as the related rules adopted by the SEC under the act, apply to anyone who is an investment adviser as defined in the act, whether or not that person is required to be registered with the SEC as an investment adviser. Sections 206(1) and 206(2) make it unlawful for an investment adviser to employ any device, scheme, or artifice to defraud any client or prospective client, or to engage in any transaction, practice, or course of business that operates as a fraud or deceit upon any client or prospective client. In addition, Section 206(3) of the act generally makes it unlawful for an investment adviser who is acting as a principal for his or her own account knowingly to sell any security to a client, purchase any security from a client, or, acting as broker for another person, buy or sell any security for the account of this client, without disclosing to the client--in writing and before the completion of the transaction--the capacity in which that adviser is acting and obtaining the consent of the client to the transaction.

Although the Investment Advisers Act does not expressly refer to the fiduciary duties of investment advisers, the Supreme Court has held that an investment adviser is a fiduciary who owes clients an affirmative duty of utmost good faith and full and fair disclosure of all material facts.[4] The Court also has stated that a failure to disclose material facts must be deemed fraud or deceit within its intended meaning.[5] Thus the duty of an investment adviser to refrain from fraudulent conduct includes an obligation to disclose material facts whenever the failure to do so would defraud or deceive a client or prospective client--in short, to place the client's interest before self-interest.

SEC Release No. IA-770 emphasizes that an investment adviser's duty to disclose material facts is particularly pertinent whenever the adviser has an actual or potential conflict of interest with a client. The type of disclosure required by an investment adviser in this situation will depend upon the facts and circumstances of the particular case. In general, however, an adviser must disclose to a client all material facts regarding the conflict of interest, so that the client can make an informed decision as to whether to enter into or continue an advisory relationship with the adviser or whether to take some self-protective action against the specific conflict of interest involved. For example, an investment adviser who is also a registered securities representative of a broker-dealer and provides investment advisory services outside the scope of that association with the broker-dealer must disclose to advisory clients that those advisory activities are independent of employment with the broker-dealer. Moreover, if the investment adviser recommends that clients execute securities transactions through the broker-dealer with which the investment adviser is associated, the investment adviser would be required to fully disclose all material facts to clients, including any compensation the investment adviser might receive from that employer in connection with the transactions. In fact, as a general rule an investment adviser must disclose compensation received from the issuer of a security being recommended--regardless of who the issuer may be.

In Release No. IA-770 the SEC also points out that, unlike other general antifraud provisions in the federal securities laws that apply to conduct in the offer or sale of any securities or in connection with the purchase or sale of any security, Sections 206(1) and 206(2) of the Investment Advisers Act do not refer to dealings in securities, but rather are stated in terms of the effect or potential effect of prohibited conduct on the client. As a result the SEC has applied these sections when the fraudulent conduct arose out of the investment advisory

---

4. See SEC v. Capital Gains Research Bureau, Inc. 375 U.S. 180, 194 (1963).

5. Ibid., 200.

relationship between investment advisers and their clients, even though the conduct did not involve a securities transaction. Moreover, the SEC has taken the position that an investment adviser who sells nonsecurities investments to clients must disclose to clients and any prospective clients all self-interest in the sale of such nonsecurities investments.

SEC ENFORCEMENT

Section 209 of the Investment Advisers Act authorizes the SEC to conduct investigations of violations and to bring actions to enjoin--that is, to cease and desist. Any person who (without just cause) does not attend and testify at an SEC investigation, answer any lawful inquiry, or produce books or records if it is in his power to do so is guilty of a misdemeanor and is subject to a fine of up to $1,000 or imprisonment for up to one year, or both.[6]

Under Sections 203(e) and 203(f) of the act the SEC may suspend or revoke the registration of an adviser, censor that adviser, or place limitations on his or her activities if the SEC finds that such actions are in the public interest and the adviser or the adviser's associates have committed any offense proscribed by the act.

Investigations and enforcement proceedings are conducted by the SEC's regional offices and by the Division of Enforcement in Washington. When deemed appropriate, criminal proceedings may be instituted by the Justice Department at the discretion of the attorney general.

CONCLUDING COMMENTS

The financial planning field is maturing and expanding, and there is an ongoing realignment of traditional major segments of the financial services industry (that is, securities, insurance, and banking) into a more homogeneous group of institutions and markets characterized by intensifying competition and cross-selling of products and services. As a result, financial services professionals will increasingly bring investment advising into play in their efforts to meet consumer needs. The Investment Advisers Act will undoubtedly have an impact on an ever-larger number of their activities in the future. In addition, other professionals whose activities on behalf of clients come under the provisions of the Investment Advisers Act, such as attorneys, accountants, and pension and employee benefits consultants, may also be subject to its compliance and enforcement procedures. Thus it is imperative that all financial services professionals have a clear understanding of the definition of an investment

---

6. 15 U.S.C. Section 80b-9(c).

adviser contained in the act, since most investment advisers are required to register with the SEC and all are subject to the antifraud provisions of the act and the SEC's antifraud rules.

Although this reading has focused on the impact of the Investment Advisers Act on financial services professionals, it should be emphasized that most of the 50 states have securities laws and regulations that define an investment adviser similarly to the way the federal law defines one. In addition, in 40 states there is also a registration requirement for investment advisers. Therefore it is imperative that financial services professionals also familiarize themselves with the particular requirements of laws and regulations in their home states.

RELATIONSHIPS BETWEEN FINANCIAL SERVICES PROFESSIONALS

by Gwenda L. Cannon*

In this reading attention will be primarily focused on comprehensive financial planners as they deal with other financial services professionals. Relationships with other financial services professionals will be primarily of two types: financial planners dealing with clients' existing advisers and financial planners dealing with members of their own financial planning team. Contact with clients' existing advisers will usually occur initially during the data-gathering process and will be most frequent during the implementation period following the presentation of the plan. During preparation of the plan, financial planners will be more involved with the various members of their own financial planning team.

Problems in relationships between planners and other financial services professionals may be exacerbated when the services offered by planners are more specialized (for example, insurance planning, investment planning, etc.). Whenever there are significant increases in problem levels and to the extent special problems seem to exist for more specialized planners, they have been noted.

In an effort to avoid repetition, the term traditional professionals has been used to describe accountants and attorneys while the term traditional advisers has been utilized to encompass accountants, attorneys, life insurance advisers, investment advisers, bankers, and other financial services professionals.

No effort has been made here to deal directly with the complexities of office politics, corporate gamesmanship, and other manipulative and/or destructive behavior that human beings are capable of inflicting on one another. Rather this is an attempt to present some stereotypical advisers whom financial planners may encounter in their professional role and with whom they will need to learn to collaborate.

Emphasis has been placed on financial planners' relationships with their clients' traditional advisers as those relationships, particularly those with the clients' accountants or attorneys, present the greatest possibility

---

*Gwenda L. Cannon, JD, is a former faculty member of The American College.

for damaging the financial planners' credibility with clients if they are mishandled.

It is axiomatic to say that human relationships are always complex. This results from the fact that each person is unique and therefore no two people ever bring exactly the same background and life experience to a situation. Verbal communication is an inexact method at best for sharing experiences. When advisers with a common client are attempting to form a working relationship, complexities such as status, preservation of livelihood concerns, and interdisciplinary suspicion present further complications. These problems are inherent and will exist regardless of the individuals involved, until each adviser has sufficient experience with the other to reach a level of confidence that neutralizes these concerns. This situation results both from the advisers' personal experiences and personalities and from traditional problem-solving methods.

TRADITIONAL PROBLEM-SOLVING METHODS VERSUS FINANCIAL PLANNING: HOW THEY DIFFER

Traditional problem solving can be characterized in two major ways: it is isolated and fragmented. This situation results not because of any failure on the part of traditional advisers, but because of the traditional methods of approaching and solving problems.

To solve a problem in the traditional way, clients must be perceptive enough, sophisticated enough, and interested enough to appreciate problems that exist, that may be lurking somewhere in the mountains of documents and red tape that pervade our lives, or that may be created by the complexities of a turbulent economy or ever-changing tax laws. If clients are sufficiently perceptive, sophisticated, and/or interested, or if problems are thrust squarely at them, they will be able to consult traditional professionals or advisers. Such advisers will be able to bring their expertise to bear upon the solution to a problem, if one is possible at that time.

When we look at the process closely, it becomes apparent that problems and potential problems are presented to advisers in a generally ad hoc manner; that is, each is examined for a specific purpose of prevention or solution. The inevitable result of such an approach is isolated and fragmented advice. Such advice cannot help being problematic, as traditional problem-solving methods do not allow the impact of the advice upon a client's total personal and financial situation to be considered at one point in time.

The process is further isolated and fragmented by the necessity of utilizing the expertise of one traditional adviser or another, because there has been no comprehensive cross-disciplinary approach to problem solving. The solutions to problems presented in such an isolated context, and fragmented among advisers with differing areas of expertise, can be conflicting or counterproductive. They can impact adversely on another aspect of the client's personal or financial situation to the detriment of the client and/or his family.

Consider a preventive approach to problem solving that is comprehensive and objective. Traditional advisers do not have an answer to that as there has been no one discipline to take a comprehensive look at a client's total financial and personal situation and to integrate all appropriate problem solutions/preventatives into a cohesive plan.

Financial planning presents a viable alternative to the traditional problem-solving methods. It seeks to prevent many problems from maturing by utilizing methods for their early detection through a comprehensive review of the client's overall family and business affairs. This approach ensures that problems are considered in the overall context of the client's total life situation and are not dealt with as isolated issues. Because the financial planner utilizes a team of experts to formulate planning recommendations appropriate for the client, the impact of advice is considered in its appropriate overall context and ceases to be fragmented.

There is an additional benefit to the client in the financial planning approach. To a great extent a professional financial planner can coordinate the efforts of many advisers with different areas of expertise, thereby freeing the client of this responsibility.

TRADITIONAL ADVISERS VERSUS FINANCIAL PLANNERS: WHY THEY DIFFER

In addition to problems inherent in traditional problem solving the traditional professional disciplines—accounting and law—have imposed upon themselves additional constraints that significantly reduce their capacity to serve the totality of a client's needs at a particular point in time. These constraints include prohibitions against solicitation of business, conflicts of interest, and the sharing of a professional practice with one who is not a member of the particular discipline. While these constraints are reasonable, they produce advice that in most cases must be initiated by the client, problems that are approached impersonally by the adviser, and solutions that are inhibited by single disciplinary expertise and specialization.

The regulatory prohibition against the solicitation of business has as its purpose the prevention of professionals' using their superior education and training to encourage laypersons to make extensive use of their services to their own benefit. A less desirable result of this prohibition is that traditional professional advice becomes almost totally client-initiated. This not only leaves the client free to procrastinate about securing advice, but as we have already mentioned, places the responsibility for knowledge about the existence of problems or potential problems on laypersons who may not have the time, opportunity, or inclination to educate themselves sufficiently. Traditional professionals do participate in educational programs concerning problems dealt with by their disciplines, to assist clients and the general public in becoming more informed. These programs, however, are not usually sufficient to overcome client apathy and procrastination because of the regulatory requirement that such efforts be addressed to broad general issues, not individual problems, and because the audience they reach is relatively small.

In addition, the nonsolicitation-of-business requirement has become so psychologically ingrained in members of the traditional professions that there are attitudinal as well as regulatory prohibitions against it. These attitudinal prohibitions can probably be traced back hundreds of years to the distinction between the learned professions and tradesmen: tradesmen solicited business; the learned professions did not.

Currently the regulatory constraints have been relaxed somewhat as a matter of law to allow for certain regulated types of advertising. It is apparent, however, that the attitudinal prohibitions have remained very strict. The majority of members of traditional professions still feel uncomfortable with any but the most discreet touting of their services. Few of them are comfortable with a situation in which professionals directly ask clients to examine their affairs to determine whether there is a need for professional services. The vast majority prefer to wait for the client to discover a problem that traditional professionals will then attempt to solve. Attorneys or accountants generally do not investigate at that time all other areas of the clients' lives, although the solutions to the problems that brought clients to their offices may have far-reaching implications.

In contrast, other advisers, such as investment advisers, insurance agents, and others who have products for sale may be very actively soliciting business by aggressively attempting to identify a problem area that requires the purchase of their product. These advisers also frequently ignore other problem areas and problems created by or ancillary to the product purchase. They can, however, be very effective at client motivation.

In short, traditional professionals lack the real capacity to motivate clients to action because of regulatory and attitudinal constraints, while other advisers (especially those who are engaged in the sale of products) often lack objectivity in delineating clients' problems because their compensation is based on the sale of a specific product.

As financial planners, part of the most basic service to clients is to reach out to them and make them aware that given the complexities of today's world, there is the potential in everyone's life and business affairs for problems that can be expensive, perhaps impossible, to resolve if not detected early. Financial planners must convince clients that no one is immune to the need to review his or her affairs in a comprehensive way at regular intervals to ensure that one aspect of planning does not impact adversely on another aspect or impinge on some important tenet of family planning. Further, financial planners must motivate clients to begin the comprehensive planning process and to keep it updated.

Solely as a result of this outreach approach, financial planners must be prepared to incur the displeasure of the more traditional professional disciplines. There can also be an element of hostility from these and other traditional advisers who feel threatened because they believe that the involvement of financial planners will disrupt the relationship they have with clients and lessen or eliminate the need for certain services and/or products. These problems can be managed, however, and there is indisputably a need for planning services that are neither client-initiated nor product-sale-dependent.

As traditional professionals essentially sell their time, it does not matter to them what advice within the area of their expertise is being solicited. They perceive this situation as an additional safety factor in that it encourages objectivity in areas where clients may be too personally involved to make prudent decisions. Objectivity, of course, is part of the required role of traditional professionals and necessarily so. The result of this approach, however, is that advice becomes not only objective but impersonal as problems rather than people are the focus of the advice.

Traditional advisers who are compensated based on the sale of a product are viewed with suspicion by traditional professionals and comprehensive financial planners, who perceive that their recommendations may be influenced by the amount of potential compensation earned rather than solely by clients' needs. To the extent compensation structures are product-dependent and/or vary from product to product, they make advisers fundamentally vulnerable to the suspicion of self-serving recommendations.

Financial planners who adhere to the comprehensive planning process become involved with their clients to a sufficient degree to become sensitive to the human aspirations of both their personal and business planning. At the same time they are not so personally involved that objectivity is lost. The balancing of personal considerations and technical objectivity produces the optimum planning result.

If the service offered is fee-only financial planning, financial planners are in much the same position as traditional professionals: they are selling their time for compensation. This should assure objectivity. If financial planners are compensated, in whole or in part, from the sale of products, the planning or product recommendations need not be subject to the suspicion that they are self-serving, as long as the comprehensive planning process is scrupulously adhered to. In either case, financial planners utilizing the comprehensive financial planning process offer a plan that has significant independent value and that should provide sufficient information to clients to allow them to assess the necessity or advisability of a particular product purchase. Moreover, any products recommended to implement clients' plans will have the rationale for their use elaborated in the plans themselves. Finally, professional planners will allow clients to compare and evaluate the quality and cost of products recommended with what is available from other sources, assuring objectivity in the procedures and outcomes of the planning process.

As the contemporary legal and financial environment becomes more complex, there is an increasing need for specialization within individual disciplines. As we have noted, traditional problem-solving methods utilizing single discipline expertise are problematic, and these problems are intensified as specialization proliferates and further fragments disciplines.

Financial planners, whatever their background, are not confined to a single discipline. Indeed in almost every case they will have primary knowledge of at least two disciplines--their background discipline and financial planning--and secondary knowledge in other areas of the financial services professions. The level of knowledge required in areas outside their background discipline and financial planning must be at least sufficient to recognize potential problem areas in those related fields. Knowledge of their background discipline should, of course, be maintained at a very high level. Regardless of the fact that financial planners are practicing in areas other than their background discipline, they will be relied on by other members of their financial planning team for current knowledge and a high level of expertise in that discipline.

As the previous sections of this reading have illustrated, there are inherent differences between traditional problem-solving methods and financial planning and between traditional advisers and financial planners. Successful financial planners must be able to understand the differences between their discipline and that of the more traditional advisers in order to recognize the problem areas that exist and still be able to work successfully with traditional advisers to serve the clients' interests.

WORKING SUCCESSFULLY WITH A CLIENT'S OTHER ADVISERS

The role of the financial planner will be primarily that of a highly skilled problem analyst, diagnostician, and coordinator. Rarely will the planner be directly responsible for implementing all, or indeed most, of the recommendations he or she has made in the financial plan. Therefore the financial planner must work closely with an otherwise unrelated group of advisers, many of whom will have some preexisting relationship with the financial planning client. This group of advisers will usually include the client's attorney, accountant, investment adviser, and insurance adviser, and may include others such as trust officers, bankers, or real estate brokers.

Working with members of this existing group of advisers as compatibly as possible generally provides the best service to the client. Establishing such a relationship can be challenging and can work to the detriment of both the financial planner and the client unless the relationship is handled in a professional and tactful manner. If other advisers are dealt with in an appropriate manner, it is usually possible to engage in productive working relationships with them that benefit all parties: the client, the financial planner, and the other advisers.

Sometimes the development and/or maintenance of these relationships is difficult, but rarely is it impossible if both the financial planner and the adviser wish to serve the client.

In an effort to promote the greatest possible cooperation between the financial planner and a client's other traditional advisers, the financial planner should be attuned, from the beginning of the relationship with the client, to the necessity of establishing the best possible rapport with the client and the client's existing advisers. This can only be done through commitment to the client and an honest and straightforward manner of dealing with the client and the client's other advisers.

Explain the Ground Rules to the Client

As early as possible in the relationship with the client and not later than the data-gathering phase, it is imperative to explain to the client the exact role of the financial planner and the precise services that will be provided as part of the financial planning process. Equally important is the necessity of explaining that certain services (for example, documents such as revised wills, insurance trusts, amended tax returns) or products, if they are recommended as part of the financial planning process, must be provided by other professionals who specialize in the preparation or sale of such items. The financial planner will review these items in draft or proposal form to assure that the recommendations they have made have been correctly understood by the other advisers. The client should also be told what the fee arrangements for financial planning will cover. It should be noted that it is likely that certain additional fees (legal, accounting, brokerage, etc.) may be payable to members of the firm or other advisers (including the client's existing advisers) when recommendations are implemented. If there are fee-sharing arrangements or commissions that may be payable to firm members, these should be disclosed.

At an early point in the data-gathering process, the financial planner should inquire about the professional advisers who are currently serving the client. The names, addresses, and telephone numbers of the client's attorney, accountant, investment adviser, banker, life insurance specialist, and other financial advisers should be obtained as a matter of course. More importantly, the relationship between the client and each of these advisers should be explored in some depth. The financial planner should remember that some clients may have long-standing relationships with some or all of their advisers that may be complicated by social or family connections. Before exploring these relationships, it is usually appropriate for the financial planner to reassure the client concerning the firm's established policy of working with a client's present advisers and further strengthening those relationships as long as the client's best interests are being served. In all fairness, it is also necessary to tell the client that if the financial planner uncovers a specific problem that requires exceptional technical expertise, the financial planner will make that fact known and attempt to assist the client in securing the services of someone with the requisite expertise for that part of the plan implementation. An important fact for the client to know, if this situation occurs, is that the financial planner will not benefit financially or otherwise from this arrangement.

With these reassurances, and with the understanding that these statements are part of the ground rules of the financial planning process, clients should be willing to discuss in some depth their relationships with each of their advisers.

The discussion must be in sufficient depth to allow financial planners to ascertain with some precision the relationship between clients and each of their advisers. For example, when gathering data about clients' attorneys, it is appropriate at a minimum to inquire into the following areas:

- whether the attorney serves the client's business needs, functions as a personal attorney, or both
- what the attorney's particular area of technical expertise is
- why the attorney was initially selected
- how long the relationship has lasted
- whether the attorney is a social friend or relative
- what the client's best assessment of the attorney's personality type is (for example, whether the attorney is conservative or aggressive)
- to what extent the client relies on and follows the attorney's advice

It can make a significant difference in developing a working rapport with the attorney whether the client answers

(a) that the attorney is involved in all aspects of the client's personal and business affairs; is an expert in corporate law; was chosen because of his affiliation with the best law firm in the city; has been with the client for many years and is always consulted on important matters; or
(b) that personal involvement is very limited in scope and/or time and the attorney merely acts as a draftsperson to implement the client's decisions.

A similar inquiry should be made regarding each of the client's advisers.

From this discussion the financial planner can begin to assess which advisers have the most influence on the client and to determine those with whom he or she may be uncomfortable or displeased.

Preparing to Make Contact with Clients' Other Professional Advisers

It is not uncommon for clients, especially those with strong ties to one or more of their advisers, to behave as if they were children playing hooky from school when seeking the advice of financial planners. These clients may prefer that information about such a visit be kept from their other advisers, as they are apparently apprehensive that the various advisers would construe such a consultation as either an indictment of the advice they have given previously or a threat to their relationship with the client with possible resulting unpleasantness and hostility. Preparation for making the initial approach to the other advisers, therefore, must be treated sensitively.

Clients should be consulted about which of their advisers are aware that they have planned to consult a financial planner. When this fact is ascertained, clients can then be asked about their responses to this information. Financial planners should preserve this data, which gives further information about the adviser's potential response should the adviser need to be contacted in the future. As to the advisers who have not been notified, clients should be asked whether there are reasons why they wish them not to be told. A list of those advisers should also be noted carefully to avoid breaching the clients' confidentiality, even inadvertently. If the list of noninformed advisers contains the names of persons from whom critical information or documents must be obtained, such as attorneys or accountants, financial planners should be prepared to assist clients in obtaining that information personally so that they can furnish it to financial planners.

Financial planners must now take steps to begin mutually favorable relationships between themselves and the advisers who have been informed and those clients wish informed.

The first step in this process is to discuss with clients the possible methods that can be employed. In general, the best first step in establishing good working relationships with the clients' other advisers is to ask clients to contact their major advisers personally and tell them that they are working with a financial planning firm, and to ask advisers to offer whatever assistance the financial planner may require to complete clients' financial plans. Clients should be advised to follow up with a written authorization to their major advisers to permit them to discuss their affairs with financial planners and to release any pertinent information to which they have access. Traditional professionals and most other traditional advisers are unable because of ethical and/or legal constraints to release information or to discuss clients' affairs with anyone without the clients' permission, and they will need a written copy of the release for their files.

A release of the following type is generally sufficient if the client is uncertain of what such a document should contain:

James A. Smith, CPA
Smith and Smith, Accountants
1430 Main Street
Anywhere, U.S.A.

Dear Mr. Smith:

We have engaged the financial planning firm of _____ to prepare a
   (name of firm, address)
comprehensive financial plan for our family.

Mary Jones, Chartered Financial Consultant, is in charge of preparing our plan. This will authorize you to discuss fully with Ms. Jones or a representative of her firm any aspect of our business or personal situation of which you or your office has knowledge.

We will appreciate your fullest possible cooperation in this matter.

                             Yours very truly,

                             /s/ Anne and George Brown
                             Mr. and Mrs. George A. Brown

If a corporation or partnership is involved, another authorization should be prepared containing the signature of the corporate president or partner. Although authorization to release information regarding a business entity can be effected by adding the client's signature in his or her corporate or partnership capacity to the personal authorization, it is better to prepare a separate authorization for each business entity. Most advisers will prefer this approach as files are kept separately, and this allows the adviser to file each authorization in the pertinent file.

The form of the authorization for a business is substantially the same as the personal authorization already illustrated. The appropriate form for the signatures is

Partnership	Corporation
ABC Partnership	Widget Makers, Inc.
_____	_____
George A. Brown General Partner	George A. Brown President

After these steps have been completed, it is time to move to the next step: making the initial contact with the client's advisers.

Making the Initial Contact

After the financial planner has ascertained that the other advisers are aware of the engagement to prepare a financial plan for a now mutual client, the financial planner, who is in direct charge of preparing the plan, should take the initiative for contacting the other major advisers. This should be done as expeditiously as possible to prevent the advisers from forming erroneous impressions about the role of the financial planner, and perhaps reacting with hostility because they feel that their relationship with the client is being endangered. The method of the initial contact with the other advisers may vary according to their accessibility to the financial planning firm and the personality and preference of the financial planner. It is not unusual, for example, for financial planning firms to have a multistate client base. If the financial planner's office is in Washington, D.C., and the client lives in Seattle, a letter or phone call is the most realistic means of introduction to the other advisers. On the other hand, if the client is a resident of the same city as the financial planner's firm, arranging a personal meeting may be advantageous.

Whatever method is chosen, a financial planner must undertake to acquaint the other major advisers with the basic concepts and philosophy of the financial planning profession and of the particular financial planning firm.

As financial planning is a new profession, a most important part of the initial contact with each adviser is to explain the services that financial planning provides. We have already discussed providing the client with this information. The same type of discussion should be held with the client's adviser to ensure that the adviser is absolutely aware of the role that the financial planner will play in the process, and which services will be performed by outside advisers after the development of the plan.

An equally important part of this initial contact is assuring the existing adviser that, as a financial planner, your objective is to work with that person to strengthen, rather than disrupt, the existing client relationship. Do not be hesitant about emphasizing this point and reassuring the adviser that generally this approach best serves the client's needs in the following manner. The financial planning process adds a fresh and comprehensive approach to a client's problems that can unearth unexpected and complex issues not readily apparent to more traditional advisers because of traditional methods of approaching and solving problems. At the same time, it does not force a client to become accustomed to dealing with an entirely new group of advisers while trying to grasp difficult concepts and make complex decisions.

Assure the adviser that, as a financial planner, you have no wish to replace the adviser in his or her relationship with the client, and that your role in the financial planning process is to act as an overall data analyst, diagnostician, problem solver, and catalyst in getting the planning process completed and the plan's recommendations implemented.

Emphasize the fact that when properly utilized, the two disciplines actually complement each other, and that there is no reason for them to become competitive. If done at an optimum level, the financial planning process encourages clients to consult their attorneys and accountants and other advisers regularly and to keep their personal and business affairs reviewed and current. This is a valuable service to the other adviser as it keeps that adviser in closer contact with the client and should, therefore, strengthen their relationship.

As a financial planner's training and background can be in a number of areas such as law, accounting, investments, or insurance, it is not inappropriate for the planner to acknowledge to the other adviser a need to draw on his or her single discipline expertise in order to effectively serve the client by implementing this plan. It is not a mistake to be candid to a degree about the limitations of one's knowledge or expertise in certain technical areas. A financial planner whose background is in insurance or investments can know a great deal, for example, about tax planning, but will not have the depth of knowledge of a tax attorney. A statement of this fact simply acknowledges your awareness of the reality of that situation. No honest human being is an expert in everything.

If a planner is engaged in more specialized planning, a description of the data-gathering process and the logical progression of this plan into a recommendation or proposal should be explained to the advisers involved.

None of the foregoing should be presented or construed to suggest in any way that a financial planner will automatically defer to any other adviser. Rather, one should seek to convey the impression that the financial planner is a bona fide professional with a high level of integrity who will put the client's interests before any issue of self-aggrandizement or self-enrichment, and who will work diligently with any other adviser whose goals and philosophy are similarly serving the client.

The initial contact will not, in all likelihood, be an exhaustive dialogue; however, its tone should give the financial planner some preliminary idea of the sort of person to be dealt with. It will also give the other adviser an opportunity to begin to form an opinion of the financial planner professionally.

When Is Conflict Likely to Develop between the Financial Planner and Other Advisers?

Although conflict can develop at any stage of the financial planning process, it may become apparent particularly in the initial contact and in the implementation stages after the financial plan has been presented and approved by the client. To the extent that narrower planning is involved, conflict is more likely to arise either in the initial contact or in the proposal stage, but can also extend into implementation.

Danger Signals in the Initial Contact and Some Possible Solutions

While some professional advisers will be reassured by a financial planner's utilization of the suggested initial approach, many will merely continue to be skeptical about your intentions and some will be openly antagonistic. If you are unable to reach a particular adviser, for example, for a protracted period for no apparent reason, this can indicate that a problem exists. Instead, you may reach an adviser and detect an extremely cold and hostile attitude. It is always better to attempt to win over a hostile or antagonistic person by demonstrating your professionalism and competence, rather than succumbing to your frustration.

The adviser who will not return your calls is more difficult. You may wish to begin writing to that adviser with a copy to the client. If you are unable to remedy the situation within a reasonable period of time through repeated calls or correspondence, it may be necessary to inform the client in a low-key way that you have been unable to reach a particular adviser. Then, ask if the client can assist you by giving the adviser a gentle reminder to cooperate with you. It is important, however, that you take the greatest care not to allow the client to become trapped in a controversy between you and another adviser. This is especially true at the beginning of the financial planning process.

If even the client's reminder does not bring a response from the particular adviser, this is an exceptional situation and is virtually impossible to defuse. It usually indicates that the client is not especially valued by this other adviser or that the adviser feels so powerful in this relationship that the individual believes that in any contest of wills, he or she will be the winning party.

If this situation should develop and persist, do not allow yourself to use the client as the channel of communication between the two of you, as technical information will inevitably be garbled in the transmission. Rather, ask the client to request the specific information you need from that adviser or to obtain it from another source.

Even in this bleak circumstance, it is not advisable to decide that this difficult adviser is expendable. When the plan has been completed, and the client has accepted those of your recommendations that are most suitable, offer the client a copy of the plan to show to the various advisers. Upon reading your carefully prepared work product, this troublesome person may then begin to be convinced that this is a matter of dealing with another professional whom he or she can respect.

Types of Advisers That You Will Meet

One of the most gratifying aspects of working with other advisers is the opportunity to become acquainted with a diversity of people and talent. If these opportunities are viewed as challenging but potentially rewarding, rather than as hurdles that must be overcome, each new working relationship can add significantly to your self-confidence and pride as a financial planner. In many cases, you will find that you enjoy the relationships immensely and in all cases, that you need each other to serve the client's needs.

It is important to remember that the essence of being a financial planner is that you are a team player. The position is roughly analogous to that of a football quarterback. It is a highly visible position, particularly in the initial stages of the planning process. It is impossible to deliver the best financial planning services for your client, however, without other members of the team participating.

It is highly unlikely that a client has chosen a particular adviser with absolutely no merit. It follows, therefore, that you must assume each adviser has some value to the client. Every attempt should be made to utilize whatever talent the adviser has, thereby reassuring the client of his or her sound judgment upon entering that relationship. No purpose is served by making the adviser appear foolish, as it reflects adversely on the client. Any such denigration can only widen an already troublesome breach between you and the other adviser and, most significantly, would reflect adversely on you as a professional. If you are sincerely interested in working successfully with another adviser, you can usually achieve a working relationship and will often learn something of value from this relationship.

The Traditional Attorney or Accountant

Many financial planners have more problems in dealing with a client's attorney or accountant than with the other advisers. This can be especially true if the financial planner does not have a legal or accounting background. If you have a legal or accounting background, discuss your training generally with the attorney or accountant. If you went to the same school or know some of the same people, you may find that the adviser will be somewhat reassured. Do not, however, assume that your problems are necessarily over. You may still find the attorney or accountant extremely skeptical. If you do not have a legal or accounting background, you may have even more difficulty.

If attorneys or accountants will be assisting in the preparation of planning recommendations, you may be able to utilize this information to reassure the traditional professional even if you do not share backgrounds.

A common initial result of these encounters is that the financial planner decides that the lawyer or accountant is adopting a completely arrogant attitude and is only interested in being an obstruction to the financial planning process.

The attorney or accountant, meanwhile, is immediately suspicious that the financial planner is proposing the financial planning process to the client merely as a method for selling something, such as insurance or investments.

It is often helpful to explain to the adviser the chronological progression of the financial planning process when it is done in a totally professional manner. The initial step in the chronology of this process is that the data are completely analyzed. Then the client's stated concerns and any other potential problems that become apparent to the financial planner in the process of looking at the client's affairs in a comprehensive manner are explored. Alternative recommendations and solutions to various problems are offered. Each recommendation discloses the potential risks and rewards if it is adopted. The client is then in a position to make an informed decision. These recommendations and suggestions may include restructuring business entities, or rearranging business transactions to allow the client to save taxes or meet other objectives. Recommendations will be offered to reduce the client's tax burden by every possible legal method that is prudent and consistent with the client's goals. If the client is still paying excessively high income taxes, that fact can be illustrated clearly by using tax and cash-flow projections before and after the recommendations are implemented. When all possible tax planning has been demonstrated in this fashion, the client can make an informed decision about the advisability of further tax reduction/deferral through various tax-sheltering vehicles that are available in the marketplace.

In addition, the client's goals will be measured against a capacity to maintain that person's living standard in a time of adversity, such as disability or death of a family breadwinner. This analysis is presented in the plan in a manner that clearly allows the client to assess the extent of personal exposures. Once potential exposures have been clearly delineated, the advisability of insuring to meet such events can be explored.

In short, a properly constructed financial plan arranges the client's personal and business affairs to best advantage in an objective manner. While the plan may ultimately disclose the desirability of some product purchases, such as insurance or tax shelters, the plan should never be designed with such an end in view. This is being less than honest with the client and reflects a lack of integrity on the part of the financial planner.

The design of a plan to promote product sales is precisely what the traditional attorney and accountant fears most when approached by a financial planner and will probably be the biggest obstacle you will encounter in dealing with these advisers. If your financial planning firm offers fee-only financial planning, divulging this fact to the attorney or accountant, and discussing it in a straightforward manner may go a long way toward allaying that person's suspicion.

If your firm offers products for sale or allows its financial planners to accept commissions on products that are sold, directly or indirectly, through their plans, you may still be able to convince the attorney or accountant that the strict chronology of the planning process is adhered to, and no decision as to the necessity of a product is ever made until the planning process has been completed. Even at that point, only those products that serve the client's interests are suggested. In other words, you need to convince the attorney or accountant that you are an advocate for your client first.

Whether your firm engages in fee-only financial planning or offers products for sale to clients, you should be able to say to attorneys or accountants that you feel the financial planning process and the recommendations embodied in the final plan have significant independent value, as they will be able to judge for themselves when they review your completed work product. You may also wish to tactfully reinforce the fact that your client has been informed of any relationship your firm has with product sales, including any commission or fee-sharing arrangements, and that the client has chosen to work with you while fully understanding these relationships.

As a professional financial planner, you should be able to make these statements with sincerity and confidence. If you cannot do so, examine your firm's policy to see if inherent bias is present as this would result in the client being served poorly.

If you or your firm does more specialized planning such as estate planning, insurance planning, or investment planning, you can expect increased resistance from attorneys and accountants. As a general rule, the closer the specialized planning is perceived by these traditional professionals as being identified with or geared to the sale of a specific product, the more skeptical they are likely to be.

Do not expect attorneys or accountants to actively facilitate a product sale effort, and do not blame these advisers unduly for their hesitance in giving even the appearance of doing so. You may not fully appreciate the severe legal and ethical implications if their conduct can be construed as inadequate representation of their clients, as a conflict of interests, or as the giving of investment advice. Unless you can convince these advisers that you are engaged in offering a bona fide service to clients, they may continue to be uncooperative. In contrast, if you have been successful in persuading traditional professionals that your services are valuable to them and their clients, you should be rewarded with allaying many of their concerns and enlisting their cooperation.

The Professional Whose Background Is Different from Your Primary Discipline

Although financial planners must deal with aspects of accounting, law, insurance, and investments, it is rarely the case that they each hold degrees or are certified in all of these fields. Usually they have a primary discipline, such as law, and have studied the other areas to a sufficient degree to recognize existing problems there.

Let us take, for example, the financial planner whose primary discipline is law. In the process of preparing a financial plan for a client, it is obviously necessary to examine other than purely legal issues. One of the areas of concern is whether the client has sufficient insurance protection to provide for the family during a prolonged period of disability, to provide for the support of the family in the event of an untimely death, and to provide sufficient estate liquidity.

A competent financial planner should be able to ascertain the type and the amount of insurance the client owns, the cash value (if any), the current death benefit, and the cost to the client per thousand dollars of death benefit. There is no guarantee, however, that the legally trained financial planner will be able to recommend whether such insurance should be maintained, or whether it is no longer cost-effective, without consulting a colleague who is familiar with the most current insurance products on the market. Indeed, it is almost a certainty that the planner would not be familiar enough with the insurance products currently available to offer such advice prudently.

Remembering that changing the type of insurance one carries on a whim is time-consuming, expensive, and foolhardy, the legally trained financial planner will wish to enlist the aid of a colleague who is an expert in the insurance field to prepare the insurance analysis and recommendations for that client's plan.

If the financial planner's firm has other financial planners who are specialists in the insurance field, they will be able to give some assistance in determining the amount and type of insurance that would be appropriate for the client's needs. If no such assistance is available from firm members, it will be necessary to have contractual or other arrangements for such assistance with an independent insurance specialist.

This makes the financial planner uncomfortable professionally. The planner is relinquishing control of part of this plan and giving it to someone whose conclusions and recommendations cannot be self-validated. The planner feels vulnerable.

The discomfort and vulnerability experienced can be exacerbated when the financial planner must deal with the client's insurance adviser. The planner is wary of any suggestion from the client's insurance adviser as it is impossible to personally assess its validity. If the planner attempts an in-depth discussion with the client's insurance adviser, this insecurity will certainly communicate itself to the other professional. The insurance adviser may then decide the financial planner is incompetent or is simply trying to take away the client.

In these situations, it is a much better tactic to allow the adviser to read the plan and to answer any general questions about the basic concepts involved in the recommendations. The adviser should be told, however, that the financial planner's area of primary expertise is law, and that specific questions concerning the insurance recommendations should be discussed with whoever within (or on behalf of) the firm was responsible for formulating them. Arrangements should be made for these two insurance specialists to discuss these issues as soon as possible. After their discussions, the legally trained financial planner must have a sufficient trust level in that person's colleague to abide by this decision.

The essence of successful cross-disciplinary professional relationships is trust--trust in the other adviser's integrity, technical capacity, and personal philosophy regarding service to one's clients. Such trust should not be given lightly and may require (1) some careful inquiry in the community, (2) inquiry from the other adviser's professional associations, and (3) astute observation of the way in which the adviser handles this particular case to form an initial opinion.

These relationships are among the most difficult to maintain, for while both parties to them may be scrupulously honest, neither has an effective way to evaluate the other's performance. For that reason, if such working relationships do flourish, rely on them and cultivate them carefully.

The Overly Aggressive Adviser Who Poses a Threat to the Client

There may be occasions when you will have to deal with an adviser who becomes so aggressive in approaching legal, tax, accounting, or other matters, that it appears to you that a client who followed the advice would actually be in violation of the law. Many times the client is not sophisticated enough to appreciate the subtleties of the situation and merely relies on the advice given. This situation can expose the client to severe penalties, both civil and criminal. As a financial planner, it is your duty to advise your client against becoming involved in any legal violation.

This does not mean that you must malign the adviser or that you should. Instead, you should concentrate on the legal issues involved and ascertain whether the adviser has some explanation or legal theory that would keep your client from being involved in an illegal act. Many times you may find that the adviser has a tenable legal theory that you believe would constitute a defensible position. It is certainly true that reasonable persons can differ regarding the interpretation of statutes and regulations.

If you genuinely feel that the adviser is pursuing an illegal course, and you are unable to persuade that person privately to a change in attitude, you have no choice but to inform your client that you believe such a course is perilous because it constitutes a legal infraction. You must also explain the possible penalties to which the client may be subjected if such a violation should result in legal action.

You cannot control the client's behavior and so cannot ensure that the client will not pursue the course you feel is improper or illegal. You have, however, informed the client of the risks and encouraged an independent decision.

These are extremely difficult situations that too often result in a great deal of ill will. They must be handled in an extremely delicate fashion. It is generally advisable to deal with the client and the adviser about these matters verbally, and not to include an extensive discussion of the alleged violations in the plan, as the plan could fall into the wrong hands and become very damaging to the client. There is also the problem of legal confidentiality. There is no legally privileged communication between financial planners and their clients.

In addition, financial planners must give some thought to protecting themselves against charges of negligence if the violations are later discovered and clients attempt to defend themselves on the grounds that they had no such knowledge. A memo to the file outlining the problem and giving the dates on which clients were informed and the advice they were given is probably prudent. If possible, it would be advisable to have clients sign a copy of such a memorandum.

A word of warning: If you believe that a client is continuing to follow advice from another adviser that you consider illegal after you have apprised that client of the facts, think carefully about terminating this counseling relationship. There are severe penalties for advisers who are convicted for aiding or abetting illegal acts. Given the severity of penalties and the personal and professional risks to the financial planner, termination of the relationship is probably the indicated course of action in these situations.

The Family Retainer--Well-Meaning and Sometimes Inept

This adviser may be a friend, relative, or simply a longtime confidant of the client. This type of adviser seems to be more prevalent in smaller cities and towns, but can occur in any setting. As a general rule, this adviser will be personally involved with the client and family, knowing and caring more about that client at this more intimate level.

This type of adviser is many times a generalist in a time when professions are moving rapidly toward specialization. You may, therefore, find the adviser lacking in technical expertise and willing to admit these limitations, or you may discern them at a fairly early stage of your working relationship.

Generally, this adviser is willing to accept assistance from the financial planner as long as it is tactful. This assistance need not undertake to totally educate the other adviser, but should be a comprehensive clarification of your recommendation. This clarification can be implemented by carefully prepared memoranda that should contain pertinent technical information and should be covered at a level that the adviser will understand. Be extremely careful not to adopt a condescending tone in these memoranda. They should clearly reflect that they are communications between professionals.

Even with this assistance, however, some projects may simply be beyond the adviser's capacities. In such cases, it may be necessary to suggest to the client that another professional be retained for a specific project on the basis that it deals with a very complex issue and requires an exceptionally high degree of technical skill to execute.

If the client agrees to retain another professional, direct that particular project to the individual promptly. This should be done in a very tactful manner, as it may not be easy for the adviser to accept. However, if the financial planner explains to the client and the existing adviser that only this one project is being moved to a specialist, while others will continue to be worked out with the existing adviser, there is generally very little difficulty. The client and the existing adviser will in all likelihood have sufficient continuing contact to maintain the integrity of their relationship. The financial planner should make every effort to provide sufficient assistance to allow the existing adviser to complete implementation of a client's plan recommendations. A specialist should only be retained when all attempts fail or when the existing adviser indicates that a particular project is outside his or her area of expertise.

Whether a particular project can be accomplished through the existing adviser with the assistance of the financial planner, or whether it must be given to a specialist, the financial planner should take the required action with as little comment to the client as possible. The less remarkable such a situation appears, the less consternation it causes both client and adviser.

Never discuss another adviser's limitations with a client unless there are compelling reasons for doing so, and then only to the extent absolutely necessary. Failure to observe this rule is not only unprofessional, but can result in making enemies of client and adviser alike.

In most cases, this adviser has functioned well considering personal limitations and has served the client adequately for many years on routine matters, and, indeed, will probably continue to do so in the future.

Never alienate such an adviser as long as that adviser is attempting to assist the client. That individual is an important member of your team, with whom your client will undoubtedly discuss your recommendations. If you have kept the adviser informed and involved, and have been courteous, that person will be unlikely to attempt to influence the client adversely. On the contrary, if the adviser feels comfortable with you, a positive attitude is likely to be conveyed to your client. Your client will be reassured by this response.

The Adviser Whose Only Interest Is Exhibiting Technical Skill

Many clients, especially those with substantial net worths and complex business or investment holdings, will have relationships with numerous advisers, some of whom are highly skilled in various technical areas. If you are working with an adviser who is highly skilled in a particular area of expertise and genuinely interested in clients as people, the experience can be a great pleasure. If, however, the adviser is one who is so entranced with displaying technical expertise that the fact that real people are attempting to understand the documents or concepts is forgotten, you may have serious difficulties.

How can you tell when you have become involved with a technical expert who is going to be a problem? The first indication may be in attempting to ascertain whether the adviser actually listens when you are relating client's goals and objectives, or simply skims over the personal and family reasons for the project you are discussing. If the adviser ignores the people involved and is interested only in the technical issues, watch out!

Another indication will occur when the adviser submits the drafts of documents or proposals you have asked for as in the example that follows. Assume that you have recommended a new will and an insurance trust for a high-income young professional who has not yet accumulated a vast net worth. Your proposal is relatively straightforward: a two-trust will (consisting of a marital trust and a residuary trust) and an insurance trust. Income from the residuary trust is to be paid to the wife for life or until she remarries, at which time it is to be continued at the discretion of the trustee; the principal of the residuary trust to be invaded for the wife and

15.24

children as necessary; and the remainder of the residuary trust to go to the children when the trust terminates. The insurance trust was designed to contain the same basic provisions.

When the draft of the will arrives at your office, it is 43 pages long and contains such complex formulae for computing trust shares, including equalization between and among all trusts in the will and the insurance trust, that it takes an expert tax attorney several hours with pad and pencil to translate and comprehend it.

The plan has been changed dramatically. Instead of allowing the trustee to invade the residuary and insurance trusts for the benefit of the wife and children, as necessary, and dividing any remaining assets between the children at the termination of the trust, the instrument requires that each payment to a child be counted as an advance against the child's eventual share. It requires that the wife exercise a special power of appointment to correct any imbalance that she perceives from this arrangement. This places a tremendous real and psychological burden on the wife. She must decide if it is appropriate to exercise the equalization power with regard to each advance made to her children. If she should exercise the power to allow parity after one child has been advanced funds for medical care or to study at Harvard, should she then exercise the power if the other child feels that a year in Europe is more meaningful than college? This plan places a tremendous responsibility on the wife, and it also places a great temptation in her path, for she has the capability to control her children's choice of life-styles through the trusts.

There may even be adverse gift tax implications should she exercise the limited power during the period when she is absolutely entitled to the income from the trust.

The primary objection, however, stems from none of these factors. This is simply not the plan that the financial planner had recommended, discussed with the family, and the family had approved. It is, without question, a plan that might be appropriate for some family--one that is much more affluent and has much more rigid control requirements than the family in question. Any financial planner should regard a document or proposal that falls short of meeting the client's needs as fatally flawed.

You should hope that the other adviser has sent you a draft copy of the document for your review and comments before sending a copy to the client. When dealing with this type of adviser, however, this is frequently not the case, and your client may be totally overwhelmed by the sheer volume of paper already received.

If your client has been sent a draft, assure that person immediately that you have received your copy and are studying it carefully. You will probably want to be candid enough to indicate that it will need some additional work and that you intend to work with the draftsperson on it. Do not let the client remain concerned and bewildered, but do tell the client not to sign the document until you have resolved the problems and received a final draft.

The best approach to take with the other adviser in this situation is to discuss the matter firmly but tactfully as soon as possible. This is without any doubt one of the most difficult conversations you will have to face, but it cannot be avoided if you are to remain a true advocate for your client.

You may wish to open the conversation by expressing some concern over the draft and some confusion as to the origin of the altered plan. It may be effective to inquire whether the client presented the other adviser with a copy of the plan containing the recommendations for the will and insurance trust or whether the client attempted to describe the recommendations to the adviser, or even whether the client merely told the adviser that a new will was needed as well as an insurance trust to minimize estate taxes. Do not immediately jump to the conclusion that the adviser has deliberately ignored the plan that had been worked out for the client and his family. Misunderstandings are always possible.

If there has been a misunderstanding, do not be unpleasant about it. Rather, you should offer to provide the adviser with the recommendations that the family indicated they wished to adopt and ask that a draft copy of the new instruments be sent when they are prepared.

If the "misunderstanding" was deliberate, point out tactfully that the draft you have received does not carry out the client's wishes as expressed to you, and see if the other adviser will relent. If there is no cooperation, you will have to go further and tell the adviser that you do not believe the proposed instruments will best serve the client's needs at this time, and that you must so advise your client. Do not rush to qualify this statement in any way that reduces its impact. It may be best at this time to allow the adviser a few seconds of total silence to consider the possibilities. The adviser may attempt a reconciliation of the matter at this point. If so, let the matter rest once and for all. Work together as pleasantly as possible for the remainder of the project.

If the situation is absolutely irreconcilable and the adviser insists on ignoring all your efforts to bring the matter to some workable conclusion, you will have no choice but to tell the client that the plan embodied in the draft instruments is not, in your opinion, advantageous. This presents immense difficulties, as the client will generally want to know what the other adviser's plan is, how it differs from yours, and why yours is better for the situation. In order to answer these questions, you will have no option but to attempt to explain these highly technical documents to the client and expose their relative merits. In the meantime, the client may also be communicating with the other adviser who is probably assuring that person that the plan is technically brilliant and requesting a signature on the documents without delay.

This places the client in the untenable position of being in a tug-of-war between two experts, neither of whose arguments are totally comprehendible. This is tremendously wearing on the client and can damage the credibility of both advisers.

If you see that the situation has reached this stage, arrange to meet with the client personally, and explain as gently and tactfully as you can that you have reached an impasse with the other adviser. Assure the client that you have tried many different approaches, without success, to move the situation forward. Explain that you have tried to relieve that person of the stress of having to make a choice between you and the other adviser, but that you remain convinced that client interests are not well served by the other adviser's overly complex plan. You should be prepared to tell the client at that point that you cannot approve such a plan, and unless the other adviser can be persuaded to draft an appropriate instrument, you cannot work with the other adviser.

To the best of your ability, communicate to the client that as far as you are concerned, this is not an egotistical contest of wills between you and another adviser. You are merely trying to serve the appointed interests in the best possible way according to your professional judgment.

The client essentially then must make a choice between you and the other adviser. This is the unhappiest of all situations, for it is extremely stressful for all parties. The client is placed in the most stressful position of all, for a decision must be reached with very little comprehension of the technical issues. This leaves the client virtually no information upon which to base a decision. The decision is reduced to which of the advisers has better established credibility as the client's advocate. There are no winners when this situation occurs; fortunately it does not occur often.

Egomaniacal Advisers

These advisers are self-styled experts at everything, whether, in fact, they are brilliant or barely competent. Such an extreme position indicates, of course, that these advisers may be overcompensating for some personal inadequacies, either real or perceived. They are almost impossible to deal with as they leave virtually no room for negotiation of any sort. Once they have made a decision, they become immovable, as any retreat could be construed as admitting that they have made a professional error, and such a thought is simply unbearable to them.

Egomaniacal advisers share many traits with the advisers who are obsessed with technical detail. In particular, such advisers tend to be so self-involved that they forget about the wishes and feelings of clients.

If you are dealing with advisers who purport to have ready knowledge on every aspect of any topic under discussion, you may be dealing with egomaniacal personalities. Such persons will resist every recommendation that you make because it did not come from them, they will battle with you over every word in a work product, and they will make it virtually impossible for you to achieve anything for your clients because they are threatened by your involvement.

If you find yourself in this situation, your options are severely limited. You may seek clients' permission to move the specific project to other advisers who will execute your recommendations under the guise of needing a more specialized technician. If you are unable to extricate yourself in this manner, you must meet with clients and put to them the same choices that were described in the section dealing with the intractable technical expert.

The Best Possible Result

As a general rule, when another adviser is properly introduced to the concept of comprehensive financial planning and is convinced of being genuinely sought after and a necessary participant in carrying that process through, that adviser will respond positively to a well-trained and competent financial planner. This does not mean that the relationship may not have some stress points, or that the other adviser will always agree with you.

If you sense that a stress point is developing or has developed in your working relationship, do not ignore it and hope it will simply go away. Explore with the other adviser the reasons for resistance or discomfort. It may be enough to simply say, "I sense you have some reservations about the _____ recommendation. Can we talk about those for a moment before going on to something else?" This gives the other adviser a polite opening to express doubts and yet does not leave the total responsibility for introducing the subject to that person.

If the adviser's reservations are valid, acknowledge that fact. If a question is raised to which you do not have the answer, agree to look into the matter thoroughly and discuss your findings with the adviser, rather than dismissing it. If the adviser has a good suggestion, indicate that you will present the suggestion to the client, affording him or her appropriate credit.

If you cannot improve on the adviser's handling of a particular part of the client's affairs, such as the estate plan, make sure that the financial plan clearly states that the estate plan is a good one. Even if you wish to make changes in some aspect of this handling of a client's problem, do it gracefully. If the estate plan, drafted in 1962, fails to take advantage of current tax laws, it is unfair to analyze the dispositive instruments, commenting merely that the current tax laws have been ignored. Point out to the client in the plan that the will or other instrument was a competent instrument embodying a good estate plan when it was originally drawn, but that time and tax law changes have made it obsolete. If the instrument is so dreadful that you can do nothing to give the adviser a graceful "out," say nothing. Remember that you will be offering the client a copy of the financial plan for this adviser to read. Another adviser may forgive you a superior knowledge of the tax laws, but will not forgive anything that can be construed as a professional slur.

Keep your discussions directly with the adviser to the greatest possible extent. This method allows you and the other adviser to settle differences in approach or technique, as well as to exchange ideas freely without taking up your client's time and energy. Even if problems develop between you and the other adviser, attempt to deal with them directly with the adviser. Part of the services that you offer your client is acting as liaison and coordinator among various other advisers in order to deliver and implement a cohesive and coordinated plan.

In the normal course of the financial planning process, a truly professional adviser and a competent and conscientious financial planner will develop an instinct for each other's level of expertise and a mutual professional respect that can result in an extremely rewarding relationship long after this client's plan is implemented.

The personality types that have been outlined have, of course, been oversimplified. No adviser is so easily categorized. Most are combinations of two, three, or more of the types. Many times, the personality that another professional adviser exhibits to you is a reflection of that person's feelings about you. Financial planners should recognize that they can produce widely different reactions in other advisers with whom they must work to implement a client's plan.

In order to produce favorable reactions in other advisers, you must become intensely conscious of the way in which people communicate. Some of the most important communication is totally nonverbal, while a constant stream of verbiage should also be telling you something. A person's tone of voice and body language should also be noted carefully, as they are indicative of attitude.

To illustrate the point, assume the following situation. You have called a client's adviser to discuss a particular aspect of implementation. When the adviser answers the telephone, you perceive by the tone of voice that he or she is annoyed. You should immediately think, "Perhaps the time is not convenient," and should ask if this is the case. If the time is inconvenient, ask when it will be convenient for you to call back, and give some estimate of the amount of time you will need. If the adviser's annoyance had nothing to do with you, your courtesy will probably be appreciated and your next call will probably be more pleasant. If the annoyed manner continues, you must look for other clues.

This may seem like a tedious and pedantic approach to advisers and other people; however, it is critically important. The essence of the financial planning profession is establishing such a level of trust with clients that they feel free to tell you some of their most intimate feelings and concerns. This trust cannot be established without becoming acutely aware of clients as persons. This concept applies equally to advisers whose trust you must also obtain.

Advisers, however impressive their accomplishments or credentials, are also people with fears and vulnerabilities. It is important that you do not maliciously or carelessly trigger their fears or intrude painfully into vulnerable areas. Not only will it impair your ability to work with those advisers, but it may touch off defense mechanisms that are unpleasant for you and your clients. Fortunately, most professional advisers are just as anxious to work well with you as you are with them.

Checklist for Dealing Successfully with a Client's Other Advisers

- Establish as early and as thoroughly as possible how your client feels about his or her present advisers.
- If possible, meet or talk with each major adviser early in the relationship. Explain the role of the financial planner, and assure the existing adviser that your objective is to strengthen rather than to disrupt his or her relationship with the client. Keep the adviser <u>appropriately</u> informed and involved in the financial planning process.
- Whenever possible settle your differences in approach or technique directly with the adviser. Do not allow your client to be caught in a battle zone between you and other advisers.
- Try to keep your ego outside the relationship as long as the client is being served adequately (for example, do not suggest repeated rewrites of a document just because you are a better draftsperson).
- Be a strong advocate for your client's interests.
- Be honest about your capabilities--no honest person pretends to know everything.
- Provide substantial services for the adviser in the planning process--do not provide the client a voluminous plan that contains no citations of authority or statistics upon which recommendations are based. This puts the adviser in the untenable position of having to spend long hours of research to validate (or legitimately disagree with) your conclusions or suggestions. It is much easier for the adviser simply to resist them.
- Ask to review items in draft or proposal form. If changes are necessary, it is easier to get an adviser to agree to change a draft or proposal than a final product.
- Behave always in a professional and courteous manner toward other advisers and be sensitive to their needs and limitations.
- Become a devout people-watcher. Observe the ways in which people communicate, especially those that are nonverbal. If this skill is sufficiently developed, it can help you to almost know what a person is thinking, and will assist you in anticipating problems with advisers and dealing with them before they become insoluble.

- Be aware of the legal and ethical constraints that are placed on various advisers. In order to do this, financial planners should read the ethical codes of the various disciplines (for example, The Code of Professional Responsibility for attorneys and Restatement of the Code of Professional Ethics for accountants).
- Believe in your own professional capacity. To maintain this belief, and to ensure its validity, financial planners must keep current in and continue in-depth study of subjects in the financial planning field.

DEALING SUCCESSFULLY WITH MEMBERS OF THE FINANCIAL PLANNING TEAM

The comprehensive financial planner is a specialist in the area of planning and in all likelihood has training or experience in one or more of the financial services professions (accounting, law, insurance, investments, etc.). The planner cannot, however, realistically expect to be an expert in all the financial services fields, and therefore must rely on other professionals who have sufficient technical expertise to help in developing the client's financial plan.

The method by which the expertise of other professionals is made available to the financial planner will vary depending on the size and type of the firm. There are generally three methods that are widely utilized: (1) a broad-based in-house team consisting of at least an attorney, an accountant, a life insurance specialist, and an investment specialist; (2) a team comprised of otherwise unrelated specialists working on a contractual basis for the financial planning firm or individual planner; and (3) a combination of 1 and 2, that is, significant in-house expertise with contractual arrangements for additional services as needed by the financial planner.

The Optimum Approach

The broad-based in-house team represents the best overall approach to the financial planning process since members of the team have easy access to each other and the client, share (at least to some degree) a common philosophy of client service, and may have developed personal and/or working relationships that facilitate sharing of information and expertise. It is unlikely, however, that any financial planning firm will ever have on staff all the advisers who can become necessary. Most firms utilizing this approach will have on-staff attorneys, accountants, and life insurance and investment specialists who will be able to handle the majority of client problems. The firms will usually have contacts with other specialists such as pension consultants, business valuation experts, etc., and will utilize their services when necessary.

Forming the Team

A financial planner with direct responsibility for the development of the client's plan should be assigned by firm management to the client when documents are originally submitted. This assignment is usually made based on those areas of the client's affairs that appear to be a significant portion of the overall planning needs. For example, if a client has multistate business interests and plans to merge these interests, the assignment of the case should go to a financial planner whose primary discipline is law, as there will be substantial areas of tax and securities law that must be explored. On the other hand, if the major problem appears to be a review and analysis of an extensive portfolio of stocks and bonds, a financial planner with an investment background is in all likelihood the better choice. Once the assignment of a financial planner to a client is made, the client becomes his or her client and the planner has total responsibility for coordinating and developing the client's plan. The planner is the team leader and will call on various team members with questions or areas of concern within their areas of expertise.

It is possible, even probable, that financial planners will be team leaders and team members for various client cases at the same time. To a significant degree this can facilitate working relationships among the various professionals--that is, each financial planner shares the experience of being in control of a client's case and lacking control of (and often contact with) another client at the same time. In this manner, the planner is given an opportunity to empathize with other team members.

Dealing with Team Members

If one is the team leader, it is important that all pertinent information, including subjective observations about the client's planning objectives, be given to other team members when their assistance is required. Some information may be pertinent to one team member but not to others. Subjective interpretations such as the client's risk attitude, for example, will be critical to an investment adviser who is asked for investment recommendations, but may be of nominal value to an accountant who is being asked to compute an income tax projection.

In requesting assistance, be sensitive to other demands on the time of team members and allow them sufficient time to adjust their work loads. For example, don't ask, even implicitly, that they drop whatever they are doing and deliver your project unless it is a genuine emergency. If that is the case, discuss the reasons for the need for immediate delivery with the appropriate team member and let that member work with you to accommodate that need.

If it is necessary for a team member to obtain additional information or clarification from the client or the client's advisers, a potentially troublesome question can arise. Who makes the contact, the team leader or team member? Although the answer may vary, the team leader's personal preference should be expressed to the various team members. It may simply require adding to the request for assistance a sentence that says "If you need further information please let me know so that I can contact the client." As a general rule, it is easier to let the team leader make such contacts as it creates less confusion for client and advisers if they deal with one person. Remember, also, that part of the financial planning service consists of utilizing the team leader to coordinate information from various advisers--the leader's and the client's--into a coherent plan. If unauthorized contacts are a problem, ask again, in writing, that requests for information be sent to the team leader in order to keep the client fully informed and minimize confusion. An additional benefit of having other team members channel all questions or requests for additional information through the team leader is that it increases communication between that leader and team members and discloses planning recommendations that are being considered.

When planning recommendations are received from other team members, the team leader must take the time to learn the basic concepts in order to present them to the client and answer general questions that the client may have about them. (Highly technical questions, when asked, should be noted by the team leader and an answer obtained from the appropriate specialist team member.) This may mean that the team leader must spend some time with particular team members, taking a concentrated and fairly sophisticated look at an insurance or investment proposal, the tax implications of certain tax-sheltered or tax-deferred investments, or a provision in the securities law. The team leader must be satisfied that there is a rational basis for the team member's recommendation. The operative word is why--why this choice? Why for this client? What else was a consideration, and why was it not chosen? The client will ask these questions, and it is better to be prepared.

If this information-gathering process is presented to the team member in terms such as those in the preceding paragraph (the team leader's need to be informed for the best presentation of the recommendation to the client), the other team member is most likely to respond positively and to provide the necessary information readily. The team leader should carefully listen to the team member, as this is an opportunity to increase in knowledge of a financial service field other than his or her own. Such knowledge accumulates over time and operates to make the team leader more attuned to clients' potential problems.

In dealing with other team members, remember that they may be your professional peers or your hierarchical superior and not subordinates. Even if they are technically subordinate to you, you need their expertise. Also keep in mind that you will not always be a team leader. This is not an appropriate situation for a power struggle, and the golden rule is a good guideline.

Obviously, on an in-house team one can encounter the same stereotypical advisers who have been discussed in the section on dealing with the client's other advisers. Fortunately in the in-house team setting, most team members are given the opportunity to work closely with other team members and to develop confidence in their colleagues much more rapidly than is possible with outside advisers. In the event that problems persist with particular team members, it may be possible for the financial planner to work with an alternate firm member with a similar background. In any organization, people who are personally compatible tend to work together whenever possible because it is a satisfying experience. The converse is also true. People who are personally incompatible tend to avoid working together whenever possible because the experience is unpleasant. If the majority are compatible, they tend to isolate a colleague who is difficult, unpleasant, or professionally weak. If these natural responses are ineffective or impossible, because a difficult person is the sole person on staff with in-house expertise on a key subject, it may be necessary to involve the firm's management in order to assure cooperation. One should, of course, make every personal attempt to win over a colleague before taking such a step.

In-house teams can easily become very close-knit groups whose members have a high degree of personal and professional regard for each other. Being a member of such a team is an extremely rewarding experience as one can feel confident in relying on colleagues and need not feel defensive in requesting assistance in an unfamiliar field.

Contractual Teams

In this situation the financial planner has chosen for reasons of economy or personal style not to have a permanent staff of advisers. Instead, the planner will have to develop a team comprised of advisers who are independent of each other and of the financial planner. The financial planner can have success with this method of developing the financial planning team; however, there are potentially more problems here than in an in-house team approach.

The financial planner is more likely with a contractual team of advisers to encounter problems such as turf-guarding, client-hoarding, and ego defense and preservation, which have been described in the section on dealing with the client's other advisers. This results because each adviser is an independent businessperson and the financial planner has much less control over such an adviser than over a staff member. It is also much more difficult for the financial planner to forge a tightly knit team from persons who may have very little contact with each other. Although members of a contractual team may share a similar philosophy of client service and similar ethical concerns, it is much harder for them to develop confidence in each other than for an in-house group that has daily opportunities to observe their colleagues in action and to evaluate both how they say they feel about client services and what they do in their relationships with clients. Consistency between what is espoused as a philosophy and what is actually done in the client's behalf builds trust in those who observe it. In the contractual team, team members are rarely able to observe each other, and confidence is built more slowly through lack of opportunity to observe and communicate with other team members. This is true not only for team members, but for the financial planner. Until and unless experience over time provides such significant positive results that almost absolute confidence in the contractual team member is experienced by the financial planner, the problems we have already discussed that are inherent in cross-disciplinary relationships will continue to exist.

The Hybrid

As we have already noted in discussing the in-house team, many financial planning firms will have both significant in-house expertise and contractual arrangements with outside advisers, which will be utilized for highly specialized problems. This is a very sound approach as it combines the advantages of an in-house team with the availability of wider client services through contractual arrangements with specialists who are not needed on a day-to-day basis by the financial planning firm.

There are no problems peculiar to this form of team that have not been discussed previously, except those of size and perhaps technicality. If such a high degree of technical expertise is required that a contractual specialist is required, the financial planner will have to prepare adequately to deal with the specialist. The planner cannot expect that a very sophisticated technician will have time to offer an education about the new field. The planner must be responsible for self-effort and self-education sufficiently to converse with this adviser. Such knowledge need not be exhaustive, but a general background in the area is essential.

The greater the number of team members working on a client's plan, the more unwieldy coordination can become. This is especially true when some of the team members are contractual advisers. The financial planner in charge of the plan must exert his or her utmost organizational efforts to assure that each adviser is provided with sufficient information to complete assignments in a timely fashion. Deadlines should be developed for projects and circulated to team members in writing, and a system for progress checks is vital. Communication and organization are the keys to a successful team effort.

ON PROFESSIONS, PROFESSIONALS, AND PROFESSIONAL ETHICS

by Ronald C. Horn

Editor's note: This reading is an abridged version of chapters 1 and 2 in the monograph On Professions, Professionals, and Professional Ethics written in 1978 by Ronald C. Horn (PhD, CPCU, CLU) for the American Institute for Property and Liability Underwriters. It is used with the permission of the American Institute, the copyright holder. While a few of the points made in the reading apply rather specifically to insurance professionals, most of the reading is relevant to all financial services professionals.

THE IDEA OF A PROFESSION

Characteristics of a Profession

In their efforts to delineate the idea of a profession, a great many writers have concentrated on identifying the distinguishing characteristics. What characteristics, traits, or attributes, they ask, distinguish a profession from other occupations? Their answers commonly take the form of a list of characteristics which professions are thought to possess.[1] While some writers explicitly or implicitly treat the characteristics as literal "prerequisites," this is probably just a poor choice of words, since most see the need to accommodate the varying degrees in which the characteristics may realistically be found in any one occupational group. The majority of writers also seem to feel that it is the collective of all characteristics, taken together, that combine to form the ultimate test. That is to say, it is seldom claimed that any one characteristic is unique to the professions, but rather that the combined set of characteristics is unique enough to distinguish professions from other occupations. Where do the lists of characteristics originate? There are a few creative products of careful thought and reflection. There are also some self-serving lists which were apparently contrived to persuade others that their authors'

---

1. Of the numerous publications which could be cited here, one of the most engaging and praiseworthy of the contemporary efforts is that of Edwin S. Overman, The Professional Concept and Business Ethics, the American Institute for Property and Liability Underwriters, Inc. The late Dr. S. S. Huebner, along with the late Dr. Harry J. Loman, left countless admirers and legacies, but their contributions to the professionalization of the insurance industry were perhaps their most priceless gifts to future generations.

occupations are professions. However, the majority have been content to use medicine, law, and theology--the so-called "learned professions"--as models or benchmarks. The usual line of reasoning goes something like this: the learned professions were the first "true" professions to be widely recognized as such; they have continued to be thought of as professions over a long period of time; they have identifiable characteristics; and, therefore, these characteristics can be taken as the characteristics of a true profession. What is left unspoken is the fact that the characteristics usually identified are not all of the characteristics of the learned professions. They are mainly what are thought to be the desirable characteristics of law, medicine, and theology. This does not mean they are accepted uncritically by everyone (for example, many have questioned certain aspects of the lawyer-client and physician-patient relationships). What it does mean is that there has been no conscious effort to use undesirable characteristics as a model for others to follow.

A complete inventory of the characteristics which have been suggested would occupy the better part of a thick book. It might also prove tedious to readers, and it probably would be an unnecessary distraction from the notions which are primary to the idea of a professional. Hence, what follows is a brief sample of views on the desirable characteristics of a profession.

A Commitment to High Ethical Standards

We will have much more to say about ethics in later sections of this reading. Here, suffice it to say that on one point there is virtually no disagreement. A sincere commitment to high ethical standards is an essential characteristic of every true profession. Indeed, this characteristic is a literal prerequisite. Without it, a profession would be little more than a way to earn a living. Surely a profession must be more than that, if it is to have any meaning and purpose at all.

A Prevailing Attitude of Altruism

A profession is also said to be characterized by a prevailing attitude of altruism. "Altruism" is a term first used, we are told, by the Positivists who were followers of the French philosopher Comte. It means unselfish concern for the welfare of others, and it is the polar opposite of "egoism," the doctrine that self-interest is the proper goal of all human actions. While there is a significant degree of overlap between altruism and a commitment to high ethical standards, altruism is often treated as being especially worthy of separate mention. It also shares with ethical standards the property of being more easily "professed" than achieved. Yet, the case for altruism rests on its inherent virtues as a desirable standard of human conduct, on its intrinsic worth as a goal, apart from the obstacles to its ultimate achievement. It is at once a case for the basic goodness of "charity," in its ancient sense of love, and a goal shared by nearly every major religion throughout the history of civilization.

What remains is the question of whether a profession is distinguished by an unselfish concern for the welfare of others. Since no profession can make good the claim that all of its members are constantly motivated by a spirit of altruism, it seems clear that the proponents of this characteristic are either naive or they are referring to an abstract ideal which has no counterpart in reality, other than where it can be identified as a prevailing attitude among members of an occupational group. It also seems clear that most proponents are using the term altruism, somewhat loosely, to convey the antithesis of "mercenary." A truly mercenary occupation is one which is pursued solely for money or other personal gain. A profession is not a mercenary occupation, it is argued, because it is pursued largely out of an unselfish desire to serve the needs of others, apart from any hope or expectation of financial or personal gain.

Although serving the vital needs of mankind may well be the most important societal value of professions, it does not necessarily follow that professions can claim exclusive rights to the role. Nor does it follow that professions are pursued largely for unselfish reasons. Skeptics still have ample reason to suspect that comparatively few persons would pursue law or medicine if doing so offered no opportunity for social status or large financial rewards (or to wonder whether more persons might aspire to the clergy if it virtually guaranteed them a spot at the top of the income distribution). Accordingly, it is probably more accurate to say that professions offer the opportunity to make a living by doing worthwhile things for which there are many rewards, including the rewards which are intrinsic to the nature of the work. Even this formulation does not, by itself, distinguish professions from other occupations. Nearly all occupational pursuits offer at least some personal rewards, other than money, and they may include rewards which are as satisfying as those enjoyed by professions. Against this it is argued that the pursuits of professions are somehow more worthwhile than other rewarding occupational pursuits, in that professions are necessarily involved in providing services to meet the vital needs of mankind. True, when a surgeon saves a young girl's life, an attorney protects her legal rights, or a clergyman gives her moral guidance and comfort, they are obviously meeting vital needs, and they are more to be admired than one who gets satisfaction from murdering for hire. But to assert that professions are therefore unique occupations can reach the stage of an arrogant and condescending attitude which contradicts the very claim to altruism. Is the lawyer who handles the legalities of a divorce serving a more vital human need than the bricklayer who builds a church, the artist who creates the timeless masterpiece, the business executive whose genius and drive create employment for thousands, the scientist who discovers a new source of energy, or the farmer whose crops feed the hungry? Which of these pursuits are the most worthy? The least worthy? Can the worthiness of pursuits serve as a meaningful basis for distinguishing professions from other occupations? In any occupational group, can it be determined whether an attitude of altruism prevails over purely mercenary goals? Such questions are not easily answered. But they do pose issues which suggest an uneasy alliance between traditional professions and the attribute of altruism.

At best, a prevailing attitude of altruism, the striving to be guided by larger values than purely mercenary ends, is a goal which traditional professions cannot claim uniquely for themselves. The idea of a profession may be partially characterized by the intrinsic nature of the work, as well as by its ultimate goal. But the same can be said of other worthwhile pursuits. Thus, the notion of profession does not fully emerge until we consider its additional characteristics.

Mandatory Educational Preparation and Training

Beginning with the earliest use of the phrase "learned" profession and continuing to the present day, a notion which has reigned largely unchallenged is that professions are distinguished by the extensive education and training required of their members. This characteristic is normally treated as a mandatory or required precondition of profession membership, and it is often said or taken to mean the specific preconditions of collegiate-level degrees, apprenticeship requirements, and qualifying examinations. For example, individuals can practice medicine only if they _first_ graduate from medical school, satisfy internship and residency requirements, and pass the various examinations which set the qualifying standards. The use of the term "practice" is noteworthy in this context, because the preponderance of opinion would reserve the profession classification for occupations which involve practical application of skills.[2] However, proponents of

---

2. Those who stress practical applications seem anxious to exclude purely theoretical or abstract pursuits from profession status. However, it is not altogether clear whether they would deny profession status to learned persons who engage in scientific research, particularly theoretical research which leads or may lead to important practical applications. Distinctions between theoretical

the latter view are quick to point out that the skill ingredient produces only a partial overlap between professions and the crafts. The work of crafts is primarily manual in nature, whereas the work of professions is primarily mental in nature. More important, the skills applied by professions are said to be based upon theoretical knowledge, analysis and understanding.

Alfred North Whitehead regarded theory as the very essence of the idea of a profession, at least in the following sense:

> ...the term Profession means an avocation whose activities are subjected to theoretical analysis, and are modified by theoretical conclusions derived from that analysis. This analysis has regard to the purposes of the avocation and to the adaptation of the activities for the attainment of those purposes. Such criticism (analysis) must be founded upon some understanding of the natures of things involved in those activities, so that the results of actions can be foreseen. Thus foresight based upon theory, and theory based upon understanding of the nature of things, are essential to a profession. (emphasis supplied)....The antithesis to a profession is an avocation based upon customary activities and modified by the trial and error of individual practice. Such an avocation is a craft, or at a lower level of individual skill it is merely a customary director of muscular labor.[3]

Whitehead recognizes that the distinction between crafts and professions is not always clear-cut. He also is one of the few writers to reject the popular assumption that professions have a monopoly on superior individuals. However, his somewhat unique definition places emphasis on the intellectual foundations of profession, and in this respect he is not alone.

The intellectual element of the profession idea is amply supported by generally accepted views on professional education. A profession is said to require a unified body of specialized knowledge which is built upon a broad

---

and practical pursuits can be so artificial that the distinctions themselves become unpractical and even useless.

3. Alfred North Whitehead, Adventures of Ideas, 1933 (New York: The Macmillan Company), pp. 72-73.

educational foundation.[4] Technical knowledge and skills are considered necessary, but they are not sufficient. They must be preceded by a solid background in the so-called "liberal" arts and sciences. The late Woodrow Wilson apparently went a step further, for he is credited with the remark: "The liberal education that our professional men get must not only be antecedent to their technical training; it must also be concurrent with it." In any case, the necessity of a broad general education is well established, as is the alternative formulation that professional education should be interdisciplinary in nature, that is, it should stress the relationships among various disciplines or fields of thought. The need to understand such relationships is especially important to the "practice" of professions, since the application of knowledge and skills is unavoidably an interdisciplinary process.

Despite general acceptance of the professional's need for both specialized training and broad education, as well as agreement on the desirability of having the broad education come first in point of time, there is by no means a consensus on the proper mix or relative emphasis which should be placed upon the two types of preparation. This issue is not unique to the professions (educators are forever quarreling about the relative mix of liberal arts, science, and vocational subjects in nearly every curriculum). Nor is the issue one which can be divorced entirely from practical constraints such as time and money. To accommodate the need for a truly adequate base of liberal education and the pressures for more technical training, one can always make a theoretical case for lengthening the required period of preparation for a profession. But this would involve a corresponding increase in costs, and, if taken too far, the aspirants would be dead or nearing retirement age before they are "ready" to practice. The preparation time in medicine has lengthened, of course, along with the trend toward greater specialization.[5] In law, where the minimum preparation

---

4. The virtually undisputed merits of this proposition are especially well expressed in the Overman monograph, op. cit., pp. 6-8.

5. Physicians also seem especially inclined to use the lengthy preparation time as a primary justification for high fees, usually on the theory that their large investment of time and money must be recovered over a shorter period of time-- or at least justifies correspondingly large returns on the investment. The argument might be a little stronger if all physicians paid for their own schooling, but it fails to account for the relatively low incomes of history professors who may spend ten years earning doctoral degrees. Students of economics will recognize that demand,

time has remained remarkably constant over the years, it is not yet clear whether the traditional resistance to recognizing subspecialties will continue. Nonetheless, the pressure toward longer minimum preparation times and more specialized training are already apparent in many occupational endeavors, including most of the recognized professions.[6] The nearly impossible task of trying to master everything inevitably forces at least some degree of specialization in our occupational pursuits, and it also helps explain the societal tendency to reserve the title "expert" for the specialist.

What persists is the nagging question of whether a specified blend of general education and specialized training sets professions apart from other occupations. Most definitions of profession ignore this issue. Their framers seem preoccupied with the existence of rigorous intellectual requirements, and they seem willing to accept as meeting this criterion a wide range of differences in the degree of difficulty, the relative emphasis on specialized knowledge, the relative emphasis as between the liberal arts and the sciences, and the length of the preparation time which is required as a precondition of the first level of practice. In point of fact, the range of accepted differences is wide enough to include many occupations which are not currently recognized as professions. Consequently, the intellectual ingredients of a profession have not been sharply defined, at least not beyond the consensus on the need for both liberal and technical preparation. Since as much can be said of nearly any occupation, is the real distinction that professions require a minimum level of intellectual preparation of all its practitioners? This cuts closer to the core of the matter, to be sure, yet it is not true of all members of all recognized professions (for example, the clergy of some religions and religious denominations). It follows from the foregoing analysis that the intellectual requirements of profession do not alone establish its status. If they are to do so, they must be combined with other characteristics.

One should not lose sight of the overwhelming agreement on the need of professionals for formal preparation and study. Experience is necessary and potentially enriching, but it is not enough. Experience is at best a hard

---

supply and other economic principles are needed to explain the distribution of income.

6. Some observers are fearful that a trend away from specialized training might disqualify insurance from professional status. For example, see Patricia P. Douglas, "Professionalism: Its Presence and Absence in the Insurance Industry," The Journal of Risk and Insurance, Vol. XXXVIII, No. 2, June 1971, pp. 218-24.

teacher. She gives the tests first and the lessons afterwards. At worst, she is no teacher at all. The latter point can be conveyed by the hackneyed notion that ten years of experience is often just one year of experience repeated ten times. Joseph Joubert said it more eloquently when he reminded us that "few men are worthy of experience; the majority let it corrupt them." It was the brilliant philosopher Kant, however, who left us with the wisdom of the following lines: "Thought without experience is empty; experience without thought is blind." Kant's message rings true after only a moment's reflection, does it not? It suggests, among other things, the futility of pretending that thought and experience can be separated and ranked in importance. Neither has any real meaning or worth without the other. If only to give professions what Whitehead called "foresight based upon theory," experience must be complemented, supplemented and preceded by careful thought and study. To rely purely on trial-and-error is to reject the accumulated wisdom of previous generations. It is to repeat their mistakes. It is to invent the wheel over and over again. And, as if its inefficiency were not enough, its barriers to progress make the case. Thus it is that professional preparation demands more than experience.

There is also another important sense in which experience is not enough to justify an entitlement to profession status, for it is now widely accepted that admission to the ranks should be based upon proof of qualifications. The proof takes the form of passing the comprehensive examinations which are among the prerequisites to certification and/or licensure (along with prior experience requirements, in some cases). Such examinations are felt to be necessary and desirable for several reasons. Although there is always the potential danger that examinations can be used to impose unwarranted restrictions on entry to a profession, examinations can serve to (1) establish and preserve the status of a profession, (2) provide an equitable means to judge candidates or aspirants to the status, and (3) give uninitiated members of the lay public a meaningful way to distinguish between qualified and unqualified practitioners. Testing is an imperfect mechanism at best, but its advantages over other alternatives have been accepted, sometimes reluctantly, at almost every level of formal education. Examinations are used from elementary school on to determine our entitlement to proceed to the next level and our status as a graduate of prior levels. So also do we have university admissions exams, bar and medical exams, and the exams to measure entitlement to CPA, CPCU, CLU, and similar professional designations. At a minimum, the existence of such examinations imposes upon non-passers and non-takers alike the entire burden of proving to the public that they are as qualified as persons who do pass the exams. Less perfectly, the various exams offer some help in defining the minimum standards to be met by professions. Very few still cling to the notion that a mere license to operate is reliable proof of professional preparation.[7] Most insist that a better form of proof lies in comprehensive exams, experience requirements, and some kind of certification. Differences of opinion continue to arise, however, in determining which certifications or designations qualify their holders for profession status. While the existence of examinations and experience requirements does not assure profession status, and while experience requirements may not be essential in the public's eye, the failure to meet the standards set by rigorous examinations seems a sure way of disqualifying occupations and individuals from the status they are seeking.

Mandatory Continuing Education

Until recently, the notion of mandatory continuing education has seldom been included in listings of the distinguishing characteristics of a profession.[8] The explanation is easy enough. Historically, in the United States at least, no recognized profession has ever required its members either to engage in continuing education or to provide tangible evidence of continuing competence. Nearly all professional associations and societies have urged upon their members the importance of maintaining and improving their professional knowledge and skills, and most have offered to their members a variety of continuing education programs and technical journals. Nonetheless, such programs frequently have not measured up to the rigor of the initial qualifying standards, and participation in them has nearly always been voluntary.

A dramatic shift in attitudes started to surface by the early 1970s, so much so that it is already safe to conclude, at this writing, that mandatory continuing education is an "idea whose time has come" for the professions. While the developments to date have been uneven among the established professions, the pattern which is beginning to take shape has all the earmarks of an

---

7. Milton Friedman, the Nobel laureate, has made a convincing case against occupational licensure in Milton Friedman, *Capitalism and Freedom*, 1965 (The University of Chicago Press), Ch. IX. Friedman's engaging thesis is that the advantages claimed for occupational licensure are outweighed by the disadvantages, thus imposing unwarranted restrictions on individual freedom. Friedman is much more receptive to certification, however, if the certification is not done by the state and is not a precondition of practicing the occupation.

8. For a notable exception, see Elmer G. Beamer, "Continuing Education--A Professional Requirement," *The Journal of Accountancy*, January 1972, pp. 33-39.

unmistakable general trend. The study of these patterns has even motivated one writer to venture the more specific conclusion that "all professions are moving in the direction of recertification based on mandatory continuing education."[9] Most knowledgeable observers seem reluctant to accept recertification requirements as a clear-cut trend, but they do not deny the increasing momentum toward some kind of required demonstration of continuing professional competence.

Accounting, a comparative newcomer to profession status, merited the recognition by playing the leading role in implementing programs of mandatory continuing education. (The fields of medicine and law have followed.)

Professions are feeling the mounting pressures to adopt some kind of mandatory continuing education programs. What are the sources of these pressures? Some have attributed the pressures partly to an intensified social consciousness and the increasing demands made by clients and patients. Most people probably know little or nothing about the existence or absence of mandatory continuing education in the professions, but many persons do tend to seek out the experts, whenever they have a choice, and such persons would undoubtedly prefer some sort of tangible evidence that a professional is "current" in his or her field. There is likewise merit in the argument that the conscience of many professionals has evolved into a tardy realization that their professional competence can become quickly outdated by the rapid changes and increasing complexity of their fields. But the potential gap between initial competence and continuing competence is hardly a new phenomenon. Hence, it could well be that the growing social consciousness of professionals has been sparked as much by the desire to maintain their professional status, alongside the professions which are moving toward mandatory continuing education, and by a fear that the failure to take the initiative will prompt government action to fill the void. Realistically, no mandatory continuing education program will be completely successful in weeding out all the incompetents in a profession, yet the failure to try may ultimately be the very thing which will disqualify some groups from profession status.

A Formal Association or Society

The greater number of observers treat the existence of formal associations or societies as an essential characteristic of professions, whether the associations are

---

9. Douglas H. Parker, Michigan State Bar Journal, October 1975, p. 794, in an article entitled "Periodic Recertification of Lawyers: A Comparative Study of Programs for Maintaining Professional Competence," reprinted from the Utah Law Review, fall 1974, No. 3.

at several levels or at the national level alone. Proponents point to the need for a unified and cohesive group to set ethical standards and provide continuing education programs and publications for its members or "alumni," as they are sometimes referred to in less formal terms. These worthy goals are best achieved, proponents feel, through elected leaders, an adequate professional staff, adequate financial resources, and the power of many persons working together toward common objectives and shared interests.

One can fully accept the validity and beneficial aspects of professional societies without overlooking that the power to do good is also the power to do evil. The associations and societies of some established professions have used their powers to impose questionable restrictions on entry into the profession, as well as to sanctify protectionism and other self-serving objectives which may not be in the public interest. To that extent, they have lost hold of their claims to altruism.

In a definitional sense, the necessity of a formal association is logically derived from the presupposition that profession is a collective or group concept. If one profession is to be distinguished from other professions and occupational groupings, it must have the kind of identity which only becomes visible in a formal organization. This conclusion is not necessarily contradicted by the splintering of medicine into subspecialities. While physicians do not constitute a completely homogeneous group, physicians (as a group) are distinguishable from other professions and occupational groups. However, a group having a very heterogeneous composition may be indistinguishable from other groups, or it may lump members who meet the tests of profession with members who do not. The latter helps explain why it might be less than convincing to treat accounting or insurance as professions per se. It also helps account for the occasional argument in support of treating insurance agents and/or brokers and consultants as a subgroup more worthy of profession status (assuming they have met the other tests), since their representation of clients makes them more like practicing attorneys and physicians than it does to, say, home office underwriters. Whether the reader or author accepts this particular view is beside the point. It is presented here merely to underscore that the struggle to find identity and purpose in a profession is a struggle for which most individuals want the assistance of a strong group. In each of the recognized professions there is a satisfying sense of fraternity or "brotherhood" which is a natural result of bringing together individuals who share common interests, problems, goals, and educational backgrounds, and who speak in the language of an esoteric technical jargon that is seldom understood outside their numbers. When this sense of fraternity is diminished by a growing diversity within the membership, the pressures to form subgroups may conflict with the desire to retain the greater strength of a larger group. In any case, the existence of associations and societies is a necessary part of giving the group a distinct identity.

Independence

Group action may be required for some purposes. It does not relieve the professional from the burden of making individual judgments. To serve the needs of those whom it is the professional's duty or privilege to serve on a daily basis, the professional must be free to exercise sound professional judgment and skill. The scholar needs academic freedom, the airline pilot needs the authority to make quick decisions, and all professionals need to be free from monetary or other external influences which inherently impair the exercise of sound judgment and skill. But no freedom can be absolute. The professional who does not operate within ethical and legal boundaries is exposed to the risks of departure.

Though one sometimes yearns for the tiller scales of justice to be equipped with the red tilt light of a pinball game, or a machine which would instantly prescribe the proper treatment for medical ills, or an electronic device which would replace baseball umpires in the calling of balls and strikes, even the best physicians and lawyers are as capable of errors in judgment as the worst baseball umpires. The difference between them lies in the gravity of consequences they may inflict upon others. The prudent professional will be mindful of his limitations, therefore, and will often seek the advice and counsel of peers or superiors. But the latter are illustrations of sound judgment, not substitutes for it. They cannot totally relieve the professional of the laboring oar of individual judgment. Accordingly, "independence" may be thought of as a distinguishing characteristic of a profession.

In public accounting, the notion of independence has a strikingly different purpose than it does in law and medicine. The professional standards of the American Institute of Certified Public Accountants (AICPA) embrace "independence, integrity and objectivity" as affirmative ethical principles, and they stipulate that "independence has always been a concept fundamental to the accounting profession, the cornerstone of its philosophical structure."[10] Independence is defined by the accounting profession as "the ability to act with integrity and objectivity." However, it should be stressed that a CPA who is engaged in the practice of public accounting is expected to be independent of those he serves (emphasis supplied). Why should CPAs be independent from their clients? If CPAs do not maintain their independence from clients, their professional opinions on financial statements will be of little value to creditors, investors, government agencies, and others who rely upon such statements, including clients. It follows that independence, as well as competence, is essential to the profession status of public accounting.

A decidedly different standard of independence is applied to the practice of law, where an undivided loyalty is said to be owed to the client. The American Bar Association's revised Code of Professional Responsibility stipulates, in Canon 5, that "A lawyer should exercise independent professional judgment on behalf of a client."[11] This broad concept is further clarified in twenty-four related guidelines, illustrative of which is the following:

> EC 5-1 The professional judgment of a lawyer should be exercised, within the bounds of the law, solely for the benefit of his client and free of compromising influences and loyalties. Neither his personal interests, the interests of other clients, nor the desires of third persons should be permitted to dilute his loyalty to his client. (emphasis supplied)[12]

Critics of the legal profession do not question the lawyer's need for freedom to make independent professional judgments. What they do challenge is the lawyer's ethical obligation to exercise that judgment solely for the benefit of his client, particularly in situations where an

---

10. AICPA Professional Standards, Vol. 2, 1976, published for the American Institute of Certified Public Accountants by Commerce Clearing House, Inc., pp. 4282 and 4291.

11. Code of Professional Responsibility, adopted by the House of Delegates of the American Bar Association in 1969 and amended in 1970. The Code, which was adopted by the Supreme Court of Pennsylvania in 1970, is included in a 1974 publication of the Pennsylvania Bar Association. In the latter publication, Canon 5 and its related "ethical considerations" and "disciplinary rules" are found on pp. 18-23. The page references would differ in the various other publications which contain the ABA Code.

12. Ibid., p. 18. The guidelines are referred to as "ethical considerations," and they are translated into more specific "disciplinary rules" of a binding nature.

undivided loyalty to the client's interests would not be, or might not be, in the public interest.

Nonetheless, it is unmistakably clear that the professional independence standards which govern lawyers are quite different than those governing public accountants. Whereas the practicing lawyer's obligation of independence is aimed at fostering and enhancing his advocacy for his client, the public accountant's independence is an independence from his client, so that the accountant's professional opinions may also serve the interests of others who rely upon them.

The general idea of independence is also a characteristic of the medical professional, yet it appears in several different forms, and the practicing physician is given considerable latitude in their application. The net effect of the various ethical principles is too complex to capture in a simple description. In fact, perhaps the only safe conclusion is that a physician's independence is tempered by a number of ethical and legal constraints, within which the physician is given considerable freedom to exercise his professional judgment. Most of the ethical constraints appear to be motivated by a desire to preserve or enhance the quality of medical care rendered to patients, while a few appear to be motivated by a desire to serve a larger public interest (for example, the ethical obligation to provide emergency treatment and the obligation to disclose confidential information to protect the welfare of the community). What emerges, in any case, is an overall concept of independence which is somewhat unique to the medical profession.

Despite the different standards of independence in public accounting, law, and medicine, many observers have preferred to stress two ways in which these professionals are ostensibly similar. Their practitioners have clients (or patients), and the practitioners are compensated on a fee-for-service basis.

Those who stress the necessity of a client or patient relationship would deny profession status to occupations which do not involve direct service to individual members of the public. By extension of their own argument, they would be forced to deny profession status to the many competent and ethical lawyers, physicians, and CPAs who are salaried employees of one employer, rather than engaged in "public practice" per se (and they would be stretching a point if they did not exclude many members of the clergy and physicians engaged solely in medical research). Actuaries would be engaged in a profession only if they were consulting actuaries, and so on, until the field is narrowed to the "chosen few" with profession status. The merits of this argument are not apparent to the writer.

What is more, the argument skirts the issue of independence, for it is entirely possible to engage in a public practice for individual clients without any measure of professional independence, and it is actually quite common for salaried employees of one employer to enjoy a large measure of professional independence and freedom to make judgments (for example, college professors).

The fee-for-service basis of compensation gets closer to an important characteristic shared by public accounting, law, and medicine, but its importance is derived from its consistency with the different types of independence which each profession is ethically obligated to exercise. The ultimate goal of the professions is to maintain and improve the quality of services rendered to those whom it is the professional's duty or privilege to serve. Achieving this goal requires not only technical competence and ethical attitudes among professionals; it also requires that professionals have the independence or freedom to make sound professional judgments, to apply their knowledge and skills, unselfishly, in ways which will best serve the needs of others. The basis of compensation is but one of the several means of fostering the required types of independence. While most of the established professions make use of the fee-for-service basis of compensation, they also make use of other systems of compensation, and they rely on ethics standards to establish and control the kinds of independence they regard as important. Thus, a distinguishable degree of independence is the characteristic which recognized professions really have in common.

Unavoidably, the foregoing analysis summons a brief consideration of the perennial controversy among proponents of fees, commissions, or fee-commission offsets as the "proper" basis of compensating insurance agents and brokers. Most readers of this essay will not need to be told that the statutes and regulations of a number of jurisdictions continue to prohibit or restrict the charging of fees by those who represent insurance buyers and/or sellers. Nonetheless, by assuming that the pertinent laws and regulations could be changed, and by avoiding the temptation to delve into other arguments which might lead the discussion astray, one can concentrate on the specific issue of whether the prevailing compensation system is a barrier to profession status for insurance agents and brokers. One of the first to suggest this issue was the late Dr. C. A. Kulp, then Dean of the Wharton School of Finance and Commerce, who often made the following observation: "As long as the insurance agent continues to receive his compensation from the seller and not the buyer, one important element of professionalism will be missing." Some immediately jumped to the premature conclusion that Dr. Kulp was making a superficial brief against the entire commission system. Others, including those of us who were made to understand his purposes, realized that Kulp's primary teaching mission was to stimulate careful thought and reflection. In any event, a lot of very thoughtful people have since taken up the cause of demonstrating a link between the fee system and profession status. And some have insisted that the fee system is a prerequisite to profession status for insurance practitioners.[13]

The usual argument presupposes that if the true professional is to serve the needs of clients, he or she must have the kind of financial detachment which is permitted only by the fee-for-service basis of compensation. Since the fee is charged, regardless of whether the advice is taken, the compensation basis does not unduly influence the nature of the advice. The advisor, having been freed from the temptation to structure the advice solely in a way which would maximize his own financial returns, can concentrate on an objective analysis of the client's needs. The commission-only system provides strong incentives for the wrong kind of self-serving advice, it is argued, because the advisor's income is based entirely on a percentage of the total number of premium dollars he or she can generate. Large premium dollars bring large incomes to producers, whereas zero premium dollars offer nothing but the hope of a future sale. Consequently, some insurance policyholders or prospective buyers get little or no advice, some pay too much for insurance coverages which meet their needs and some end up with the wrong kinds of coverage. Such results can be attributed largely to a lack of knowledge and skills among numerous insurance producers and buyers, as well as to the questionable ethics of a portion of both groups. But proponents of the fee system cling to the idea that the commission-only system is a major barrier to professionalism, at least in the minds of the general public. Highly competent and ethical producers must face the practical implications of giving free advice. And skeptical buyers, aware that the producer's income depends upon a sale, are quite reluctant to follow even the best advice, perhaps especially if it is given free of charge.

---

13. For example, see William Peet, "Insurance--Present or Potential Profession," CPCU Annals, Vol. 13, No. 2, fall 1960, pp. 165-72. See also Peet's follow-up communication, "A Profession for CPCUs," CPCU Annals, Vol. 16, No. 1, spring 1963, pp. 82-87. For a scholarly look at the fee vs. commissions controversy, an analysis of the legal restrictions and proposed solutions, see E. J. Leverett, Jr., and James S. Trieschmann, "Fees vs. Commissions: Are They Legal?" CPCU Annals, Vol. 27, No. 4, December 1974, pp. 266-70.

The obvious merits of such arguments are received with varying degrees of enthusiasm in the community of sophisticated corporate insurance buyers. Some do favor the fee system, for the general reasons already noted. Others would prefer a fee-commission offset system, under the terms of which a producer would be free to charge a fee for consulting services rendered. If the corporation places some of the recommended insurance through the producer, and the commission is larger than the fee, the commission is accepted as full payment for the producer's services, with no additional cost to the buyer. If the commission on the insurance is less than the fee, the buyer is billed for the difference. Some corporate insurance buyers also favor a sliding-scale commission system of the kind which has long been used in group life insurance, that is, a system where the commission <u>rate</u> declines with higher levels of premium volume (in other words, the rate of commission varies inversely with premium volume). Still other corporate insurance buyers are indifferent about which compensation system is used. Sophisticated buyers will get what is best for the corporation under any of the producer compensation systems, according to this rationale, because knowledgeable buyers know what the fee or commission will be, and they will not allow the producer's compensation to get out of line with the quantity and quality of services the producer actually provides.

That it is far easier to be ethical without any temptations to be unethical is axiomatic. However, if public opinion gives profession status to some occupations and denies it to insurance producers because of the commission system, it could be that the public is less aware of quite similar systems among the established professions. For example, it is common practice to compensate hospital pathologists with a percentage of the gross pathology charges of the hospital (35 percent in one hospital for which this author sat on a budget review committee). This approach obviously provides incentives for higher pathology rates and the ordering of unnecessary diagnostic tests, particularly now that "defensive medicine" is a widely used safeguard against malpractice claims. Yet, abuse can be minimized by the ethics of the pathologist, efficient hospital administration, hospital review boards, peer review, insurance companies, and government agencies. Less controllable is the office practice of many general practitioners and medical specialists. Most rely heavily on fees (and insurance to pay them) and the overwhelming demand for their services. Some increase their hourly rates to maintain the desired gross income and keep the demand for their services at a manageable level. Many will accept no new patients. But some continue to charge a flat rate per patient or varying flat rates for different types of service; and, as the jam-packed waiting rooms of physicians' quarters will confirm, their incomes can be increased or maintained only if they see a certain number of patients each day. Their incomes are just about as closely linked to "production" or volume as the insurance producer's, and this can lead to a deterioration in the quality of medical service they provide each patient. Attracting physician-partners to ease the load is very difficult in less desirable communities, which in turn leaves the physician with an ethical choice that the majority of insurance producers may never have to make. Faced with excessive demand for his or her services, the physician must decide whether to see more patients and spend less time with each, increase the number of working hours at the risk of the physician's own health, turn away patients who want and seriously need medical attention, or some combination thereof, even if total income is not a primary factor in making the decision.

Practicing ophthalmologists sometimes derive no small portion of their incomes from ownership interests in optical businesses situated on or near the premises, a sort of "locational quasi-monopoly." The compensation of law and medical partners is often related, respectively, to the volume of law business they generate or the amount of surgery they perform. Every recognized profession has its share of book authors who receive substantial percentage royalties (a noble word for commissions) on the sales volume. Every recognized profession has a large share of members who participate in profit-sharing plans financed from the profits of their own practice. Plaintiffs' attorneys take a percentage of dollar amounts they recover for clients and call the commission a "contingent fee." And these are just a few illustrations of professional compensation arrangements which are not fundamentally different, in terms of their potential effect, from the commission system for insurance producers. Sure, one could pick at the illustrations by observing that some of them do involve percentage payments of a seller directly to an intermediary, or that an author does not normally peddle his own books. The shortcomings of the analogies do not alter the basic point, however, about the variety of compensation arrangements used by established professions. Nearly all of these arrangements, including hourly fees, offer strong financial incentives for the professional to do some very unprofessional things, and each of the recognized professions has its share of members who succumb to the temptations. There are surgeons who perform totally unnecessary surgery, pathologists who order unnecessary tests, lawyers who "chase ambulances," accountants who falsify financial statements, teachers who take bribes for good grades. Would such persons be any more inclined to do these things if the money came in an envelope stamped "commission from the seller?" Would insurance producers automatically enjoy profession status if they, like physicians, were ethically obligated to charge the client a fee based on his ability to pay?

Members of the general public are probably not aware of the full extent to which established professions make use of commission-type compensation arrangements, whereas they are aware that insurance producers are compensated by commissions. Furthermore, most insurance buyers are well aware of the fact that the requirements for an agent's or broker's license are quite minimal compared to the extensive time, education, and testing required to practice law or medicine. They likewise perceive some sharp differences in the kinds of ethical standards which are applicable to practicing insurance producers, lawyers, and physicians. A physician who overtly solicits individual patients is known to be violating explicit ethical standards; an insurance producer who solicits customers is known to be doing what is expected of a producer. Physicians are ethically obligated to expose quacks among their numbers, and they should bring pressure to revoke the quack's license to practice medicine. Insurance agents and brokers are seldom under any explicit ethical obligation to expose "quackery" within their ranks, and few bother to try, unless it has affected them directly (for example, where an agent loses a life insurance policy because of the statutory "twisting" of a competitor). Indeed, some producers seem to look upon "squealers" with contempt; or they at least prefer to govern their own conduct by the unwritten ethic of "mind your own business," leaving it largely up to the regulatory authorities to discover incompetence or wrongdoing. Public perceptions of all producers are also tainted, undoubtedly, by the conduct of overly-aggressive insurance salespersons (where their impact on public perceptions has overshadowed their numbers). Thus, while it could be that the public would like to take away the profession status of the pathologist who gets a percentage cut of the hospital's gross pathology charges, it seems more likely that the commission system of insurance producers is a secondary issue in the public's eye. To further dramatize the point, let us make the highly unrealistic and untrue assumption that the insurance producer group eventually became composed entirely of high school dropouts who operate under no ethical or legal constraints, solicit customers aggressively, and charge each customer an hourly fee for services rendered. Would they now qualify for profession status? Conversely, if all producers could demonstrate mastery of knowledge and skills and adherence to very high ethical standards, would a commission basis of compensation deny them profession status in the public eye? One cannot be sure. One only suspects.

The foregoing discussion is not intended to be an argument in support of either commissions or fees. It will instead suggest why independence, not compensation per se, may play a more crucial role in the concept of a profession. The importance of professional independence was expressed succinctly by the Committee on Ethics of the American Psychiatric Association when, in speaking of a particular type of contractual arrangement, it said:

> The ethical question is not the contract itself but whether or not the physician is free of unnecessary nonmedical interference. <u>The ultimate issue is the freedom to offer good quality medical care.</u> (emphasis supplied)[14]

The kinds of independence a professional needs (and does not need) have been fairly well defined in public accounting, law, and medicine, mostly by their written codes of ethics. However, the nature of the independence required by insurance producers remains controversial, vague and essentially undefined.

If the insurance producer is to be free to offer the best quality of "insurance care" to clients, does this require the insurance producer to be an "independent" agent or broker in the insurance sense of the term? Does an agent who represents one insurance company exclusively have sufficient professional independence? Does either the exclusive agent or the independent agent have sufficient control over the supply of insurance or the quality of insurance contracts and insurer services? Would a fee system of compensation give the producer better control over the supply of insurance or the quality of insurance contracts or the quality of insurer services? Glib answers to such questions may continue to pose barriers to profession status and progress.

For a variety of reasons, the independence models of medicine, law, and public accounting may not be completely transplantable for the insurance producer. With the partial exception of medicine and drugs, the physician is not an intermediary for a company or companies, and he has direct and substantial control over the supply and quality of health care rendered to his patients. Maybe some producers could charge fees for writing "insurance prescriptions," but the absence of a counterpart for local drugstores would require buyers to find purchasing agents, unless the producer also served as the pharmacist. If the advocacy role of a practicing attorney were to be emulated as a model of independence, the producer would have to be a broker with undivided loyalty to the client he represents, and he probably would have to charge fees for his

---

14. "The Principles of Medical Ethics with Annotations Especially Applicable to Psychiatry," <u>American Journal of Psychiatry</u>, 130:9, September 1973, p. 1062.

services.[15] However, the independence model of CPAs offers some interesting insights which have scarcely been mentioned in insurance publications. The ethical standards applicable to CPAs, remember, require them to be independent <u>from their clients</u>, so that they may serve the best interests of creditors, stockholders, and others who rely upon their professional opinions, including clients. There are interesting parallels here to the kind of independence which insurance producers truly need. For example, just as creditors, stockholders, and outsiders rely upon CPA opinions, so also do these same parties rely, consciously or otherwise, on the insurance recommendations of the producer. In fact, the same can be said of all third-party "beneficiaries" of insurance. The injured claimant relies upon liability insurance, the injured worker on compensation insurance, the spouse and children on life insurance, the mortgagee on fire insurance, the importer on ocean marine insurance, and even the hospital relies on the health insurance of its patients. In each case, the insurance producer is serving the insurance needs of others, as well as his clients. Maybe commissions are a necessary incentive for that reason alone (perhaps especially in life insurance, where most people need to be motivated to buy). But commissions may serve less effectively than fees to provide the producer with independence <u>from</u> his client. And so the web of complexity is spun.

The reality is that one currently finds aspects of various models of independence among insurance producers. In this respect, they are not as homogeneous as the recognized professions. Whether the homogeneity of independence which might merit profession status would be a better servant of mankind than the current diversity of approaches is a question which deserves careful and deliberate study.

<u>Public Recognition as a Profession</u>

Students of the profession concept have placed a considerable amount of emphasis on the matter of public recognition. Surprisingly, the very notion they are trying to emphasize is almost never defined. The pronounced tendency of writers to avoid the meaning of "public" implies a contentment with the use of weasel words like "general public," "public opinion," the "public as a whole," or the "public at large," so as to permit them to get on with the business of advocating a particular role of the public in distinguishing a profession.

---

15. For a scholarly analysis by an experienced CPCU-lawyer who is highly respected by his fellow CPCUs, including this writer, see Robert M. Morrison, "The Anomalous Position of the Insurance Agent--An Invitation to Schizophrenia," <u>Villanova Law Review</u>, spring 1967, pp. 535-44.

There are undoubtedly situations and purposes for which casual references to the general public provide an acceptable convenience of language. The preceding pages contain many such references, to be sure. However, where the objective is to understand a position on the role of public opinion, it would be helpful to know whether its advocates are thinking about the opinions of a substantial majority of the entire U.S. population, a simple majority, a majority of adults, a plurality, or some other measure of opinion. At this level of specificity, the various advocates may have very different measures in mind. They obviously do not feel that profession status is conferred by a vote to Congress or by a 5 to 4 decision of the U.S. Supreme Court. They have a larger public in mind, and they may not be thinking of anything more specific than their own intuitive feelings about what portion of the population determines such things as profession status.

The writers are united in the belief that profession status comes gradually to its aspirants, if at all, and that shifts in public opinion can change the list of occupations which qualify. Yet, once again, they stop short of raising or addressing several troublesome issues. For instance, is the lay public really able to confer social status? Ordinary persons have little more than a remote and indirect influence on the matter of who is accepted in "high society" and put on the social register. Those who confer such social status are the people who already have it, and the conferees may or may not be popular choices or admired, either within the group of previous initiates or by members of the lay public who have not been accepted into the fold. Therefore, is it not conceivable that profession status may be conferred in a similar way?

Among the people who are not in the recognized professions, a majority or a vocal minority may greatly influence those who are in positions of power. The "non-profession" people are also perfectly free to view any occupation with admiration, indifference, or contempt, whether or not it is a recognized profession. They may aspire to become business executives, lawyers, or physicians, for whatever reasons they may have, and they may seek profession status for a previously unrecognized occupation. Nevertheless, members of the established professions probably will have the final say on which occupations are admitted. Or, to put it another way, aspirants of profession status would hardly be satisfied if their occupations were not recognized as professions by those who already hold the distinction. Aspirants would like to be thought of as professionals by everyone, no doubt, especially by clients, but acceptance by nonprofessionals would not be enough. It would have all the emptiness of knowing that everyone believes you are a great athlete, except the great athletes.

In the ebb and flow of published materials on the subject, one finds a wide range of opinion concerning the impact of "the" public (that is, whichever public each author had in mind) on the idea of a profession. Some writers treat public acceptance as but one of several characteristics of a profession, while others see it as the only characteristic or the only one which truly matters. Seemingly, the weight of authority supports the view that public recognition of profession status is important, yet it is based upon whether an occupation adequately meets various criteria. The latter view is well illustrated by the following:

> ...an entire society decides which vocations deserve true professional status. If that is true, it is impossible for proponents, opponents or scholars sitting on the sidelines to make this decision until or unless society as a whole is ready to make it. Of the characteristics examined (in the article), only two appear fairly consistently to have governed society's decisions and at the same time to have furnished society with the requisites of a profession.[16]

This author goes on to suggest the two requisites used by society; namely, the practitioners must be paid directly for the services or commodities they sell, and society must have direct control over the right to practice. In speaking of barriers to profession status faced by the insurance industry, another writer applied somewhat different tests (public service, educational requirements, and codes of ethics), but he expressed a very common feeling about the importance of public recognition:

> We cannot say we are professionals because this is, in the end, a status that is conferred by the public on a particular group. If the public does not recognize us as a profession, nothing we can say will gain that coveted status for our group.[17]

The reader will note, in both of these quotes, the idea that profession status cannot be self-declared by the group itself, or even by outsiders, if the general public disagrees. Of course, it is entirely possible to have profession status within a group; it just would not be worth much without wider recognition.

The seeking of instant recognition has led some rather disreputable occupations to rely entirely on advertising

---

16. William Peet, CPCU Annals, fall 1960, op. cit., pp. 171-72.

17. Ronald T. Anderson, "The Professional Urge," CPCU Annals, Vol. 29, No. 6, June 1976, p. 121.

and public relations campaigns, as though a billion dollar advertising budget could buy profession status for any group, whereas the majority of aspirants with a fighting chance for public recognition seem to accept as fact that it must first be earned. As to the best way for a group to "earn" the distinction, there is considerably less agreement. Again, one major reason for this disagreement is the fuzziness with which the "public" is defined, as well as the lack of hard evidence on which standards the public uses.

From this writer's perspective, the public's role in determining a profession would be a fertile area for in-depth research. To say that the profession status of an occupation is conferred by public recognition is to say very little. Indeed, one yearns to know whether the advantages of group recognition are worth the costs. One would first need to know, specifically, the exact "public" which decides the question of recognition. One would then need to know the standards this public uses in making the decision, as well as the relative weight or importance of each standard in this public's eye. In the absence of such data, your author is unwilling to entrust the idea of a profession to any public opinion poll. Some of the finest books in history never made anybody's best seller list, and some which did would not be able to pass any other meaningful test of good literature. Musicians have stayed at the top of the record charts for years, as popular entertainers, with music "talents" which would be judged as poor or mediocre by highly skilled and highly disciplined musicians (and this should not all be dismissed as mere jealousy). Racism is very prevalent among all races, but this does not make it right and proper, or even a characteristic to be desired. Similarly, if profession status is to be decided by the number of people who "buy" it, like a best seller list, occupations seeking the status may find that the advantages are outweighed by the compromises it may require.

For example, careful research might reveal that the public accepts occupations as professions based primarily on their television image, the life and death drama of their work, the fact that they must meet rigorous occupational licensure requirements just to "practice," their high incomes, their political power, the large public demand for their services, whether the work seems to be interesting and challenging, the fact that they do not knock on your door to solicit business, the fact that they charge fees, or other characteristics perceived by the public. Are all of these characteristics desirable to the aspirants of profession status? Are they the only desirable traits? What if the public left out or gave very small weight to education? What if they gave comparatively little weight to ethics? If that sounds farfetched,

TABLE 1

Honesty and Ethical Standards of Eleven Occupations*
(Percent of total nationwide sample who rated occupations as very high or high; average; low or very low in honesty and ethical standards.)

	Very High or High	Average	Low or Very Low
Medical doctors	56%	35%	9%
Engineers	49	43	4
College teachers	44	44	9
Journalists	33	49	16
Lawyers	25	48	26
Building contractors	23	54	21
Business executives	20	58	20
Senators	19	51	29
Congressmen	14	47	38
Labor union leaders	12	38	48
Advertising practitioners	11	43	44

*Adapted from "The Gallup Opinion Index," Political, Social and Economic Trends, Report No. 134, September 1976, pp. 17-29. Perhaps out of charity, Dr. Gallup did not include the clergy in his listing. Unfortunately for our purposes, there were no separate ratings for the insurance industry or for particular occupational categories within the industry.

consider the excerpt from a recent Gallup opinion poll, where people were asked to rate the "honesty and ethical standards" of individuals in eleven occupations, in table 1.

While the "no opinion" column is not shown above, it is significant that very few people said they had no opinion (less than 2 percent each for most of the occupations listed). Of particular interest are the ratings for medical doctors and lawyers, the two most widely recognized as professions of the eleven occupations. Doctors were at the very top of the list, yet only a slight majority of the people gave the honesty and ethical standards of doctors high or very high ratings. Lawyers were given a slightly higher percentage of low or very low ratings than they were high or very high ratings, and the highest ratings of lawyers were less than half the comparable ratings for doctors. Both groups got a surprisingly high percentage of average ratings.[18]

18. Not shown above are various other tables in the Gallup survey results, which reveal important variations in the honesty and ethics ratings according to the income, age,

16.25

The Gallup survey results become even more interesting when we compare them with the prestige ratings of a 1978 Harris poll.[19] Harris found that 90 percent of the people regard doctors as having "very great or considerable prestige." Gallup results say only 56 percent felt doctors have "very high or high" honesty and ethical standards. Some 73 percent feel lawyers get the highest prestige ratings, whereas only 25 percent feel they deserve the highest honesty and ethics ratings. Of course, there are some dangers in comparing the sample results of two different organizations, and there are doubtless some sampling errors in each of the surveys. But suppose they had asked a statistically representative sample of the entire population the following question: "Which of the following occupations are _true_ professions?" One suspects that nearly 100 percent of the people might have said medical doctors and lawyers are true professions. If so, in the light of the other evidence summarized above, it appears that people may not place much weight on honesty and ethical standards when they are deciding which occupations they accept as professions or prestigious. It would not necessarily mean that people have a low regard for honesty and ethics. It would seem to mean that they put as much or more weight on other factors which they perceive as characteristics of true professions. Or, it could mean that traditional professions are still regarded as such, but losing their social status. Or, it could mean some vastly different things which are not readily apparent in the data now available. What is apparent is the need for new and reliable research data.

In the meantime, it would seem only prudent to focus on the desirable characteristics of the profession idea. Apart from what the public thinks about the totality of a given occupation at any time, these desirable characteristics need to be sharpened, so that they may better serve as worthwhile goals for individuals and occupational associations.

Characteristics of a Profession: A Brief Summary

Since the foregoing discussion of profession characteristics has been lengthy, a brief summary may be in order. The occupational idea of a profession is probably best defined by identifying its set of distinguishing characteristics. The idea of a profession emerges more clearly when these characteristics are viewed together as a collective set, because some of the characteristics are not

---

education level, politics, geographical location, occupation, race, and sex of the persons doing the rating.

19. See the article by Louis Harris, _Chicago Tribune_ release, January 12, 1978.

unique to professions. The characteristics identified here were as follows:

1. a commitment to high ethical standards
2. a prevailing attitude of altruism
3. mandatory educational preparation and training
4. mandatory continuing education
5. a formal association or society
6. independence; and, with reservations
7. public recognition as a profession

There is some overlap among these characteristics, and no attempt was made to make them mutually exclusive and collectively exhaustive categories of formal logic. Each was considered by the author to be worthy of separate treatment. Other authors use somewhat different lists.

Above all, these are desirable characteristics of a profession. They are not absolute prerequisites, because (a) no established profession meets all the criteria perfectly, (b) some unrecognized occupations meet some or all of the criteria fairly well and (c) there are considerable differences in the degrees to which each criterion is met among the established professions. Each characteristic also poses a number of questions which have not yet been answered satisfactorily.

No conscious attempt has been made to assign relative weights or priorities to each and every characteristic. However, the general notions of competence and ethics standards are almost universally agreed to be at the top of the importance scale. Mandatory continuing education is the newest of the characteristics to be identified, yet it may soon be widely recognized as one of the most important attributes by which to judge whether an occupation deserves the title of profession. The oldest item on the list, public recognition, undoubtedly started the search to find what it is that is distinctive about theology, law, and medicine. Whether public recognition is thought of as a prerequisite to social status, the goal to be achieved by an occupation having specified characteristics or just one of several characteristics which are desirable, the notion of "public" recognition has not been defined well enough to determine the nature and extent of its role. Allowing a public majority to define the idea of a profession is a particularly debatable approach if one's reason for defining profession is to find desirable characteristics to aspire to and emulate. More reliable research data would be very helpful, if not essential, in the resolution of the remaining troublesome and largely unanswered questions concerning the profession-public recognition relationship.

Insurance and the Characteristics of a Profession

A few members of recognized professions have shared in published words their concerns about a potential loss of profession status.[20] Vastly larger numbers of pages have been occupied by commentaries on the aspirants to profession status. In this respect, the insurance industry need not feel lonely. A long list of occupations marks the ceaseless indulgence in the exercise of putting them to various tests of profession adequacy.[21]

For three reasons, this section will be brief. First, there is a very ample supply of published commentary on the extent to which the insurance industry has, or does not have, the desirable characteristics of a profession.[22] Second, to put the tape measure on the insurance industry as a whole does not take much time. One does not need to go much further than the notion of mandatory educational preparation and training as a precondition of the right to "practice insurance." A significant segment of the industry clearly does not measure up to this or other accepted characteristics of a profession. Moreover, those who still want proof would not be convinced by anything which has not already been said. Third, a rehash of what others have expressed better would blow this ship off course.

---

20. One thoughtful example is provided by W. A. Paton, "Earmarks of a Profession--And the APB," The Journal of Accountancy, January 1971, pp. 37-45. Paton is concerned about activities of the Accounting Principles Board which may impair the professional status of public accountants and the quality of services rendered by CPAs. Specifically, he worries about the erosion of professional independence among public accountants.

21. For examples in a field closely related to insurance, see Douglas A. Hayes, "Potential for Profession Status"; Marshall D. Ketchum, "Is Financial Analysis a Profession?"; and C. Steward Sheppard, "The Professionalization of the Financial Analyst," all in the November-December 1967 issue of the Financial Analysts Journal.

22. For a cross-section of opinions, see Ronald T. Anderson, "The Professional Urge," op. cit.; William Peet, "Insurance--Present or Potential Profession," op. cit.; Patricia P. Douglas, "Professionalism: Its Presence and Absence in the Insurance Industry," op. cit.; and Edwin S. Overman, The Professional Concept and Business Ethics, op. cit. See also William E. Brandow, "Insurance as a Profession," CPCU Annals, Vol. 17, No. 4, winter 1964, pp. 374-75; and Duke N. Stern and David R. Klock, "Public Policy and the Professionalization of Life Underwriters," American Business Law Journal, Vol. 13, 1975, pp. 225-38.

16.28

One constantly struggles at the wheel to keep the trip interesting without losing sight of the pilot's destination. But the reader, as well, has the right to know where we are headed. So, perhaps it would be wise to describe the next port.

It soon will become obvious that the next section is rigged. It will make no apologies for trying to make you and me think deep thoughts about ourselves, as <u>individuals</u>. Elbert Hubbard once said: "If I supply you with a thought, you may remember it and you may not. But if I can make you think a thought for yourself, I have indeed added to your stature." In the section the reader is about to complete, much was said about the idea of a profession as an occupational group. A few thoughts were supplied. Many questions were raised to stimulate additional thinking. However, if the effort was successful, it served to pave the way for the more personal and important notion of professionalism, each individual's quest for an unrealized and worthwhile ideal. As Aldous Huxley said, "There's only one corner of the universe you can be certain of improving, and that's your own self." It would be arrogant and presumptuous, indeed, for this author to suggest a bundle of neat little rules for improving one's self, even in connection with the smaller tasks of one's occupational pursuits. What one can hope to do is serve up a small but solid chunk of meat to chew on.

PROFESSIONALISM AND THE PROFESSIONAL

The preceding section stressed the idea of a profession as a distinctive occupational <u>group</u>. Although such a group may be identified by a set of desirable characteristics, individuals within the group may or may not qualify for profession status. Truly significant differences in the degrees of professional competence and ethics can be found among the individual members of every profession. There are likewise varying degrees of competence and ethics among individual members of occupations which are not widely recognized as professions. And virtually every occupation has its share of incompetent charlatans and highly competent thieves. These are facts of life. Consequently, there is little to be gained by the common and indefensible pretense that the desirable characteristics of an occupational group belong to everyone who pays the annual membership fee. Such characteristics, in the end, have their greatest value as definers of standards which each <u>individual</u> may seek to achieve, if he or she desires them and is willing to pay the price.

Professionalism

As a part of speech, "professionalism" is a noun. It is a word used to denote the conduct, aims, or qualities which mark or characterize a professional. A "professional," in turn, is a person who conforms to the technical and ethical standards of a profession. Professionalism refers to the qualities themselves; a professional is a person who has the specified qualities.

It was suggested earlier that a profession is an occupational group which has, in varying degrees, the following desirable characteristics: a commitment to high ethical standards; a prevailing attitude of altruism; mandatory educational preparation and training; mandatory continuing education; a formal association or society; independence; and (subject to the author's reservations) public recognition as a profession. For the purpose of translating these into a workable notion of professionalism, it is both necessary and helpful to shorten and simplify the list of applicable characteristics. One needs to dispense with the group orientation and concentrate, instead, on the qualities which characterize the professional as an individual with a personal identity, an identity which is separate and distinct from the group(s) of which the individual may be a part.

The many advantages of a formal association or society have already been acknowledged. The belonger who actively participates in the functions of a formal association will reap many personal rewards, not the least of which is the opportunity to serve others who are inside and outside the group. But trade associations per se, valuable as they may be for other purposes, do not get to the core of the idea of professionalism, and professional societies suffer from two important handicaps. First, though such societies frequently have high admissions standards, most of them do not regulate the right to practice an occupation, and they do not control certification (that is, the conferring of specialty and professional designations). It follows that their power to enforce professional standards is limited to the power of expulsion of individuals from membership in the society. Moreover, the expulsion of members can hurt the society more than the individuals who are expelled, by reducing the number of dues-paying members without affecting the former members' right to practice the occupation.

Second, membership in a professional society is not as essential to the idea of professionalism as it is to the group idea of a profession. One can certainly argue that a professional has an ethical obligation to assist in maintaining and raising the professional standards of his or her occupation, but this notion does not need to be a separate characteristic of professionalism, since it is easily folded into the ethics characteristic. A more troublesome issue is whether any ethics code should require professionals to be members of specified professional societies. Although it would be impossible for most professional societies to impose such a requirement on nonmembers, many society leaders have been tempted by the possibilities of getting membership in their own society imposed as an ethical or legal requirement of state licensing boards, national specialty certification boards, organizations conferring professional designations, and/or educational institutions. The reluctance of the latter organizations to oblige the societies is perfectly understandable. Society membership per se seldom has any appreciable influence on the professional's competence and ethics, and requiring the professional to belong to a particular society is felt to be a serious infringement on his or her professional independence. It also would be difficult to require membership in one society, because each occupation normally has several societies for which the professional is eligible. Should a physician, for instance, be required to join the American Medical Association? Other medical societies? Many physicians have been harshly critical of the AMA's involvement in various political matters. A physician could even feel ethically obligated not to belong to the AMA. In any case, it is abundantly clear that a physician can be highly competent and ethical without belonging to the AMA, which brings us back to the central point, to wit: membership in a particular society is not essential to the idea of professionalism. To the extent that society membership requirements are considered essential by a given occupation, they should be treated as part of a broader ethics characteristic, not as a separate quality of professionalism. The assertion that they "should" be so treated is deliberate here, if only to force a brief consideration of the alternatives.

One extreme is represented by the dictionary definition of professionalism, which is far too general either to apply in our daily lives or to define the idea. The other extreme would be a lengthy list of specific qualities for each and every occupation. Such a list invariably takes the form of an ethics code that sets the standards to which the individual is expected to conform. While this writer would be the last to deny the important role of ethics codes, and while much of the remainder of this essay is devoted to them, it is the commitment to observe such codes which all aspirants to professionalism have in common, not the specific code standards themselves. In fact, the codes of various occupations probably should be different, so that they will best address any unique needs of each occupation. But that is exactly what makes the specifics of each code too different to incorporate in a common notion of professionalism. Some occupations may wish to require society membership. Others may think such a requirement would be unethical or otherwise unprofessional. Thus, in the interest of defining professionalism as an idea which may be applied by individuals in every occupation, one "should" concentrate on the desirable qualities that are common to all occupations.

When the public recognition characteristic of a profession is considered in the context of an individual, two aspects of public recognition come to mind. The first is not a quality of the professionalism idea. The second is just a part of a more fundamental quality.

The first aspect has to do with the well-known and significant fact that many people are motivated to seek the qualities of professionalism largely because they want to be publicly recognized as professionals. For some individuals, such public recognition may even be the only motivation toward professionalism. In either case, it is not a quality of professionalism. It is a goal or reason for seeking it. The second aspect of public recognition concerns the tangible recognition which comes from earning degrees and designations such as MD, CPCU, CLU or CPA. This is a most significant aspect of public recognition, to be sure, but it is not really a separate quality of professionalism. It is better thought of as a "proof-positive" part of the professional competence and ethics qualities of professionalism. That is to say, such degrees and designations give tangible evidence to laymen that their holders have met the qualifying standards which each degree of designation entails. To that extent, they have earned a measure of professional status.

Mandatory continuing education, as well as mandatory formal preparation and training, can be thought of as aspects of the more fundamental notion of professional competence. This simplification is not only logical. It also has the advantage of permitting a broader perspective on the various types, degrees, and sources of professional competence among various occupations. Different occupations may require, of aspirants to professional status within the occupations, different mixes of manual and mental skills, different types of preparation and training and varying degrees of preparation, apprenticeship, and subsequent work experience. Yet, in every occupation, professional competence is central to the idea of professionalism. It is a quality to be acquired and maintained by every deserving professional.

Altruism, an unselfish concern for the welfare of others, is frequently treated as a separate quality of professionalism. Some writers also treat "performance" as a separate quality, on the admittedly logical grounds that a true professional is not merely a competent spectator sitting on the sidelines. The real professional is a performer, and he or she lives up to high standards of performance. However, in order to define professionalism broadly enough to be equally applicable to all occupations, it is helpful to view altruism and performance, along with the concept of independence, as elements of the more fundamental quality of professional ethics. Altruism is more of a theme or broad goal of ethics codes, whereas performance and independence are standards which are necessary to achieve broad and specific goals of a professional nature. Again, the specific ethics standards are better left to each occupation, because professionalism in different occupations may require different standards of altruism, performance, and professional independence.

Primary Characteristics of the Professional

When the focus of attention is on the desirable qualities which may be possessed by individuals in virtually every occupation, it becomes apparent that professional competence and ethics are fundamental qualities of professionalism. Implicitly, this formulation invites the hasty conclusion that a "professional" is a person who meets the minimum competence and ethics standards which are required to obtain and maintain the right to practice the occupation in question. But acceptance of such a conclusion would lead full circle back to the common usage of a dictionary definition, and it would mean that a "professional" is any person who is employed for compensation. A person who lost the right to practice one occupation could still be a "professional," simply by getting another job with lesser competence and ethics requirements. The customary way to avoid this conclusion is to assert that such an individual is not a "true" professional. The trouble is, the very same convenience of language is used, in a sharply contradictory way, in referring to practicing lawyers and physicians as the only "true" professionals, despite the fact that some among them do not even meet the minimum standards of their own professions (they just have not been caught yet).

The paradox here is rather easily explained. Many of those who use the term "true" professional are trying, often self-servingly, to reserve professional status exclusively for all members of a limited number of occupations. In contrast, your author wishes to reserve the term "professional" for a limited number of individuals in a large number of occupations. There is little to be achieved by the preoccupation with learned vocations, while there is a lot to be gained by emphasizing the deserving individual in every honorable vocation. Who, then, is the "deserving" individual? What are the "honorable" vocations?

Since observance of the bare minimum standards of competence and ethics would not make any individual special, extraordinary, or admirable, let us first stipulate that honorable and high standards of professional competence and ethics are the most essential qualities of professionalism. Accordingly, the deserving professional is a person who meets and maintains competence and ethics standards which are significantly higher than the minimums required to engage in the occupation, and the standards themselves are honorable, that is, capable of honor. When it is presumed or understood that the author is implicitly thinking of honorable standards, the primary characteristics of a deserving professional may be reduced to two, as follows: A professional in an individual who (1) has a high level of competence and (2) adheres to high ethical standards in the application of that competence. Above all else, these two qualities distinguish the deserving professional from the ordinary merchant of products or services. Once a professional, always a professional? Not necessarily! An individual "has" professional competence at a point in time. Unless it is maintained and improved, it may be lost more easily than it was acquired. Moreover, the quality of competence is inexorably interrelated to the quality of ethics, if only because competence is an ethical obligation which is owed to those whom it is the professional's duty or privilege to serve in a professional capacity. Stated another way, individuals who hold themselves out to the public as "professionals" have an ethical duty of competence; otherwise, they are engaging in a factual misrepresentation of the worst sort.

One of the essential qualities of professionalism cannot be held by individuals who work in occupations which a democratic society has declared illegal. The murderer for hire, the seller of harmful drugs to children, and the petty thief may be highly competent in their fields. They may even be admired in some quarters. But neither their occupations nor their ethical standards are ultimately capable of honor. However, this author categorically rejects the snobbish and condescending view that professionalism is the exclusive property of individuals who are engaged in the traditional professions or other learned occupations. Both of the essential qualities of professionalism may be held by the construction worker, the surgeon, the secretary, the judge, the used car dealer, the minister, the insurance agent, the engineer, the senator, the journalist, the supermarket manager, and the clerk alike. To deny the aspiration of professionalism to the used car dealer is to miss the point. No truly learned person would attempt such a denial, for it would deny the car dealer the human satisfaction of an altruistic concern for his customers and the opportunity to pay his daughter's way to medical school. Furthermore, every truly learned person realizes that the moral measure of a man or woman goes far beyond the occupation in which each is engaged, despite the fact that his or her morality may be reflected in its pursuit. If dairy farming is a "lesser" calling than obstetrics, then obstetrics is a lesser calling than motherhood. If the lawyer who defends the twice-convicted rapist is engaged in a "higher" calling, the lawyer is less to be admired than the competent and ethical television repairman who can also be trusted alone with the lawyer's wife. No, a person's worth or morality is not measured by the number of years he spends in school or the number of degrees he holds. Nor should the notion of professionalism be confined to those whose calling it is to engage in a learned vocation. Indeed, learning alone is not the measure of professional competence. Persons in some fields may be highly competent without much formal learning. No person may be competent without the skills which his or her occupation requires. And every competent person who deserves the label "professional" is deeply committed to high standards of professional ethics.

The Price of Professionalism

Generally

Professionalism does not come to its seekers free of "charge." It exacts standards for which all aspirants will have to pay the toll. Furthermore, the price of professionalism will not be the same for every occupation. The larger prices will be paid by members of occupations which (1) require extensive learning and/or (2) involve more complex questions of ethics. Yet, the nonmonetary benefits to the professional may ultimately be the same in every honorable occupation.

Surgeons who wish to specialize in organ transplants must first spend many years in school, meet internship and hospital residency requirements, work long hours, develop extraordinary manual skills, and make many personal sacrifices along the way. Their incomes will be larger than most, but they also face some of the most complex ethical choices. Appreciably smaller learning and skill demands, as well as simpler ethical choices, may lower the price of professionalism for the kindergarten teacher, the photo engraver, the concert pianist, the typist, or the concrete finisher of a construction crew. Nonetheless, the deserving professional in all these fields, beyond the price each pays, can reap the priceless benefits of blending extraordinary competence with extraordinary ethical standards. Each will know the pride and satisfaction of a durable job well done in the service of others. Call it the personal rewards of altruism, if you wish, or the necessity of "man's humanity to man." Or, perhaps there is an even better and more direct explanation. In the pursuit of an occupation, an individual can truly care for others only by combining the competence and ethics ingredients of professionalism. And men and women must care for others, if they are ultimately to care for themselves.

For Insurance Professionals

Insurance professionals are in an enviable position in many respects. They may know all of the ultimate rewards of caring for others. They normally pay a smaller price than the surgeon does for professionalism, yet they may make a substantial amount of money, some more than the surgeon. Insurance professionals also have the satisfaction of knowing that they serve vital needs of mankind. It would be stretching a point to contend that every insurance professional directly serves a more vital need than the physician, the clergyman, or the defense attorney. However, one could certainly argue that the insurance advisor serves more vital and more universal needs than the lawyer or the accountant does in the rendering of advice to others. While insurance alone cannot save a life, it can pay for the medical treatment that will. Insurance can hold families together. It can permit the mother to raise the children of their deceased father without being forced to take a job. It can replace the income of a disabled breadwinner, send a son or daughter to medical or law school, pay for quality medical and legal care. It can protect the owners of homes and automobiles from lawsuits. It can replace the dwelling destroyed by windstorm so that the family will have a decent place to live. It can, indeed, protect the individual, the family, the business, the law firm, the medical firm, the accounting firm, and the church from financial ruin. But such things cannot be achieved by the insurance advisor alone. The quantity and quality of insurance necessarily and heavily depends upon underwriters, claims representatives, safety engineers, company executives, and many other insurance professionals. Additionally, proper insurance protection depends upon the proper education and training of insurance professionals and insurance consumers.

The need of insurance practitioners for education and training, along with the public's need for proof thereof, has had an obvious effect on the way insurance professionalism has been defined. A growing number of people obviously feel that insurance professionalism is the meeting of the standards initially required to obtain the CPCU, CLU, FSA, FCAS or similar professional designations.

Thus, they tend to view the price of insurance professionalism as the price of obtaining such designations.

There can be little doubt that obtaining an <u>earned</u> professional designation involves the sort of "blood, sweat, and tears" which men and women will not engage in without strong motivations. Those who fear failure may not even try, and those who fail examinations may give up in despair. The designations demand personal sacrifices, monetary costs, and long hours of quiet study. The latter poses a dilemma of particular import to the family man or woman. Single individuals need only resolve that professional studies are more important to them than the alternative ways they would otherwise spend their leisure time. Married persons, especially those with small children, have family obligations to consider. The natural tendency is to rationalize that professional studies will ultimately benefit the family more than would the spending of the same amount of time in ministering to the needs of the spouse and children. Dr. Noah Langdale, president of Georgia State University, put the matter into perspective with the following cogent observation: "There is no success outside one's family that will compensate for a failure with it." Since a failure with one's family is too high a price to pay for professionalism, perhaps one way to resolve the dilemma is suggested by the following quote from Longfellow:

> The heights by great men reached and kept
> Were not attained by sudden flight,
> But they, while their companions slept,
> Were toiling upward in the night.

It is the notion that great men and women reach and maintain great heights only by "toiling upward in the night." Such toiling, in the late of night or the first breath of morning, does not require one to ignore his or her family. Toil is a price of professionalism, however, and it requires a willingness to sacrifice at least some of the time one would otherwise spend at the bowling alley, at the golf course, or in front of a television set.

There are other potential consequences of insurance professionalism which have not been widely discussed in insurance circles, at least not as "prices" of professionalism. Four such prices will be briefly described under the following headings: the increasing vulnerability to the unauthorized practice of law; the increasing vulnerability to professional liability in tort; the growing demands for proof of continuing professional competence; and the price of adherence to increasingly demanding codes of professional ethics. The first of these prices or costs of professionalism probably has greater impact on life insurance producers. The second has impact on all insurance producers and company executives. The third and fourth are prices which are likely to be paid by all insurance practitioners who desire to achieve and maintain the essential qualities of professionalism.

Concerning the unauthorized practice of law, Dr. Snider aptly observes: "...the life underwriter may be tempted to serve his client in those areas beyond the limit of his authority but well within the scope of his knowledge and training."[23] A life underwriter who has completed CLU and post-CLU courses will have studied, in addition to individual and group life and health insurance, pension planning, wills, trusts, estates, taxation, economics, investments, and life insurance law; and equally important, he or she will have demonstrated an ability to *apply* these areas to the financial needs of clients. The life insurance professional who does the best job for clients is the most likely to be accused of the unauthorized practice of law. Yet, other than prohibitions against the acceptance of insurance commissions, practicing attorneys may (and do) give all sorts of life insurance and retirement planning advice, despite the fact that the vast majority of law schools do not require education or training in either area. The "team approach" to estate planning seems to be gaining ground among responsible life insurance agents, attorneys, trust officers, CPAs and investment advisors, but its merits are by no means as widely accepted among the traditional professions as they are among CLUs. In the meantime, life insurance agents will continue to face the dilemma of better serving clients at the risk of the unauthorized practice of law.

All insurance producers are also exposed, increasingly, to the legal consequences of their negligence. Under the law of torts, professionals have long been held to higher standards of care than nonprofessionals.[24] Therein lies another potential price of professionalism. To the extent that insurance practitioners succeed in convincing the public that they are professionals, they may become

---

23. H. Wayne Snider, "Problems of Professionalism," *The Journal of Insurance*, Vol. XXX, No. 4, December 1963, p. 566. For an excellent analysis of how a life underwriter may avoid or engage in the unauthorized practice of law, see Ralph J. Chittick, "Responsibilities of Professionalism," *The Journal of the American Society of CLU*, winter 1964, esp. pp. 35-40.

24. See Donald Malecki, James Donaldson and Ronald Horn, *Commercial Liability Risk Management and Insurance*, American Institute for Property and Liability Underwriters, Inc., 1978.

increasingly vulnerable in professional negligence suits.[25] Such vulnerability has already affected not only insurance producers but also the corporate officers and directors of insurance companies.

Every insurance practitioner must face the growing pressures for proof of continuing competence long after the obtaining of CPCU or CLU designations. Because the development of mandatory continuing education was discussed at length earlier, it will not be repeated here. Suffice it to say that the American Institute's new Code of Professional Ethics imposes upon CPCUs an ethical obligation to maintain their professional competence. It stops short of requiring them to certify such competence periodically, as has already been done by other professions. It does not require or provide for voluntary self-assessment examinations. Nor does it require or provide for peer review.

Editor's note: The American College and the American Society of CLU & ChFC recently developed and jointly sponsor a program of continuing education called Professional Achievement in Continuing Education (PACE). Participation in the PACE program is mandatory for those who first enroll in the CLU or ChFC program after June 30, 1989. It is voluntary for others but becomes mandatory for them once they elect to participate in PACE.

However, all of these means of proving continuing competence are rapidly being adopted by many professions, through an ethics code or otherwise. And any or all of these means may also become part of the price of insurance professionalism, sooner or later, voluntarily or by statute. As Palmer observed:

> ...it should be clear that the public no longer takes any of the professions for granted. The public is demanding proof of concern for their interest. That concern must be evidenced by results, not conversation.[26] (emphasis supplied)

25. For a recent case in point, see Tannenbaum v. Provident Mutual Life Insurance Co., 53 App. Div. 2d 86, 386 N.Y.S. 2d 409 (1976), aff'd mem., No. 218 (May 5, 1977). In its ruling, the court noted that the insured had relied heavily on the agent, and the court also stressed that as a CLU, the agent had a special duty of care and disclosure to the applicant. The potential implications should be obvious! For an analysis of earlier court decisions, see Ralph J. Chittick, "Responsibilities of Professionalism," op. cit., pp. 29-35.

26. Russell E. Palmer, "It's Time to Stop Talking," The Journal of Accountancy, October 1975, p. 65.

That the public no longer takes any of the professions for granted is an unmistakable trend, if not a current fact of life. Members of the public are beginning to make distinctions. They are beginning to focus more on the demonstrable ethics and competence of each professional, as an individual, and they seem to want tangible proof of concern for the public interest. All this is happening at the very same time when insurance practitioners are doing their utmost to convince everyone that they are professionals. The implications should be rather obvious. Insurance professionalism is likely to demand much more rigorous forms of public accountability than have been historically supposed.

Finally, there are the potential costs of adherence to increasingly demanding codes of professional ethics. Written codes of ethics have existed for many years. Some of them have never been enforced. Some, indeed, offer little more than a superficial and insincere lip service to broad and vague standards which attempt to anoint the members of an organization with the indisputable virtues of motherhood, country, morality, and the good dog, Lassie. Among codes which have been enforced or otherwise adhered to, some have had to be revised due to the results or threats of antitrust actions. Trade association codes have historically provided numerous illustrations of conspiracies in restraint of trade and other antisocial restrictions of competition. More recently, the traditional professions have been taken to task for such things as uniform minimum fee schedules, ethics code prohibitions of advertising, and other practices with similar effects. A great many trades have adopted new codes of ethics, while traditional and newer professions have effected massive overhauls of their previously existing codes. In fact, ethics code adoptions and revisions seem to have totally dominated the activities of literally hundreds of occupational organizations. They have been busy at the task of defining and altering the standards themselves. They have been changing their disciplinary rules and procedures to comply with the constitutional requirements of due process, and some have been attempting to toughen enforcement practices, procedures, and penalties.

With the notable exception of the codes of membership organizations which do not have strong enforcement powers (for example, the American Medical Association), professional ethics codes generally seem to be moving in the direction of making greater demands on the individuals to whom they apply. Especially in the most recent revisions of the ethics code of CPAs, one finds considerably less self-protectionism and a much greater emphasis on the welfare of the public at large. One also finds evidence, among the recognized professions, of a growing resolve to put teeth in the ethics enforcement mechanisms. Such developments have not exactly been celebrated by all whom they directly affect. They have been met by angry and irrational cries of protest. And, at the other extreme, they have provoked thoughtful concerns about whether the additional restrictions on professional independence are really in the public interest. The latter concerns may force a healthy recognition of the need of professions to redefine their traditional notions of professional independence. Further restrictions of professional independence, along with adherence to higher standards of ethics generally, are likely to emerge as modern prices of professionalism.

Many people have drawn hasty and superficial conclusions about the question of why there has been such a marked increase in the public's interest in occupational ethics. For instance, hundreds of journalists and media personalities, through their endless utterings, turned the phrase "Watergate morality" into a popular cliché. They likewise showed a fondness for the indefensible contention that this sort of "morality" is unique in our society, particularly among presidents and high public officials. Then, with additional revelations which confirmed that wrongdoings had become more of an epidemic than a unique disease, the phrases "Watergate morality" and the "new morality" became catchalls to describe widespread corruption among Washington lawyers and politicians.[27]

The thoughtful columnist Vermont Royster was one of the few who was able to penetrate the two-edged wall of political bias which surrounded the underlying issues. Other journalists had already acknowledged the widespread existence of the phenomenon in virtually every

---

27. Years before Watergate appeared in the national spotlight, scholars had already exploded the myth that there is anything new about the "new morality" (which makes one wonder whether some very prominent newspaper journalists ever read anything beyond the newspapers). To take just one for instance that falls into the category of "must" reading for insurance professionals, see John D. Long, "Insurance and the New Morality," CPCU Annals, December 1970, pp. 303-21. Dr. Long, for whom this writer has great affection and respect, suggests that a resurgence of the new morality poses a long-range threat to the proper functioning of the insurance mechanism. Though Dr. Long has authored numerous other publications on the insurance-ethics relationship, the cited article has particular relevance to the nature of widespread ethical relativism in our society.

occupation.[28] Few had dealt so openly with the nature of the phenomenon. Though it is a lengthy quote extracted from a longer article, it truly deserves the reader's careful evaluation:

> ...the shock, I believe, was not so much that a few lawyers might deliberately violate the law; there are shysters in every profession and craft. Rather it was that so many of them seemed to go astray unthinkingly. Their behavior was not that of the intentionally dishonest man, the bank robber who knows full well what he is doing. Rather it arose from a kind or moral myopia that led them to do things without seeing any ethical questions at all....
>
> It's true, of course, there's nothing novel in immoral behavior.... Corruption is as old as civilization. The difference lies in the morality we profess. Today for so many people in so many places corruption steals upon them unawares. They are not so much consciously immoral as unconsciously amoral.
>
> If there's any moral standard at all today it lies in the doctrine that short of obvious injury to another one is free to do one's thing. That has an appealing sound, but under such a standard how does one teach the young not to cheat?
>
> Under this morality...no moral injunction comes with any authority...whatever one does to one's self is free from moral fault.
>
> This also absolves guilt for the corruption of others. The dope pusher excuses himself by saying if I don't push it someone else will. Not far different from saying if I don't pay this bribe somebody else will. Besides, if everybody's doing it, who is to be blamed?
>
> We have come to this by a devious route. We began in good cause to remove the law's punishment

---

28. For example, on the front page of The Wall Street Journal, June 10, 1975, there is a prominent reference to a study conducted by Archie Carroll, a professor at the University of Georgia. Professor Carroll reportedly found that three out of five of the corporate executives surveyed said that young managers would have committed the same kind of unethical acts that the junior Nixon aides committed. A striking 65 percent of the executives agreed that managers today feel under pressure to compromise personal standards to achieve company goals.

for people's private conduct. But <u>having removed
the law's proscription we have come to say what is
not proscribed is to be approved, even promoted.</u>
We began by asking sympathy for the misguided
thief or murderer, we end by excusing theft or
murder by the misguided....

The danger here is that every society, from the
most primitive to the most advanced, depends for
its survival on an accepted moral base....
Without a sense that some things are wrong simply
because they are wrong...I am tempted to say,
without a sense of sin--then every man is cast
adrift. Not just the young; the lawyer, doctor or
public servant has no inner standard to measure
whether what he does is ethical or unethical. Why
should we be surprised, then, at what some men do?

I do not know why we have gone so far on this
road.... But to look around at the common
behavior is to see what we have put in jeopardy.[29]
(all emphasis is supplied)

Yes, it is tempting to conclude that the rampant corruption
of Washington lawyers and politicians provided a rude
public awakening to the ultimate dangers of "doing one's
own thing." But if it did, it was only because many people
saw the same kind of corruption in their neighbors, in
their families, and in themselves. Perhaps there is, at
last, a growing sense of a critical need to make vast
changes in the ethical standards which individuals and
occupations "profess." If not, perhaps the renewed
interest in written codes of ethics is at least one giant
step in the right direction.

A Summary

Professionalism is a concept which refers to the
qualities which mark or characterize a professional.

---

29. Vermont Royster, "The Common Behavior," <u>The Wall Street Journal</u>, September 17, 1975. See also Floyd G. Lawrence, "Whose Ethics Guide Business," <u>Industry Week</u>, October 27, 1975, wherein an extensive survey shows that an overwhelming majority of business managers feel that "they are a better judge than anyone else of what's right and wrong for them." Theoretical writers were concluding, at about the same time, that executive behavior is "learned in significant degree through observation." See George Strother, "The Moral Codes of Executives: A Watergate-inspired Look at Barnard's Theory of Executive Responsibility," the <u>Academy of Management Review</u>, Vol. 1, No. 2, April 1976 (submitted on June 20, 1975).

Despite the historical tendency to reserve professionalism for all members of the recognized learned professions, your author has argued that honorable and high standards of professional competence and ethics are the most essential qualities of professionalism. Accordingly, a professional is an individual who (1) has a high level of professional competence and (2) adheres to high ethical standards in the application of that competence.

The personal benefits of professionalism go far beyond the increased financial returns it may bring to its achievers. The larger benefits come from a personal pride in excellent craftsmanship, the deep inner satisfactions of serving the needs of others, and the knowledge that individuals will care for themselves only if they care for others.

While the nonmonetary benefits of professionalism are ultimately the same for members of every honorable occupation, the price paid for professionalism is likely to be larger for members of occupations which involve extensive learning and complicated questions of ethics. For insurance practitioners, the prices or costs of professionalism may include the following:

1. the necessity of extensive educational preparation and training
2. an increasing vulnerability to the unauthorized practice of law
3. an increasing vulnerability to professional liability in tort
4. the growing demands for proof of continuing professional competence
5. the price of adherence to increasingly demanding codes of professional ethics

A few of these costs will be borne more by insurance producers than they will be by other insurance practitioners. However, all insurance practitioners will pay a price, if they wish to reach and keep the heights of professionalism. They will pay for obtaining and maintaining high levels of competence and ethics, and they may, as Longfellow forewarned, be toiling upward in the night. Is it worth it? That is ultimately for each individual to decide. In so doing, perhaps each should remember that the best things in life are not always free.

CODE OF ETHICS

by the American College

Throughout the life span of The American College education and ethics have been inextricably combined. Dr. Solomon S. Huebner, the pioneering educator who founded the College, seldom spoke of education without also speaking of ethics. To him a professional relationship between agent and client had to be based on sound ethical principles.

The ethical underpinnings of the CLU designation gained greater meaning in 1960 when the American Society of CLU adopted a formal Code of Ethics. Since 1960 the Society has endeavored to strengthen its Code, foster adherence to it among members, and promulgate it widely.

At the College courses and designations have changed over the years but the ethical emphasis has remained constant and all new students enter a designation program aware that becoming a CLU or a ChFC involves more than just education.

Until recently that has been enough.

Now a new climate surrounds financial services. Institutional lines and prerogatives have become blurred. The role of those who serve the financial needs of the public has changed. Competition has increased. New products and services abound.

In this climate The American College and the American Society of CLU & ChFC have felt an imperative to be more forceful in the application of long-standing ethical principles. What was once a matter of persuasion is now a matter of requirement.

RATIONALE FOR THE CODE OF ETHICS

The American College's major programs are of two distinct types. Some lead to degrees that are irrevocable because they are based solely on educational achievement and have no ethical requirements. Those that lead to designations, however, have not only educational and experience prerequisites but also ethical requirements that continue beyond graduation and require the maintenance of ongoing standards of conduct. The display of a designation is a continuing indication that the holder will act competently and ethically in all business relationships.

Before conferment the College has historically examined the experience as well as the educational and ethical qualifications of candidates for its designations. Unless an individual has acted fraudulently to obtain a designation, however, no postconferment action to remove a designation has ever been taken.

More recently, with adoption of the new Code of Ethics, the board of trustees acted to assure postconferment fidelity to the ethical standards that exemplify the CLU and ChFC designations. The Code, which was adopted in June 1984, following a study and report by a special committee on ethical policy, received the unqualified endorsement of the board of directors of the American Society of CLU.

THE PROFESSIONAL PLEDGE AND THE CANONS

The Code consists of two parts: The Professional Pledge and eight Canons.

The Pledge to which all CLU and ChFC designees subscribe is: "In all my professional relationships, I pledge myself to the following rule of ethical conduct: I shall, in light of all conditions surrounding those I serve, which I shall make every conscientious effort to ascertain and understand, render that service which, in the same circumstances, I would apply to myself."

The eight Canons are:

I. Conduct yourself at all times with honor and dignity.
II. Avoid practices that would bring dishonor upon your profession or The American College.
III. Publicize your achievement in ways that enhance the integrity of your profession.
IV. Continue your studies throughout your working life so as to maintain a high level of professional competence.
V. Do your utmost to attain a distinguished record of professional service.
VI. Support the established institutions and organizations concerned with the integrity of your profession.
VII. Participate in building your profession by encouraging and providing appropriate assistance to qualified persons pursuing professional studies.
VIII. Comply with all laws and regulations, particularly as they relate to professional and business activities.

ADMINISTRATION

The certification officer of the College is empowered by the board of trustees to implement the Code by investigating complaints and reports of violations, which may originate with state commissioners of insurance, other public and judicial bodies, individuals, and established institutions or organizations. In certain instances the College itself may initiate action based on an apparent violation.

Violations that may cause the certification officer to begin an investigation include conviction of a misdemeanor or felony, suspension or revocation of a license, or suspension or revocation of membership in an established institution or organization.

Although only actions that occur after October 1, 1984, are subject to the Code of Ethics, the standards established by the Code of Ethics apply to students in the CLU and ChFC programs who matriculated on July 1, 1982, or later. All earlier CLU and ChFC matriculants have been invited to subscribe to the Code and to accept its mandates voluntarily. Jurisdiction does not extend to pre-1982 matriculants who have not consented to the Code.

PROCEDURES

I. Initiation of Action
   The American College, acting through the certification officer, investigates all alleged violations of its Code of Ethics that are reported by state or federal authorities, individuals, and/or established financial services institutions or organizations.

II. Step 1: The Certification Officer

   A. The certification officer of The American College makes a preliminary appraisal to determine whether

      1. the complaint involves a violation of the Code of Ethics
      2. there is sufficient evidence for presentation to the certification board

   B. The certification officer determines the facts of the complaint by

      1. reviewing the charges with the complainant(s)
      2. relaying the complaint to the person charged and permitting him or her to respond
      3. examining all facts that appear relevant to the complaint

C. After completing the above steps the certification officer

1. determines whether to discontinue action or to present the case to the certification board
2. transmits the determination in writing to all parties involved in the complaint
3. reviews the earlier steps if new information comes to light
4. prepares the file and presents the complaint to the certification board if the case so warrants

III. Step 2: The Certification Board

A. Membership. The certification board is composed of a chairman, who must be a trustee of the College, and three to five members, including one senior administrative officer of the College. (Note: The College's legal counsel may serve in an advisory role.)

B. Duties

1. The certification board reviews the case and requests any additional information that it considers necessary.
2. After reviewing the case the certification board may either dismiss the complaint or decide that the Code of Ethics has been violated and impose an appropriate sanction.
3. The decision is conveyed in writing to all parties involved in the complaint.

C. Action. The certification board decides to impose a sanction only by unanimous vote.

IV. Sanctions

A. The certification board may order temporary or permanent suspension of the right to use the CLU designation, the ChFC designation, or both. The suspension notice is sent by registered mail.

B. If no appeal is received, a copy of the suspension notice is sent to the complainant(s) and made a part of the College's permanent records.

C. The College reserves the right to transmit the decision to other parties such as government agencies and relevant institutions or organizations.

V. Appeals

A. A suspension may be appealed by notifying the chairman of the certification board in writing within 30 days of receiving the suspension notice.

B. When an appeal is received, the chairman of the certification board notifies the chairman of the board of trustees, who appoints a hearing committee composed of no fewer than three members who may be trustees but not College staff members. The members may have no prior connection with the case or with any company with which the appellant has been associated.

C. The certification officer or a member of the certification board who voted the sanction presents the case and may answer questions but may not participate in the deliberations.

D. The appellant may present his or her position, call witnesses, and point to alleged errors in the decision.

E. If the appellant has counsel, the hearing committee must also be so represented. Counsel to the committee may be present to clarify issues even if the appellant is not represented.

F. A recorder who is not a member of the hearing committee keeps minutes of the proceedings.

G. The hearing committee sets the rules for conduct of the hearing.

H. A majority vote based on information provided during the hearing is required and is final and binding on the College and the appellant.

I. The decision and a statement of reasons for the decision is sent by the chairman to the College, the appellant, and the complainant(s) by registered mail within 15 days of the hearing.

J. The College reserves the right to convey the decision to other parties such as government agencies and relevant institutions and organizations.

CODE OF ETHICS AND ETHICAL GUIDANCE PROCEDURES

by the American Society of CLU and ChFC

CODE OF ETHICS

Introduction

Men and women who have chosen to enter into membership in the American Society voluntarily bind themselves to this the Code of Ethics of their professional organization.

The purpose of the Code is to give further force to the Pledge taken by all holders of the CLU and ChFC designations and to provide a series of standards by which those involved in providing insurance and financial planning and economic security may conduct themselves in a professional manner. The Code is founded upon the two Ethical Imperatives of competent advice and service to the client and enhancement of the public regard for the CLU and ChFC designations.

Competent advice and service to the client is at the very essence of any professional calling. Enhancement of the public regard for professional designations gives voice to the concept that in accepting Society membership an obligation is also accepted to all other holders of similar and allied professional designations and degrees.

In its design, the Code presents the two Ethical Imperatives, supported by Guides which give specificity to the Imperatives, and interpretive comment which is intended to aid in a uniform understanding of the Guides.

A violation of the Code would expose a member to sanctions which range from reprimand to revocation of membership in the American Society. A member is in violation of the Code when a final judgment is made that the member has breached an Ethical Imperative through failure to adhere to one or more of the Guides.

For ease of drafting and reading, the masculine gender and singular number have been used. When appropriate, masculine is to be read as feminine and singular as plural. The word "client" is used under the First Imperative since standards concerning advice and service have greatest applicability to the relationship of client to professional life underwriter.

FIRST IMPERATIVE: TO COMPETENTLY ADVISE AND SERVE THE CLIENT...

GUIDE 1.1: A MEMBER SHALL PROVIDE ADVICE AND SERVICE WHICH ARE IN THE CLIENT'S BEST INTEREST.

Interpretive Comment.

A. A member possessing a specific body of knowledge which is not possessed by the general public has an obligation to use that knowledge for the benefit of the client and to avoid taking advantage of that knowledge to the detriment of the client.

B. In a conflict of interest situation the interest of the client must be paramount.

C. The member must make a conscientious effort to ascertain and to understand all relevant circumstances surrounding the client.

D. A member is to accord due courtesy and consideration to those engaged in related professions who are also serving the client.

E. A member is to give due regard to any agent-principal relationship which may exist between the member and such companies as he may represent.

GUIDE 1.2: A MEMBER SHALL RESPECT THE CONFIDENTIAL RELATIONSHIP EXISTING BETWEEN CLIENT AND MEMBER.

Interpretive Comment.

A. Competent advice and service may necessitate the client sharing personal and confidential information with the member. Such information is to be held in confidence by the member unless released from the obligation by the client.

GUIDE 1.3: A MEMBER SHALL CONTINUE HIS EDUCATION THROUGHOUT HIS PROFESSIONAL LIFE.

Interpretive Comment.

A. To advise and serve competently a member must continue to maintain and to improve his professional abilities.

B. Continuing Education includes both the member adding to his knowledge of the practice of his profession; and, the member keeping abreast of changing economic and legislative conditions which may affect the financial plans of the insuring public.

C. A member may continue his education through formal or informal programs of study or through other professional experiences.

GUIDE 1.4: A MEMBER SHALL RENDER CONTINUING ADVICE AND SERVICE.

Interpretive Comment.

A. Advice and service to be competent must be ongoing as the client's circumstances change and as these changes are made known to the member.

B. A client with whom a member has an active professional relationship is to be informed of economic and legislative changes which relate to the client-member relationship.

SECOND IMPERATIVE: TO ENHANCE THE PUBLIC REGARD FOR PROFESSIONAL DESIGNATIONS AND ALLIED PROFESSIONAL DEGREES HELD BY MEMBERS...

GUIDE 2.1: A MEMBER SHALL OBEY ALL LAWS GOVERNING HIS BUSINESS OR PROFESSIONAL ACTIVITIES.

Interpretive Comment.

A. Business activities are non-personal activities carried on outside the life insurance community; professional activities are non-personal activities carried on within the life insurance community.

B. A member has a legal obligation to obey all laws applicable to his business and professional activities. The placement of this Guide within the Code raises this obligation to the level of an ethical obligation.

GUIDE 2.2: A MEMBER SHALL AVOID ACTIVITIES WHICH DETRACT FROM THE INTEGRITY AND PROFESSIONALISM OF THE CHARTERED LIFE UNDERWRITER DESIGNATION, THE CHARTERED FINANCIAL CONSULTANT DESIGNATION, OR ANY OTHER ALLIED PROFESSIONAL DEGREE OR DESIGNATION HELD BY MEMBERS.

Interpretive Comment.

A. Personal, business, and professional activities are encompassed within the scope of this Guide.

B. Activities which could present a violation of this Guide might include:

1. A member's failure to obey a law unrelated to the member's business or professional activities.
2. A member impairing the reputation of another practitioner.
3. A member unfairly competing with another practitioner.
4. Actions which result in the member discrediting his own reputation.
5. A member discrediting life underwriting as a profession, the institution of life insurance or the American Society of Chartered Life Underwriters.
6. A member advertising the Chartered Life Underwriter or Chartered Financial Consultant designation or membership in the American Society in an

undignified manner, or in a manner prohibited by the Bylaws of the American Society.

GUIDE 2.3: A MEMBER SHALL ENCOURAGE OTHERS TO ATTAIN THE CHARTERED LIFE UNDERWRITER AND/OR THE CHARTERED FINANCIAL CONSULTANT DESIGNATIONS.

Interpretive Comment.

A. Enhancement of the public regard for the CLU and ChFC designations depends upon a continuing increase in the number of holders of the designations who are available to advise and serve the public.

B. Encouraging others who might be qualified to enter into a practice is one hallmark of a professional.

GUIDE 2.4: A MEMBER SHALL AVOID USING THE CHARTERED LIFE UNDERWRITER OR CHARTERED FINANCIAL CONSULTANT DESIGNATION IN A FALSE OR MISLEADING MANNER.

Interpretive Comment.

A. The CLU and ChFC designations are granted by The American College to specified individuals. Acts which directly or indirectly extend the member's personal designation to others would present a violation of this Guide.

B. Chartered Life Underwriter (CLU) or Chartered Financial Consultant (ChFC) may not be used in a name of a business in a manner which would reasonably lead others to conclude that someone other than the named member held the designation. Example:

1. John Jones, CLU & Associates is permissible.
2. John Jones & Associates, Chartered Financial Consultants is not permissible.

ETHICAL GUIDANCE PROCEDURES FOR CHAPTERS OF THE AMERICAN SOCIETY OF CLU

I. Initiation of Action.

    A. In those cases involving conviction for felony, or involving revocation for cause of a license to sell insurance or other financial products or services by an appropriate State or Federal Authority, or involving a member who is not also a member of a local Chapter, action will be initiated at the national level upon receipt of this information. In such an event:

        1. Chapter action would be limited to the forwarding of this information to Society headquarters; and,
        2. the individual concerned will be advised that membership will be suspended or revoked in ninety days unless the member requests a hearing before the National tribunal.

    B. In all other cases, an action arising out of a possible violation of the Code of Ethics is initiated by filing a written complaint with the Chairman of the Chapter's Ethical Guidance Committee.

II. Investigation of the Complaint.

    A. Upon the filing of a complaint with the Chairman, it becomes the responsibility of the Chapter's Ethical Guidance Committee to determine whether the complaint made against the member:

        1. alleges a violation of the Code of Ethics, and
        2. is supported by sufficient facts to warrant a hearing.

    B. To determine the factual sufficiency of the complaint, the Chapter Committee should:

        1. interview the party or parties bringing the complaint;
        2. interview the member against whom the complaint was filed. The member shall be notified in writing by the Committee that a complaint has been filed and an investigation is to be conducted. A summary of the letter of complaint shall

be included with the notification to the member;
3. examine all other matters relevant to the complaint.

C. If the Committee determines, as a result of its investigation, that there are grounds to support a charge of ethical misconduct, then the Committee recommends to the Chapter Board of Directors that a hearing be held.

D. If any member of the Chapter Committee has a business, financial or familial relationship with either the complainant or the member against whom the complaint was filed, that Committee member shall be replaced for the proceedings.

III. Determination to Conduct a Hearing.

A. The Chapter Board of Directors shall, upon the recommendation of the Ethical Guidance Committee, establish the time and place of the hearing.

B. The Board of Directors shall at this time determine whether:

1. it (the Board) shall serve as the tribunal to hear the case, or;
2. to create an ad hoc tribunal, which may consist only of Chapter members, to hear the case.

C. The ad hoc tribunal, if created by the Chapter Board:

1. shall consist of no less than three Chapter members;
2. shall act, in this matter, with the same authority as the Chapter Board of Directors. Its decision shall have the same weight and effect as a decision made by the Chapter Board.

D. The purposes of the hearing are to:

1. determine if the member has violated the Society's Code of Ethics;
2. decide upon or recommend an appropriate discipline for a member judged to have violated the Code of Ethics.

E. If any member of the tribunal selected to hear the case has a business, financial or familial relationship with either the complainant or the member against whom the complaint was filed, that tribunal member shall be replaced for these proceedings.

IV. Notification of the Accused Member.

A. Upon the Board's approval of the Ethical Guidance Committee's recommendation, the Chairman of the Ethical Guidance Committee shall serve notice upon the member in writing, via registered mail, with return receipt requested.

B. The notification to the member shall state that:

1. the Ethical Guidance Committee has examined complaints brought against the member concerning violation(s) of the Code of Ethics, and that, as a result of its investigation, the Committee has recommended that a hearing be held;
2. the member is charged with violation of a specified Ethical Imperative and specified Guide(s) under that Imperative as a result of specified acts or conduct, which acts or conduct shall in this notification be disclosed to the member;
3. the Chapter Board has approved the Committee's recommendation for a hearing, and that a Chapter tribunal shall hear the case;
4. the tribunal is empowered to:

   a. impose the discipline of reprimand or censure;
   b. refer the record of the hearing to the American Society for revocation or suspension of Chapter and National membership;

5. the member may be represented by counsel or appear on his own behalf, may present and interrogate witnesses; and
6. indicate the date, time, and place of the hearing.

C. The notification shall be signed by the Committee Chairman, as Chairman, and shall be sent to the member sufficiently far in advance of the hearing date so that he may:

1. schedule his appearance;
2. obtain counsel; and
3. adequately prepare his presentation.

D. Copies of the notification shall be sent to:

1. the Chapter Board of Directors;
2. the Executive Vice President of the American Society.

V. Conduct of the Hearing.

A. Quasi-Judicial Nature:

1. parties testifying are to be sworn;
2. the member may not be required to testify against himself;
3. a verbatim transcript is to be made;
4. specific charges against the member are to be read into the record;
5. the case against the member is to be presented first with the member given the opportunity to interrogate witnesses;
6. the member is to be given an opportunity to present his case;
7. written evidence is to be made part of the record;
8. a "Legal Officer" may be utilized by the Chapter to guide the course of the hearing.

B. Roles of the Parties.

1. The Chairman of the Ethical Guidance Committee, or his delegate, is responsible for presenting and moving the case against the member. He shall:

    a. state the specific violations with which the member is being charged;
    b. present and interrogate witnesses against the member;
    c. introduce into the record nonverbal testimony against the member;
    d. interrogate witnesses testifying on behalf of the member.

2. The Chapter tribunal functions as an impartial hearing body charged with the responsibility of determining whether, on the facts presented, the member violated the Code of Ethics as charged.

a. The tribunal's decision is to be based solely upon matters introduced in the course of the hearing.
   b. The tribunal may ask questions of any party testifying for purposes of clarification or amplification.
   c. After all testimony has been given and the hearing has been concluded, the tribunal shall not consult with or refer to any outside person or agency.
   d. Issues left in doubt are to be resolved in favor of the member.
   e. The decision of the majority is the decision of the tribunal.

VI. Effect of the Chapter Tribunal's Decision.

   A. If the tribunal decides that the member did not violate the Code of Ethics:

   1. this decision is binding upon the Chapter and the American Society;
   2. there shall be no subsequent rehearing of these charges brought against the member;
   3. the member shall be advised of the tribunal's decision;
   4. the complainant shall be advised of the tribunal's decision;
   5. a copy of the record along with supporting materials and notification of the tribunal's decision shall be forwarded to Society headquarters.

   B. If the tribunal decides that the member did violate the Code of Ethics:

   1. at the same time and place that the tribunal reaches this decision, the tribunal must vote upon a penalty;
   2. a majority decision is the decision of the tribunal.

VII. Penalties.

   A. The types of penalties which may be imposed because of unethical conduct are:

   1. Reprimand -- a formal rebuke given limited publication.
   2. Censure -- a formal rebuke of a more serious nature given wider publication.
   3. Suspension of membership -- a suspension of the member from membership in any Chapter and from membership in the

American Society for a stated period of time and/or until the occurrence of a stated event.

   4. Revocation of membership -- a permanent barring of the member from membership in any Chapter and from membership in the American Society.

B. In voting upon a penalty the tribunal is to consider all such factors as are necessary so that the agreed upon penalty matches the severity of the misconduct.

C. If the tribunal votes the penalty of reprimand or censure, the Chapter proceeds to impose the penalty.

D. If the tribunal votes the penalty of suspension or revocation, then the Chapter:

   1. forwards its decision and a complete record of the hearing to Society headquarters;
   2. notifies the member that the matter has been referred to the American Society.

VIII. Chapter Imposed Penalties: Not Appealable to the American Society.

A. Reprimand.

   1. The decision of the Chapter tribunal to impose the penalty of reprimand shall be final and binding upon:

      a. the Chapter and
      b. the American Society.

   2. A letter of reprimand will be sent to the member.
   3. Notification of reprimand will be disseminated to:

      a. the complainant
      b. Society headquarters.

   4. A copy of the record will be sent to Society headquarters.

      a. From time to time there will be Society-wide publication of ethical actions taken by Chapters. This will be done for educational purposes only and the publication will not identify the member.

B. Censure.

1. The decision of the Chapter tribunal to impose the penalty of censure shall be final and binding upon:

   a. the Chapter and
   b. the American Society.

2. A letter of censure will be sent to the member.
3. The act of censure will be reported at the next business meeting of the Chapter and published in the next Chapter Newsletter or other official Chapter communication.

   a. Such reporting and publication shall limit itself to the statement that: a named CLU/ChFC, member of the named Chapter, has, as a result of a hearing held before the Chapter tribunal, been censured by the Chapter for named violations of the Code of Ethics; that a letter of censure has been sent to the named member, and that notification of this Chapter action has been given to the parties complaining and to the American Society.

4. Effective the date of the decision of the tribunal, a member who has received a letter of censure shall be barred from Chapter and/or National office or service.
5. Notification of censure will be disseminated to:

   a. the complainant
   b. Society headquarters.

6. A copy of the record will be sent to Society headquarters.

   a. From time to time there will be Society-wide publication of ethical guidance actions taken by Chapters. This will be done for educational purposes only and the publication will not identify the member.

IX. Actions Referred to the American Society.

A. Upon receipt of the record and vote of a Chapter tribunal for suspension or revocation, or upon request of a member charged under Section I.A. of these Procedures, the President of the Society shall create a National tribunal to decide the case.

B. The decision of the National tribunal shall be final and binding upon:

1. all Chapters of the American Society, and
2. the American Society

C. In response to actions referred to the American Society by a Chapter, the National tribunal shall decide one of the following:

1. that membership in the Chapter and Society shall be suspended;
2. that membership in the Chapter and Society shall be revoked; or
3. that membership in the Chapter and the Society shall be neither suspended nor revoked.

    a. If the National tribunal neither suspends nor revokes membership, the Chapter tribunal may, without further hearing, reprimand or censure the member.
    b. A majority decision is the decision of the National tribunal.

D. In response to alleged violations by a member who is not also a member of a local Chapter (Member-at-Large), the National tribunal shall follow the procedures outlined in Sections II through VII of these Procedures, substituting the word "Society" for the word "Chapter" as applicable. Penalties imposed as a result of any tribunal decision involving a Member-at-Large may also be those of reprimand or censure, not appealable. Notification of the penalty of reprimand or censure of a Member-at-Large shall be made by letter to the member and to the complainant and Society headquarters. If a tribunal recommends a penalty of suspension or revocation of membership for a Member-at-Large, such penalty shall not be imposed until reviewed and sustained by a special panel of three members of the Executive Committee of the Board of Directors of the Society appointed by the President of the Society.

X. **Penalties Imposed by the American Society.**

   A. Suspension of Membership.

   1. A letter of suspension will be sent to the member from the President of the Society.
   2. Notification of suspension will be disseminated to:

      a. the complainant,
      b. the Chapter referring the action, and
      c. all other Chapters of the Society.

   3. From time to time there will be Society-wide publication of the act of suspension. This will be done for educational purposes, only, and the publication will not identify the member.
   4. Upon expiration of the suspension period the suspended member shall be eligible to apply for membership.

   B. Revocation of Membership.

   1. A letter of revocation will be sent to the member from the President of the Society.
   2. Notification of revocation will be disseminated to:

      a. the complainant,
      b. the Chapter referring the action, and
      c. all members of the Society.

   3. The act of revocation shall be reported at the next meeting of the Society's Board of Directors.